Implementing SAP™ R/3: The Guide for Business and Technology Managers

Vivek Kale

800 East 96th St., Indianapolis, Indiana, 46240

Implementing SAP™ R/3: The Guide for Business and Technology Managers
Copyright © 2000 by Sams Publishing

International Standard Book Number: 0-672-31776-1

Library of Congress Catalog Card Number: 99-64583

Printed in the United States of America

First Printing: January, 2000

07   06   05   4   3   2

Trademarks

Warning and Disclaimer

ASSOCIATE PUBLISHER
Angela Wethington

EXECUTIVE EDITOR
Tim Ryan

ACQUISITIONS EDITOR
Steve Anglin

DEVELOPMENT EDITOR
Tiffany Taylor

MANAGING EDITOR
Lisa Wilson

PROJECT EDITOR
Dawn Pearson

COPY EDITOR
Michael Brumitt

INDEXER
Craig Small

TECHNICAL EDITOR
Wolfgang Haerle

TEAM COORDINATOR
Karen Opal

INTERIOR DESIGNER
Gary Adair

COVER DESIGNER
Aren Howell

COPY WRITER
Eric Borgert

PRODUCTION
D & G Limited, LLC

Overview

Contents

PART III   The Pre-Implementation Stage   225

10   Initiating the SAP Project   227

About the Author

Vivek Kale has a total professional experience of 19 years including three years of experience in SAP FI-CO modules and project managing SAP projects. Kale has experience managing large application software development and implementation projects. He brings a rich experience of IT as well as consulting experience in various capacities in the U.S., India, and Europe. He has handled and consulted on all aspects of enterprisewide information modeling, enterprise architectures, business process re-design, and, more recently, foundations of e-business. With his breadth of expertise and experience, he is deeply interested in the information revolution wrought by the Internet, and the consequent transformation of markets and businesses. Kale also holds a Masters in Science and a Pre-Doctoral in Physics.

Dedication

To
Girija
and our beloved daughters
Tanaya and Atmaja

Acknowledgements

I would like to thank many people who helped in creation of this work, but especially my wife Girija and our daughters Tanaya and Atmaja for their patience and understanding. This book could not have been possible without the continued love, support, and sacrifice of my wife, who gave up a great deal of our time together while I was writing this book.

I am thankful to many colleagues especially Deepak Bhomkar who helped me in reviewing the technical chapters of this book. I also thank the various reviewers, including Wolfgang Haerle, for their comments and suggestions that helped in improving the book. I thank my senior colleagues Sam Mahajan, Dr. D. G. Mahajan and Ulhas Yargop for their interest and encouragement. Thanks to Chris Van Buren, my agent, and the various helpful people I worked with at Sams. These include Steve Anglin, Tim Ryan, Tiffany Taylor, Dawn Pearson, Mike Henry, and Karen Opal. Any book like this requires the work of dozens of people, and those working in the background at Sams did a great job. I thank them all.

Vivek Kale
Iselin, NJ
October 10, 1999

Tell Us What You Think!

As the reader of this book, *you* are our most important critic and commentator. We value your opinion and want to know what we're doing right, what we could do better, what areas you'd like to see us publish in, and any other words of wisdom you're willing to pass our way.

As an associate publisher for Sams Publishing, I welcome your comments. You can email or write me directly to let me know what you did or didn't like about this book—as well as what we can do to make our books stronger.

Please note that I cannot help you with technical problems related to the topic of this book, and that due to the high volume of mail I receive, I might not be able to reply to every message.

When you write, please be sure to include this book's title and author as well as your name and phone or fax number. I will carefully review your comments and share them with the author and editors who worked on the book.

Email:	feedback@samspublishing.com
Mail:	Michael Stephens
	Associate Publisher
	Sams Publishing
	800 East 96th Street
	Indianapolis, IN 46240 USA

Introduction

One of the most important decisions that a senior executive of a millennium enterprise will have to make is related to the selection and implementation of an enterprise resources planning (ERP) package. It is one of the investments that will contribute to every aspect of business from the operations and transactions of a company to its product and services. However, many managers are ill equipped to make a sound decision on these issues. This book provides a framework and a plan that will enable business and technical managers to make the optimal decisions that are necessary for the successful implementation of SAP in their organizations.

The approach adopted in this book will be useful to any professional who must present a case for implementing SAP to higher management or to those who would be involved in a SAP project.

Within the two covers of this book, you will find all the details that you need to confidently plan and present a case for choosing SAP, without ever asking the software vendor or involving the vendor's personnel. Rather than gaining help, approaching the vendor often turns out to be the best prescription for stirring up a hornet's nest! For readers who are actually involved with any aspect of a SAP project, this book can be used as a road map that will enable them to make a more meaningful contribution to the success of their SAP implementation project.

By millennium enterprise, I mean those companies that have annual revenues between $50 million and $1 billion; they are also referred to as small and medium enterprises (SME). In the last few years, most of the Fortune 1000 companies have already implemented SAP or some other competing product. Thus, in the new millennium, the growth in ERP market will primarily be coming from SME segment companies; hence, I am calling them millennium enterprises. The reader may be well advised to keep this in mind while he or she is reading the book, because some facts stated here may seem contrary to what has been the norm for ERP implementations up to now. For instance, many SAP consultants seem to believe that the post-Y2K SAP implementations will be no different than the affairs of the past that involved 70 to 100 people. The point is that SAP implementations in the new millennium are *not* going to require the efforts of 100 people.

What Makes this Book Different?

This book interprets the 1990's phenomenon of ERP software packages from the point of view of business as well as technology. This book unravels the mystery of ERPs like SAP and their power and potential to transform business enterprises. Customary discussions on ERP systems do not address the key differentiator of ERPs from the earlier mission-critical systems: ERPs, for the first time, are able to treat enterprise-level information not merely as records of information, but as a tangible resource.

This book also touches upon certain aspects of SAP implementation that would be of interest to company executives and decision makers. In Part VI, we touch upon return on investment (ROI) issues for implementing ERP within an organization. The last chapter covers many aspects that will become significant for the extended millennium enterprise, or what I term as the *extended collaborative enterprise*, including supply-chain management (SCM), customer relationship management (CRM), enterprise application integration (EAI), and SAP's mySAP.com Internet environment. I also introduce the powerful concept of a *customer-triggered company*.

SAP is the one of the best ERPs on the market. It has a very advanced architecture and design that enables it to not only provide both comprehensiveness and flexibility of adoption, but also permits it to evolve and release upgrades in functionality from different modules without disrupting its already functioning system. SAP, however, has not developed in isolation from the IT industry in general. The design and architecture of SAP picks from the best of development in IS/IT in the latter half of the 20th century. At various stages I have taken the opportunity to highlight the connections with parallel developments in software development technologies and methodologies to make the context of several outstanding features available in SAP more meaningful.

This book also gives you an introduction to SAP's rapid implementation methodology called AcceleratedSAP (ASAP). ASAP is mainly targeted at the millennium enterprises with revenues between $50 million to $1 billion.

In this book, you will also encounter concepts that may pique your interest since they might have been used for the first time in the context of ERP systems. These include management by Enterprise Standard Time (EST), collaborative enterprise, extended collaborative enterprise (ECE), Critical Value Determinants (CVDs), the Web User Interface (WUIs) and many more. Some terms and concepts, however, have been newly developed during the course of writing this book, such as management by collaboration, introduced in the first chapter, and customer-triggered company, described in the last chapter of the book.

In the last section of the book, with the reader's indulgence, I speculate on the reasons why Internet is begetting the revolutionary changes that we are witnessing today not only for individuals, but also for enterprises.

How Is this Book Organized?

Part I: Setting The Stage

Chapters in the first part of this book give the context and significance of ERPs and SAP in particular for increasing the competitiveness of organizations. Chapter 1 introduces the key idea of information as a substitute for traditional resources and the consequential productivity-multiplying and performance-enhancing features of ERPs.

Chapters 2 and 3 present a framework for the evaluation and selection of ERPs. Chapter 4 presents support for the claim that SAP is the best ERP system on the market. Chapter 5 presents an overview of a SAP implementation project, which can help your understanding of how all the other pieces, discussed in the following chapters, fit into the overall scheme. Chapter 6 touches upon enterprise reengineering, which is an important aspect of any ERP implementation project, especially for rapid implementation methodologies like ASAP.

Part II: SAP R/3

This part contains three chapters that respectively cover the three main components of SAP. Chapter 7 introduces Basis for the administration and management of a SAP system. Chapter 8 is on Advanced Business Application Programming (ABAP), which is the complete development environment within SAP. Chapter 9 is on the heart of the SAP R/3 system, the various application modules catering to the functional requirements of different areas of the enterprise.

Part III: The Pre-Implementation Stage

This part presents the various activities that are prerequisites for starting a SAP project. Chapter 10 discusses various activities and tasks that need to be readied for the SAP implementation effort. Chapter 12 provides a brief on SAP installation its administrative aspects.

Part IV: The Implementation Stage

This part presents in detail SAP's ASAP implementation methodology through all its stages. Chapter 12 introduces the concept and context of ASAP and, along with the other chapters in this section, it provides details on ASAP's five stages: Project Preparation, Business Blueprint, Realization, Final Preparation, and Go Live and Support.

Part V: The Post-Implementation Stage

Chapter 18 gives a brief overview of the post-implementation issues associated with a SAP system in production. Chapter 19 presents the enhancements and interface systems provided by SAP to maximize the benefits of a SAP-enabled integrated, enterprise-wide, process-oriented, information-driven, real-time enterprise.

Part VI: SAP Implementation and Beyond

Chapter 20 presents various aspects related to valuing the ROI of a SAP implementation using the Balance Scorecard method recommended by SAP. SAP implements the Balance Scorecard via its SAP strategic enterprise management solution. In the last chapter of the book, Chapter 21, we visit several aspects of the extended collaborative enterprise and how SAP is gearing up for enabling millennium enterprises to address these emerging challenges through a slew of product initiatives like Advanced Planning and Optimization (APO) and mySAP.com. With SAP finally abandoning the monolithic approach to developing systems and embracing a more symbiotic strategy vis-à-vis other players in the market, mySAP.com marks a watershed in the history of SAP.

Who Should Read this Book?

This book can be read by all stakeholders of the SAP project.

Here are the minimal recommendations for the chapters that should be read by different categories of stakeholders:

- Executives and business managers should read Chapters 1, 4, 20, and 21.
- Operational managers should read Chapters 1, 4, 5, 6, 10, 20, and 21.
- SAP evaluation and selection team members should read Chapters 1, 2, 3, 4, 5, and 21.
- Project managers and module leaders should read Chapters 1, 4, 5, 6, and 9 through 21.
- Functional members of the SAP team should read Chapters 1, 2, 4, 5, 6, 9, 10, 12 through 17, 20, and 21.
- Technical managers should read 1, 2, 3, 4, 5, 7, 8, 10 through 19, and 21.
- Technical members of the SAP team should read 1, 2, 4, 5, and 7 through 19.
- Professionals interested in SAP should read Chapters 1, 4, 5, 6, 9, 10, 11, 12, 16, 20 and 21.
- General readers interested in the phenomenon of ERP and SAP should read 1, 4, 5, 10, 12, 18, 20 and 21.

Vivek Kale

Iselin, NJ

October 15, 1999

Setting the Stage

IN THIS PART

The Millennium Enterprise

In the postindustrial and postmodern era, organizations are undergoing fundamental transformation and will undergo even further changes in the new millennium. The enterprises of the new millennium will be characterized by their primary emphasis on value-adding in every process and activity within the organization. Consequently, millennium enterprises will foster the ability to change and then leverage the organizational expertise and experience. Members of these enterprises will be partners rather than employees, with high involvement and participation in the operations of the company. This will demand a new kind of enterprisewide architecture that will act as an enabler for all the flexibility and resilience essential for survival in the new millennium. ERP packages, such as SAP R/3, provide essentially such an empowered architecture for the millennium enterprise.

SAP the Company and its Product R/3

SAP has become the leading vendor of standard business applications software. Throughout the last decade, it has reported sales and profit growth rates in excess of 40% every year. The sales for 1998 were reported to be $8.47 billion. As reported by SAP, there are more than 10,000 customers with more than 19,000 installations of SAP across the world. And, world wide, more than 1 million users work on SAP systems. By any standards, these are impressive numbers coming from a company that has a great vision and is destined to play a significant role even in the Internet-driven markets of this century as well.

SAP has two main products: R/2 and R/3. The R/2 system runs on mainframes like IBM, Siemens, and so on. R/3 system, which is the client/ server variant of the older system, was introduced in 1992. However, subsequent to the major enhancements during versions 3.0 and 3.1, it became the flagship product of the company garnering a lion's share of the total revenues earned by SAP every year. Throughout this book, I will refer to SAP as a company as well as its products R/2 and R/3 by the same term 'SAP.' This should not lead to any confusion because I believe that, at any point, the context would make it clearwhich meaning is intended. Also, unless specifically mentioned, SAP the product would usually refer to its client/server product R/3.

The phenomenal success of SAP comes from the fact that SAP systems are comprehensive but at the same time configurable to the specific needs of any company. Companies prefer off-the-shelf packages like SAP because it is flexible and can be configured to satisfy most requirements of any company in any industry. SAP can be deployed on various hardware platforms providing the same comprehensive and integrated functionality, flexibility for addressing individual company-specific requirements, as well as ensuring independence from specific technologies deployed in the company.

SAP implements a process-oriented view of the enterprise. It is remarkable that right from the beginning, SAP focused on developing enterprisewide software to integrate all business processes within the enterprise. This integration was also to result from real-time processing of data rather than the batch-mode processing that was dominant at that time. And, they also adopted very early on the layered model for the application architecture as a fundamental design principal that promised inherent flexibility and openness.

At every stage in its history, SAP made critical decisions in adopting barely emerging ideas and technologies as the core strategies for its products even though these concepts had not proven themselves in the market. For instance, in the beginning they decided on the concept of an enterprisewide centralized database as well as real-time updates into this centralized database. They embraced the truth about GUIs being the focus of all interactions between the system and the users long before hardware and technologies made this viable without sacrificing the critical virtue of scalability. Also SAP always kept internationalization and related issues like multi-currency on its active agenda while developing and enhancing its products. The SAP systems were fundamentally architectured to be multi-lingual right from their initial offerings and versions.

SAP is one of the best ERP packages that there is on the market; but it also shares this market-space with a handful of other packages. In the last few years, the characteristics of such packages called Enterprise Resources Planning (ERP) have become well established. In this chapter, we will look in detail at the nature of ERP packages and the reason for their predominant position in the IT landscape in the '90s.

The Concept of Enterprise Resources Planning Systems

There have never been commensurate gains accruing to an enterprise corresponding to the level of its investments in IS. This has also come to be known as the productivity paradox of IT. It has been a reality that all of us in the IT industry have lived uncomfortably with for the major part of our professional lives.

In the past few decades, all of us have witnessed a procession of different methodologies, tools, and techniques emanating from this industry that have had tremendous impact on the very nature and operations of business enterprises. But in midst of all this turmoil, one fact has remained constant, and that has been the lack of productivity improvements, irrespective of the extent and nature of computerization.

But right from the start, there was an even more basic problem in terms of the number of software applications that were actually completed and implemented successfully. Much has been written on the software crisis that was engulfing information service groups in the '80s. The reasons were multifold:

- With the advent of PC-like functionalities, users were becoming more complex and demanding.
- Consequently, applications were becoming bigger and more complex.
- Correspondingly, productivity was reducing rather than increasing.
- Software development times were increasing, and cost and time overruns were fairly routine.
- Quality, trained professionals were always in short supply, resulting in increased costs for programmers; hence, systems development costs were ever-increasing.
- Mortality of systems was very high.

On average, out of the total number of IT systems under development, more than half used to be cancelled; out of the remaining half, only about two-thirds was delivered. Half of the delivered systems never got implemented, whereas another quarter were abandoned midway through the implementation. Out of the residual quarter of the delivered systems, half failed to deliver the functionality required by the management and, therefore, were scrapped. Only the remaining half of the systems were used after great modifications, which entailed further delays and costs in an almost never-ending process.

One of the root causes identified for these problems was the inherent weakness of the phase in which requirements were captured and analyzed. This phase never seemed to get the correct and complete requirements. As a result, completed projects never seemed to deliver promised functionality and had to be recycled for more analysis and development. Maintenance and enhancements were called for indefinitely and became harder to achieve as time passed by. Because individuals changed midway both on the development and user sides, system requirements changed and the whole process continued indefinitely. This is primarily because there is a fundamental disconnect between the business and the IT/IS people. Notwithstanding how much both the parties try to bridge the gap, there is a fundamental gap between the perception of a business user and what is understood by the systems staff; both classes of people speak different languages. Even if the systems personnel tried to increase precision by using methodologies and specification tools, because users were unfamiliar with these tools, they were never able to ratify the documented requirements completely.

Typically, surveys found that 50% to 80% of the IT/IS resources were dedicated to application maintenance. The return on investments in IT was abysmally low by any standard of measurement and expectations. With IT/IS budgets stretching beyond the capabilities of most organizations, there was a compelling need for a radically new approach that could result in actual usable functionality that was professionally developed, under control, and on time.

This is the postmodern version of C. P. Snow's 'two cultures', which he had initially mooted to talk meaningfully about the worlds of art and science in the middle of the last century.

The traditional software implementations involving the development of applications were characterized by:

- Requirement-driven functional decomposition
- Late risk resolution
- Late error detection
- Use of different languages or artifacts at different phases of the project
- Large proportion of scrap and rework
- Adversarial stakeholder relationship with non-IT users
- Priority of techniques over tools
- Priority of quality of developed software rather than functionality per se
- Great emphasis on current, correct, complete and consistent documentation
- Great emphasis on testing and reviews
- Major effort on change control and management
- Large and diverse resource requirements
- Schedules always under pressure
- Great effort on projected or estimated target performance
- Inherent limitations on scalability
- Protracted integration between systems

Many alternate strategies were devised like CASE and prototyping; however, none were able to cross this basic hurdle. CASE provided more rigorous environment for requirements analysis and design, and, automated to a large extent the subsequent development of code, testing, and documentation efforts. The increased time spent on requirements definition with the users was envisaged to lead to systems that were closer to the users' actual requirements. On the other hand, prototyping was designed to address the requirements capture issue by making the users directly participate in the process of defining the requirements. This was focused mainly on the screen and reports design because these were the elements that could be visualized directly by the user. But, none of these strategies really resolved the problem. ERP packages adopted a totally different approach by providing the most comprehensive functionality within the package. Company personnel were only expected to pick and choose whatever was required by the company actually using the package. Thus, ERP packages effectively short-circuited the whole issue of capturing requirements. The traditional project life cycle—consisting of analysis, design, development, testing, and implementation—was transformed to the ERP implementation life cycle consisting merely of requirements mapping, gap analysis, configuring and customizing, testing, and implementation. Figure 1.1 shows a comparison of effort expended during ERP and the traditional software development life cycle.

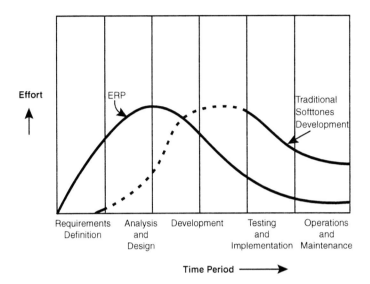

FIGURE 1.1
Comparison of effort expended during ERP and the traditional software development life cycle.

This ultimately led to the ERP revolution that we are witnessing today.

Unlike the traditional systems, the ERP software implementations involving the implementation of pre-developed comprehensive software applications are characterized by:

- Primacy of the architecture; process-oriented configurability
- Primacy and direct participation of the business user
- Early risk resolution
- Early error and gap detection
- Iterative life-cycle process; negligible proportion of scrap and rework
- Changeable and configurable functionality
- Participatory and cohesive stakeholder relationship with non-IT users
- Priority of functionality over tools followed by techniques
- Quality of the functional variability and flexibility of the available functionality
- Great emphasis on current, correct, complete, and consistent documentation of customizations

- Great emphasis on integration testing
- Actual demonstration of functionality at all phases of the project
- Twin categories of resource requirements: functional and technical
- Schedules devoid of long-term cascading impact
- Demonstrated performance
- Larger span of scalability
- Efficient integration between systems

What Is ERP?

So, what is ERP? Not only is there little agreement on what it really stands for, but also there is even less agreement on what constitutes an ERP package, how it should be used, the potential of productivity gain, the impact on the organization, the costs involved, the personnel needed, and the training needed for the ERP personnel. ERP characteristics are not limited to the ERP products and tools that are currently available in the market, and ERP is certainly not a technique or methodology. There is every reason to believe that the boundaries described for ERP in this book will be constantly enlarging in the coming years (see "The Anatomy of an ERP System" in Chapter 2). Notwithstanding all these caveats, ERP could be defined reasonably as follows:

An Enterprise Resources Planning (ERP) software application package is a suite of pre-engineered, ready-to-implement, integrated application modules, catering to all the business functions of an enterprise and possessing the flexibility for configuring and customizing dynamically the delivered functionality of the package to suit the specific requirements of the enterprise. ERP enables an enterprise to operate as an integrated, enterprisewide, process-oriented, information-driven, and real-time enterprise.

An ERP package can provide this comprehensiveness and flexibility because at the heart of the system resides a CASE-like repository that stores all details of these predeveloped applications. These details include every single data-item, data-table, and software program that is used by the complete system. For instance, SAP 4.0B has more than 800 application process definitions stored in about 8000 tables within its repository. It also has additional support subsystems that help it manage, secure, and maintain the operations of this package on a day-to-day basis.

Off-the-shelf packages, and especially enterprisewide solutions such as ERP, were considered as the best approach for confronting the software crisis of the '80s. This was because of the following:

- ERP ensures better validation of user requirements directly by the user
- ERP ensures consistent quality of delivered functionality
- ERP provides a cohesive and integrated information system architecture

- ERP ensures a fair degree of standardization
- ERP provides a consistent and accurate documentation of the system
- ERP provides outstanding quality and productivity in the development and maintenance of the system

A decade later, as companies are reporting their experiences in implementing ERP, a base of experience seems to support the fact that companies that plan and manage the use of ERP are usually successful. It is no longer a matter of learning only new technology; it is now about applying the new technology effectively and addressing the problems of inertia and resistance to change across the organization. In fact, ERP has the potential to enforce cross-functional interaction, consistency, structure, processes, and above all, good management practices. Today, the recognized management decision is not *whether* to use ERP, but rather *when* to use ERP and *which* ERP package to use. As you go through the book, it will become evident that SAP R/3 is the best-of-breed product in this genre.

The success of ERP packages is based on the principle of reusability. The origin of reusability goes back almost to the beginning of the computer era, when it was recognized that too much program code was being written and rewritten repeatedly and uneconomically. Very soon, most of the programming languages provided for routines or packets of logic that could be reused multiple times within individual programs or even by a group of programs. Databases enabled the reuse of data, resulting in a tremendous surge in programmer productivity. Similarly, networks permitted reuse of the same programs on different terminals or workstations at different locations.

ERP basically extended the concept of reusability to the functionality provided by the package. For instance, SAP R/3 was based on the essential commonality observed in the functioning of companies within an industry. SAP built a reusable library of normally required processes in a particular industry, and all implementing SAP customers had to do was to select from this library all those processes that were required by their company. From the project effort and cost that were essential for the development and implementation using the traditional software development life cycle (SDLC), ERP reduced the project effort and cost to that associated with the implementation phase of the SDLC.

Even though the cost of implementing ERP might seem higher than that of traditional systems, ERP is implemented sooner, and therefore, starts delivering all its benefits much earlier than traditional systems. The fabled library of 800 best-of-business processes made available by SAP R/3 is like building blocks that can be reused by any customer to build its system quickly and at a considerably reduced cost.

Although there have not been any published results yet, it became an accepted fact that enterprises that implemented ERP packages for only a part of their organizations, or for only a few select functions within their organizations, did not benefit greatly. For the first time in the history of IT, ERPs recognized the fact that business processes of an organization were much more fundamental than data characterizing various aspects of the organization. Most importantly, ERP packages elevated IS from a mere enabler of the business strategy of an organization to a significant part of the business strategy itself.

Thus, ERP packages brought to an end the subsidiary and support role that IT had played throughout the last few decades. But in turn, the very nature of IS has also undergone a complete transformation. Implementing an ERP within an enterprise was no longer a problem of technology; it was a business problem. ERP packages have been the harbingers of a paradigm shift in the role of the IS/IT function within an enterprise. This book was motivated by the need to address these fundamental changes in the very nature of IS/IT activity within an enterprise.

The distinguishing characteristics of ERP are as follows:

- ERP transforms an enterprise into an information-driven enterprise
- ERP fundamentally perceives an enterprise as a global enterprise
- ERP reflects and mimics the integrated nature of an enterprise
- ERP fundamentally models a process-oriented enterprise
- ERP enables the real-time enterprise
- ERP elevates IT strategy as a part of the business strategy
- ERP represents an advance on the approaches to manufacturing performance improvement
- ERP represents the new Department Store model of implementing computerized systems
- ERP is a mass user-oriented application environment

In the remaining part of this section, we deal with each of these characteristics of ERP systems. There is also a need for a unifying framework that brings together the various aspects of an ERP implementation. In the section "Management by Collaboration," I introduce the unifying framework for the various aspects of the ERP-enabled collaborative enterprise, and set the tone for the rest of the book as well. I end this chapter with a discussion of how ERP packages such as SAP R/3 provide the new organizational architecture essential for the enterprise of the new millennium, or what I will call the millennium enterprise.

ERP Transforms an Enterprise into an Information-driven Enterprise

All computerized systems and solutions in the past were using past-facing information merely for the purpose of referring and reporting only. ERP, for the first time in the history of computerized systems, began treating information as a resource for the operational requirements of the enterprise. But, unlike the traditional resources, information resource made available by ERPs can be re-used and shared multiply without dissipation or degradation. The impressive productivity gains resulting from the ERPs truthfully arise out of this unique characteristic of ERPs to use information as an inexhaustible resource.

ERP Perceives an Enterprise as a Global Enterprise

In these times of divestitures, mergers, and acquisitions, this is an important requirement.

Unlike some of the earlier enterprisewide solutions available on mainframes, ERP packages cater to corporation-wide requirements even if an organization is involved in disparate businesses such as discrete industries (manufacturing, engineering, and so on), process industries (chemicals, paints, and so on), and service industries (banking, media, and so on). ERP packages enable the management to plan, operate, and manage such conglomerates without the impediment of mismatching systems for different divisions.

Although it might seem a minor point, ERP packages also permit the important functionality of enabling seamless integration of distributed or multi-location operations; I consider this aspect in the next subsection.

ERP Reflects and Mimics the Integrated Nature of an Enterprise

Notwithstanding the different ways in which the enterprises are structured and organized, enterprises function essentially in an integrated fashion. Across the years, the turf-preservation mentality has caused a motley array of information systems to mushroom within organizations, reinforcing rather than lessening the heterogeneity of systems. This has led to problems of incompatibility, differing standards, interfacing issues, limited upgrade paths, costly maintenance, high operating costs, costly training and support activities, inconsistent documentation, and so on. Instead of providing the strategic leverage necessary for the business operations of the enterprise, IS/IT systems were a constant drain on the enterprise.

ERP, with its holistic approach and its demand for integration, dissolves all such inefficiency by dissipating spurious processes, not only in their IS/IT aspects, but also in their actual functions. With its laser-like focus on best-of-breed practices, SAP demonstrates the essential futility of routine bureaucratic mechanization within organizations. For instance, whereas finance might aim for minimizing stock, the purchasing function might want to maintain a buffer stock to avoid out-of-stock situations. Similarly, marketing might want production of more varied product models to cater to the requirements in the market whereas production function will want to lessen the number of different kinds of products for reducing set-up times and related costs. By promoting cross-functional processes and work teams, ERP, like SAP R/3, provides a powerful medium for supporting, reconciling, and optimizing the conflicting goals of different functions of organizations.

ERP Fundamentally Models a Process-Oriented Enterprise

As organizational and environmental conditions become more complex, globalized, and competitive, processes provide a framework for dealing effectively with the issues of performance improvement, capability development, and adaptation to the changing environment. Process modeling permits the true comprehension of the characteristic structure and dynamics of the business.

Conventional systems primarily store only snapshots of discrete groups of data at predefined or configured instants of time, along a business process within an organization. This predominating data-oriented view of the enterprise as implemented by traditional IT systems is a most unnatural and alien way of looking at any area of human activity. The stability of the data models, as canonized in the conventional IT paradigm, might have been advantageous for the systems personnel, but for the same reason it would have been unusable (and unacceptable) to the business stakeholders within the organizations. Traditional systems could never really resolve this simple dichotomy of the fact that systems based on leveraging the unchanging data models, although easy to maintain, can never describe the essentially dynamic nature of businesses. Business processes are the most important portions of the reality that had been ignored by the traditional information systems. The traditional IT process modeling techniques, methodologies and environments, are a misnomer; for they truly model only the procedures for operating on the data associated at various points of the business sub-processes which themselves are never mirrored within the system.

ERP packages for the first time recognized the fundamental error that was perpetuated all these past decades. Although many ERP packages still carry the legacy of the data-oriented view, the parallel view of business process and business rules is gaining prominence rapidly. This is the reason for the rapidly maturing groupware and workflow sub-systems within the core architecture of current ERP systems.

ERP Enables the Real-Time Enterprise

ERP packages have engendered the earlier, only imagined possibility of a real-time enterprise. Even before the arrival of ERP packages, companies witnessed the power and perils of operating an online system that provided on-the-system direct registration of business transactions, as well as immediate updates and posting to the relevant master and transaction data files. ERP packages have made this possible on an enterprisewide scale, and have realized tremendous gains in efficiencies and productivity by extending the concept of "just in time" (JIT) to the whole organization.

Every system is a collection of many subsystems and processes, with life-cycle times of varying duration. A system that can respond effectively within the life-cycle time of some of the smaller life cycles can be considered to be functioning essentially in a real-time mode. This would result in the kinds of customer responses that would be unimaginable earlier.

In analogy with this, for better appreciation of real-time responsiveness, enterprises could define Enterprise Standard Time (EST). This could be defined based on the following:

- A central reference location within the organization
- An optimal cycle time in days or weeks suitable for all functions within the organization

All responses within the enterprise could be measured with reference to this EST. Enterprises that can cut down their EST relentlessly would be able to sustain their competitiveness in the market. And, this would become achievable to a large extent because of the instant availability of relevant information to all concerned members of the company provided by the ERP. Information is only relevant when it is available within a cycle of EST; information furnished after this period ceases to act as a resource and rapidly ends up being of value only for recording and reporting purposes (see the last paragraph in the section "Information as the New Resource"). A continuous effort for reducing EST would result in the kind of customer responsiveness that would be unimaginable in earlier times.

Furthermore, the real-time responsiveness of the enterprise coupled with the earlier mentioned enterprisewide integration also enable enterprises the powerful capability of *concurrent processing* which would be impossible without ERPs like SAP. Enterprises can obtain tremendous efficiencies and throughputs because of this ability to administer in parallel many related processes that are not interdependent fully or partially. In non-ERP enterprises, such closely related processes are typically done sequentially because they are usually handled by the same set of personnel, who might obviously be constrained to address them only in a sequence. An illustration of this could be ad-hoc analysis that might have to be done simultaneously on a set of purchase orders (PO) and corresponding vendors/suppliers, deliveries, invoices, and so on. ERPs like SAP can perform all these concurrently because of ready availability of all relevant, complete, and consistent information at the same time.

ERP Elevates IT Strategy as a Part of the Business Strategy

The coming of SAP heralded an enhanced role for IT systems. They are no longer the support functions of earlier years. If someone is under that illusion, he or she will pay a very high price. Today, the real focus of IS/IT systems is no longer its alignment with the business strategy of the enterprise, but on how to give it a competitive edge; it is part of the business necessities and priorities. Because of the complexity of increasing business change and uncertainty, IS/IT is business strategy incarnate!

This arises primarily from the fact that information itself has become a vital resource for an enterprise. Information is now in the same league as the traditional resources, such as manpower, materials, money, and time.

ERP Advance on the Earlier Approaches to Manufacturing Performance Improvement

ERP is the latest in the succession of approaches that has been adopted throughout the history of enterprises for improvement of enterprise-level performances. ERPs have realized the failed dream of improvements that were expected from the MRP-II based Manufacturing Resources Planning systems of the '70s. ERP has enabled combining the 'hard' approach of MRP-II with the more broad-scoped 'soft' approaches of World Class Manufacturing (WCM) that were widely adopted during the '80s. The WCM included such powerful approaches as JIT, TQM, Benchmarking, Lean Manufacturing, Human Resources Development movement, and, later in the '90s, Business Process Re-engineering. Table 1.1 gives a list of major enterprise performance-improvement movements during the last century. ERPs provide the basic platform for devising techniques and tools for better implementations of the earlier approaches.

TABLE **1.1**   Timeline of Performance Improvement Movements in the 20th Century

Year	Performance Improvement Movement	Founder(s)
1690	Division of Labor	Adam Smith
1890	Scientific Measurement	Frederick Taylor
1900	Mass Production	Henry Ford
1920	Industrial Engineering	F. Gilbreth and Fredrick Taylor
1930	Human Relations Movement	Elton Mayo
1950	Japanese Quality Revolution	J. M. Juran and W. E. Demming
1960	Materials Requirement Planning	William Orlicky
1970	Manufacturing Resources Planning	Oliver Wright
1970	Focused Factory	Wickham Skinner
1980	Total Quality Management	Philip Crosby
1980	Just In Time	Taiicho Ohno
1980	Computer Integrated Manufacturing	
1980	Optimized Production Technology	Eliyahu Goldratt
1980	ISO 9000	NASI
1980	World Class Manufacturing	Richard Schonberger

continues

TABLE **1.1** Continued

Year	Performance Improvement Movement	Founder(s)
1990	Mass Customization	Stan Davis and B. Joseph Pine II
1990	Lean Manufacturing	Jones & Roos
1990	Business Process Re-engineering	Michael Hammer
1990	Supply Chain Management	

ERP Represent the Departmental Store Model of Implementing Computerized Systems

The coming of ERP has been the death knell of the development model of IS systems. Along with it went the concept of requirements capture, modeling languages, development of software programs, testing, and so on that have usually been associated with the conventional developmental model. In its place, for the first time, is the end-user friendly model of what one could call the Department Store model of computerized systems. From the array of functional goodies on display, you pick and choose the functionality you require.

An ERP is the analogue of the great Department Store of functionalities or processes required within an organization. ERP makes the transition from the world of carefully engineered and running systems to the world of consumers, in which the value of the delivered functionality is based not on its pedigree, but only on what, how, where, and when it can be used gainfully. This then is the final commoditization of the IS/IT products and services!

ERP Is a Mass-User Oriented Application Environment

Compared to the degree of involvement of functional managers and end users in traditional software project implementations, their participation in SAP implementations might seem unusual. SAP brings computerization to desktops, and in this sense is an end user-oriented environment in the true sense of the word. Unlike traditional systems in which users accessed the system directly only in well-defined pockets within the enterprise, in SAP, end users are truly the personnel actually involved with the operations of the business. Because of the intense involvement of a sizable portion of the workforce of the company with the SAP implementation from the beginning, the probability of users embracing the system and not struggling against it is much higher. Users also act as the advocates and facilitators during and after the implementation phase.

Management by Collaboration (MBC)

The business environment has been witnessing tremendous and rapid changes in the '90s. There is an increasing emphasis on being customer focused and on leveraging and strengthening the company's core competencies. This has forced companies to learn and develop abilities to change and respond rapidly to the competitive dynamics of the global market.

Companies have learned to effectively re-engineer themselves into flatter organizations, with closer integration across the traditional functional boundaries of the organization. There is increasing focus on employee empowerment and cross-functional teams. In this book, I am proposing that what we are witnessing is a fundamental transformation from the manner in which businesses have been operating for the last century.

This change, which is primarily driven by the information revolution of the past few decades, is characterized by the dominant tendency to integrate across transaction boundaries, both internally and externally. The dominant theme of this new system of management with significant implications on organizational development is *collaboration*. I will refer to this emerging and maturing constellation of concepts and practices as Management by Collaboration (MBC). ERP packages such as SAP R/3 are major instruments for realizing MBC-driven organizations.

MBC is an approach to management primarily focused on relationships; relationships by their very nature are not static and are constantly in evolution. As organizational and environmental conditions become more complex, globalized, and therefore, competitive, MBC provides a framework for dealing effectively with the issues of performance improvement, capability development, and adaptation to the changing environment. MBC, as embodied by ERP packages such as SAP R/3, has had a major impact on the strategy, structure, and culture of the organization.

The beauty and essence of MBC are that it incorporates in its very fabric the basic urge of humans for a purpose in life; for mutually beneficial relationships; for mutual commitment; and for being helpful to other beings, that is, for collaborating. These relationships could be at the level of individual, division, company, or even between companies. Every relationship has a purpose, and manifests itself through various processes as embodied mainly in the form of teams; thus, the relationships are geared towards attainment of these purposes through the concerned processes optimally.

Because of the enhanced role played by the individual members of a company in any relationship or process, MBC promotes not only their motivation and competence, but also develops the competitiveness and capability of the organizations as a whole. MBC emphasizes the roles of both the top management and the individual member. Thus, the MBC approach covers the whole organization through the means of basic binding concepts such as relationships, processes, and teams. MBC addresses readily all issues of management, including organization development. The issues range from organizational design and structure, role definition and job design, output quality and productivity, communication channels, and company culture to employee issues such as attitudes, perception, values, and motivation.

The basic idea of collaboration has been gaining tremendous ground with the increasing importance of business processes and dynamically constituted teams in the operations of companies. The traditional bureaucratic structures, which are highly formalized, centralized, and functionally specialized, have proven too slow, too expensive, and too unresponsive to be competitive. These structures are based on the basic assumption that all the individual activities and task elements in a job are independent and separable. Organizations were structured hierarchically in a "command and control" structure, and it was taken as an accepted fact that the output of the organization as a whole could be maximized by maximizing the output of each constituent organizational unit.

On the other hand, by their very nature, teams are flexible, adaptable, dynamic, and collaborative. They encourage flexibility, innovation, entrepreneurship, and responsiveness. For the last few decades, even in traditionally bureaucratic-oriented manufacturing companies, teams have manifested themselves and flourished successfully in various forms as super-teams, self-directed work teams (SDWT), quality circles, and so on. The dynamic changes in the market and global competition being confronted by companies necessarily lead to flatter and more flexible organizations with a dominance of more dynamic structures like teams.

People in teams, representing different functional units, are motivated to work within constraints of time and resources to achieve a defined goal. The goals might range from incremental improvements in efficiency, quality, and productivity to quantum leaps in new-product development. Even in traditional businesses, the number and variety of teams instituted for various functions, projects, tasks, and activities has been on the increase.

Increasingly, companies are populated with worker-teams that have special skills, operate semi-autonomously, and are answerable directly to peers and to the end customers. Members must not only have higher level of skills than before, but must also be more flexible and capable of doing more jobs. The empowered workforce with considerably enhanced managerial responsibilities (pertaining to information, resources, authority, and accountability) has resulted in an increase in worker commitment and flexibility. Whereas workers have witnessed gains in the quality of their work life, corporations have obtained returns in terms of increased quality, productivity, and cost improvements.

Consequently, in the past few years, a new type of non-hierarchical network organization with distributed intelligence and decentralized decision-making powers has been evolving. This entails a demand for constant and frequent communication and feedback among the various teams or functional groups. An ERP package such SAP R/3 essentially provides such an enabling environment through its modules like SAP Office, SAP Workflow, and SAP Business Warehouse.

The Information-Driven Enterprise

The combined impact on companies of increasing product complexity together with increased variety has been to create a massive problem of information management and coordination. Information-based activities now constitute a major fraction of all activities within an enterprise. Information-based organizations alone can enable companies to survive in the dynamically changing global competitive market. Only integrated, computer-based, postmodern information systems such as SAP R/3 are (and can be) enablers for this kind of enterprise-level collaboration.

The information-based organization as proposed by management theorist Peter Drucker is a reality today; correspondingly, companies are compelled to install both end user- and workgroup-oriented, enterprise-level, integrated computing environments. Only information-based organizations can possibly store, retrieve, analyze and present colossal amounts of information at the enterprise-level that is also up-to-date, timely, accurate, collated, processed, and packaged dynamically for both external and internal customers. It should be noted that this sub-section title uses the phrase "information-driven" rather than "information-based." The primary reason for that is technology in the '90s permits us to use information as a resource that is a legitimate substitute for conventional resources. We visit this aspect in the section "Information as the New Resource."

The Process-Oriented Enterprise

ERP packages enable an organization to truly function as an integrated organization—integration across all functions or segments of the traditional value chain such as sales order, production, inventory, purchasing, finance and accounting, personnel and administration, and so on. They do this by modeling primarily the business processes as the basic business entities of the enterprise, rather than by modeling data handled by the enterprise (as done by the traditional IT systems). Every ERP might not be completely successful in this, however; in a break with the legacy enterprisewide solutions, every ERP treats business processes as more fundamental than data items.

Collaborations or relationships manifest themselves through the various organizational processes. A *process* might be generally defined as the set of resources and activities necessary and sufficient to convert some form of input into some form of output. Processes are internal, external, or a combination of both; they cross functional boundaries; they have starting and ending points; and they exist at all levels within the organization.

The significance of a process to the success of the company's business is dependent on the value, with reference to the customer, of the collaboration that it addresses and represents. Or, in other words, the nature and extent of the value addition by a process to a product or services delivered to a customer is the best index of the contribution of that process to the company's overall customer satisfaction or "customer collaboration."

Thus, MBC not only recognizes inherently the significance of various process-related techniques and methodologies such as Process Innovation (PI), Business Process Improvement (BPI), Business Process Redesign (BPRD), and Business Process Re-engineering (BPR), but also treats them as fundamental, continuous, and integral functions of the management of a company itself. A collaborative enterprise enabled by the implementation of an ERP is inherently amenable to business process improvement, which is also the essence of any Total Quality Management (TQM)-oriented effort undertaken within an enterprise. We will deal with such process improvement related issues in Chapter 6, "SAP and Enterprise Re-engineering."

The Value-Add Driven Enterprise

Business processes can be seen as the basis of the value addition within an organization that was traditionally attributed to various functions or divisions in an organization. As organizational and environmental conditions become more complex, globalized, and competitive, processes provide a framework for dealing effectively with the issues of performance improvement, capability development, and adaptation to the changing environment.

Along a value stream (that is, a business process), analysis of the absence, creation of added value, or (worse) destruction of value critically determines the necessity and effectiveness of a process step. The understanding of value-adding and non-value–adding processes (or process-steps) is a significant factor in the analysis, design, benchmarking, and optimization of business processes in the companies leading to the BPR. As will be discussed in Chapter 6 SAP R/3 Business Analyzer provides an environment for modeling, analyzing, and optimizing business processes.

Values are characterized by value determinants such as time (cycle time and so on), flexibility (options, customization, composition, and so on), responsiveness (lead time, number of hand-offs, and so on), quality (rework, rejects, yield, and so on), and price (discounts, rebates, coupons, incentives, and so on). I must hasten to add that I am not disregarding cost (materials, labor, overhead, and so forth) as an value determinant. However, the effect of cost is truly a result of a host of value determinants such as time, flexibility, responsiveness, and so on.

Consequently, in this formulation, one can understand completely the company's competitive gap in the market in terms of such process-based, customer-expected value and the value delivered by the company's processes for the concerned product or service. I will refer to such customer-defined characteristics of value as Critical Value Determinants (CVDs). Therefore, we can perform market segmentation for a particular (group of) product or service in terms of the most significant of the customer values and the corresponding CVDs.

Enterprise Change Management

Strategic planning exercises can be understood readily in terms of devising strategies for improving on these process-oriented CVDs based on the competitive benchmarking of these values. The strategies resulting from analysis, design, and optimization of processes would in turn result in a focus on the redesign of all relevant business process at all levels. This could result in the modification or deletion of the concerned processes or even the creation of new processes.

Initiating change and confronting change are the two most important issues facing the enterprises of today. The ability to change business processes contributes directly to the "innovation" bottom line. The traditional concept of change management is usually understood as a one-time event. But if an organization is looking for the capability not only to handle change management, but also management of changes on a continual basis, then ERP, like SAP R/3, is a must.

SAP R/3 enables the essential changing of processes that are extremely critical to the success of the enterprise. Business processes that "reside" or are internalized within an organization's employees are difficult to change simply because human beings naturally find it more difficult to change. However, processes that reside within any computerized systems are easy to change.

The Learning Organization

MBC also underlies the contemporary notion of the learning organization. To compete in an ever-changing environment, an organization must learn and adapt. Because organizations cannot think and learn themselves, it is truly the individuals constituting the organization who have to do this learning. The amount of information in an organization is colossal. A single individual, however intelligent and motivated, cannot learn and apply all the knowledge required for operating a company. Moreover, even this colossal amount of information does not remain constant, but keeps changing and growing.

The only effective solution is collaborative learning; that is, sharing this learning experience among a team of people. This not only caters to differences in the aptitudes and backgrounds of people, but also allows them all learn simultaneously, thus drastically shortening the turnaround time on the learning process itself. If organizational learning is seen in terms of the creation and management of knowledge, it is very easy for us to see the essential need to share the learning experience among the various member teams at the company level and, within each team, among the members of the teams.

As I will discuss in Chapter 4 in the section "Other Significant Aspects of SAP," SAP R/3 provides facilities and tools for quickly incorporating such learned variations on the primary business processes. Moreover, while incorporating these variations of the basic process in terms of various parameters, SAP would automatically suggest the selection of parameters for configuration that would permit the variation to become as generic as possible. Thus, ERP would not only assist in the immediate problem-solving problems in the present, but would also define the problem in a new way. The essential difference between the two types of learning is between being adaptive and having adaptability. ERP provides and increases the adaptability of an enterprise. This also automatically transforms the tacit knowledge within an enterprise to its explicit form for every one to know it, feel it, analyze it, and if possible, improve it further.

Thus, we see another reason for collaboration among and within teams for contributing effectively in the learning process of the organization as a whole. Furthermore, what distinguishes learning from mere training is the transformation that results from the former. This, again, can be implemented successfully only by collaborations between various teams as becomes apparent when such collaborations are embodied in the form of an ERP package, such as SAP R/3, and are implemented within enterprises.

The Virtual Organization

Along with the general economic growth and globalization of markets, personal disposable incomes have increased, so the demand for product variety and customization have increased appreciably. Additionally, technological progress driven by the search for superior performance is already increasing the complexity of both products and processes. Because volume, complexity, and variety are mutually exclusive, this has invariably led to collaborative endeavors for achieving this with greater flexibility in terms of enhancing capabilities, minimizing of risks, lowering costs of investments, shortening product life cycles, and so on.

These collaborative endeavors, which have been known variously as partnering, value-added partnering, partnership sourcing, outsourcing, alliances, virtual corporations, and so on recognize the fact that optimization of the system as a whole is not achievable by maximization of the output at the constituting subsystem levels alone. Only mature ERP packages such as SAP R/3 can provide a backbone for holding together the virtual value chain across all these collaborative relationships. In Chapter 21, "Beyond the Enterprise," we look at issues that are beyond the borders of the conventional enterprise.

Outsourcing will become a dominant trend in the millennium enterprise, whereby the enterprise concentrates only on being competitive in its core business activities and outsources the responsibility of competitiveness in noncore products and functions to third parties for mutual benefit. The development and maintenance of its core competencies are critical to the success of its main business; an enterprise cannot outsource these because it is these core functions that give it an identity. On the other hand, competitiveness in noncore functions, which is also essential for overall efficiencies, is outsourced to enterprises that are themselves in business of providing these very products or services; the outsourced products and services are *their* core competencies.

Most of the major manufacturers the world over have become to a large extent "systems integrators," providing only some of the specialized parts and final assembly of subsystems from a network of suppliers. Their economic role has transformed mainly into the basic design, marketing, and service, but not complete production *per se*. For the existence and growth of such virtual organizations, it is important that the company be able to manage the complexities of managing such relationship on day-to-day basis. An ERP system provides all the functionality and processes for managing and accounting for such outsourced jobs. But, more significantly, only an ERP can make it possible for such a collaborative enterprise to exist and grow to scales unimaginable with traditional organizational architectures. This will be dealt with in the last section of this chapter on "The Collaborative Enterprise, or Competing by Organizational Design."

Why Use ERP?

The implementation of ERP engenders the following business and technical advantages:

- Reconciles and optimizes the conflicting goals of different divisions or departments.

- Standardizes business processes across all constituent companies and sites, thus increasing their efficiencies.

- Provides the ability to know and implement global best practices.

- Alters the function-oriented organization toward a more team-based, cross-functional, process-oriented organization, thus leading to more flexible, flatter, and tightly integrated organization.

- Provides a responsive medium for undertaking all variants on process improvement programs and methodologies, including process innovation, process improvement, business process, and so on.

- Provides a responsive medium for quality improvement and standardization efforts including QC, QA, and TQM.

- Is process-oriented, and therefore is fertile ground for implementing Activity Based Management (ABM) efforts be they for budgeting, costing, efficiency, or quality.

- Provides the best conduit for measuring the benefits accruing to an organization by monitoring the Return on Investment (ROI) of not only money, but also manpower, materials, time, and information. This could be in terms of various parameters like cost, quality, responsiveness, cycle time, and so on. Thus, ERP could assist in the implementation of, for instance, the balanced scorecard within the enterprise.

- Customarily implements best-of-class practices and provides the best means for benchmarking the organization's competitiveness.

- Enables an enterprise to scale up its level of operations drastically, or even enter into different businesses altogether, without any disruption or performance degradation.

- Enables real-time creation of data directly during the actual transaction or processes by the persons who are actually responsible for it.

- Pushes latest data and status to the operational-level persons for better and faster decisions, at least on routine issues; empowers and gives ownership to the operational personnel at the level of actual work (this automatically does away with problems associated with collection of voluminous data, preparation, entry, corrections of inaccuracies, backups, and so on).

- Integrates data of the organization into a single comprehensive database.

- Provides online availability of correct and up-to-date data.

- Provides the most current, correct, consistent, and complete operational data that could be populated into the enterprise data warehouse for analysis and reporting.

- Greatly reduces the cost of maintaining systems.

As mentioned in the introduction to this chapter, all these characteristics of SAP-implemented organizations arise primarily from the fact that what they handle is not merely organizational data, but a resource that is of strategic significance to the enterprise.

In the next section, we turn to this aspect of the postmodern integrated organizations.

Knowledge as the New Capital

Adam Smith started the industrial revolution by identifying labor and capital as the economic determinants of the wealth of a nation. In this century, however, the size of the land, mass of labor, and materials that you may possess might be worthless if you do not control the related know-how. In the 21st century, know-how will reside and flourish in people's minds; what might matter more are how many enterprising and innovative people you have and the freedom they have in realizing their dreams. It will be the century of information economics.

ERP, like SAP, also acts as a transformer of the knowledge which resides in the heads of the operational and subject experts into a more explicit and accessible form. This corresponds exactly to the *tacit knowledge* talked about by I. Nonaka and H. Takeuchi in their book titled *The Knowledge Creating Company*. These could be learning experiences, ideas, insights, innovations, rules of thumb, business cases, concepts or conceptual models, analogies, and so on. They exhort companies to convert the illusive, unsystematized, uncodified and 'can-be-lost' knowledge of the corporation into *explicit knowledge* that can be codified, collated, and managed like any other capital investment. This could be in the form of documents, case studies, analysis reports, evaluations, concept papers, internal proposals, and so on. Most importantly, it is available for scrutiny and can be improved upon on an on-going basis. SAP performs the invaluable service of transforming the implicit knowledge into the explicit form.

Information as the New Resource

Having covered the context of ERP in this chapter, it's time to state that the importance of ERP packages such as SAP are not because of the total integration of various modules, single-point data entry, data integrity, ad-hoc reporting, instant access to information, end-user computing, and so on. The importance of ERP packages arises primarily from the fact that information is by now the *fifth resource* (the first four being manpower, materials, money, and time). And, unlike other resources, information is inexhaustible—*it can be shared infinitely without any reduction.* Thus, if we can use information as a substitute for other resources (which we can, see the following discussion), we can use it many times over without any appreciable further cost. Among all resources, this is one resource, which in practical terms almost defies the universal law of increase of Entropy as understood in the physical sciences.

Traditionally, competitive advantage came from strategies based on the following value determinants:

- Cost—Ownership, use, training support, maintenance, and so on
- Time—Cycle time, lead time, and so on
- Response time—Lead time, number of handoffs, number of queues, and so on
- Flexibility—Customization, options, composition, and so on
- Quality—Rework, rejects, yield, and so on
- Innovation—New needs, interfaces, add-ons, and so on

Everyone has squeezed (and continues to do so) as much as they can from these value determinants in the last few decades. Now the only source for competitive strategy of substantial value that remains to be exploited in a major way is from the latest new-found resource:

- Information—Correctness, currency, consistency, completeness, clarity, availability, security, and so on

For instance, Just-in-Time (JIT) inventory permits us to order for just the right kind of material at the right time at the right place. Therefore, it reduces inputs of manpower in ordering, handling and storing, and so on. It also results in reduced materials inventory and, hence, cost of storage mechanisms, cost of locked capital, and so on. The availability of detailed and up-to-the-minute information on (for example) production runs can result in up-to-the-minute information on

- Production plan for the next run
- Material requirements for next run
- Issue of materials from the main stores for the next run

- Stock-on-hand in the stores for the next run
- Material to be ordered for the next run, and so on

It is not difficult to see that this ultimately results in drastically increased throughputs and reduced business cycle times, which is equivalent to improved production or technological processes through use of improved resources. Traditionally, appreciably higher throughputs and lower production/business cycles were possible only through innovation in technology or production methods or processes. How information, as provided by ERPs, is a resource of an organization can be seen from the analogy with fuel which drives automobiles: Information, as made available by SAP R/3, greatly increases the velocity of business processes within the organization. Evidently, this is a class apart from what is achievable with the manual or even fragmented legacy computerized systems. enterprisewide JIT, and not just the one confined primarily to the production department, is impossible without integrated postmodern computerized systems like ERP packages for correct, current, consistent, and complete information.

We can take this analogy even further. In any industry, just as with any other traditional raw material, companies need the "information" resource preprocessed in massive amounts that has to be correct, current, consistent, and so on. Only complete and integrated ERP packages such as SAP R/3 can provide this operational raw material required in massive amounts. It should be specially noted that only an ERP implemented within an enterprise enables the optimal utilization and efficient conversion of such a seemingly intangible resource as *information* into a tangible commercial product, which is also a highly *perishable* resource!

ERPs as Keepers of Organizational Knowledge Assets

Vendors and ERP consultants strongly advise organizations not to customize ERP systems to fit the business but, as far as possible, change the business to fit best-practice functionalities and processes provided by the ERP system. However, ERP implementations must ultimately be business driven and not dictated and driven by technology issues.

The survival and success of an enterprise depends on how it differentiates itself and its products and services from those of its competitors. In this era of mass customization, what organizations need is not more standardization and generic processes, but the capability to be more dynamic, more flexible, more proprietary, and more customized. Because ERP basically embodies the "theory of business" of a company (à la Peter Drucker), it must also mirror these differences in strategies and processes. This is counter to the general emphasis on standardization and generic processes. To leverage their competencies, distinct advantages, edges, or competitive advantages, companies cannot abandon the corresponding differentiating processes and will have to incorporate such fundamental variants in their ERP implementations or interface with such systems (see the section "Enterprise Application Integration [EAI]" in Chapter 21). SAP's Industry Specific (IS) solutions were primarily efforts driven by recognition of this fundamental need along with the realization that SAP cannot be 'everything to everybody.' With the introduction of mySAP.com, SAP has finally abandoned the monolithic approach to developing systems, and it is adopting a more symbiotic strategy vis-a-vis other software players in the market.

All these unique value propositions and differentiating factors are organizational information assets, and are captured and configured into the ERP system. These information assets include the business rules and procedures or methods of operations, analysis, and making decisions, parameters of analysis, ranges for defining credit limits, credit periods, discounting structures, ratings, and so on. Like any other assets, ERP packages register, maintain, monitor, and report on these informational assets. This helps to maintain these assets to be current and useful.

The Collaborative Enterprise, or Competing by Organizational Design

ERP provides the design and architecture for the collaborative enterprise as discussed in this chapter. It provides the basic platform for enabling the enterprisewide, integrated, information-based, process-driven, real-time enterprise. This has a direct impact on many aspects that traditionally have been more relevant to issues of organizational development.

- Vision—ERP enables the realization of an organization that has a vision to be competitive by raising the level of skills and competencies of its personnel so that they can respond better, faster, and at the optimal cost to the changing business situations every day.

- Strategic Goals—ERP enables access to data to all concerned personnel to keep track of the organization's overall performance, with reference to the company's goals as well as their own contribution to the same on a daily basis. This engenders a sense of involvement and transparency that wasn't achievable earlier.

- Culture—ERP truly makes it possible to operate a collaborative, value-add driven organization in real-time mode. SAP permits learning that is happening in any part of the enterprise to be incorporated into the system, even on a daily basis.

- Structure—For the millennium enterprise, the ERP system provides visibility to the responsibility-oriented organization structure rather than the designation-oriented structure of earlier times. It provides instant communication and interaction with all members who are involved in a particular activity or process, irrespective of their reporting department or designation.

- Systems—ERP implements all essential systems and procedures to their bare minimum. It provides for adequate control without encumbering the work that directly contributes in the value–add delivered to the external or internal customers.

- Processes—ERP enables the process-oriented enterprise that might not always be feasible to realize physically; for instance, by locating all concerned members of a team in one place. It makes it possible for members to participate in more than one business-critical process efficiently and effectively.

Summary

In this chapter, I introduced the concept of Management by Collaboration (MBC) as a unifying framework in the context of the enterprise. The real power of this concept can be seen when we go beyond the boundaries of an enterprise. In the last chapter of this book, we look beyond the physical confines of an enterprise to include its partners like vendors and customers into an extension of the enterprise to the next higher level of what I term as the Extended Collaborative Enterprise (ECE). There I also introduce the powerful notion of the *Customer Triggered Company* as an even-driven enterprise in which all actions are triggered by the 'click of the customer' on the personalized Web user-interfaces (WUIs) of the enterprises like the SAP's mySAP.com Workplace. With the launch of mySAP.com, SAP has adopted a symbiotic strategy to go beyond simple integration to collaboration between enterprises.

ERP Evaluation

IN THIS CHAPTER

This chapter outlines the concepts and criteria for evaluating the ERP package most suitable to the requirements of a company. Managers must initially make a careful decision on the functional requirements that are desired and the characteristic features and facilities expected of the ERP system as a whole. Managers can then make an objective selection of the best ERP to deploy, considering the various factors described in this chapter.

The Anatomy of an ERP System

A functional ERP system is massively complex. Chapter 1's section "What is ERP?" shows that ERP essentially treats an application development environment as an application *in itself*. The integrated application repository holds a full set of correlated information regarding the application as well as the data that will reside in the system when it's in production, which also greatly facilitates documentation, testing, and maintenance. In this section, I briefly give an overview of the various systems constituting a fully functional ERP like SAP R/3. Every system described in the following has two simultaneous aspects: managing the application data and also the metadata related to the very nature and configuration of the implemented ERP itself.

The exhaustive list provided in the following illustrates the complexities of modern off-the-shelf packages. It can also act as a reference list when we look at the issues related to the evaluation and selection of ERP packages in later sections of this chapter.

Application Repository System

The application repository system forms the core of the ERP system. It provides the essential information on the structure and design of the whole application to all other modules or systems. It records the information regarding the information model of the system in terms of the entities, attributes, relations, processes, views, user scenarios, and so on. It also promotes a methodology that is native to the development and maintenance of the ERP system. It contains information on every single program, file, and data item in the system. This includes information on the various components and elements: identity, purpose, type and nature, defining attributes, "where used" list, tables accessed, processing cycles and times, sizing, and so on.

This module provides facilities to check the consistencies and integrity of definitions for all system components and elements within the ERP.

The application repository needs analysis and design modeling subsystems. It also needs a graphics environment to represent the processing requirements of the company operations. The graphic module provides a diagram representing the processes that enables rapid changes whenever necessary. Detailed requirements can be defined and stored in a related database that can be analyzed for dependencies, consistencies, impact analysis, and so on. This is usually called the *data dictionary* and provides support for the database and data tables or file design (including forming data tables, normalization, indices, referential integrities, and so on).

Graphical User Interface (GUI) Management System

This module provides the standard facilities of any presentation manager in terms of layouts, navigation among and within screens, help features, error recoveries, and so on. The graphical user interface (GUI) management system controls the design and functioning of the dialog flow on the screen, validations and table look-ups, default values, lists of values, and so on. This system will usually be one of the standard Relational Database Management Systems (RDBMS) like Oracle, DB2, and so on.

Menu Management System

This system presents the various choices that are available in various areas of functionality. It also lets you dynamically define the choices that are available to a particular user, depending on his level of access and authorization in different areas within the ERP.

Help Management System

This system provides the specific or contextual help at every field or processing step within the system. At any moment, it provides information on programs, screens, or particular fields of interest. This system also incorporates the architecture to report on errors and warnings, as well as give more specific diagnosis or suggestions on resolving problems encountered during the usage of the system.

Database Management System

This module is responsible for the storage of information required or supplied by all other modules of the ERP product. This will usually be one of the standard RDBMSs like Oracle, DB2, and so on.

Fourth-Generation Language Development Environment

This environment provides facilities to customize or extend the ERP system's functionality to meet the specific requirements of an enterprise. This has the standard tools set for the development, testing, debugging and documentation of the programs, especially data-entry programs.

Query Management System

This system provides extensive querying facilities on the system details stored in the application repository (and data dictionary). These details include process information, entities, data tables, programs, and also the data stored in the tables of the application database. This query management system enables the painting of query screens; the specification of tables to be accessed, fields to be displayed, and their sequences; the selection of a set of records to be displayed; and so on.

Report Management System

This report management system is similar to the query management system, except that it permits the queried information to be printed for reference. It defines customized reports for specific requirements of the company related to pre-printed documents like purchase orders, invoices, and so on. It provides advanced features for rapidly programming break totals, page breaks, line details, and so on within a report.

Application Administration and Management System

This provides facilities to guide and assist in installation, upgrades, system maintenance, printer/spool management, and so on. This application administration and management system interfaces with other related systems for managing software distribution, configuration and change releases, versions, security and authorization, disaster recovery, archival, and so on. It also provides facilities for operational requirements of performance monitoring, back-ups, background processing, creating and managing jobs, and so on.

Software Distribution Management System

This system enables the facility to upgrade the client-based software automatically from a centralized place. The system can enforce the access and authorization profiles at the various users' PCs.

Configuration Management System

This permits the ERP to be configured to the specific organizational structure of a company. This might include the physical locations; operational divisions; profit/loss (P/L) entities and accounts; the fiscal period; the taxation and discount structures; the categories of customers, suppliers, and products; and so on. All subsequent reporting and analyses are based on the details of configuration defined at the time of inception. This system also customizes the ERP system to embody the various functions and processes specific to an enterprise.

Change Management System

This system provides the facility to register, release, and control all changes introduced into the system. This permits control over system components being changed or tested and those that are released in the production environment for access and use by all. It also enables gathering and monitoring details on dates, persons, and the duration required for affecting changes. This helps both in the security as well as the productivity of the ERP operations.

Version Management System

This system provides facilities to keep track of the current versions of the various systems constituting the ERP. This enables prompt diagnosis of any malfunction that might arise because of incompatible systems, wrong interfaces, non-compliant systems, and so on.

Security and Authorization Management System

In an integrated environment of ERP, this system provides the architecture for the security and hence the access and usage available to the system. This enables maintaining the profiles of authorized access, assigning such profiles to specific user accounts, authenticating the users in the production environment, logging user access and usage, tracking attempts to breach the system security, changing access profiles and passwords, and so on.

Audit Management System

This system provides monitoring for user access and usage, system processing and updates, system and data changes management, error logs, and so on.

Disaster Recovery Management System

This provides the facility to define the alternate disaster recovery servers and systems, triggering or initial response procedures, databases recoveries, activating back-up resources, full recovery procedures, and so on.

Archival Management System

This provides the facility to archive system and application data that has been identified as essential for future reference. This defines details on data, the data sources, duration, frequency, the target archival system, and so on.

Communications Management System

This provides the communication layer for the ERP system. It provides features like distributed processing, distributed databases, security, and so on.

Application Programming Interface (API) System

This system provides facilities for a standardized interface of the ERP to upload or download data from legacy systems; specific application systems like supply-chain management (SCM), customer relationship management (CRM), electronic data interchange (EDI), and so on; high-end project management systems; or scientific and industrial application systems. These interfaces could be in batch or asynchronous modes or, for ongoing operations, in synchronous mode. Even multiple installation of the same ERP at different sites for the organization will need such interfaces. These might also be needed as basic enablers for such sophisticated facilities like data replication, database mirroring, and so on.

Online Documentation System

This provides the ability to make system documentation available on the system while one uses it and, more importantly, in the context of the particular functionality being used at any moment. This system provides links to related issues as well as the facility to pursue individual topics in full detail.

Print Documentation System

This provides facilities for printing the full technical details and the application design of the system for offline reference. Moreover, it enables updates to this documentation depending on upgrades, enhancements, and new releases of functionality in any of the above systems.

Online Tutorial, Training, and Demonstration Management System

This system provides an online tutorial carefully designed to highlight the comprehensiveness of the application and also advanced features that are available within the system. This training and demonstration system provides a path to be followed during the learning phase on the ERP. The system also provides the ability to measure and assess the progress made by the trainees during such exercises.

Office Automation System

This system provides the functionalities provided by word processors, document formatters, spreadsheets, and so on. This office automation system is used for recording annotations on the system or for project management, defining preformatted letters generated by the systems, and so on.

Groupware and Workflow System

This system provides extensive communication between users of the ERP system. More significantly, it provides direct interfaces between itself and the mail system in order to inform and alert concerned personnel about pre-defined events occurring during processing, like released purchase orders, dunning notices, alarms on exceeding credit limits, and so on.

This system also provides for broadcasting mail to multiple persons, routing mail in the operating sequence, triggering reminders at various stages along the workflow, soliciting approvals or authorizations, and so on.

Data Warehouse and Data Analysis System

This system provides for mapping and populating operational data from the ERP tables into the multidimensional tables of the data warehouse for manipulation and analysis. It provides advanced tools for detecting data patterns, trends, co-relations, and so on within the available data and prospecting for any significant relationship between data across the organization.

Implementation Project Management System

This system provides integrated capabilities for monitoring and managing the progress during the implementation of the ERP. It provides the capability to define the work steps, dependencies, schedules, estimates on duration and effort, work in progress, work completed, work under testing, and so on.

ERP Acquisition Decision Process

The evaluation and selection of the ERP packages for implementation within organizations are major exercises. Specific effort needs to be taken for the evaluation of highly complex ERP packages, like SAP R/3, in terms of their functionality and technology. The package needs to be selected by judiciously balancing, on both the dimensions of functionality and technology, the mutually contradictory requirements for complexity and flexibility of the ERP packages. Manufacturing companies have processes ranging from make-to-order to continuous flow. For certain shortcomings in functionality, they might also have to decide to build, rather than buy, some applications.

In the following section, I discuss the various aspects to be considered when evaluating the ERP packages suitable for an organization. The actual process of selecting an ERP is the topic of the next chapter.

General Considerations of ERP Evaluation

The general characteristics of ERP packages to be reviewed include the following:

- Comprehensive functionality
- Ease of use
- Capability for customizing
- Controls and reliability
- Ease of installation
- Efficiency of operation
- Ease of user management

- Open system architecture
- Open system interfaces
- Year 2000 compliance and Euro currency
- Online documentation and contextual help
- Future upgrades and enhancements
- Skill transfer and training programs
- User group activity

Checklists for ERP Evaluation

The exercise of evaluating ERPs becomes easier if detailed checklists of major points of interest are prepared beforehand. These checklists can be used to gather relevant information that can be analyzed and used as the basis for the selection process.

Tables 2.1 through 2.8 are included for reference:

- ERP vendor issues are illustrated in Table 2.1.
- ERP product issues are illustrated in Table 2.2.
- ERP technical issues are illustrated in Table 2.3.
- ERP installation and operation issues are illustrated in Table 2.4.
- ERP integration and interface issues are illustrated in Table 2.5.
- ERP modification and maintenance issues are illustrated in Table 2.6.
- ERP audit and control issues are illustrated in Table 2.7.
- ERP standards and documentation issues are illustrated in Table 2.8.

The meaning of the column headings is as given below:

- Available: indicates that the functionality is currently available as standard functionality in the ERP system.
- Configured: indicates that the functionality is not available as the standard functionality, but the ERP system can be configured easily to deliver the required functionality.
- Upgraded: indicates the functionality is planned and would become available in future named upgrades or release versions of the ERP system.
- Third-party: indicates that the functionality is not available in the ERP system but is available with third-party packages that have been specifically qualified for the ERP system.

TABLE 2.1   ERP Evaluation: Vendor Issues

Item No.	*Description*	*Available*	*Configured*	*Upgraded*	*Third-Party*	*Absent*
1	How long has the ERP under consideration been sold by the vendor in the market?	_____	_____	_____	_____	_____
2	Has it been developed in-house or acquired? Is the core development team still with them?	_____	_____	_____	_____	_____
3	What is the gross annual turnover and profit of the company? What is the ratio of sales to support revenue?	_____	_____	_____	_____	_____
4	How long has the vendor been in the packaged solution market?	_____	_____	_____	_____	_____
5	What is the installed base of this ERP?	_____	_____	_____	_____	_____
6	What are the hardware and operating systems that it is currently available on?	_____	_____	_____	_____	_____
7	How are they distributed: industry-wise or location-wise?	_____	_____	_____	_____	_____
8	What is the geographical spread of the vendor's development, sales, and support offices?	_____	_____	_____	_____	_____

continues

TABLE 2.1   Continued

Item No.	Description	Available	Configured	Upgraded	Third-Party	Absent
9	How many employees does the company have in technical and support functions?	_____	_____	_____	_____	_____
10	What are vendor's support and service policies?	_____	_____	_____	_____	_____
11	Does the vendor provide online modem-based support?	_____	_____	_____	_____	_____
12	What are vendor's training programs and facilities?	_____	_____	_____	_____	_____
13	How many employees does the company have in development, technical support, training, and commercial areas?	_____	_____	_____	_____	_____
14	Does the company's products have user groups? How are they organized?	_____	_____	_____	_____	_____
15	Who are the technical and business partners of the vendor?	_____	_____	_____	_____	_____
16	What is the company's strategy for industry-specific solutions?	_____	_____	_____	_____	_____
17	Is the vendor itself ready to implement the ERP package within the company?	_____	_____	_____	_____	_____

TABLE 2.2   ERP Evaluation: Product Issues

Item No.	Description	Available	Configured	Upgraded	Third-Party	Absent
1	How many actual package users are there?	_____	_____	_____	_____	_____
2	How many years have they been using the package? How many locations has the package been operational?	_____	_____	_____	_____	_____
3	Have the users been satisfied with the package?	_____	_____	_____	_____	_____
4	Can the vendor provide references of companies where the ERP under consideration is in operation?	_____	_____	_____	_____	_____
5	Can the vendor provide details of installations at these customer sites?	_____	_____	_____	_____	_____
6	Can the vendor provide professional references who can be contacted in these companies?	_____	_____	_____	_____	_____
7	Can the vendor arrange a visit to one or two sites where the package has been operational? Can this visit include detailed demos and a review of experiences, operations, and problems?	_____	_____	_____	_____	_____
8	Is the package user-friendly?	_____	_____	_____	_____	_____
9	What is the product map? Is it comprehensive?	_____	_____	_____	_____	_____
10	Does it cover all functions of an enterprise?	_____	_____	_____	_____	_____

continues

TABLE 2.2 Continued

Item No.	Description	Available	Configured	Upgraded	Third-Party	Absent
11	How scalable is the ERP in terms of the number of users that can be supported as well as its ability to be deployed as a company-wide solution?	_____	_____	_____	_____	_____
12	Does it follow the principle of one-point data entry?	_____	_____	_____	_____	_____
13	Does it have a centralized database for enterprise data?	_____	_____	_____	_____	_____
14	Are the transactions updates done in batch or online mode?	_____	_____	_____	_____	_____
15	Can it be integrated? Can its modules work in a standalone mode?	_____	_____	_____	_____	_____
16	How easy is it to integrate with third-party systems and solutions?	_____	_____	_____	_____	_____
17	Does it have an open architecture with adherence to worldwide standards?	_____	_____	_____	_____	_____
18	Is it based on non-proprietary technology? Can it work on standard hardware and operating system platforms?	_____	_____	_____	_____	_____
19	Does it follow standard protocols and interfaces? Can it interface with legacy and other systems like SCM, CRM, EDI, and so on?	_____	_____	_____	_____	_____

Item No.	Description	Available	Configured	Upgraded	Third-Party	Absent
20	Does the source code come along with the system?	_____	_____	_____	_____	_____
21	Is it accessible for making modifications? How will modifications and corrections be made?	_____	_____	_____	_____	_____
22	Will modifications of the ERP be necessary to obtain efficient and effective operations?	_____	_____	_____	_____	_____
23	Will the ERP markedly affect other user services?	_____	_____	_____	_____	_____
24	How easy is it to configure the ERP to the specific requirements of a company quickly and simply?	_____	_____	_____	_____	_____
25	Does the system enable the uploading of data from the legacy systems used by the enterprise?	_____	_____	_____	_____	_____
26	Does the system have utilities for doing the data conversion? What is the cost of such utilities?	_____	_____	_____	_____	_____
27	What is the development status of the product? Is it slated to go through a major revamping or through major additions?	_____	_____	_____	_____	_____
28	Does the package contain current technological features?	_____	_____	_____	_____	_____
29	What is the enhancement and upgrade strategy of the product?	_____	_____	_____	_____	_____

continues

2

ERP EVALUATION

TABLE 2.2 Continued

Item No.	Description	Available	Configured	Upgraded	Third-Party	Absent
30	How many releases or upgrades have been introduced in the last two years?	_____	_____	_____	_____	_____
31	Did the releases meet your schedule?	_____	_____	_____	_____	_____
32	What is the design strategy for addressing Y2K compatibility, Euro currency, and international languages?	_____	_____	_____	_____	_____
33	What is the product strategy to make it Web-enabled?	_____	_____	_____	_____	_____
34	Does the system have e-commerce functionality or does it have third-party e-commerce solutions?	_____	_____	_____	_____	_____
35	What is the product strategy to introduce and enhance country-specific functionality?	_____	_____	_____	_____	_____
36	What is the product strategy to introduce industry-specific functionality?	_____	_____	_____	_____	_____
37	How often are the new releases introduced?	_____	_____	_____	_____	_____
35	What is the market view of the product? Has it been analyzed, compared, and benchmarked?	_____	_____	_____	_____	_____
36	Does the package rate well in surveys?	_____	_____	_____	_____	_____
37	What is the cost of the package?	_____	_____	_____	_____	_____

Item No.	Description	Available	Configured	Upgraded	Third-Party	Absent
38	Is the cost based on the envisaged number of users?	_____	_____	_____	_____	_____
39	What are the licensing policies of the product?	_____	_____	_____	_____	_____
40	What is the cost of additional features and modules required by the enterprise?	_____	_____	_____	_____	_____
41	What are the annual recurring costs?	_____	_____	_____	_____	_____
42	What is the cost of periodically purchasing updated versions?	_____	_____	_____	_____	_____
43	What is the cost of installation?	_____	_____	_____	_____	_____
44	What is the cost of training?	_____	_____	_____	_____	_____
45	What is the cost of system documentation?	_____	_____	_____	_____	_____
46	What is the cost of vendor support and services?	_____	_____	_____	_____	_____

TABLE 2.3   ERP Evaluation: Technical Issues

Item No.	Item Description	Available	Configured	Upgraded	Third-Party	Absent
1	Does the ERP run on the target platform identified by the enterprise?	_____	_____	_____	_____	_____
2	What is the minimum configuration required for the target computer for installing the ERP?	_____	_____	_____	_____	_____

continues

TABLE 2.3 Continued

Item No.	Description	Available	Configured	Upgraded	Third-Party	Absent
3	Does the package need any optional features from the O/S?	_____	_____	_____	_____	_____
4	Does the ERP have an application repository system?	_____	_____	_____	_____	_____
5	Does it have a GUI system?	_____	_____	_____	_____	_____
6	Does the system provide for defining default screen characteristics, function keys, fonts, and so on?	_____	_____	_____	_____	_____
7	Does the menu have pictures or icons? Is the status information displayed on the screen for reference?	_____	_____	_____	_____	_____
8	Does it have a menu management system?	_____	_____	_____	_____	_____
9	Is the system startup satisfactory, including date, time, operator identification, control numbers, security controls, and so on?	_____	_____	_____	_____	_____
10	Are there clear, brief, and well-documented instructions to guide the user through the system?	_____	_____	_____	_____	_____
11	Are error messages well formatted, clear, and well documented?	_____	_____	_____	_____	_____
12	Are the error correction options and instructions satisfactory?	_____	_____	_____	_____	_____
13	Are single-key action commands used to speed the interaction of the user?	_____	_____	_____	_____	_____

Item No.	Description	Available	Configured	Upgraded	Third-Party	Absent
14	Does it have a help management system? Is contextual help available on a field or a program?	_____	_____	_____	_____	_____
15	Does it have a database management system?	_____	_____	_____	_____	_____
16	Does it have facility for database reorganization?	_____	_____	_____	_____	_____
17	Does the system provide direct access to the data within the database outside of the system?	_____	_____	_____	_____	_____
18	Are the record sizes, key structures, and other elements relatively independent of the target environment?	_____	_____	_____	_____	_____
19	Are the detailed layouts available for all data tables?	_____	_____	_____	_____	_____
20	Do the data tables contain sufficient audit trails including date changed, by whom, and the type of change?	_____	_____	_____	_____	_____
21	Does the system test for the existence of numbers such as account numbers, document numbers, and code numbers?	_____	_____	_____	_____	_____
22	Does the package have adequate input and output edits and controls?	_____	_____	_____	_____	_____
23	Does the package have adequate controls for maintaining the integrity of tables and data?	_____	_____	_____	_____	_____

continues

2

ERP EVALUATION

TABLE 2.3 Continued

Item No.	Description	Available	Configured	Upgraded	Third-Party	Absent
24	Does it have a 4GL development system?	_____	_____	_____	_____	_____
25	Does it have a query management system?	_____	_____	_____	_____	_____
26	Does it have a report management system?	_____	_____	_____	_____	_____
27	Can the user select documents. formats. and fields and control the output to the screen the printer?	_____	_____	_____	_____	_____
28	Does it have an application administration system?	_____	_____	_____	_____	_____
29	Does the system provide mirroring or data replication?	_____	_____	_____	_____	_____
30	Can the system tolerate errors and difficulties at the terminals and continue operating?	_____	_____	_____	_____	_____
31	Does the system save the data needed for recovery in case of power failure. entry of improper data. and so on?	_____	_____	_____	_____	_____
32	Are terminal users prevented from stopping. disrupting. or destroying the operation of the system?	_____	_____	_____	_____	_____
33	Are there simple non-destructive methods for EXIT or GO BACK or PREVIOUS SCREEN?	_____	_____	_____	_____	_____
34	Does it have a software distribution system?	_____	_____	_____	_____	_____
35	Does the system provide for defining an access profile at specific terminals?	_____	_____	_____	_____	_____

Item No.	Description	Available	Configured	Upgraded	Third-Party	Absent
36	Does it have a configuration management system?	_____	_____	_____	_____	_____
37	Does the system help in guiding through the configuration system?	_____	_____	_____	_____	_____
38	Does it have a change management system?	_____	_____	_____	_____	_____
39	Does the system have facilities to control the release of new or changed programs into production?	_____	_____	_____	_____	_____
40	Does it have a version management system?	_____	_____	_____	_____	_____
41	Does it have a security and administration system?	_____	_____	_____	_____	_____
42	Does the system provide for defining and maintaining access profiles and passwords?	_____	_____	_____	_____	_____
43	Does it have an audit management system?	_____	_____	_____	_____	_____
44	Does it have a disaster recovery system?	_____	_____	_____	_____	_____
45	Does the system provide automatic recovery procedures?	_____	_____	_____	_____	_____
46	Does it have an archival management system?	_____	_____	_____	_____	_____
47	Does it have a communications management system?	_____	_____	_____	_____	_____
48	Does it have an API system?	_____	_____	_____	_____	_____
49	Does it have an online documentation system?	_____	_____	_____	_____	_____

continues

2

ERP EVALUATION

TABLE 2.3 Continued

Item No.	Description	Available	Configured	Upgraded	Third-Party	Absent
50	Does it have a powerful search facility as well as suggestions on related topics?	_____	_____	_____	_____	_____
51	Does it have a print documentation system?	_____	_____	_____	_____	_____
52	Does it have an online tutorial, training, and demonstration system?	_____	_____	_____	_____	_____
53	Does it have an office-automation system?	_____	_____	_____	_____	_____
54	Does it have a facility for voting?	_____	_____	_____	_____	_____
55	Does it have a GroupWare and Workflow system?	_____	_____	_____	_____	_____
56	Does the Workflow system interface with the e-mail system?	_____	_____	_____	_____	_____
57	Does it have a data warehouse and data analysis system?	_____	_____	_____	_____	_____
58	Does it have an implementation project management system?	_____	_____	_____	_____	_____
59	Does the system report on missed milestones, schedules, and so on?	_____	_____	_____	_____	_____

TABLE 2.4 ERP Evaluation: Installation and Operation Issues

Item No.	Description	Available	Configured	Upgraded	Third-Party	Absent
1	Are the vendor's and purchaser's installation responsibilities clearly defined?	_____	_____	_____	_____	_____

Item No.	Description	Available	Configured	Upgraded	Third-Party	Absent
2	Are installation specifications defined clearly?	_____	_____	_____	_____	_____
3	Does the vendor have a manual or computer-assisted installation procedure?	_____	_____	_____	_____	_____
4	Does the configuration of the installation depend on the specifics of the enterprise and is there enough assistance available via documentation or vendor personnel?	_____	_____	_____	_____	_____
5	Are the acceptance criteria clearly defined?	_____	_____	_____	_____	_____
6	Does the operation of the system need extensive training for computer operators and system programmers?	_____	_____	_____	_____	_____
7	Does the vendor provide sample operating standards and procedures that can be adapted and used?	_____	_____	_____	_____	_____
8	Does the system documentation conform to the installation's documentation standards?	_____	_____	_____	_____	_____
9	Can the system be installed in the operating system environment, database, LAN, and so on without major modifications?	_____	_____	_____	_____	_____
10	Are the system's performance criteria for acceptance clearly stated?	_____	_____	_____	_____	_____

continues

2

ERP EVALUATION

TABLE 2.4 Continued

Item No.	Description	Available	Configured	Upgraded	Third-Party	Absent
11	Does the vendor promise full support until the system is installed satisfactorily?	_____	_____	_____	_____	_____
12	Will the vendor be available for the data conversion effort?	_____	_____	_____	_____	_____

TABLE 2.5 ERP Evaluation: Integration and Interface Issues

Item No.	Description	Available	Configured	Upgraded	Third-Party	Absent
1	Does the ERP system provide an interface to its database?	_____	_____	_____	_____	_____
2	Does the ERP system provide an interface to other databases and systems?	_____	_____	_____	_____	_____
3	Does the ERP system conform to known communications protocols and standards?	_____	_____	_____	_____	_____
4	Does it conform to known standards of encryption?	_____	_____	_____	_____	_____
5	Does the system provide online or batch interfaces?	_____	_____	_____	_____	_____
6	Does the system provide for controlling the upload of data into the system?	_____	_____	_____	_____	_____
7	Does it provide facilities for quickly mapping the external data into the system tables and vice versa?	_____	_____	_____	_____	_____

Item No.	Description	Available	Configured	Upgraded	Third-Party	Absent
8	Does the system provide for defining and scheduling the upload or download of data in an online mode?	_____	_____	_____	_____	_____
9	Does the system provide a report or audit trail on the transfer of data?	_____	_____	_____	_____	_____
10	Does the system provide an interface with e-mail?	_____	_____	_____	_____	_____
11	Does the system provide an interface with the workflow system?	_____	_____	_____	_____	_____
12	Does the system provide an automatic interface for loading data into a data warehouse system?	_____	_____	_____	_____	_____

TABLE 2.6 ERP Evaluation: Modification and Maintenance Issues

Item No.	Description	Available	Configured	Upgraded	Third-Party	Absent
1	Can the system function on an as-is basis without modification?	_____	_____	_____	_____	_____
2	Can the users change the administrative procedures to suit their requirements?	_____	_____	_____	_____	_____
3	Are all the system requirements defined through parameters and tables, making modifications easy to accomplish?	_____	_____	_____	_____	_____
4	Does the vendor inform others that customers have made similar modifications that may be available rapidly?	_____	_____	_____	_____	_____

continues

2

ERP EVALUATION

TABLE 2.6   Continued

Item No.	Description	Available	Configured	Upgraded	Third-Party	Absent
5	Are customers advised of outstanding problems that other users have discovered?	_____	_____	_____	_____	_____
6	Are new releases available regularly and automatically to all the purchasers?	_____	_____	_____	_____	_____
7	Can a system dump be sent to the vendor for review?	_____	_____	_____	_____	_____
8	Does the vendor provide onsite support and maintenance?	_____	_____	_____	_____	_____
9	Will the vendor support an installation that has the package modified by a customer?	_____	_____	_____	_____	_____

TABLE 2.7   ERP Evaluation: Audit and Control Issues

Item No.	Description	Available	Configured	Upgraded	Third-Party	Absent
1	Does the system have adequate backup if the operational version of the system is destroyed? Are all transactions properly recorded at the point of origin?	_____	_____	_____	_____	_____
2	Does the system have controls to ensure that all data recorded enter the computer for processing?	_____	_____	_____	_____	_____
3	Does the system provide for determining the proper authorization of transactions?	_____	_____	_____	_____	_____

Item No.	Description	Available	Configured	Upgraded	Third-Party	Absent
4	Does the system provide facilities to ensure that all data received by the system are accurate and complete?	_____	_____	_____	_____	_____
5	Can the system ensure the complete and accurate processing of data through the system?	_____	_____	_____	_____	_____
6	Does the system provide controls to detect the loss of data or non-processing of data?	_____	_____	_____	_____	_____
7	Does the system ensure that all transactions are recorded in the proper accounting period and also posted to the proper records?	_____	_____	_____	_____	_____
8	Can the system ensure that the organization's procedures and processing rules have been followed?	_____	_____	_____	_____	_____
9	Can the system ensure that the data in the tables are accurate and complete?	_____	_____	_____	_____	_____
10	Does the system have information on when the file was created, modified, by whom, and for what purpose?	_____	_____	_____	_____	_____
11	Does the system provide safeguards such as passwords or authorized terminals, to protect the tables from unauthorized access?	_____	_____	_____	_____	_____

continues

2

ERP EVALUATION

TABLE 2.7   Continued

Item No.	Description	Available	Configured	Upgraded	Third-Party	Absent
12	Does the system ensure that the processed data do not include unauthorized alterations?	_____	_____	_____	_____	_____
13	Does the system have controls to ensure that all the errors detected by the system get corrected?	_____	_____	_____	_____	_____
14	Do the transmitted messages include sufficient identification including the message number, terminal, date, transaction type, and so on?	_____	_____	_____	_____	_____
15	Does the system maintain logs to ensure that lost or garbled messages can be recreated?	_____	_____	_____	_____	_____
16	Does the system retain information to permit the reconstruction of transactions to prove the accuracy and completeness of the processing?	_____	_____	_____	_____	_____

TABLE 2.8   ERP Evaluation: Standards and Documentation

Item No.	Description	Available	Configured	Upgraded	Third-Party	Absent
1	Does the package have standard documentation that is available online and in printed form?	_____	_____	_____	_____	_____
2	Does the package provide documentation on the system's functionality, technical design, and operating environment?	_____	_____	_____	_____	_____

Item No.	Description	Available	Configured	Upgraded	Third-Party	Absent
3	Is the documentation easily referenced?	___	___	___	___	___
4	Does the system provide extensive cross-referencing facilities?	___	___	___	___	___
5	Does the system provide the capability to automatically change the relevant documentation when making modifications in the system, such as to tables, fields, screen formats, and report layouts?	___	___	___	___	___
6	Does the user documentation have clear representations of menus, screens, and so on?	___	___	___	___	___
7	Does the system provide the ability to prepare relevant training material on the modified system?	___	___	___	___	___
8	Does the system describe the programming standards and procedures in sufficient detail to establish conformity and make documentation easy?	___	___	___	___	___
9	Does the system enable easy maintenance of the modifications in the system as well as the corresponding documentation?	___	___	___	___	___

2

ERP EVALUATION

Checklists for ERP Functional Requirements

When evaluating the suitability of an ERP package, the detailed functional requirements of an enterprise need to be analyzed and enlisted for detailed scrutiny later. It is also useful to compare the various ERP packages under consideration.

A detailed checklist of functional requirements needs to be compiled for the various functional areas within the company. An example of the different functional requirements include

- Accounting Function:

  General Ledger

  Fixed Assets

  Financial Statements

  Cash Flow Statements

  Product Costs

  Profitability Analysis

  Management Information System

  Balance Sheet Analysis

  Yearly Financial Statements

  A sample checklist of General Ledger requirements is shown in Table 2.9.
- Customers Function:

  Customer Masters

  Sales Order Processing

  Order Deliveries

  Sales Invoices

  Customer Receipts

  Dealers Commission

  Sales Forecasting
- Vendors Function:

  Vendor Masters

  Vendor/Material Analysis

  Vendor Quality

  Vendor Rating

  Vendor Payments

  Vendor Credit Status

  Vendor Reports

  Vendor Ledger
- Materials Function:

  Material Masters

Purchase Requisitions

Purchase Orders

Non-Stock Items

Pricing

Quality Control

Purchase Ledger

Inventory Control

Tools and Gauges

- Manufacturing Function:

Master Production Schedule

Materials Requirement Planning

Work Center Planning and Scheduling

- Engineering Function:

Engineering Bill of Materials

Manufacturing Bill of Materials

TABLE 2.9   ERP Functional Requirements: General Ledger Accounting

Item No.	Description	Available	Configured	Upgraded	Third-party	Absent
1	Does the system provide a chart of accounts? Does it have a provision for subcodes within this?	_____	_____	_____	_____	_____
2	Does the system provide multiple levels when producing reports and summaries?	_____	_____	_____	_____	_____
3	Does it provide subledger facilities for designated accounts?	_____	_____	_____	_____	_____
4	Does the system provide for recording, validating, and posting accounting transactions?	_____	_____	_____	_____	_____

continues

TABLE 2.9 Continued

Item No.	Description	Available	Configured	Upgraded	Third-Party	Absent
5	Does the system provide for printing documents created in the system?	_____	_____	_____	_____	_____
6	Does the system provide for generating document-wise registers (payment vouchers, receipt vouchers, debit notes, credit notes, journal vouchers, and so on) and account-wise summaries (general ledger accounts, and so on)?	_____	_____	_____	_____	_____
7	Does the system provide bank reconciliation with automatic batch- and screen-based matching?	_____	_____	_____	_____	_____
8	Does it provide interfaces for bank data and cash-flow systems?	_____	_____	_____	_____	_____
9	Does the system provide for securing data on posting and update account balances on posting?	_____	_____	_____	_____	_____
10	Does the system provide for analyzing party accounts and report on the same?	_____	_____	_____	_____	_____
11	Does the system provide follow-up letters and details for a confirmation of balances?	_____	_____	_____	_____	_____
12	Does the system enable system-generated entries?	_____	_____	_____	_____	_____
13	Does the system provide for a generation of standard, recurring entries?	_____	_____	_____	_____	_____

Item No.	Description	Available	Configured	Upgraded	Third-Party	Absent
14	Does the system provide for the planning and analysis of variances?	_____	_____	_____	_____	_____
15	Does the system provide reporting on variances?	_____	_____	_____	_____	_____
16	Does the system provide for consolidated reports and inquiries at all levels of the organization?	_____	_____	_____	_____	_____

Significant Issues to be Considered While Evaluating ERP

In this section, I describe a set of issues that need to be considered while evaluating an ERP.

ERP Product Functionality and Features

Just as a vendor company, a similar exercise would have to be taken for the company's suite of ERP products. Product evaluation criteria would involve queries as illustrated in Table 2.2.

Unlike the traditional computerized systems, which take a data-oriented view of the operations of the company, the enterprisewide systems primarily emphasize the process-oriented view of the organization. Hence, special attention needs to be paid to ascertain whether the ERP package can configure, support, and maintain business process of the organization.

Support for Standard Processes and Best Practices

Companies that are multidivisional and multilocational develop differently at different sites and acquire a character of their own at each site that might not fit into a uniform mold across the organization. An ERP package must have the capability to provide a comprehensive functionality to implement such deeply ingrained, differing ways of operations at different locations. It should be able to provide ready-to-use, best-practice processes that incorporate such varying ways of executing any business transaction or process.

A standardization of processes usually leads to tremendous gains in terms of maintenance, future upgrades, documentation, training, and even routine operations and the administration of the ERP applications system.

Support for Customizing the Processes

This custom support is counter to the general emphasis on standardizing the processes and implementing generic ones. It's a business truism that the survival and success of a company depends on how it differentiates itself and its products or services from those of its competitors. To leverage on their competencies or advantages, companies cannot abandon the corresponding differentiating processes and will have to incorporate such fundamental variants in their ERP implementations.

Therefore, in addition to the best-of-class processes, an ERP package must provide a basic framework and philosophy for the customization of processes for a company or even for a different division of the company. As suggested in Chapter 10, "Initiating the SAP Project," a company should rationalize, standardize, and, as much as possible, use the process configurations that have been made available in SAP.

Customization requirements could arise because of

- Country-specific rules and regulations
- State-specific differences, if any
- Country-specific business requirements
- Company-specific business strategy and tactics
- Division- and location-specific business and operational requirements

Support for Cinderella Processes

Theses processes are also known as *exception* processes or *strange* processes. Process scenarios occur in an organization that might result from particular or peculiar circumstances at any moment of time. Such exceptions could either be treated as erroneous scenarios or could be handled as specifically identified exception processes. For instance, occasionally, every organization makes or is required to make an exception in the procedures for selection of suppliers, proposals submitted to prospective customers, delivering supplies to defaulting but otherwise loyal customers, releasing of delayed payments, partial payments against unverified invoices and so on.

Exception processes are major targets for customizations. However, as discussed in relation with customizations above, decisions on customizations need to be taken after assessing the resulting complexity in terms of use, training, and maintenance of these and dependent processes.

Vendor Credibility

An organization might select an ERP primarily on the basis of the product credibility to be discussed in the next section. However, the credibility of the vendor-company to upgrade and continuously improve its suite of offerings is important because of the rapid changes in the technology and market requirements. The relevant issues are listed in Table 2.1 for reference.

ERP Architecture and Technology

The ERP system should been implemented using the latest technology, architecture, and methodology. As technology keeps on undergoing rapid change, the product architecture becomes very important because this enables relevant portions of the monolithic packages like SAP to be upgraded modularly without disrupting the function of the full package.

Three-Tier Architecture

Client/server computing permits tremendous advantages in terms of load balancing as well as scalability and flexibility for growth.

The three-tier architecture, consisting of the presentation, application, and database layers, is the optimal implementation of the client/server computing model. The characteristics of each layer are as follows:

- The presentation layer manages the dialog between the end-user and the application program (see the next section, "Graphical User Interface (GUI)").
- The application layer performs the actual transformation of the data that make the application work.
- The database layer stores, updates, and retrieves required data by using the programs in the application layer.

See Chapter 4's section "Client/Server Principle."

Graphical User Interface (GUI)

It might seem strange that I am talking about the importance of GUIs, but what are generally accepted standards of GUI functionality today were not available even a few years back. This was more so for ERP-like solutions, where the emphasis tended to be on comprehensive functionality and flexibility to make changes. The GUIs basically enable the systems to become more user friendly by providing and controlling the features such as

- Structuring and nesting of menus
- Facilitating cursor movement on the screen
- Navigating between different screens
- Providing context-sensitive help
- Flashing of error messages

There are essentially five variations on the theme of client/server three-tier architecture. These are

- Distributed Data Management: The data is split between the server and the client.

- Remote Data Management: The user-interface and application logic are on the client and the database is on the server. This is the traditional model of client/server architecture.

- Distributed Logic: The logic is split between the server and client. This variation is more suitable to the distributed nature of enterprises.

- Remote Presentation: The application and the database are on the server and the presentation-related logic and presentation management software resides on the client.

- Distributed Presentation: The presentation logic is split between the server and the client; the presentation management system is on the client and the presentation logic server is split between the server and the client.

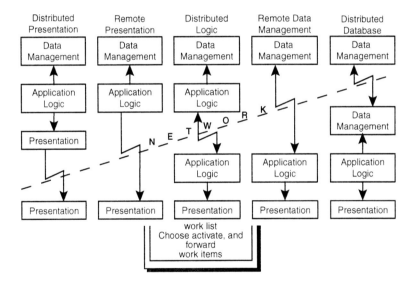

FIGURE 2.1

Types of client/server architectures.

Figure 2.1 shows the five basic variations of the three-tier client/server architecture. See Chapter 4's section "SAP Architecture" for more details on the GUI layer. SAP is closer to the last two variations.

With the advent of the Internet, the importance of a separable GUI has become even more pronounced.

Open System Interfaces and APIs

The information technology (IT) developments in the past decade have amply demonstrated the importance of open systems; that is, the need for non-proprietary systems, protocols, and interfaces. ERP systems are conceptually easy to understand, but very difficult to deliver. Developing such monolithic products at one instance is simply inconceivable. Therefore, ERP architecture and interfaces must permit the evolutionary development of the various components of the ERP system without disrupting its integrated functionality.

The ERP systems should permit easy interfacing with legacy systems and other specialized systems like SCM, CRM, product development management (PDM), automatic data recording (ADR), data capturing like bar codes, EDI, computerized telephony, and so on. It is impossible for any vendor to develop a suite of products to address all these functionalities provided by all these systems with the same panache as its core product.

Web-Based Functionality

With the growing importance of the Web as a primary medium of interaction and executing transactions, ERPs have to be flexible by design to enable not only business-to-business commerce, but also enable personalized interactions with end-customers. The architecture of ERP should permit easy conversions to Web-enabled functionality. In this regard, an ERP like SAP with a user-interface layer, which is separate from the underlying business logic, just as the corresponding database layer, is ready for its functionality to be seen on an Internet browser.

ERP Implementation and Use

In ERPs, which are end-user–oriented systems, there is a major emphasis on the ease of implementation and use. This refers especially to the ease of operations and management of the end users.

Ease of Installation

Although the installation of packages like ERPs are not envisaged to be simple, a systematic and menu-driven facility for installation of the various components of the system is in vogue. But more importantly, the installation application component should make the installation process independent of, for example, the operating system on which it is being installed (see Chapter 11's section "SAP Installation").

Ease of Configuration

After the installation, facilities for configuring the system for the existing or envisaged IT infrastructure of the company is very important. The system should have an easily understandable path and method for gathering the company-specific details of the IT infrastructure. Using present empirical models or theoretical models and the information furnished at the various stages, the system should be able to suggest various default values that would define the configuration of the installation for a particular company.

Ease of Operations

The ERP system should provide sample procedures and documentation for routine operations of the system. The system should also provide for automated backup and recovery procedures.

Ease of User Management

ERP, being an enterprisewide and end-user–oriented system, must enforce complete control on the access and authorization profiles of its users. Unlike the traditional computerized systems, the number and categories of people who operate the ERP system on a routine basis have undergone a change. Earlier the usage was confined to systems personnel or, at most, data entry operators, but ERP is now operated directly by the end-user operational persons. They create all the business transactions and functions directly on the system or with the help of the ERP system.

The ERP system must provide a judicious mixture of role-oriented and individual-oriented access profiles. This is necessary to cater to the needs of personnel working in rotation on different production shifts during a month.

Investments and Budgets

The ratio of the implementation expenses is as broadly as follows:

- Hardware Infrastructure   x
- SAP license and other software infrastructure   x
- SAP Implementation Project   2 to 5 x

The breakup of the SAP implementation project cost could be as follows:

External consultants	25%
In-house consultants	15%
Travel and local expenses	15%
Training	7%
Miscellaneous	3%
Contingency	5%

For capital equipment, the operating costs not directly related to the implementation effort are as follows:

Annual maintenance contracts	10%
Depreciation	20%

The ERP Infrastructure

An important element that must be considered while evaluating the ERP for an organization is the type and size of the envisaged hardware infrastructure essential for the enterprisewide operations.

Hardware

This is the central horsepower required to drive the functioning of the ERP throughout the enterprise. The nature of ERP will dictate this to be either a monolithic server or a cluster of servers, each focusing on a part of the envisaged load. The number of computers within the cluster can be based on either the particular functional areas or the sublocations that are to be served by the cluster as a whole. The sizes of the individual computers might be dependent upon

- The envisaged processing load of the system
- The number of terminals through which the system will be accessed

System Software

Usually, deciding on the system software is coupled with the selection of the hardware boxes. The operating system environment should have the capability to provide fault-tolerant operations with facilities for automatic backup, mirroring, and replication across sites and automatic failure recovery features.

Networking

Because ERPs are end-user–oriented systems, the usage and load expected on the terminals will be substantial. The network should be able to provide enough throughput so as not to impair the performance of access at these terminals.

The ERP Implementation Time

The time required for implementing a whole suite of ERP applications within an organization is important. As will be discussed later, this book recommends that for real payoffs from an ERP implementation, an organization should adopt the big-bang strategy of implementing all the SAP modules that cater to the company operations. This includes basic modules like Finance and Costing, Materials Management, Sales and Distribution, and Production Planning as well as other relevant modules like Assets Management, Quality Management, Plant Maintenance, Service Management, Warehouse Management, and so on.

The ERP project duration is dependent upon the characteristics of the company, such as its cultural, organizational, and technical readiness, as well as on the innate complexity of the ERP product. The cultural readiness of an organization is dependent upon its vision of its future as well as its willingness to embrace change towards that end. The organizational readiness has to do with the management's commitment, empowerment of the employees, streamlined systems and procedures, standardized processes, and so on. Technical readiness deals with the maturity of the infrastructure for hardware and communications, training, help desks, office automation, groupware, and so on.

The complexity of ERP products arises because of the multiple demand for comprehensiveness as well as flexibility of customization. When implementing ERP, it becomes critical to have prior familiarity with the functionality provided by the ERP system. In an integrated system, any wrongly configured process might have adverse and unforeseen effects on processing in some other related function. And this might not get detected until a rigorous integration-testing phase of the implementation or, worse, when the system is in actual production! Consequently, the effort to identify the all-functional gaps between the required and available functionality, coupled with the effort required to configure the resulting processes in an integrated ERP package, leads to comparatively longer implementation times.

Summary

In this chapter, I introduced the concept and criteria for evaluating an ERP package that is suitable for the requirements of a company. After considering the basic characteristics of a full-featured ERP system, we considered in detail various checklists for ascertaining the technical and functional requirements expected of the envisaged ERP system. In the latter part of this chapter, I discussed several dimensions of an ERP that are essential for any enterprisewide solution.

ERP Selection

IN THIS CHAPTER

SAP for the Small and Medium Enterprises (SME)

The majority of companies that will be implementing enterprise resource planning (ERP) systems in the millennium will be the small and medium enterprises (SMEs). SMEs are usually defined as companies that have revenues ranging from $200 million up to $1 billion. These companies have modest IT/IS resources and budgets and are expected to benefit the most from implementing off-the-shelf application products like ERPs. This is because they do not have the depth of experience and a constant availability of adequate expertise to be able to handle the in-house development of an enterprisewide system.

Like the large enterprises within their markets, SMEs are impacted by the rapidly changing marketplace and their own ability to respond to these changes. ERPs provide the platform for SMEs to address the competitive demands of the rapidly changing marketplace and be successful in terms of

- Improved customer relations and management
- Reduced cycle time
- Improved quality
- Increased sales volumes
- Improved margins
- Reduced product development time
- Reduced manpower for routine operations
- Improved market share

ERP implementations in SME enterprises also need a completely different type of skills set as compared to the implementation of the same system in a Fortune 500 company. I will touch on this aspect again in Appendix A, "Selecting SAP Implementation Partners."

The ERP Selection Process

The objective of a systematic selection of ERP is to optimize the benefits for the organization. Careful selection to acquire the most acceptable enterprisewide system is important, as it has a salutary effect on the overall acceptability, usefulness, cross-functionality, and collaboration within the enterprise.

An enterprise must select the most suitable ERP system based on the predefined, predetermined and pre-agreed criteria of evaluation. The process should follow the organizational policies and procedures in reaching the final decision.

The use of checklists for such purposes has proved especially valuable. I discussed a handful of checklists in Chapter 2, "The ERP Evaluation," to evaluate the different characteristics of the ERP systems. These checklists should be supplemented or altered depending on the requirements of the organizations. It is important, however, to use such checklists because it helps in focusing discussions on issues that matter objectively. Later in this chapter I discuss using metrics to compare ERPs.

The process of selecting an ERP system for an enterprise involves the following steps:

- Establish the ERP selection team (discussed later in the section entitled, "The Selection Team").
- Establish the functional requirements of the envisaged enterprisewide system.
- Search and screen for prospective ERP systems.
- Prepare detailed checklists of different class characteristics in order of priority, such as necessary, desirable, good-to-have, and great-to-have.
- Screen the available ERP products that most nearly meet the agreed criteria against the necessary requirements that have been established. The company can also partner with the vendor companies in this stage by issuing an RFP based on the finalized checklists.
- Evaluate the resulting short list of ERP products against the detailed desirable requirements like those presented in Chapter 2, "ERP Evaluation."
- Select the few remaining ERP systems for demonstrations, site visits, and hands-on trials.
- Direct and help the vendors to conduct script tests and stress tests and report on the results of these tests using the same test data provided by the company to all of the ERP vendors.
- Conduct a comparison and rating of the various ERPs using metrics by compiling, collating, and analyzing the submitted information.
- Compile the findings of the product ratings and test reports with special emphasis on the cost of installing and operating the ERP, the timeframe for implementing the package, the experience and strength of the vendor, and the risks associated with each of the alternative ERPs.
- Prepare the recommendations report to the management.

A systematic and metrics-based approach would not render the decision process as foolproof, but it would help in making the decision clearer. The recommendation report will give clear descriptions of how the ERP systems were rated, for what reasons, and how the selection decision was reached. At a later stage, others can know the principal points that were considered, and why certain ERP systems were rejected while others were considered more suitable. This approach leaves a clear "audit trail" of the route taken in the decision process used for the final selection of the ERP for the organization.

The Selection Team

Implementation of enterprisewide systems like SAP can be successful only when all stakeholders are willing participants in such an effort. It is necessary for ensuring the future interest and involvement of all concerned that all stakeholders and their views should be properly represented and incorporated during the planning, organizing, executing, and managing the implementation of the ERP system. In the millennium enterprise, the mistakes committed while implementing computerized systems in the last century should be avoided. In the remaining part of this section, I discuss the important constituents of the selection team.

Functional Team

This team is the major constituent of the selection team. Its members should consist of senior officers who are knowledgeable of the company's business operations, manufacturing technology, competencies, and the competitive gaps. Because the ERP implementation projects are user-driven, involving the functional team members in the evaluation and selection phase is the best prescription for ownership during the implementation of the selected package. They should preferably be members who have participated in similar enterprisewide performance improvement efforts like TQM, BPR, and so on.

Technical Team

The members of this team should be members who have extensive experience at least in the traditional application development and implementation projects. They should be familiar with conventional development environments and the traditional methodologies employed during the software development life cycle (SDLC). They should be perceptive of the rationale for deploying ERP solutions in the organization and the reasons for the implementation project to be driven and led by the functional users.

Technology Team

The members of this team should be conversant with the latest hardware, networking issues, and solutions. They should be familiar with issues of portability, scalability, and interoperability. They need to be aware of the latest standards and protocols to make an informed judgment on the infrastructure issues for the ERP implementation within the organization. They must be comfortable with issues of compatibility, upgrade paths, network traffic on LANs and WANs, and estimating systems loads and system responses.

Technology team members should also be familiar with solutions for backup, archival, and disaster recovery systems. The members of this team need to be conversant with site preparation, cabling, installation, maintenance, and support requirements for the ERP system installation.

Commercial Team

The members of this team need to be conversant with the issues of negotiating with vendors, signing commercial contracts, defining deliverables and milestones, laying out acceptance criteria and approval procedures, performance guarantees, payment terms, legal liabilities, licensing procedures, upgrades and releases, regulatory issues and taxes, and so on.

ERP Core Selection Methodology

As ERP fundamentally implements a process-driven enterprise, the selection of processes for implementation is of primary significance. The selection team will make its choice depending on how easily the ERP can implement the process considered critical for the company operations. It will depend upon how flexibly the system implements the business processes of interest to the organization.

Process Selection

This involves systematically compiling all processes and variants that are prevalent within the organization. These could be processes at every level within the organization, irrespective of whether it has been computerized or not.

Enterprise Process Mapping

This involves painstakingly mapping a selection of processes that are considered critical for the business operations of the company. This entails detailing each process in terms of its name, purpose, responsible owner, process description (including inputs and outputs), quality and efficiency, subprocesses, interfaces with other functions and systems, exceptional conditions, areas for improvement, impact analysis of suggested scenarios, and so on. This compilation of process mapping is helpful in preparing the script tests. The topic of process mapping is discussed in detail in Chapter 6, "SAP and the Enterprise Reengineering."

Script Tests

Script tests are process scenarios that have to be demonstrated by the vendor in the product licenses. These tests are a handful of process scenarios that are considered especially critical for the business operations and are not easily configurable within the standard functionality provided by the ERP systems.

The approach recommended for handling these specifically identified processes indicates the robustness, depth, and inherent flexibility of the ERP systems. ERP systems might have the following approaches for mapping a process within the package:

- Provide it as a basic or standard functionality.

- Suggest a workaround for achieving the same functionality and configure it accordingly.

- Indicate if this functionality is to be introduced in the next scheduled release of the system.

- Suggest third-party add-ons or plug-ins that provide the desired functionality and have been qualified for compatibility with the concerned ERP.

- Program the required functionality in ERP system by developing the same in the 3GL/4GL native to the ERP system.

ERPs that can accommodate such processes, albeit even if these are achieved only by resorting to workarounds are preferable to others where the only options are to either wait for these functionalities to be addressed, possibly in the next released version of the system, or for the company to customize the package itself by programming such functionality directly into the system.

Stress Test

This is similar to the stress test administered for traditional systems. This involve estimating the load anticipated in the production environment and simulating the same in the test environment to ascertain whether the suggested configuration can handle the expected load. This test can involve predictable volumes of data in the database, transaction throughputs on the LAN/WAN, or interactive sessions on the terminals serviced by the central servers. Industry-level benchmarks for the relevant areas should be used for reporting on the observed performances. This could be a full-scale test conducted on the company site or at the technology demonstration centers of the concerned vendor.

ERP Selection Report

When reporting on a selection of systems like ERP, which are large, complex, and integrated, functionalities are not very easy to compare. Moreover, the participation of members from different functional areas into the selection team also brings forth widely differing views on every aspect of the envisaged enterprisewide system.

As noted in the section entitled, "The ERP Selection Process," it is best to state the variables involved as objectively as possible and to apply some sort of measuring scale for each of these variables. A metrics approach is the best way to assign values and resolve disputes. Although the assigned numbers are only comparisons on a relative scale and not actual costs, they help in focusing the discussions more on the specific numbers assigned to definable points. The relative scale or the weighty factors assigned to various aspects could always be reworked until most participants are satisfied with the scale. The resulting conclusions will arise from all such smaller agreements made along the way.

In the next subsection, I discuss a metrics approach for comparison of the ERP systems.

ERP Systems Comparative Chart

Table 3.1 presents a form that can be used for comparison of ERP systems.

The steps to be used by the selection team for using this form are as follows:

1. Using the information gathered in response to the various criteria for evaluation, as suggested in Chapter 2, prepare a list of characteristics that are mutually acceptable as important for the envisaged enterprisewide systems.

2. Place these characteristics in the order of importance as agreed by all the members of the selection team.

3. Decide on which of these characteristics are necessary.

4. Decide on which of these characteristics are desirable.

5. Assign factors on a scale of 1 to 10 for each of the characteristics; the higher the factor is, the more important the characteristic for the envisaged ERP. Characteristics that are considered necessary should definitely be assigned a factor closer to 10, using a scale like the following:

   ```
   Vital = 10
   Critical = 9
   Essential = 8
   Significant = 7
   Important = 6
   Mandatory = 5
   Required = 4
   Useful = 3
   Desirable = 2
   Optional = 1
   ```

   The actual weights should be decided by consensus.

6. Next, rate the various ERP systems for each of these characteristics on a scale of 1 to 5. Five indicates excellent, whereas 1 denotes poor or unacceptable. A good rule of thumb is to agree on the best package for a particular characteristic and give only that package a rating of 5:

   ```
   Excellent / Best = 5
   Remarkable = 4
   Moderate = 3
   Acceptable = 2
   Poor / Worst = 1
   ```

   Then, agree on ratings for other packages by consensus.

7. Compute the score for each ERP system by each characteristic by multiplying the weighting factor by the corresponding rating as follows:

```
Score = Weighting Factor X Rating
```

8. Total all the scores for each ERP system.

TABLE 3.1 Comparative Chart of ERP Systems

ERP System Characteristics	*Weighting Factor*	*SAP R/3*		*BaaN*		*PeopleSoft*		*Oracle Apps.*	
		Rating	*Score*	*Rating*	*Score*	*Rating*	*Score*	*Rating*	*Score*
Technical									
Comprehensive functionality	____	____	____	____	____	____	____	____	____
Ease of use	____	____	____	____	____	____	____	____	____
Extendibility, flexibility, and configurability	____	____	____	____	____	____	____	____	____
Ability of customization and modification	____	____	____	____	____	____	____	____	____
Open systems architecture and interfaces	____	____	____	____	____	____	____	____	____
One-point data entry	____	____	____	____	____	____	____	____	____
Centralized database	____	____	____	____	____	____	____	____	____
Interfacing of other devices, barcodes, EDI, and so on	____	____	____	____	____	____	____	____	____
Year 2000 and Euro compliance	____	____	____	____	____	____	____	____	____
Online documentation and contextual help	____	____	____	____	____	____	____	____	____
Future upgrades and enhancements	____	____	____	____	____	____	____	____	____
Skill transfer and training programs	____	____	____	____	____	____	____	____	____
Users group activity	____	____	____	____	____	____	____	____	____
Total Score	____	____	____	____	____	____	____	____	____

ERP System Characteristics	Weighting Factor	SAP R/3		BaaN		PeopleSoft		Oracle Apps.	
		Rating	Score	Rating	Score	Rating	Score	Rating	Score
Operational									
Controls and reliability	____	____	____	____	____	____	____	____	____
Ease of installation	____	____	____	____	____	____	____	____	____
Efficiency of operations	____	____	____	____	____	____	____	____	____
Ease of performance tuning	____	____	____	____	____	____	____	____	____
Ease of user management	____	____	____	____	____	____	____	____	____
Security and authorization	____	____	____	____	____	____	____	____	____
Backup and disaster recovery	____	____	____	____	____	____	____	____	____
Availability	____	____	____	____	____	____	____	____	____
Resource requirements	____	____	____	____	____	____	____	____	____
Total Score	____	____	____	____	____	____	____	____	____
Financial									
System costs									
Hardware, system software, and networking	____	____	____	____	____	____	____	____	____
Base license	____	____	____	____	____	____	____	____	____
Enhancements	____	____	____	____	____	____	____	____	____
Third-party solutions	____	____	____	____	____	____	____	____	____
Site preparation	____	____	____	____	____	____	____	____	____
Installation	____	____	____	____	____	____	____	____	____
Services									
Staffing	____	____	____	____	____	____	____	____	____
Training	____	____	____	____	____	____	____	____	____

continues

3

ERP SELECTION

TABLE 3.1 Continued

ERP System Characteristics	Weighting Factor	SAP R/3		BaaN		PeopleSoft		Oracle Apps.	
		Rating	Score	Rating	Score	Rating	Score	Rating	Score
Financial									
Services									
Implementation consultancy	____	____	____	____	____	____	____	____	____
Documentation	____	____	____	____	____	____	____	____	____
Travel	____	____	____	____	____	____	____	____	____
Communications	____	____	____	____	____	____	____	____	____
Maintenance	____	____	____	____	____	____	____	____	____
Spread of investment	____	____	____	____	____	____	____	____	____
Total Score	____	____	____	____	____	____	____	____	____
GRAND TOTAL	____	____	____	____	____	____	____	____	____

Script and Stress Test Reports

The results of the script test and stress test reports could also be included as one of the characteristics for comparing the ERP systems. This should be considered if the test results vary widely among the various ERP systems.

Recommendations Report

The report on the recommendations for the ERP submitted to the company's management should include the following:

- The advantages and disadvantages of the selected ERP system. This would be based on the information collected on evaluation criteria presented in the earlier chapter.

    A detailed profile of SAP R/3 is presented in the next chapter; by the end of the chapter, it will be clear why SAP R/3 is a winner amongst all other ERP systems available on the market today.

- The ERP systems comparative chart.

- The estimate of cost and benefits for the implementation of the ERP. This would be based on the information collected in Table 2.2 for costs of the requisite hardware, system software, ERP software, networking software, installation, training, yearly maintenance, implementation consultancy services, travel, communications, and so on.

- The implementation project schedule with dates of key milestones. An overview of a SAP R/3 implementation project is discussed in Chapter 5, "The SAP Implementation Project Cycle."
- A recommendation for the approval by the management.

Summary

In this chapter, you saw the methodology for selecting the ERP package most suitable to the requirements of a company. In the later part of the chapter, I discussed the preparation of the ERP systems comparative chart and the final recommendation report.

In the following chapters, I talk about SAP AG and its client/server product R/3. I will talk in sufficient detail about the architecture, structure, and design of SAP R/3 to understand the comprehensiveness and complexity of this system. Chapters 4 through 9 will amply demonstrate why SAP was the leading ERP product on the market in the last decade. It will also substantiate to a great extent my claim that SAP R/3 will be the ERP system of choice even for the millennium enterprises of the twenty-first century.

The SAP Solution

IN THIS CHAPTER

In this chapter, and in the remaining part of the book, I talk in detail about SAP AG's ERP product SAP R/3. First, I relate briefly the history of SAP AG and the products introduced by SAP since its inception in 1972. Thereafter, I present the architecture and salient features of the R/3 system in sufficient detail to highlight its overwhelming superiority.

It will become evident by perusing this chapter and the following ones that SAP R/3 is indeed the best ERP system on the market today. With its three-tiered, flexible client/server architecture, excellent repository-driven ABAP/4 development environment, and comprehensive business functionality covering all functions across several industries, SAP R/3 represents perhaps the best of the software development efforts since the inception of computer industry in the middle of the last century.

SAP the Company

SAP has become the leading vendor of standard business applications software. Throughout the last decade, it has reported sales and profit growth rates in excess of 40 percent every year. The sales for the year 1998 were reported to be $8.47 billion. As reported by SAP, there are more than 10,000-plus customers with more than 19,000 installations of SAP across the world and more than 300,000 users work on SAP systems worldwide. By any standards, these are impressive numbers coming from a company that has a great vision and is destined to play a significant role even in the Internet-driven markets of the next century as well.

The phenomenal success of SAP comes from the fact that SAP systems are comprehensive but at the same time configurable to the specific needs of any company. Companies prefer off-the-shelf packages like SAP because it is flexible and can be configured to satisfy most requirements of any company in any industry. SAP can be deployed on various hardware platforms (see Figure 4.3), providing the same comprehensive and integrated functionality, the flexibility for addressing individual company-specific requirements, and independence from specific technologies deployed in the company. Moreover, SAP also implements a process-oriented view of the enterprise.

SAP has two main products: R/2 and R/3. The R/2 system runs on mainframes like IBM, Siemens, and so on. R/3 system, which is the client/server variant of the older system, was introduced in 1992. However, subsequent to the major enhancements during versions 3.0 and 3.1, it became the flagship product of the company, garnering a lion's share of the total revenues earned by SAP every year. The SAP R/3 product map is shown in Figure 4.1.

In the following discussion, I will refer to SAP as a company as well its products R/2 and R/3 by the same term, "SAP." This should not lead to any confusion because I believe that, at any point, the context will clarify which meaning is intended. Also, unless specifically mentioned, SAP the product will usually refer to its client/server product R/3.

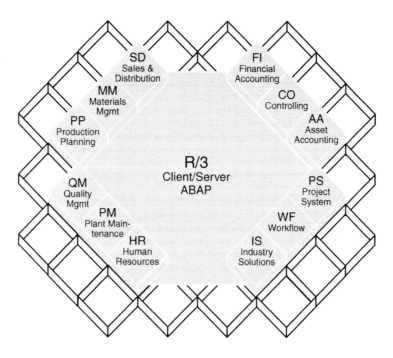

FIGURE **4.1**

SAP product map.

History of SAP

In the following, I relate a brief chronological history of SAP AG.

- 1972   Five systems analysts leave IBM to found Systemanalyse and
  Programmentwicklung (System Analysis and Program Development) at Mannheim. The
  company introduces a system for financial accounting that utilizes real-time data within
  an integrated enterprise. It is based on the commonality that was observed by them in the
  functional requirements of companies in similar businesses.

- 1973   SAP introduces the Material Management System, followed by Purchasing,
  Inventory Management, and Invoice Verification modules. In line with its philosophy, the
  MM module shares data directly and in real-time with the FI module with consequent
  benefits.

- 1977   The company changes its name to Systeme, Anwendungen, Produkte in der
  Datenverarbeitung (Systems, Applications, Products in Data Processing) and also moves
  its head office from Mannheim to the present location at Walldorf.

SAP introduces the Assets Accounting module.

SAP gets its first foreign customers in Austria.

SAP also develops the French version of the accounting module. Thus, the internationalization of its products becomes the hallmark of SAP.

- 1978   SAP introduces its first truly enterprisewide solution, called R/2, for the mainframes.

  SAP adds the Cost Accounting module.
- 1980   SAP's products are listed at 50 in the top 100 customers in Germany.
- 1984   SAP gets its first production planning and control system customer.

  Work commences on the Personnel Management and Plant Maintenance modules.
- 1985   SAP has presence in most European countries and begins to address markets outside of Europe with customers in Canada, the U.S., South Africa, and Kuwait.
- 1986   SAP exhibits R/2 at the world largest information technologies (IT) trade fair, CeBIT, for the first time.
- 1987   IBM announces Systems Application Architecture (SAA), which introduces the concept of layered architecture for application software; this entails the use of platform-independent applications, graphic user interfaces (GUIs) as the front-ends, and standard database management systems (DBMS) as the back-ends. It is similar to the OSI Reference model for open computer networks published at the beginning of the 1980s. SAP adopts the concepts behind SAA as the framework for the planned R/3 system.

  SAP decides to develop all business applications in ABAP/4, but the runtime environment is to be in C.
- 1988   SAP becomes a publicly held corporation.

  SAP opens an international training center in Walldorf.
- 1989   SAP presents the R/3 application system at the CeBIT Conference in Hanover. SAP organizes the first SAPPHIRE conference in the U.S.
- 1992   SAP revenues equal DM831 million, half of which are generated outside of Germany. The R/2 software is now available worldwide in 14 different languages, including Russian.

  SAP introduces the client/server enterprisewide solution called R/3 for the UNIX platform. It is the most significant event in the history of the company and leads to explosive growth in revenues.
- 1993   SAP and Microsoft (MS) begin joint cooperations to integrate PC-based MS applications like Word, Excel, Project, and Access with SAP business applications.

  SAP and MS also port R/3 to Windows NT. SAP R/3 becomes available on Windows NT platforms.

SAP America establishes a development center in Foster City in Silicon Valley, California.

SAP introduces the Kanji version of R/3.

- 1994   SAP has more than 1,000 R/3 customers.

SAP R/3 development receives an ISO 9000 certification.

SAP R/3 Release 2.2 is introduced with major enhancements in logistics.

- 1995   SAP R/2 has 2,000 customers and R/3 reaches a worldwide customer base of 4,000.

SAP releases R/3 Release 3.0, making a quantum jump in functionality, especially in the Production Planning module.

SAP makes R/3 available on the widely used IBM AS/400 platform.

SAP announces industry solutions for the process industry (including the chemicals, pharmaceuticals, and food and beverage industries).

SAP also introduces the Application Link Enabling (ALE) solution for the linking of applications running on different computers. ALE allows SAP to preserve its core strategy of integrated applications, even in the client/server environment through message-based, asynchronous linking of essentially distributed but still integrated applications across different computers.

The complete implementation environment, consisting of the R/3 Reference Model, R/3 Business Navigator, Procedure Model, and the Implementation Guide, is introduced to aid in project implementations.

SAP opens a service and support center at Walldorf.

- 1996   SAP introduces the business framework architecture with the goal of making it faster and easier for customers to introduce new functionalities into the system. This also makes the system even more flexible and open.

SAP introduces Internet applications.

SAP introduces Accelerated SAP methodology for rapid implementation by leveraging on experiences gained from thousands of SAP projects.

SAP becomes no. 1 vendor for manufacturing systems solutions.

- 1997   SAP has 750 customers going live in a month.

SAP introduces TeamSAP.

Motorola implements SAP HR with 25,000 users.

- 1998   SAP launches SAP Solution maps for 19 industries.

SAP releases SAP R/3 4.0

SAP introduces EnjoySAP that aims at making SAP easy to learn, customize to individual preferences, and easy to use.

SAP announces New Dimension Initiatives such as SAP Customer Relationship Management Initiative, SAP Business Intelligence Initiative, SAP Supply Chain Management Initiative, SAP Advanced Planner and Optimizer, Management Cockpit, SAP Strategic Enterprise Management, SAP Business Information Warehouse, and Enjoy SAP.

- 1999 SAP launches mySAP.com which extends the power of SAP to the Internet.

SAP also introduces partnership program for application hosting and outsourcing services.

SAP unbundles SAP licenses so that they can be procured as per needs.

It is remarkable that right from the beginning, SAP focused on developing enterprisewide software to integrate all business processes within the enterprise. This integration also resulted from real-time processing of data, rather than the batch-mode processing that was dominant at that time. They also adopted very early on the layered model for the application architecture as a fundamental design principal that promised inherent flexibility and openness.

At every stage in its history, SAP made critical decisions in adopting barely emerging ideas and technologies as the core strategies for their products, even though these concepts had not proven themselves in the market. Right at the beginning they decided on the concept of an enterprisewide centralized database as well as real-time updates in this centralized database, even though the mainframe-oriented infrastructure prevalent then was not really suitable for this kind of application framework.

They were quick to adapt the SAA philosophy (which itself was inspired by the OSI Reference model for open computer networks) as the central tenet for ensuring the innate flexibility and openness of their products. They embraced the truth about GUIs being the focus of all interactions between the system and the users well before hardware and technologies made this viable without sacrificing the critical virtue of scalability. SAP also always kept internationalization and related issues like multi-currency on its active agenda while developing and enhancing its products. The SAP systems were fundamentally architectured to be multilingual right from their initial versions.

The Significance of SAP R/3

In the remaining part of this chapter, I provide an overview of the salient features and advantages of SAP's R/3 as an ERP system. Although not patterned on our discussions in Chapter 2, "ERP Evaluation," and Chapter 3, "ERP Selection," for the evaluation and selection of an ERP system, it will become evident that SAP excels in all of those dimensions compared to any other competing product on the market today. This chapter covers the most significant characteristics of the SAP R/3 product and the related services provided by SAP. Certain aspects like query facilities, reporting facilities, online help, documentation, training, and so on will be covered later in the book. The transfer of knowledge to the customer's personnel involved in SAP implementation through comprehensive training materials, programs, and certifications is discussed in Chapter 5 section "Project Management."

Client/Server Principle

Client/server computing is a style of computing where the computer processing load is distributed across several synchronously or asynchronously cooperating computer programs running on a single computer or on a group. During the last decade of development, this has become one of the architectures of choice for computerized systems because of the tremendous flexibility permitted by this approach. Applications can be installed, configured, and run on a central computer or distributed across several numbers, depending on the type and load of the applications. Moreover, as the processing requirements and loads change, the corresponding systems can be upgraded selectively. This approach provides a path for the companies to achieve greatly enhanced performance at only incremental costs, while preserving the investments made in the earlier hardware.

In SAP R/3, client/server computing forms the basis of cooperative processing of disparate software components that could reside either on a centralized or distributed configuration on many servers that are networked to each other. The communication between the servers could be based on synchronous program-to-program communication, asynchronous message exchange, or Remote SQL. These disparate software components could be meant for graphical presentation, for processing applications, or even for the storage of data. Special application servers can also be installed for individual work areas as well. Allocating separate servers not only helps in balancing loads, but also enables allocating individual server configurations that are appropriate for the concerned tasks. This not only helps in improving the throughput and response times, but also optimizes costs.

The three-layer client/server approach, with its distribution of presentation, applications, and database functions on separate computers, truly provides a viable foundation for enterprisewide client/server solutions. For integrated systems like SAP R/3, however, the real achievement is to implement the multi-layer client/server concept without losing the integration of data and the processes across the entire system.

Comprehensive Functionality

SAP R/3 covers all of the business processes within several industries and businesses. Organizations can utilize divisional operations that are discrete or continuous in nature, or both.

Within the discrete industries, a company can have lot-sized–based operations, be repetitive manufacturers, or practice Kanban manufacturing techniques. Similarly, a company can also have operations in service industries like banking, financial services, and so on. Such organizations, and many such enterprises exist now, need a uniform enterprisewide system that can span all such disparate business activities and help in controlling and managing them on a day-to-day basis. It's understandable that organizations that have interests in heterogeneous business activities across different regions of the world can be handicapped when managing day-to-day operations if different, incompatible, and non-integrated systems are functioning at all these locations.

Application Modules

SAP's standard application modules address functionality that is commonly used across a broad spectrum of industries. They are mainly divided into three major groups: Financials, Logistics, and Human Resources. SAP Financials consists of standard modules like Financial Accounting, Controlling, Assets Management, Investment Management, and Treasury. SAP Logistics consists of major modules like Materials Management, Production Planning, Quality Management, Plant Maintenance, Project System, Sales and Distribution, Service Management, Warehouse Management, and so forth. SAP Human Resources consists of modules like Personnel Planning and Development, Personnel Administration, and Payroll Accounting. We will be discussing more details of these modules in Chapter 7, "SAP R/3 Package."

Cross-Application Modules

Cross-application modules (CA), as the name suggests, are not related to any specific modules mentioned above but have relevance across the whole of the SAP system. Important CA modules include

- SAPoffice   Provides mailing facilities and interfaces with the SAP system
- SAP Business Workflow   Provides Workflow functionality and also interfaces with the SAP system
- SAP Business Information Warehouse   Provides data warehousing functionality and interfaces with the SAP database
- SAP ArchiveLink   Provides data archiving from the SAP database as per requirements

SAP Business Engineer is also considered to be a CA module. Other CA modules are systems like Plant Data Collection (PDC), Process Control Systems (PCS), IDoc interfaces for EDI, Application Link Enabling (ALE), CAD interfaces, Document Management Systems, and so forth. We will discuss more on these modules in Chapter 19, "Enhancements and Interfaces to SAP."

Industry Solutions

Almost every industry has characteristic requirements that are specific to the companies operating in that industry. SAP provides a wide array of industry-specific vertical solutions that address such unique requirements through industry solutions (IS) that are complementary to the base R/3 solution. A company in the oil and gas sector can implement a combination of SAP R/3 and IS-Oil, achieving the objective of obtaining a solution that is a standard package as well as specific to the requirements of their industry. SAP partners with customers, consulting companies, and other software developers to develop and enhance IS solutions at established industry centers of expertise (ICOEs).

SAP has IS in its stable for several industry segments including Oil and Gas, Auto, Pharmaceuticals and Chemicals, Retail, Consumer Goods, Healthcare, Telecommunications, Utilities, Construction and Engineering, Banking and Insurance, Media, High Technology and Electronics, Public Sector, and so forth (refer to Chapter 9's sections "Industry Specific (IS) Solutions" and "SAP Solution Maps").

Customizability

SAP has comprehensive functionality, but for individual companies, the real test of SAP is to be able to customize it quickly for their specific requirements. SAP provides the tools for a company to tailor SAP to its specific requirements by configuring the parameters at the time of implementation.

SAP Business Engineer provides a complete environment for analyzing, designing, and configuring your business processes quickly and efficiently. The 800 best-business practices or scenarios that have been referred to numerous times in the text are scrutinized here. Business Engineer provides different models and views of these processes in different forms (including graphical representations) for facilitating the selection of the right processes. These selections are also automatically embodied in the corresponding Implementation Guide (IMG) that subsequently handles the actual work of customizing the configuration of the system.

Chapter 1's section "What is ERP?" mentions the application development environment, which in the case of SAP is the Business Engineering Workbench, functions like a complete application and consists of the following:

- The R/3 Reference Model is part of the R/3 repository and incorporates the following models: function, process, information flow, communication, organization, distribution, and data.
- The R/2 Business Navigator
- The R/3 Analyzer uses the Reference Model and process selection matrices for recording the requirements and their analysis for selection of the optimal solution.

4

THE SAP
SOLUTION

- The Procedure Model (now superseded by Accelerated SAP (ASAP) Methodology especially for the SME enterprises) provides a methodology and a framework for managing SAP implementation projects. This model provides the sequence of activities for different phases of the project. Each of these activities can be executed by interfacing with the IMG.

- The Implementation Guide (IMG)

- The Model Company is a full SAP implementation for a model company International Demo and Education System (IDES), which is mainly used for demonstrating SAP capabilities and technology, testing out real-world scenarios, and for training users on the functioning of the system.

We discuss these components in Chapter 5's "Implementation Environment" and Chapter 12's "Implementation Guide (IMG)."

These modifications to the functionality do not alter the SAP system itself, but SAP also provides enhancement of the system through custom development using the ABAP/4 Development Workbench.

World-class Practices

SAP consists of a repository of more than 800 world-class practices that are available for reference and use. These have been compiled by SAP across several years while designing the R/3 repository in order to be able to address the requirements arising in several industries. The value of this library of processes can be judged from the fact that SAP had at one time been working seriously on introducing a scaled-down version of R/3 targeted to small and medium enterprises (SMEs). However, work on R/3 Lite, as it was to be called, was abandoned after realizing that SMEs have requirements that are quite similar to larger companies. Moreover, success in business, contributed in no small part by implementing SAP, may lead to rapid growth of such SME companies and expansion of their business activities, which may in turn require enhanced functionalities that are available only in the full-featured R/3 system.

Application Integration and Real-Time Operations

SAP provides real-time integration across all modules, owing to its single, centralized database and also to its strategy of immediate updates that are available instantly to all logically related processes and modules. This enables businesses to respond to the latest changes and statuses without any intervening delays. As an accompanying benefit, it eliminates efforts and processes like reconciliations that result from delayed communication of information within or between organizations. All decisions, projections, and plans based on such real-time information are more accurate and can also be fine-tuned further in real time.

SAP Architecture

Figure 4.2 shows SAP components from a functional as well as an infrastructural point of view. From a functional point of view, the topmost layer is the presentation layer that is made of the GUI system. The middle layer is the application layer that handles not only business applications, but also the middleware layer called Basis. Integration of all business applications relies on the Basis system. This system includes components such as the ABAP/4 Development Workbench, system administration tools, system management tools, authorization and security systems, and cross-application systems. The lowest layer is made up of the network, the database, and the operating system.

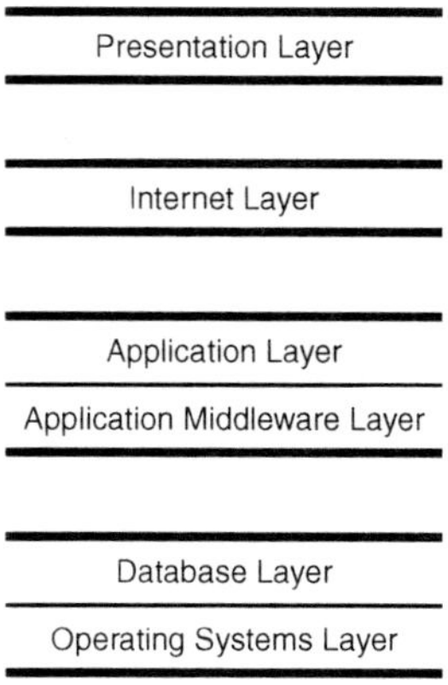

```
┌─────────────────────────────┐
     Presentation Layer
└─────────────────────────────┘


┌─────────────────────────────┐
       Internet Layer
└─────────────────────────────┘


┌─────────────────────────────┐
      Application Layer
 Application Middleware Layer
└─────────────────────────────┘


┌─────────────────────────────┐
       Database Layer
    Operating Systems Layer
└─────────────────────────────┘
```

FIGURE 4.2

SAP architecture.

Since the client/server is primarily a software-driven concept, we can very easily picture the functional view also in terms of the widely used three-tier architecture of SAP implementations whereby the system computers are partitioned into three functional groups for handling the presentation, application, and database services, respectively. R/3 also enables the distribution of presentation and application layers over multiple computers. Communication between the three tiers of computers is achieved through standard protocols such as CPI-C or TCP/IP.

The presentation layer deals with the following services: SAPGUI, SAPLOGON, and the SAP Session Manager. The Applications layer deals with business applications and is grouped into the following services: Financials, Logistics, and Human Resources. The Application Middleware layer deals with the following services: dialog, update, enqueue (lock management), background processing, message server, gateway, and spool. The database layer deals with native and open SQL services. Application layer will be tackled in Chapter 9," SAP R/3 Application Modules," while the Middleware layer is described in Chapter 7, "Basic for SAP Administration" and Chapter 8," ABAP for Custom Development."

Scalability

SAP's scalability on the technical front is easy to grasp. The multilayer client/server architecture enables SAP to easily scale the operations from a configuration for few hundred users to a few thousand. On particular sites, this scaling might also be dictated by the implementation of additional modules or third-party specialized applications that are interfaced with SAP.

SAP, however, also provides scalability on the business front as well, where an SME might commence using only a subset of the functionality provided by the SAP system. As a result of business successes, an organization might witness rapid growth and expansion in terms of volume, type, and the complexities of business activities. SAP can keep pace with such positive developments in the nature and structure of a company's business by customizing its delivered functionality on an ongoing basis suitable to the increased scale and complexity of its business. This is the genesis of SAP's configure-to-order strategy for SMEs.

Graphical User Interface (GUIs)

SAP GUI is the standard GUI of the R/3 system. SAPGUI's design logic and element definitions are independent of the presentation system, and hence the SAP user interfaces have the same look and feel, irrespective of the presentation software used at any installation. The graphical systems could be from any platform, including MS Windows, OS/2 Presentation Manager, OSF/Motif, and Apple Macintosh. SAPGUI includes all the graphical capabilities of modern Windows interfaces, with menu bars, toolbars, push buttons, radio buttons, online help, value lists, and so on.

Moreover, because SAP does not transmit fully prepared screen images between R/3 application servers and presentation systems, the volume of data transmitted for every screen is very low, approximately 1 to 2 KB. This results in minimal network traffic, which is another major contributing factor towards the overall scalability of the SAP system.

Internationalization

As I have noted while relating the history of SAP in Section 4.1, SAP has always had as a part of its core strategy a plan to support multiple languages and related aspects of currencies, taxation, legal practices, and import/export regulations within its systems. The same logic of presentation mentioned above also has enabled SAP to provide multilingualism as an innate capability of the system. All onscreen text is maintained separately in several languages, and the presentation screens are assembled only at the time of display, depending on the language version chosen by the user at the time of logging into the system.

SAP also maintains programs for the development and enhancement of country-specific functionalities in different parts of the world. As more and more companies have facilities operating in different parts of the world, such country-specific functionalities are becoming critical for obtaining the promised benefits of implementing solutions like SAP R/3 worldwide.

R/3 Repository

As mentioned in Chapter 2's section "The Anatomy of an ERP System," the R/3 Repository is the central collection area for access or information on every kind of development object in the SAP system. These development objects include the data and process models, the ABAP/4 dictionary, function libraries, user exits, Workbench organizer objects, and so on. The Repository Information System also provides a comprehensive cross-reference facility that delivers information on all of the points of use for a specified object.

Comprehensive Application Development Environment

SAP has a centralized, integrated, full-featured development environment for custom development or enhancement of SAP standard functionality.

ABAP/4 Development Workbench

The Advanced Business Applications Programming (ABAP/4) Language is a full-featured 4GL available for custom development in the SAP R/3 environment. The ABAP/4 Development Workbench provides all the necessary facilities, tools, and aids for the design, development, and testing of application data tables, screens, programs, inquiries, reports, and so on. At the heart of the Workbench is the ABAP/4 data dictionary. The data dictionary stores the descriptions of the table structures used throughout the system. It is the central metadata repository that I talked about in Chapter 2, "The Anatomy of an SAP System."

In addition, the Workbench has an object repository that stores all objects under development, be they programs, dynpros (dynamic programs), documentation, and so on. This controls the actual development and testing of programs directly. On successful completion of the development, another component called the Workbench Organizer handles the transfer of new developments and customizations into productive systems or to other SAP systems. The Workbench Organizer maintains facilities for version control.

Open Architecture

SAP enables the cooperation and portability of applications, data, and interfaces across different computers, because they use internationally accepted standards for definitions of interfaces, services, and data formats.

Because of the open architecture, SAP can work flexibly with multiple solutions options at all levels:

- Graphical interface level
- Desktop level
- Application level

- Database level
- External interfaces level
- Communication protocol level
- Hardware and O/S level

Figure 4.3 gives the various platforms supported by SAP.

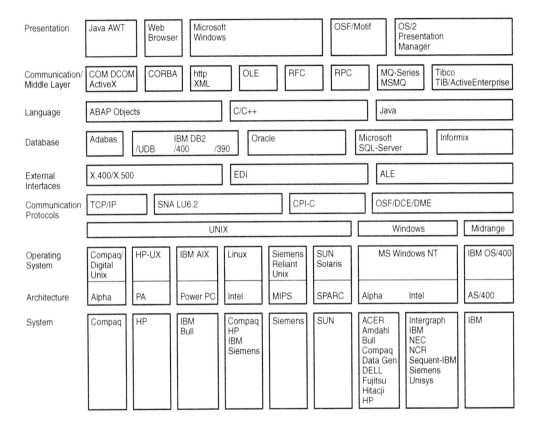

FIGURE 4.3

SAP R/3 supported platforms.

Portability

The R/3 system can be used on a variety of systems. In fact, its platform independence permits the use of different hardware or O/S platforms for presentation, application, and database servers with tremendous advantages in terms of performance and costs. This also enables any installations to benefit from the latest developments in infrastructure technologies (hardware, O/S, networking, DBMS, and so on) without disrupting the SAP system in production. Owing to the client/server architecture of the R/3 runtime system, the R/3 can also run on multi-processor systems.

Interoperability

Open system interfaces permit SAP to be integrated with other applications using earlier-noted industry-standard interfaces like Object Linking Enabling (OLE) and Remote Function Call (RFC).

The R/3 system follows internationally recognized standards like

- CPI-C for program-to-program communication across computers
- SQL and ODBC for access to databases
- TCP/IP for transport protocol in networks
- RFC for high-level programming interfaces
- OLE/DDE and RFC for integration with PC-based applications
- x.400/ x.500 as the open electronic mail interface
- The EEDIFACT EDI protocol for the exchange of structured business-oriented data at the application level
- ALE for online integration of decentralized applications across computers
- Open interfaces for interfacing with systems like process control systems, plant data collection systems, CAD, and so on

Figure 4.4 shows the standard protocols used by SAP with reference to the OSI-layered model for networks.

R/3 System Controls

Every user has a valid user identity and password that is authenticated when logging in to the system. The R/3 authorization concept is implemented on the basis of the authorization objects. This ranges from general access down to the level of access to individual tables, fields, and values. Authorization could be for access to particular set of enterprise data or for a set of operations or both.

An authorization object consists of several system elements that need to be protected like parametric or configuration data, master data, transactions, processing tasks, and so on. For efficient authorization, authorization objects are packaged into predefined authorization profiles. SAP supports an array of standard profiles for a wide range of applications and activities. These profiles can be maintained independently and can be assigned to the appropriate users on demand. Users can also be given authorizations to create, change or view objects. Authorization profiles are further combined into composite profiles for personnel who are required to work in areas that are not covered by one profile.

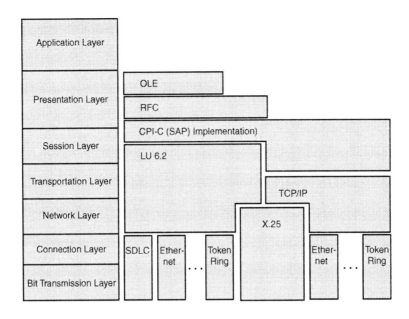

FIGURE 4.4
Protocols used in SAP R/3.

More importantly, SAP's transport and release system controls and manages all programs that are released into production as well as changes that are to be made from time to time on the system. This transfer can only be done under the strict control of the transport and release system. The transport system has a strict version control on all development objects that are transferred to the production system. The transport system is subject to the R/3 authorization concept.

All activities occurring in an R/3 system get recorded in the system logs and can be listed according to the user or transaction. Similarly, every change to the R/3 startup profile, the customizations, database parameters, and the operating system parameters is also recorded and is available for analysis.

To ensure protection from unauthorized tampering, the R/3 system as a whole is stored in separate directory structures of the operating system with exclusive access authorizations.

SAP Services

SAP provides companies with a comprehensive set of services during the implementation and support phases of their R/3 implementations. SAP delivers support services mainly on remote connections between customer SAP installations and the network of SAP support servers spread throughout the world.

Online Service System (OSS)

This OSS service is provided by SAP via customers logging into the nearest SAP support servers. This is basically a service for registering problems as well as accessing information, including solutions to registered problems. It is also the forum for disseminating up-to-date release, installation, and upgrade information.

OSS provides 24-hour Hotline support to assist users in determining solutions to problems faced in the system. A problem is logged with all the relevant information. When logging a problem, the customer states how important the problem is and how quickly a solution is required (low, medium, high, very high). When a customer is in a live-production environment and a resolution to the problem is critical, SAP will respond immediately, resolving most issues in less than an hour. SAP support staff can be given access to log directly into a customer's system and assist in resolving issues for the customer. Using OSS, customers have access to download patches and code corrections to known errors in the release of SAP that is being implemented.

EarlyWatch

EarlyWatch is a service offered by SAP, wherein SAP experts from SAP support centers connect to your SAP systems. They access customers' SAP installations and gather numerous data on various aspects of system performance data and system operations. This information is analyzed and processed for diagnosing problems or detecting potential problems and bottlenecks. This is largely useful at the time of initial installation or whenever major changes occur in the infrastructure or configuration of a SAP installation.

The EarlyWatch specialists analyze customer installations and provide a written report on the optimal parameterization of the system, on performance improvement, and on bottlenecks that might appear in the future.

Partnering for Growth

Partnering has been one of the driving forces in the growth of SAP. SAP has adopted partnering as a growth strategy not only with its business and technology partners, but also with its customers. This partnership with customers has led to the success of its ISs. SAP combines the horizontal functionality of its base solution with focused, vertical functionality provided by ISs that are developed along with specific, best-in-class SAP customers in each industry.

Until recently, SAP did not consider itself to be in the implementation business per se. Most of the SAP implementations have been undertaken by SAP implementation partners that range from the erstwhile Big Six accounting firms and Big IT firms to national-level consulting companies. Most of them have built exclusive practices for providing SAP implementation and support services (see Appendix B and C for the list of SAP Partners).

Technology partners are the leading software vendors of products that form the standard components of the multi-tier client/server architecture of SAP implementations. These include vendors of operating systems, databases, and networking products.

SAP has the following types of partners: hardware, consulting, technology, development, and the traditional value-added resellers. Development partners are companies that participate along with SAP's personnel in the development and enhancement of R/3. Additionally, SAP also has partnerships with third-party product developers called Complementary Software Program (CSP) partners. These are parties with specialized solutions like CAD, plant data collection systems, process control systems, identification and access control systems, mobile data collection systems, geographical information systems (GIS), and so on.

Other Significant Aspects of SAP R/3

In this section, I will mention briefly some aspects of SAP system operations that might not get highlighted in SAP literature yet are nonetheless, in my opinion, of great value in terms of their potential for leading to major gains in productivity. They are also indicative of the exactness of the research done by SAP in the usability engineering of their system.

SAP Document

In analogy with the integrity of an accounting transaction document in accounting systems, SAP has defined the concept of a SAP Document. A SAP Document contains all information pertaining to a transaction and is always retained in its complete form. This enables tremendous advantages in traceability, audit and maintenance of document history.

Recording by Example (RBE)

SAP by design is oriented towards screen-based interactions. It religiously follows the principle of recording any data only once. The system recognizes that this data entry effort is substantial, however, and goes further to help in expediting this data entry effort by providing a facility that I would term as Recording by Example (RBE).

Across the entire system, while doing data entry of any master or transaction record, SAP R/3 provides a facility to essentially provide a copy of relevant data from similar data items created earlier. For instance, when creating a new vendor, the system prompts you to optionally give a reference of an existing vendor whose details are similar to the new one being created. After providing an existing vendor number, the system provides a copy of *all relevant details* from the referred vendor record for you to accept or override for the new vendor record being created. This is a novel application of software engineering's basic guiding principle of reusability to as mundane an issue as that of data entry. It reduces keystrokes, minimizes individually keyed errors, automatically inputs standard information, and assures that none of the mandatory items are missed by an oversight. All this leads to tremendous gains in productivity, even in routine operations of data entry.

Variants

Here is another variation on the concept of reusability. A group of data items that may be required, often even in differing contexts, is packaged and identified uniquely as *variants*. This can then be retrieved and employed quickly at the required stages of processing, without having to specify all the minute details again and again free of errors. Variants are useful for situations like printing using specified format layouts, posting in a predefined manner to a set of accounts, and so on. It is amazing to witness how a little amount of reusability enlivens the drudgery and tediousness of routine operations.

Drill-down Reporting

Drill-down reporting is another facility that makes the inquiry and reporting functions in SAP very powerful. Any inquiry or report in SAP can be chosen at any point with a mouse click to access the supporting details of the source transaction. One can continue doing the same further, or, in other words, drill down to a level where the relevant supporting information is located.

For instance, in a statement of accounts for a customer, a user can click on any outstanding amount to immediately scrutinize the corresponding invoice and then go on to the customer order, the specific line item detail, and so on. After finishing, the user can return to the initiating program screen. This is of great value, especially for finance and accounting reports where an audit trail becomes available almost instantaneously without leaving the report or enquiry program of immediate interest.

Recent SAP Strategic Initiatives

In the past couple of years, SAP has taken the initiative to address the concerns reported by their customers. These initiatives have also been based on the experiences gained from thousands of SAP implementation projects that have been undertaken by SAP and its partners in the last few years. The thrust of all these initiatives has been to increase the efficiency of project efforts, decrease project completion times, and make SAP easy to use and operate.

TeamSAP

TeamSAP has been introduced to get the best of SAP and their partner's resources in three key areas—people, processes, and products—for the ultimate benefit of their customers. It enables SAP to deliver faster and at a lesser cost, without sacrificing its quality and benefits (also refer to Chapter 12 for information on SAP's rapid implementation methodology Accelerated SAP).

Accelerated SAP (ASAP) Implementation Methodology

The ASAP implementation methodology represents the process component of TeamSAP. ASAP is a comprehensive solution to achieve successful SAP implementations with optimal resources, costs, and time periods. It is based on the experiences obtained from thousands of SAP implementations in the past few years. It includes technical guides for expediting all stages of the ASAP methodology, especially the business blueprint and realization phases. It contains detailed project plans that guide you through project management in order to optimize time, ensure quality, and make efficient use of resources throughout the duration of a project.

SAP Ready-to-Run R/3 (RRR)

The Ready-to-Run R/3 (RRR) program, which is complementary to ASAP, has been especially designed and targeted for SMEs. The main feature of this program is that it is a combined hardware and SAP R/3 solution that comes with an already installed SAP system on a properly sized hardware system. This infrastructure contains a complete two-system landscape with development and production systems.

SAP has a range of RRR packages that can support R/3 production operations ranging from 12 to 200 users. Optionally, the RRR program also provides pre-installed front-end PCs or even network servers and software. Many procedures involved with the system operations also come predefined at the time of installation.

SAP has also introduced a special tool called the System Administration Assistant to aid in managing the system administration function. It is also useful to have the system up and running without any usual delays to permit the system administration function to get defined and stabilized properly.

EnjoySAP

The initiative behind EnjoySAP focuses on addressing the design and usability issues of using the SAP R/3 environment. Its objectives are to permit the dynamic customization of user-interfaces in accordance with users' role-based needs. This is intended to lead to an increase in the intuitiveness and also the speed with which a user can complete any interactive task.

MySAP.com

SAP introduced MySAP.com to enable SAP customers to do business on the Web. It combines the functionality of SAP with standard Internet technologies. It uses the EnjoySAP user interface to provide a common interface for both normal as well as Web-based interactions of the user within the system. More importantly, MySAP.com launches SAP into the application outsourcing market where SAP customers can outsource their operations to SAP outsourcing partners. The customers are then charged for the processes utilized by them, rather than the cost of owning and administering the whole suite of SAP systems.

Summary

In this chapter, we looked at several aspects of SAP to substantiate the fact that SAP is the best ERP solution that there is on the market. Even though it is not directly patterned on various evaluation criteria discussed in Chapter 2, "SAP Evaluation," this chapter clearly demonstrates the overwhelming superiority of SAP in all those criteria.

The intelligent use of Internet technology for business operations has already become a critical success factor for many enterprises. The sudden explosion in e-business implies that beyond-the-enterprise issues such as supply-chain management (SCM) and customer relationship management (CRM) have already become crucial for the competitiveness of many companies. SAP has always worked with the tremendous foresight and vision that have powered its growth to its present position as the number one business applications software company. With the advent of Internet, SAP truly stands challenged not only to provide competitive solutions, but also to keep on changing and upgrading them continuously on Internet-time.

The SAP Implementation Project Cycle

IN THIS CHAPTER

In this chapter, we consider an overview of an SAP implementation project life cycle. First, we consider the context of launching such a project, which includes the objectives of the project, implementation strategies, and the resource requirements for a company. We also provide an overview of the pre-implementation, implementation, and post-implementation phases of the project. The chapter ends by identifying some of the aspects involved with the deployment of SAP at remaining sites, as well as the issues of supporting an SAP production environment.

It is assumed that after the evaluation and selection of the ERP system for the company, the company has decided to implement SAP R/3 as the core solution throughout the company. All other systems, whether they are legacy or that might be implemented in the future, have to interface with the SAP backbone that will be implemented within the company. We will also assume that the company has evaluated, selected, and contracted for the hardware and networking infrastructure and the SAP implementation partners, as well as any other vendors for training, testing, system and network management support and services, and so forth.

It must be noted that the approach being presented here is based on my experience and perception of SAP projects. The situations in particular projects might certainly be different, and the measures presented here might not be applicable. SAP projects should still be considered recent phenomena, and no one is in a position to take a definitive stance on various aspects of such projects. I urge readers to modify the prescriptive message, particularly of this and subsequent chapters, to suit the particular circumstances of individual companies. This might also be true by reason of the fact that SAP implementations for millennium enterprises might differ qualitatively from implementations for the earlier Fortune 500 enterprises.

Mission and Objectives of the SAP Project

The mission of the SAP project should dovetail into the mission and objectives set forth by the company for the following 3–5 years.

The SAP implementation project itself could have a mission similar to the following:

To prepare, implement, and support SAP R/3 throughout the organization in the planned period of 2 years, with the full participation of all stakeholders of the company and to the satisfaction of all of these stakeholders.

Project objectives set for the SAP effort are quantifiable items such as

- Increasing process throughputs by 30%
- Reducing inventory by 30%
- Increasing stock turnover by 100%
- Increasing yield by 1% to 3%
- Reducing transaction turnaround times by 50%; these could be related to collecting or making payments, responding to internal requisitions or external queries, and so forth

Examples of Cited Reasons for Implementing SAP

By now there are more than 20,000 SAP installations through out the world. The reasons cited for undertaking SAP vary markedly from company to company. Some of the cited reasons are

- The existing applications have too many limitations.
- Application should be able to function on heterogeneous hardware and infrastructure.
- Application should provide companywide uniform user-interface across incompatible front-end hardware.
- Application should provide all business events online.
- Application should provide access to real-time information.
- Application should provide support for cross-functional processes.
- Application should enable flexible adjustment of business processes to market demands.
- Application should provide integration of back-office systems with customer-facing systems.
- Application should ensure that business processes should not be hampered by system or national boundaries.
- Application must support country-specific functionality.
- Application should lead to reduction in lead time.

Project Initiation and Planning

For business-driven projects such as SAP, it is vital that the top management should not only be involved, but should also be driving the project at every stage. Therefore, the project initiation would start with the appointment of an executive sponsor for the project. Usually the executive sponsor should be the CEO of the company. That appointment should be followed by the formation of a project executive committee and a steering committee. These should be followed by the appointment of a Chief Project Officer (CPO) and also the finalization of the scope of the project.

The CPO, under the guidance of the executive and steering committees, should assemble the implementation team, including the identification of module and site managers. The project management policies and guidelines should be finalized. The central project office should be established, including the critical support staff such as the training manager, the resources manager, and the project administrative staff. This team will have to prepare a plan and schedule for the implementation project, including the various activities, the manpower required, the duration, and the schedule for completing each of these activities.

The CPO will have to form another team to look after the procurement, installation, and productive operation of the basic infrastructure, including the hardware servers and clients, networking hardware and software, operating systems, databases, office automation software, and so forth.

Critical Success Factors

Various factors are considered critical for the success of the SAP projects. We'll look at each of them in this section.

Direct Involvement of the Top Management

SAP implementation is not an IT project but a business strategy project. As with any other business strategy project for new product development, new marketing strategy, BPR project, and so on, an SAP project should get the direct attention and involvement of the senior management. If this involvement is confined only to the initial stages of the project, the project is certain to falter later.

One of the issues in which top management is required to demonstrate and encourage full commitment to the SAP project is the deputation of key managers from different departments. Particularly in manufacturing concerns, participating in IT-oriented projects might be considered a non-value-adding activity in terms of its ability to further managers' career goals. This perception must be corrected because SAP implementation is not an IT-driven effort. Furthermore, the number of employees who would use SAP for their routine operations would be very large and their full participation in the project is very critical. This can be ensured only by deputing the key managers of the company for this effort.

Clear Project Scope

It is very important for a project to have a well-defined scope. Any ambiguities lead only to diffusion of focus and dissipation of effort. There are always adherents for increased scope and a series of such increments in scope would render any project unsuccessful. This is also referred as "scope creep." Hence, the CPO must be vigilant on any creep in the scope of the project.

Covering as Many Functions as Possible Within the Scope of the SAP Implementation

I have mentioned that the more functions are integrated and performed in real time, the more competitive the organization would be. For this, it is essential that as many functions as possible should go productive together on SAP. This "big bang" strategy will have to be adopted in a beginning stage of the projects, such as the Business Blueprint stage. Hence, it is critical that at least all the basic modules of SAP, like FI-CO, MM, PP, and SD, should be implemented in the pilot site.

Standardizing Business Process

Every plant or office site of a company develops its own character and culture, which are the results of the company's recommended corporate environment blending with the local situations. Such local practices have strong adherents and generate fierce loyalty and pride. These factors often harm the progress of a system implementation across the organization at all of its sites and offices, even if it is a computerized system such as SAP. As a prerequisite, it's important to streamline and standardize a business process.

Proper Visibility and Communication on the SAP Project at All Stages

It is important to give proper visibility to the SAP project. This might entail communicating about the strategic direction of the company, the relevance of SAP, the SAP implementation project and team, and the implementation plan and schedule. Either there could be a bulletin exclusively focused on the SAP project or the company's in-house newsletter must have regular features and articles on SAP project-related issues and milestones.

Allocation of Appropriate Budget and Resources

After the company has made the strategic decision to undertake the SAP implementation effort, it must also prepare and approve the budget plan and estimates for the complete SAP project. Because the project schedules are dependent nonlinearly on the prerequisite at all stages, any changes or deferment of release of funds, and therefore resources, will always have an adverse effect on the successful commencement of the project.

Many times the controllers or decision makers will withhold sanction for the resources at a particular stage at a pilot site or for other sites for optimization of costs. It must be noted that when any business project is launched, and SAP implementation is no exception, any deferment of such strategic programs only *increases the opportunity cost* for the period that the project is delayed. Moreover, for an integrated project such as SAP, that opportunity cost is not confined only to the local activity or site that contributes to the delay, but at the level of the whole company. Thus, for a company with a turnover of $500 million, after launch of the SAP project, that company would effectively be incurring an opportunity cost of $50 million for every delayed month in the schedule.

Full-Time Deputation of Key Managers from All Departments

In traditional IS/IT projects, the personnel normally allocated to such efforts are either members who were young and newly joined or are older members who could be spared from the department. In either case, this did not help in a large way to lead the projects to success. SAP, being a strategic project, should get allocation of the key personnel of different departments because only if the inputs are accurate and functionally correct will the SAP system truly deliver when it goes in production. For millennium enterprises, whose staff numbers (unlike the large enterprise) are small, must allocate their best people with the conviction that after SAP is in production correctly, it will give better returns not only in terms of money, but also other resources such as materials, manpower, time, and information.

Completing Infrastructural Activities in Time and with High Availability

Consistent with the approach being taken in this book, the infrastructure for an SAP project—whether it's the computers and networking infrastructure or human infrastructure in terms of skills acquisition and training—must not be treated as an IS/IT infrastructure. It must be monitored like any other non-IS/IT infrastructure. Any mismatch between the readiness of the infrastructure and the overlaying SAP system will only lead to delays in the project and, hence, incur opportunity costs.

Instituting a Company-Wide Change Management Plan

Like any other strategy implementation plan, SAP implementation is a prime case of an organizational change. It should be recognized and planned as such. In parallel with the SAP implementation effort, it makes sense to undertake a change management program to address the disorientation and lost sense of direction that might be experienced by a large number of members. If not managed properly, this could jeopardize the success of the whole project.

Top management should note that unlike traditional IS/IT projects, most SAP implementations do not have *parallel runs* in which incumbent systems are run along with the older ones for a predetermined time period until the new systems are declared operational and the company switches over to the new regime. This happens because after SAP goes productive, the transactions and the actual operational tasks are done on the SAP system itself; any major error could turn fatal for the company. The situation might seem alarming based on the past experiences of the traditional IT systems going productive; however, that is the exact point that I am trying to make in this book. SAP is not like a traditional IT/IS project; it represents a totally different model of computerization (see the section in Chapter 1 entitled, "ERP Represents the Departmental Store Model of Implementing Computerized Systems").

Training of SAP Team Members

All training needs for all the members of the team should be identified and corporate training programs should be arranged, either on site or members should be nominated for external training programs. For the millennium enterprise, in which project schedules are shorter and the manpower base in the organization is smaller, it is essential that training of the team members is initiated and completed before the scheduled start of the program. Members should be encouraged to take certification tests in their concerned area of activity.

Training of User Members

Awareness as well as familiarity training for all users who might use the SAP productive system are important. Training plans should not only have training programs, but should also budget refresher courses for all members. Sometimes, when an SAP project is reaching critical mass, the user community as a whole might be put to disadvantage because of a time lag between the actual training and the commencement of SAP going into production. In such cases, refresher courses might have to be undertaken either very close to the actual commencement of implementation or, if all sites and offices go live on SAP, on a staggered schedule. Again, top management should allocate a good contingency training budget in light of the fact that when SAP goes into production, there is no fallback arrangement; when launched, it has to reach "critical mass."

Scheduling and Managing Interface of SAP with Other Systems

There are many legacy systems, non-SAP systems, external systems, and even manual functions that might be considered out of the scope of the SAP project. SAP does not address all the functional requirements of a company. This might be involved with solutions for physical security and access control, plant data collection, mobile data collection, process control systems, CAD, digitizing systems, and so on. SAP has a complete program of interfacing with, and qualifying, third-party products to leverage on companies with special expertise and products. Interfacing these systems should be scheduled in such a way that the interfaces are operational when SAP goes into production.

In cases in which a peripheral or support system could be replaced by some functionality provided by SAP, the steering committee must make the judgement as to the schedule of that functionality's implementation in SAP. Considering the onerous agenda of the SAP project itself, the committee could decide to continue using the earlier system and transit to the functionality in SAP at a more appropriate time.

Transition Plan for Cut-Over to SAP

The company must have a subsidiary project plan for transitioning from the earlier systems, whether they are computerized or manual, to the SAP system. This might entail uploading data in a timely fashion into the SAP system. The timeliness of the data might be dictated by whether it is master unchangeable data or transaction data; or, it might be like opening balances for general ledger (GL) accounts and party ledger accounts. It could also be processing jobs that are done on a periodic basis, which might have to be transferred to the SAP production system. Because everything cannot just be transferred automatically to SAP, a phased approach—starting with uploading of data, to transactions, to posting statuses and subsequent processing steps—might have to be designed and executed.

Implementation Strategy

In this section, we consider what should be adopted by a millennium enterprise for its SAP implementation projects.

Big Bang Implementation of SAP Modules

The organization should consider a "big bang" implementation of SAP, wherein all the base modules of SAP are implemented and put in production together. As I have pointed out elsewhere in this book, by implementing only certain modules of the system, the company should not hope to reap more significant benefits than those accruing from the traditional systems. If SAP is not to be used as a past-facing system merely for recording and reporting purposes but more as a future-facing handler of an important enterprise resource, implementation of all the basic modules corresponding to the businesses of the company is essential. SAP system is modular and allows module-wise implementations. However, this is one feature that I recommend that should be ignored unless it is unavoidable because of extreme circumstances. A piecemeal approach of progressive implementation should be abandoned because delaying the implementations of all basic modules together only delays the benefits of a fully functional SAP and, therefore, incurs opportunity costs.

However, it must be noted that "big bang" being recommended here means implementing vanilla SAP or at the most with minimal customization.

Base Modules Implemented First

This strategy clearly dictates that the base modules should be implemented with highest priority, though the definition of base module may vary from industry to industry. But, in contrast, other modules or interfaces to other systems could be handled more appropriately after the based modules as a whole have stabilized.

Implementation of SAP Standard Functionality

As far as possible, avoid the bugbear of customization by altering and additional programming in ABAP/4. Additional programming should be evaluated and adopted only as a last resort. SAP keeps upgrading its suite of products and if custom software is built for a particular version, it will have to be upgraded every time SAP releases new upgrades. Like any other product, SAP goes through oscillating cycles between major functional upgrades followed by technical upgrades and vice versa. The best solution is to

- Use SAP standard functionality
- Accommodate the variation of the business process by using SAP's flexibility for configuring variant processes
- Adopt a workaround that indirectly takes care of the required functionality; for example, in the absence of the HR module, some accounts-interfacing HR functions can be managed by treating employees as customers
- Use third-party products that are properly certified and qualified by SAP

Pilot Site Implementation Followed by Rollouts at Other Sites

This strategy entails implementing as comprehensive functionality as possible at the pilot site and preparing the base-reference SAP configuration at the first site. This configuration is merely rolled out rapidly, with minimal changes at other sites. These changes might have to do, for instance, with loading separate master data for a different portfolio of products that may be manufactured at different sites. Thus, subsequent to the implementation at the pilot site, the project effort at the other sites will mainly involve

- Installing SAP
- Functional training of super users and end users
- Training technical personnel in SAP Basis and system administration and management functions
- Uploading corresponding data
- Integration testing

Utilize External Consultants to Primarily Train In-house Functional and Technical Consultants

No external consultant can match the know-how of the functional and operational requirements of the company better than its own members, who have the requisite expertise and experience working in various capacities and on different functions in the company. External consultants should be used as facilitators for getting their own key members familiarized with the functionality and navigation of the SAP system.

Considering the tight schedules, external consultants would have to shoulder the main effort and deliverables during the business blueprint and realization stages of the ASAP methodology.

But the focus of their participation should be in transferring the SAP product know-how to the key members of the implementation team. The key members of the implementation team will have the key responsibility of not only rolling out SAP to other sites, but also of providing the necessary support for the SAP effort in the future. As you will see later, it is not as simple as it might sound because after gaining expertise on SAP product know-how, such key members have a marked tendency to quit their jobs and join the growing number of independent SAP consultants or join one of the SAP consultancy firms.

Because of their backgrounds, the IS/IT professionals have a critical role in acting as facilitators for non-IS/IT-savvy functional members to clarify, define, and decide on their business requirements, and in assisting the functional members in configuring the system to obtain the desired functionality.

Centralized or Decentralized SAP Configuration

SAP installations have had centralized database servers. The enterprises of the millennium with distributed database servers might need to use the decentralized configuration. As we have noted in Chapter 4, "The SAP Solution," R/3 also allows the distribution of the presentation and application layers over multiple computers. For integrated systems such as SAP, it is a great achievement to be able to implement the multilayer client/server concept without losing the integration of data and processes across the entire system. SAP accomplished this with the Application Link Enabling (ALE) technology, introduced in 1995.

User-Driven Functionality

In marked contrast to traditional IS/IT projects, SAP projects are user driven. The key members from functional and business departments on the implementation team play the critical role of documenting and mapping the AS-IS (or existing) processes and deciding on the TO-BE processes. The mapping and configuration of the desired functionality proceeds by an approach closer to the Joint Application Development and prototyping methodology of the '80s.

SAP Implementation Project Bill of Resources (BOR)

Taking a cue from the Bill of Materials (BOM) employed in Production Planning and Control (PPC) functions, we can define a generalized version of the same for the SAP implementation project called the Bill of Resources (BOR). It enables one to define the hierarchy of the inputs, resources, and costs in the same structure. In this section, I provide an overview of what resources are needed for an SAP implementation project.

SAP recommends the AcceleratedSAP methodology as the primary implementation methodology for SME enterprises (which will be discussed in detail in Part IV, "The Implementation Stage"). The Accelerated SAP Project Estimator evaluates the scope of the project and other influencing factors, such as available expertise, implementation strategy, and so on to give an estimate of the project duration and costs.

Money

Although it is obviously dangerous to make any kind of generalization, an average SAP project for SMEs might range from $3 million to $7 million.

A possible breakdown could be as follows:

Hardware Infrastructure	30%
Software License Costs	30%
Implementation Services (both internal and external)	40%

Materials

The material inputs needed would be

- Hardware: Servers (database, application, network, email, and so on) and client PCs
- Networking: Hardware and software
- Software: ERP, front-end GUI software, operating system, office automation systems, and so on
- Project Office and SAP Center infrastructure

Manpower

The manpower resources essential are

- Executive management
- Senior officers
- Technical personnel
- System administrative and support personnel
- Office administrative and support personnel
- Super users
- End users

Time Period

The duration of an SAP project for SMEs might range from 4 to 9 months.

Information

The significant input is the documentation of business process for the whole of the enterprise. This includes documentation on each process, including inputs, outputs, duration, labor, frequency, processing, purpose, interfaces, initiator, supervisor, and so on.

Implementation Environment

The implementation environment consists of several components, discussed in the following sections.

R/3 Reference Model

All the processes that are available for implementation within SAP have been modeled and documented in this model for reference. There are several views for looking at the same processes. The following views or models are available for reference:

- Functional model
- Process model
- Data model
- Organization model
- Information flow model
- Communication model
- Distribution model

R/3 Business Navigator

This component gives the context for accessing the reference model. It provides for two different views:

- Process View
- Component View

Figure 5.1 through 5.7 present sample screens for the process and component view.

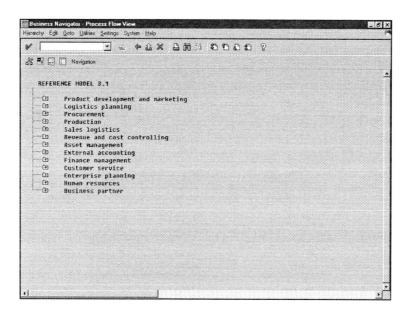

FIGURE 5.1

Process View of Reference Model.

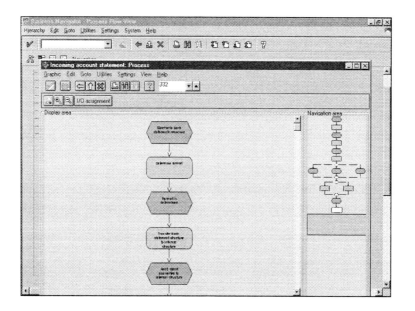

FIGURE 5.2

Sample Processes within the Reference Model.

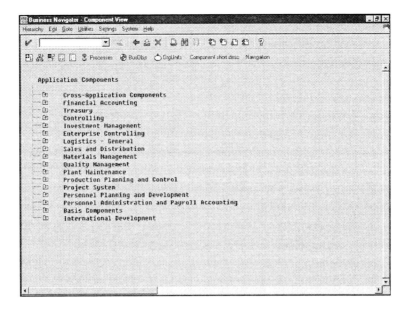

FIGURE 5.3

Component View of Reference Model.

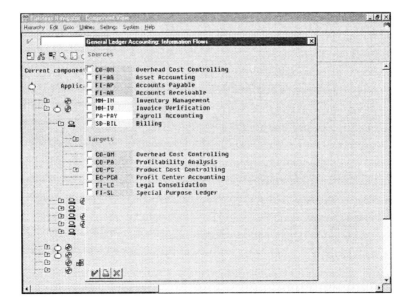

FIGURE 5.4

Sources and targets for sample Information Flows.

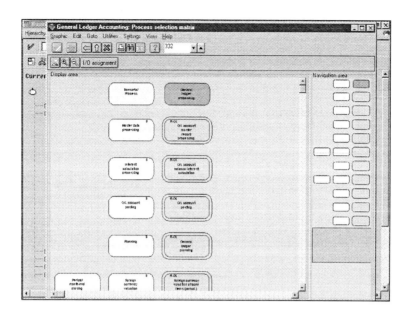

FIGURE 5.5

Selection of Business Processes.

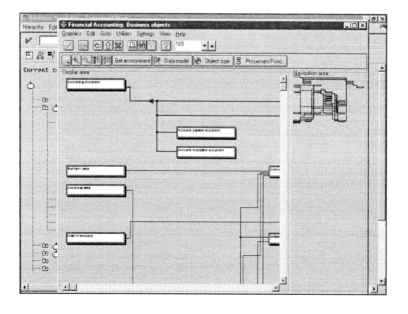

FIGURE 5.6

Sample Business Objects.

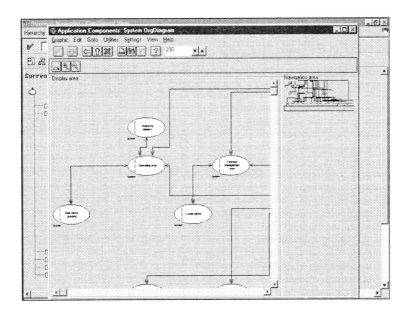

FIGURE 5.7

Sample Organization Diagram.

Function view starts from a top-down view of activities within a function. This view can be navigated down through the transactions to the level of the data model.

Process view primarily goes into details of a particular process.

R/3 Analyzer

This component is used during the analysis and mapping of requirements of a company on to the processes available in the library of best-business practices. By utilizing the R/3 reference model along with process selection matrices, the business analyzer enables the analysis and proper selection of SAP processes that are suitable for the implementation of SAP for the company.

Implementation Guide (IMG)

This is the core of the implementation environment, which permits customization of the functionality on the basic, full-featured SAP system. The system provides for different versions of IMG. The IMGs could be at the enterprise, project, or even individual level.

In every IMG, the system provides facilities for documentation, annotations, activity scheduling, resource management, monitoring of project status, and so forth. Also refer to Chapter 12's section "Implementation Guide (IMG)."

International Demo and Education System (IDES)

This is a full SAP implementation for a model company called International Demo and Education System (IDES). It is mainly used in demonstrating SAP capabilities and technology, testing out real-world scenarios, and training users on the functionalities of the system.

SAP Implementation Methodologies

Under ideal conditions, projects can be completed in the most efficient manner in time and on budget. However, it is essential to have a standardized approach of systems and procedures to help a company new to SAP to implement SAP successfully. Such an approach (called a *methodology*) may not be the most efficient one but it ensures success under *optimal conditions*. Companies survive and grow not by planning for the most ideal or adverse conditions, but by planning for optimal conditions. In the case of an SAP implementation project, the implementation methodology must ensure success given the usual complexity of businesses, resources, organizational structures, deadlines, and so on.

An enterprise implementation methodology broadly covers the following:

- Modeling Business Processes: The company defines the envisaged or TO BE business processes.
- Mapping Business Processes onto the Processes supported by SAP: The company identifies the SAP standard processes and functionality that address the requirements of the modeled process.
- Performing the Gap Analysis: The company assesses the difference or gap between the SAP standard and functionality and the requirements of the modeled processes.
- Finalizing the scope of the SAP implementation project: The company decides on the scope of the SAP implementation in terms of what processes would be implemented in the SAP system.
- Customizing the SAP system: The company configures the basic parameters in the SAP through Implementation Guide (IMG) for catering to the requirements identified (see the section in Chapter 12 entitled, "Configuration through Implementation Guide (IMG)"). All customizing is performed in client 001.
- Testing the customized SAP system: The configured system is tested for delivered functionality with actual data.

The identified gaps in functionality can be rectified by any of these measures:

- Devise a work-around for achieving the same functionality and configure it accordingly.
- Program the required functionality in ERP system via user exits.

- Suggest third-party SAP add-ons or plug-ins that provide the desired functionality and that have been certified for compatibility through SAP's Complementary Software Program (CSP).

- Defer its implementation to the next wave or defer it until the SAP release update that will introduce this functionality becomes available.

- Change the business process radically so it is suitable to the functionality available in SAP to achieve the same objectives

- Modify SAP software directly, although this is not recommended because changes in SAP sources invalidates SAP's warranty. Moreover, the modified software may lead to incompatibility with future releases of SAP.

SAP provides a full-featured R/3 Business Engineer environment for assisting in the implementation of SAP. For the purpose of modeling business process, SAP permits use of any of the following: ARIS toolset from IDS Sheer, VISIO from Microsoft, LiveModel from IntelliCorp, and Enterprise Charter. They are based on R/3 Reference Model and provide a direct interface with the R/3 system functionality. This enables easy understanding of the system because it permits specific SAP transactions to be started directly from these modeling environments; on the other hand, the process models provided by these systems give the whole context of particular SAP transaction.

The R/3 Reference Model and the tools mentioned above use the modeling technique called Event Process Chain (EPC) diagrams that is recommended by SAP. This technique primarily models processes as an ordered set of procedures that are triggered by events within the systems. These events could be database events like updates or screen selection events like menu-selection by user or even clicks on the Web page.

SAP Procedure Model

This is the traditional methodology for implementing SAP and is fully integrated with SAP. It was introduced in 1995 along with SAP R/3 3.0. There is some confusion as regards to the use of SAP Procedure Model: sometimes there is a feeling that the SAP Procedure Model methodology of SAP implementation is dated and should be discarded in favor of ASAP. However, it must be noted that ASAP is typically targeted for companies in the SME segment, whereas for the higher-end of the market, SAP Procedure Model continues to be the best methodology for implementing SAP. Because we are focusing on the SME segment, we present here only a brief summary of the SAP Procedure Model, which is suitable for larger companies having revenues in excess of $1.2 billion.

The Procedure Model consists of four phases:

1. Organization and Conceptual Design

- Project preparation
- Set up development environment
- Train project team
- Determine processes and functions
- Define interfaces and enhancements
- Quality check organization and conceptual design

2. Detailed Design and System Set up

- Configure global settings
- Establish Organization Structure
- Prepare Master Data
- Configure processes and functions
- Implement interfaces and enhancements
- Establish reporting
- Organize archive management
- Organize authorization management
- Perform final testing
- Quality check detailed design and system setup

3. Preparations for Going Live

- Create user documentation
- Prepare for going live
- Set up production environment
- Train end-users
- Establish system administration
- Upload data
- Quality check preparations for going live

4. Productive Operations

- Support live operations
- Organize Help Desk
- Establish systems operations

Figure 5.8 shows a schematic of the SAP Procedural Model.

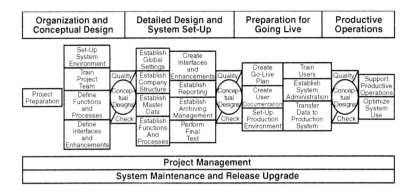

FIGURE 5.8

SAP Procedure Model.

Accelerated SAP

Accelerated SAP (ASAP) is the rapid implementation methodology introduced by SAP primarily for the American market in 1996. It provides a large number of tools and utilities to assist in the implementation process. Some examples are

- Implementation Assistant
- Question & Answer Database (Q&Adb)
- Issues Database
- Guidelines
- Knowledge Corner

We discuss ASAP methodology in detail in Part IV of this book.

Project Management

The purpose of project management is to help define the tasks that are necessary to complete a project, control the progress of the activities, and account for the resources expended through the project.

Project Organization

Project organization consists of constitution of the various teams that are assigned to different tasks of the project. It entails nominating the various members of all teams, appointing team leaders, and reporting structures for compiling the progress reports of each team, which are consolidated progressively into higher-level progress reports. Usually, the team will consist of the Basis technical team, the ABAP/4 programming technical team, and many teams corresponding to major modules within SAP. Each of these later will contain subteams for performing analysis and design, as well as undertaking documentation and testing of the various modules.

Project Control

It is essential that the work of all teams and groups of teams in different areas be controlled for gauging the progress, or lack of it, in the corresponding tasks. For this, the effort and time expended will have to be recorded and monitored on a daily basis. This would be helpful in detecting delays and slippage, reconstituting the teams, and reinforcing any team with additional resources wherever necessary.

Time Recording

Time recording involves recording the time expended under various categories of activities by every member of the team. This is essential not only for the external consultants, but also for company members as well. An analysis of the time expended in various activities could be helpful in identifying the effort and cost expended in identifying gaps, resolving gap issues, talking with end users, configuration, documentation, functional and technical testing, debugging functional and technical errors, and so forth.

Meetings

Project meetings could be for all project related issues, such as

- Scope of the project
- Project strategy
- Constitution of teams
- Project schedule and milestones
- Requirements and business processes
- Gap issues
- Resolution of gaps issues
- Issues that have not been resolved
- Decisions on standardizing processes
- Preparation of test plans and data
- Test reports
- Debugging and candidate solutions
- Documentation and updates

- Software upgrades
- Scheduling training programs
- Nominating team members for training
- Resource availability and utilization
- Conflicts and resolutions
- User accounts, access, and authorizations
- Performance and availability
- Hardware and networking vendors
- Providers of implementation services and consultancy
- Bill payments
- Leave and resignations

Project Monitoring

The actual effort and time expended need to be compared to the planned effort and schedule on a frequent basis. Any observed deviations, or pattern of deviations, are corrected immediately. Any rescheduling of the project plan is addressed only in the project reviews.

Project Reviews

The main objective of project reviews is to ascertain the progress made with reference to the planned schedule. Progress on the action points of the last review is reassessed. Any shortfalls in achieving milestones or delays are diagnosed for the reasons, and corrective measures taken are endorsed or changed. Any suggestions for changing strategies are considered during the reviews. Any unforeseen problems cropping up during the project are analyzed here.

SAP Implementation

Unlike the traditional software development project, this involves three main phases: pre-implementation, implementation, and post-implementation. The pre-implementation phase will be discussed in Chapters 10 and 11. Implementation by using ASAP methodology is presented in Chapters 12 through 17. The post-implementation phase is discussed in Chapter 18 and 19.

Pre-Implementation

Pre-implementation involves the formation of the project and steering committees, the constitution of the implementation project team, and the installation of hardware and SAP software.

The latter involves readying the hardware and infrastructure, installing the operating systems, database software, client software, and SAP R/3 software. The SAP administration function entails systems administration, R/3 instance administration, network administration, database administration, printer administration, client administration, user administration, security administration, and so forth. Another major activity during this phase is training for the implementation team and other users, which is very critical to the success of the project.

Training

Considering the short time frames of the SAP implementation projects, SAP has identified training as an important determinant in the success of any project. SAP offers a broad spectrum of training courses covering all stakeholders of a SAP project. These courses cover a range of topics from a general overview to in-depth coverage of individual topics.

The training courses are divided into three levels of difficulty:

- Level 1—One- to two-day training courses introducing R/3 technology
- Level 2—Three- to five-day training courses providing initial specialization in an area
- Level 3—Three- to five-day training courses providing in-depth knowledge of an area covered by a level 2 training course

The level 1 training courses are meant for decision makers and it is recommended that they be taken before the start of the SAP project.

SAP also offers Partner Academy Courses, which are five- to seven-week intensive training courses on a particular module (FI, CO, HR, SD, ABAP, Basis, and so on). These courses cover the most important aspects of a module, from the introduction to a case study involving configuration of a sample business case. Successful graduates of the Partner Academy are considered "Certified Consultants" in that module. These courses were previously open only to consulting partners of SAP, but are now open to all customers.

SAP Installation

This basically involves installing the base license and designing the system landscape. This helps the SAP system to maintain a strict control on the separation of development, quality, and the production system.

Implementation

For the SMEs, the Accelerated SAP implementation methodology is recommended by SAP. It consists of the following five stages:

- Project Preparation
- Business blueprint
- Realization
- Final preparation and
- Go live and support

Post-Implementation

The post-implementation phase involves instituting support and services such as the SAP Help Desk, Disaster Recovery Systems, and Archival Systems. Following the implementation of the base modules, other modules such as SAP Business Warehouse, SAP Workflow, and so on can be implemented. We also get acquainted with SAP's business framework architecture, which has the goal of making it faster and easier for customers to introduce new functionalities into the system.

For effective SAP operations, training of implementation team and user personnel is essential.

SAP Support

Support includes various measures or activities that are undertaken to ensure availability of the application functionality or continued functioning of the system.

It deals with design, organization, and operation of a help desk for the SAP users within the company. Users can register their complaints and queries, and get specific responses that can be implemented by the end users with the help of the super users in their respective departments.

Hardware availability is ensured by various measures, such as disaster recovery systems and archival of data.

SAP Deployment

After SAP goes into production at the pilot site, it is important to have scheduled the focus to immediately shift to the other sites. In fact, at those other sites certain activities, including training of super users and preparation of data for uploading into the SAP system, should be undertaken in parallel with the last stages of implementation at the pilot site. It is advised to immediately commence implementation at other sites because doing so enables the company to leverage the momentum generated by the implementation at the pilot site. Moreover, any breaks between the implementations might cause members of the core team to look for other challenging opportunities.

If training super users and data loading are done parallel with the finishing stages of the implementation at the pilot sites, what remains during the actual SAP project at the sites is

- Deploying the base configuration prepared at the pilot site
- Conducting the integration test
- Conducting the training of the end-users at the concerned site
- Going live

Why SAP Projects Might Sometimes Be Less than Successful

There are various reasons why SAP projects might be less than successful. This might be because of the following reasons:

- Top management involvement and interest falters or is perceived as faltering
- Lack of clear project scope and strategies; project is too narrowly focused
- Implementation of nonoptimized processes in SAP
- Decisions regarding changes in processes and procedures may not be effected; they might be ignored or subverted
- Lack of proper visibility and communication on the SAP project at all stages
- Lack of adequate budget and resources such as for training of large group of envisaged end users
- Not deputizing the key managers on the implementation team
- Support infrastructure and systems are delayed inordinately
- Disputes and conflicts in the team are not resolved quickly
- Company members of the team might not get along with the external consultants
- External consultants might have differences with end users or user managers
- Core team members might have differences with user departments
- A company-wide change management plan is not implemented
- Too much time between the implementation at the pilot site and rollout sites
- Members of the company do not participate actively because

    Members feel the system has been implemented in haste and that it does not address their requirements; they feel they have not been taken in confidence

    Members feel they have not been given adequate training

    Members of the company are apprehensive of their future roles

Members of the company are afraid that they not be able to learn the new system and perform satisfactorily

Members of the company feel unsettled by the lack of hierarchy in the system

Members feel they have been reduced to data entry operators

- Members of the core implementation team might resign and leave the company

- Members of the core team might be averse to moving on projects at rollout sites

- Inexperienced consulting resources

- Slow decision-making process

- Scope creep

The solutions for tackling these problems will vary from company to company. The approach to be adopted will depend upon the industry, culture, and history of the company. An approach for handling these kind of issues is discussed in Chapter 14's section "Organizational Change Management."

Summary

This chapter gave an overview of the complete implementation cycle of SAP. The pre-implementation issues are discussed in Part III. Chapters of Part IV discuss the various phases the Accelerated SAP methodology during the implementation stage. The post-implementation issues are dealt with in Chapter 18, "Supporting SAP" and Chapter 19, "Enhancements and Interfaces of SAP" of Part IV.

SAP and Enterprise Reengineering

IN THIS CHAPTER

This chapter clarifies the role played by SAP in the Business Process Re-engineering (BPR) effort within a company that is driven by SAP. After introducing the concept of BPR, we look at the full cycle of an enterprise's BPR methodology. Throughout the chapter, we pause at various stages to note the relevance and the role that SAP can play at every stage in the reengineering effort within an organization.

The Background of Business Process Reengineering (BPR)

Although BPR has its roots in information technology (IT) management, it is basically a business initiative that has major impact on the satisfaction of both the internal and external customer. Michael Hammer, who triggered the BPR revolution in 1990, considers BPR as a "radical change" for which IT is the key enabler. BPR can be broadly termed as the rethinking and change of business processes to achieve dramatic improvements in the measures of performances such as cost, quality, service, and speed.

Some of the principals advocated by Hammer are as follows:

- Organize around outputs, not tasks.
- Put the decisions and control, and hence all relevant information, into the hands of the performer.
- Have those who use the outputs of a process to perform the process, including the creation and processing of the relevant information.
- The location of user, data, and process information should be immaterial; it should function as if all of it were in a centralized place.

As will become evident when perusing the above points, the big-bang implementation of SAP possesses most of the characteristics mentioned above.

The most important outcome of BPR has been viewing business activities as more than a collection of individual or even functional tasks; it has engendered the process-oriented view of business. However, BPR is different from quality management efforts like TQM, ISO 9000, and so on that refer to programs and initiatives that emphasize bottom-up incremental improvements in existing work processes and outputs on a continuous basis. In contrast, BPR usually refers to top-down dramatic improvements through redesigned or completely new processes on a discrete basis. In the continuum of methodologies ranging from ISO 9000, TQM, and ABM on one end and BPR on the other, SAP implementation definitely lies on the BPR side of the spectrum when it comes to corporate change management efforts.

An SAP implementation can result in BPR, or top-down dramatic improvements through re-designed or completely new processes. However, it all depends on the approach taken by the company. Some companies will implement SAP while trying to duplicate their existing business practices. Although implementing SAP will result in some improvements in this case, BPR will not result. Top-down management focus on BPR during the implementation of SAP is required for BPR to be achieved. In this case, the timeframe and project plan must reflect the goal of BPR.

Value-Added View of Business Processes

As discussed in Chapter 1's "The Value Add Driven Enterprise," business processes can very easily be seen as the basis of the value addition within an organization that has been traditionally attributed to various functions or divisions. As organizational and environmental conditions become more complex, globalized, and therefore competitive, processes provide a framework for dealing effectively with the issues of performance improvement, capability development, and adaptation to the changing environment. Along a value stream (that is, a business process), the analysis of the absence, creation, addition of value, or (worse) destruction of value critically determines the necessity and effectiveness of a process step. The understanding of value-adding and non-value-adding processes (or process steps) is a significant factor in the analysis, design, benchmarking, and optimization of business processes in the companies leading to BPR.

As organizational and environmental conditions become more complex, globalized and, therefore, competitive, processes provide a framework for dealing effectively with the issues of performance improvement, capability development and adaptation to the changing environment.

Value Added can be defined typically as

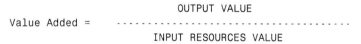

```
                              OUTPUT VALUE
        Value Added =   - - - - - - - - - - - - - - - - - - - - - - - - - - - - - - - - -
                          INPUT RESOURCES VALUE
```

Figure 6.1 shows the relationship between Output Value Vs Input Resources Value for SAP-driven business processes as compared with business processes based on traditional IT systems.

As discussed in Chapter 1's "Information as the New Resource," information made available by ERPs like SAP is not only a substitute for tangible resources like money, manpower, materials and time, but is also employable many times over. This clearly explains why the Value Added in Figure 6.1 shoots almost vertically for SAP-driven organizations. This also indicates that only when the basic modules of SAP are operational and fully integrated does the system truly begin to utilize information as a resource resulting in massive gains in productivity. Until then the system is only functioning as a recording system albeit an efficient one (see Chapter 5's sub-section "Big Bang Implementation of SAP Modules").

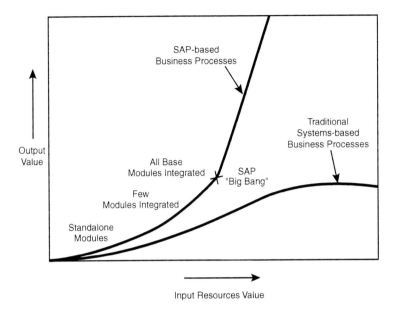

FIGURE 6.1

Relationship between Output Value versus Input Resources Value for SAP-based Business Processes.

Values are characterized by value determinants (VDs) like

- time (such as the cycle time)
- flexibility (options, customization, and composition)
- responsiveness (lead time and number of hand-offs)
- quality (rework, rejects, and yield)
- price (discounts, rebates, coupons, and incentives)

I must hasten to add that I am not disregarding cost (such as materials, labor, and overheads) as an value determinant, but the effect of cost is truly a result of many value determinants like time, flexibility, responsiveness, and so on.

The nature and extent of a value addition to a product or service is the best measure of that addition's contribution to the company's overall goal for competitiveness. Such value expectations are dependent upon

- The customer's experience of similar product(s) and/or service(s)
- The value delivered by the competitors
- The capabilities and limitations of the base technological platform

However, value, as originally defined by Michael Porter in the context of introducing the concept of the value chain, is meant more in the nature of the cost at various stages. Rather than a value chain, it is more of a cost chain. Porter's value chain is also a structure-oriented and hence a static concept. Here I mean value as the satisfaction of not only external but also internal customers' requirements as defined and continuously redefined as the least total cost of acquisition, ownership, and use.

Consequently, in this formulation, one can understand the company's competitive gap in the market in terms of such process-based, customer-expected levels of value and the value delivered by the company's process for the concerned products or services. Therefore, we can perform market segmentation for a particular product or services in terms of the most significant customer values and the corresponding value determinants, or what I term as critical value determinants (CVD). We look at CVDs in detail in the next section.

Strategic planning exercises can then be understood readily in terms of devising strategies for improving on these process-based CVDs, based on the competitive benchmarking of these "collaborative" values and processes between the company and customers. These strategies and the tactics resulting from analysis, design, and optimization of the process would in turn focus on the restrategizing of all relevant business process at all levels. This can result in the modification or deletion of the process or creation of a new one.

BPR and AcceleratedSAP (ASAP)

While using SAP's rapid implementation methodology ASAP, it is advisable that the company should avoid undertaking a Business Process Re-engineering (BPR) effort in conjunction with the SAP implementation. It is recommended that the company should implement vanilla SAP functionality initially.

When a company adopts ASAP methodology for implementing SAP, their success depends on how quickly the company can implement changes in its business processes that are in line with the best-of-business processes in SAP. When the implementation stabilizes, custom functionalities could be introduced later judiciously. The vanilla approach cuts down on maintenance, as well as speeds the time to production and benefits of the new system.

An Enterprise BPR Methodology

In this section, we look at the full life cycle of an enterprise's BPR methodology. We will indicate opportunities where SAP can be of assistance in an ongoing BPR effort within the company. We present an overview of the eight steps in a BPR methodology. These steps are as follows:

1. Develop the context for undertaking the BPR and in particular reengineer the company's business processes. Then identify the reason behind redesigning the process to represent the value perceived by the customer.

2. Identify the concerned business processes within the company.

3. Select the business processes for the reengineering effort.

4. Map the selected processes.

5. Analyze the process maps to discover opportunities for reengineering.

6. Redesign the selected processes for increased performance.

7. Implement the reengineered processes.

8. Measure the implementation of the reengineered processes.

The eight steps of the enterprise BPR methodology are shown in Figure 6.2.

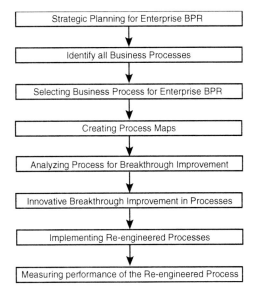

FIGURE 6.2

A cycle of Enterprise BPR Methodology.

BPR-effort within a company is not a one-time exercise but an on-going one. One could also have multiple BPR projects in operation simultaneously in different areas within the company. The BPR effort involves business visioning, identifying the value gaps and, hence, selection of the corresponding business processes for the BPR effort. The re-engineering of the business processes might open newer opportunities and challenges, which in turn trigger another cycle of business visioning followed by BPR of the concerned business processes. Figure 6.3 shows the iteration across the two alternating activities without end.

SAP and Enterprise Reengineering

CHAPTER 6

137

6

SAP AND
ENTERPRISE
REENGINEERING

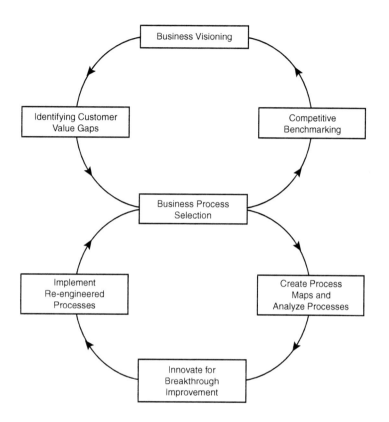

FIGURE 6.3

The alternating activities of Business Visioning and BPR.

Strategic Planning for Enterprise BPR

All markets are fluid to some degree, and these dynamic forces and shifting customer values necessitate changes in a company's strategic plans. The significance of a process to the success of a company's business is dependent on the nature and extent of the value addition to a product or service. Consequently, as stated earlier, one can understand the competitive value gap in terms of the customer-expected level of value and the value delivered by the company for the concerned product or service.

The competitive gap can be defined as the gap between the customer's minimum acceptance value (MAV) and the customer value delivered by the company. A good illustration of the concepts in this section could be the turn-around times or response times (RT) for queries from the various external as well as internal customers. Companies that consistently surpass MAVs are destined to thrive, those that only meet the MAVs will survive, and those that fall short of the MAVs might fail.

CVDs are those business imperatives that must happen if the company wants to close the competitive gap and are similar to the critical success factors (CSF) at the company level. CVDs are in terms of factors like

- Time (lead time, cycle time, and so on)
- Flexibility (customization, options, composition, and so on)
- Responsiveness (lead time, number of hand-offs, number of queues, and so on)
- Quality of work (rework, rejects, yield, and so on)

Market segmentation is performed based on the customer value and the corresponding CVDs. Such a market segmentation helps in suggesting corrective strategic and tactical actions that might be required, such as in devising a process-oriented strategic business plan. The strategic plan can in turn help identify the major processes that support these critical value determinants that must be innovatively improved and reengineered.

Identifying the Business Processes in the Company

All business processes in an organization are identified and recorded. A process can be defined as a set of resources and activities necessary and sufficient to convert some form of input into some form of output. Processes can be internal or external, or a combination of both. They cross functional boundaries, they have starting and ending points, and they exist at all levels within the organization, including section, department, division, and company levels. In fact, processes exist across company boundaries as well. Processes evolve and degrade in terms of their efficiency and effectiveness.

A process itself can consist of various substeps. The substeps in a process could be

- Value-added steps
- Non-value added steps
- Legal and regulatory steps (which are treated as value-added steps)

Selecting Business Processes for BPR

Selecting the right processes for an innovative process reengineering effort is critical. The processes should be selected for their high visibility, relative ease of accomplishing goals, and, at the same time, their potential for great impact on the value determinants.

Customers will take their business to the company that can deliver the most value for their money. Hence, the MAVs have to be charted in detail.

In our example of the response times (RT), MAV is dependent upon several factors, such as

- The customer's prior general and particular experience base with RT in an industry, product, and/or service

- What competition is doing vis-à-vis RT in the concerned industry, product, or service
- What effect technological limitations have on setting the upper limit for RT

As mentioned earlier, MAVs can be characterized in terms of the CVDs; only four to six value determinants may be necessary to profile a market segment. CVDs can be defined by obtaining data through

- The customer value survey
- Leaders in non-competing areas
- The best-in-class performance levels
- Internal customers

A detailed Customer Value Analysis analyzes the value gaps and helps in further refining the goals of the process reengineering exercise. The value gaps are as follows:

- Gaps that result from different value perceptions of RT in different customer groups
- Gaps between what the company provides and what the competition provides by way of RTs
- Gaps between what the organization perceives as the MAV of RTs for the identified customer groups and what the customer says are the corresponding MAVs

It must be noted that analyzing the value gaps is not a one-time exercise; neither is it confined to the duration of a cycle of the breakthrough improvement exercise. Like the BPR exercise itself, it is an activity that must be done on an ongoing basis.

As a goal for the improvement effort, a clear, competitive advantage can be gained if best-in-class performance levels can be achieved in some key customer value areas and at least some MAVs can be achieved in all others.

Creating Process Maps

A process map documents the flow of one unit of work (the unit may be one item, one batch, or a particular service that is the smallest unit possible to follow separately) or what actually happens to the work going through the process. A process map is developed at several process levels, starting at the highest level of the company. It documents both value-added and non-value-added steps. A process map could either be sequential or concurrent in nature.

Process could be mapped in two forms:

- Workflow chart form
- Work breakdown structure form

Process Workflows fall into three categories: continuous Workflows, balanced Workflows, and synchronized Workflows.

Workflow becomes non-synchronized because of

- steps or tasks produced at different rates, that is, an imbalanced workflow
- physical separation of operations causing work to move in batches, that is, a non-continuous workflow
- working in batches, causing intermittent flow
- long setup or change-over times resulting in batched work along with its problems
- variations in process inputs in terms of quality availability on time

All these add time and costs to the process and reduce flexibility and responsiveness.

Using the value-added Workflow analysis of the process map, we can

- identify and measure significant reengineering opportunities
- establish a baseline of performance against which to measure improvement
- determine which tools may be most useful in the reengineering effort

Evidently, the major goal in reengineering the process is to eliminate non-value added steps and wait-times within processes. A good rule of thumb is to remove 60 to 80 percent of the non-value added steps, resulting in the total number of remaining steps to be no more than one to three times the number of value-added steps. Even this would be a credible goal for the first iteration of the BPR effort.

SAP's strategy is to integrate all business operations in an overall system for planning, controlling, optimizing and monitoring a given business. SAP has included over 800 best-of-business practices or scenarios that could help company to restructure the its processes. These scenarios provide logical models for the optimization of the specific business processes and can be modeled around primary and support business activities. SAP guides a company to automatically integrate all primary and support functions of logistics like customer order, production, procurement, packaging, warehousing, delivery, service, accounting and so on. Companies can simply print out the relevant process models and analyze the most critical processes quickly and efficiently. The customizing features of SAP can then help in implementing the required changes

The SAP R/3 Reference Model can help companies define their process needs and develop solutions; business solutions are already built into the reference model eliminating the need for organizations to start from scratch. The components of the R/3 reference model, not only cover the process view but also function view, information view, data view and organization view.

For purpose of modeling business process, SAP permits use of any of the following: ARIS toolset from IDS Sheer, VISIO from Microsoft, LiveModel from IntelliCorp and Enterprise Charter. They are based on R/3 Reference Model and provide a direct interface with the R/3

SAP and Enterprise Reengineering

CHAPTER 6

141

6

SAP AND
ENTERPRISE
REENGINEERING

system functionality. The R/3 Reference Model, and the tools mentioned previously, use the modeling technique recommended by SAP called Event-driven Process Chain (EPC) diagrams. An EPC, as the name suggests, is a sequence of pre-defined processes that is triggered by the occurrence of a pre-defined event. These events could be a user-created event, a database update event or another EPC itself.

A typical ERP diagram is constituted of the following symbols:

- Event   indicated by a hexagonal block
- Functions   indicated by rectangle with rounded corners
- Information or material objects   indicated by a rectangle
- Organizational units   indicated by an ellipse
- Control flows   indicated by a dotted line with arrowhead
- Informational or material flows   indicated by a continuous line with arrowhead
- Logical operators   indicated by circle enclosing a symbol
- Assignment   indicated by a continuous line

Figure 6.4 shows a list of these EPC symbols. A sample of an EPC diagram is shown in Figure 5.2 earlier.

Analyzing Processes for Breakthrough Improvements

A company's competitive strength lies in eliminating as many costly non-value added steps and wait-times as possible. The key to eliminating any non-value added steps is to understand what causes them and then eliminate the cause.

For breakthrough improvements, the process maps are analyzed for

- Organization complexity: Commonly organizational issues are a major deterrent to efficiency of the processes.
- Number of handoffs
- Work movement: Workflow charts are utilized to highlight move distances, that is, work movements.
- Process problems: Several factors may have a severe affect on the continuity, balance, or synchronicity of the workflow. Examples are loops of non-value added steps designed to address rework, errors, scraps, and so on. These might be on account of
  - Long changeover times
  - Process input/output imbalances
  - Process variabilities
  - Process yields

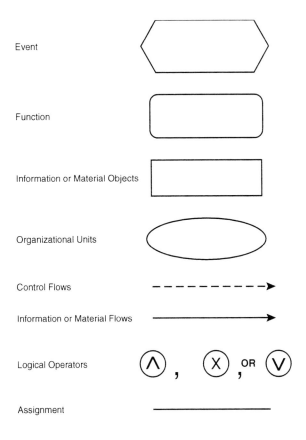

FIGURE 6.4
Symbols constituting an Event-driven Process Chain (EPC) Diagram.

These problems need to be identified, measured, analyzed, and resolved through innovative problem-solving methodology.

Innovative Breakthrough Improvement in Processes

The steps involved in innovative problem-solving methods are as follows:

1. Define a problem.
2. Find alternate solutions.
3. Evaluate the solutions.
4. Implement the best solution.
5. Measure and monitor the success.

SAP and Enterprise Reengineering

CHAPTER 6

143

6

SAP AND
ENTERPRISE
REENGINEERING

Business problems that need to be solved typically fall into three basic categories:

- System problems (methods, procedures, and so on)
- Technical problems (engineering, operational, and so on)
- People problems (skills, training, hiring, and so on): these problems arise because if you change what a person does, you change what he or she is.

Implementing Reengineered Processes

This step involves implementation of the following:

- Reengineered vision and policies
- Reengineered strategies and tactics
- Reengineered systems and procedures
- Reengineered communication environment
- Reengineered organization architecture
- Reengineered training environment

While perusing the various tasks presented earlier, it becomes evident that SAP can play a critical role in enabling and assisting any BPR effort in an organization in a major way. SAP can assist in almost all areas identified previously through facilities for defining organizational structures and processes through configuration and customizations (refer to Chapter 14's "Business Process Definition" and Chapter 15's "Baseline Configuration and Confirmation").

Measuring the Performance of Reengineered Processes

Measuring the performance of any process is very important, because lack of measurement would make it impossible to distinguish such a breakthrough effort from an incremental improvement effort of an Total Quality Management (TQM) program.

Measurements are essential because they are

- useful as baselines or benchmarks
- a motivation for further breakthrough improvements, which are important for future competitiveness

The measures for innovative process reengineering should be

- visible
- meaningful
- small in number

- applied consistently and regularly
- quantitative
- involve personnel closest to the process

SAP permits monitoring and management of hundreds of user-defined measures of performances (MOPs) that can be indicators of the excellence of processes. The MOPs can also vary depending on the market conditions or because of alterations in the emphasis and focus of the measures already implemented. Chapter 20 focuses on the important issue of valuation of an SAP-driven enterprise.

Changeability of SAP-driven Organizations

SAP-driven organizations are fundamentally enabled for managing changes in the operations of the business. These changes could be driven by external market conditions or they could also be planned and generated internally. You have already seen many aspects of this in Chapter 1, "The Millennium Enterprise." In this section, I highlight two characteristics of SAP-driven organizations that achieve a measure of BPR simply by implementing SAP in the first place.

Real-Time SAP Operations Make Processes Transparent

SAP transactions are immediately updated in the concerned functional areas, be they inventory, party ledgers, accounting, and so on. SAP reengineers the business immediately to eliminate all wait times and minimize the time period required for communication between various functions. All of these postings are done simultaneously so that a consistent view is always available for any transactions; there is no lag among the material, management, or financial accounting of any transaction. All this adds up to tremendous transparency and visibility in the functioning of the SAP system and hence the organization.

With traditional systems, which were not integrated and had batch-oriented processing cycles, a consistent picture was available only for a short period of time near the close of a month or a year. It also permitted different functions a certain latitude in exercising a manner of ownership and a degree of authority, even to the detriment of the overall functioning of the company's operations.

By making all transactions in real time, SAP enables an organization to minimize reaction times to changing situations in the market and take immediate corrective action. This also makes the organization more efficient, which is discussed in the following subsection.

Integrated SAP Operations Eliminate Handoffs

The integration of an organization's functions and processes through SAP eliminates various kinds of handoffs between departments, wherein tasks and copies of related documents are

SAP and Enterprise Reengineering

CHAPTER 6

145

6

SAP AND
ENTERPRISE
REENGINEERING

handed over to the next department for further processing. At every stage, this generates the need for inwarding, reconciliation, negotiations and follow-up with upstream and downstream activities along the process path, and so forth. All this merely adds more overheads, elapsed time, manpower effort, information overload, and, therefore, costs. The inherent integration provided by SAP eliminates all such overheads and non-valued-added activities. Reduced time cycles encourage various operational decision-makers not to inflate plans, projections, estimates, requisitions, material and purchase orders, production orders, and so on in order to accommodate contingencies. Overall, implementing SAP helps companies become more lean and efficient. However, one cannot discount the possibility that an organization, under some misguided zeal for accountability, may enforce highly restrictive authorization and access profiles that might essentially negate the advantages of the basic transparency, real-time interfaces, and integration provided by SAP.

SAP and Change Management

In the last chapter, which gave an overview of a SAP implementation project, we identified the fact that a SAP implementation project is like any other business performance improvement program. Because of the enterprisewide character of these projects, the issues arising out of SAP project necessitate that a formal change management program be undertaken within the company.

Change Champions—Core Team

The key members from the various functional departments of the SAP team are the ideal "change champions" for the SAP project. They can best communicate to the end users of their department, with whom the key members already have a good standing. After mapping and configuring the processes in SAP suitable for their requirements, the key members are also in the best position to talk to the other members of their respective departments and quickly address their particular common requirements and apprehensions. The change process is furthered by the core team members being directly involved in training the super-users from their respective departments.

Change Facilitators—Super-Users

Super-users are the key to a full-scale implementation and subsequently the productive operation of SAP. The super-users are trained by the key members of their respective departments. Their training consists of an overview of their module (and related modules) and all the critical processes of interest within their departments.

Under the guidance of the key users, the super-users participate in the full-scale testing and integration testing with other departments. This will help them to see the power and potential of SAP through actual experience with the system. It will also help them understand the practical implications of the tight integration, immediate updates, and transparency available in the SAP system. The super-users can then convey the real power of the system as experienced by them, especially during the integration-testing phase, to the end users in their respective departments. The super-users would be the messengers who would not only advocate changes in the processes, but would also demonstrate its actual functioning and its benefits.

Change Agents—End Users

The super users train the end users in their respective departments, covering an overview of the processes in their area of operation, the details of the process, and programs of direct relevance to their daily operations.

The transparent and instant access to relevant information that SAP provides from other departments is always a great motivator, but the implications of instantaneous updates and integration also make all members conscious of the enhanced responsibility and discipline that the system demands from all the concerned participants. Although new systems are always viewed with suspicion, the sense of involvement and ownership inherited from contacts and interaction far outweighs all misgivings about using a SAP system in production.

Summary

This chapter introduces the concept of BPR and details the full cycle of an enterprise BPR methodology. You also saw the relevance and role that SAP can play at various stages in the re-engineering effort within an organization. In the later part of the chapter, we looked into the change management aspects enabled by implementation of SAP within an organization. The valuation of processes and measurement of performances (MOPs) has been tackled in greater detail in Chapter 20 of this book.

SAP R/3

IN THIS PART

Basis for SAP Administration

IN THIS CHAPTER

The application layer sits on top of the middleware layer of SAP called the SAP R/3 Basis system. The Basis system is the layer that truly makes the applications portable or independent of a particular operating system, networking system, database system, or even presentation system. The Basis system provides the interfaces that enable the application layer to become independent of the heterogeneity of such satellite systems that are essential for the application system to function.

The Basis system provides the following:

- Operating system interfaces.
- Network interfaces.
- Database interfaces.
- Graphical user interfaces.
- SAP system administration, monitoring, and management tools.
- User authorization and profile management tools.
- ABAP/4 development environment, which includes the ABAP development workbench and the ABAP/4 dictionary. It also includes the workbench organizer and the transport system that manages the development, as well as the release, of modifications into the production system.

I have referred to many of these interfaces in Chapter 4, "The SAP Solution," but in this chapter, I focus more on the SAP interfaces to the operating system. More issues related to installation and routine administrative activities of SAP are covered in Chapter 11, "Installing and Administering SAP." This includes installation of SAP and administration of SAP instances, clients, users, jobs, printers, databases, and so on. Chapter 18, "Supporting SAP," covers topics related to support of SAP installation such as upgrades, Help Desk, and so on. Interfaces to external systems like ALE, I-Doc, SAP ITS/ IAC and so on are covered in Chapter 19, "Enhancements and Interfaces to SAP." The ABAP/4 Development Workbench is the topic for Chapter 8, "ABAP/4 for Custom Development." In the later part of the chapter, I touch briefly on SAP interfaces to the database, networks, and presentation systems.

Operating System Interface

In this section, I cover the SAP Basis that constitutes the interface to the underlying O/S.

Transactions in SAP

The functioning of the Basis system is based on a few concepts, such as a SAP transaction and Logical Unit of Work (LUW). We will consider these concepts before discussing the various services provided by the Basis layer.

SAP transactions are associated with interaction of users with the screens because in SAP, any business process-oriented event is fundamentally related to some screen interaction. Application transactions, as understood in SAP, are different from the transactions we are familiar with from the context of databases, although they are ultimately tied up with the concept of the changes to the database.

An SAP transaction might consist of multiple logically related dialog box steps with accompanying database updates.

Each of these steps is really a dynpro (dynamic program) that consists of a screen. Each screen consists of information on screen layout, fields, field definitions, field validations, cross validations, and other processing logic.

The execution of an SAP transaction consists of two phases: the online phase and the update phase. The transaction is not considered complete until all the logically related steps are completed successfully. Thus, all the database updates in the individual steps, even if they are individually completed, are reversed if the SAP transaction itself does not conclude successfully.

SAP Logical Units of Work (LUW)

SAP defines an application-oriented Logical Unit of Work (LUW), which might contain more than one dynpro and corresponding database updates. Thus, one SAP LUW might contain multiple database LUWs, but not the other way around. Database LUWs are no different from what we know for standard databases such as Oracle, Informix, and so on.

However, if the SAP LUWs do not conclude properly, all constituting database LUWs that are typically performed in the last dialog step are also reversed. This ensures that not only do individual tables remain consistent, but also that the SAP system as a whole remains consistent at all times.

The reason for defining a generalized application LUW in SAP is because different dynpros within a single SAP transaction might be handled by different processes (see "Dispatcher and Work Processes"). In contrast, in a DBMS, only a single process always handles a database LUW. Additionally, SAP transactions permit both synchronous (that is, real time) and asynchronous posting for performance reasons or updates, even on different computers within the same SAP transaction.

The Dispatcher and Work Processes

The R/3 runtime system handles many functions such as scheduling, memory management, lock management, and so forth that are usually handled by the operating system. But SAP executes them itself by reason of ensuring portability and control on performance. The R/3 runtime system has been developed in C/C++, whereas the SAP application modules have been written in ABAP/4 or ABAP for SAP 4.0 and later.

An application server consists of a dispatcher and multiple work processes. The runtime system of R/3 operates like a group of cooperating parallel processes. The dispatcher is a process that functions like a transaction monitoring system; it assigns tasks to other processes and coordinates and controls their activities. Every SAP instance has one dispatcher, which in turn can have many work processes. The dispatcher enables optimal utilization and balancing of the system load. It does the latter through the message handler that receives the request for logon by a user from the presentation server. Figure 7.1 displays a schematic on the dispatcher and work processes.

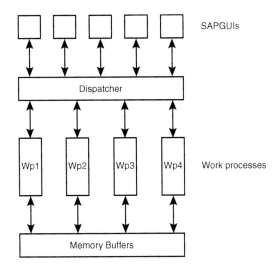

FIGURE 7.1
The SAP Dispatcher and work processes.

For instance, the dispatcher optimizes the interaction between the presentation and the application layers. After the dispatcher receives the data fed by the user, the dispatcher queues the request for processing that data and allocates it to the first-available work process of the appropriate type, on a first-come-first-served basis. On completion of the processing, the data is piped back to the corresponding screen and the work process is released for the next request in the queue. All communication between the work processes and other systems, such as the SAP GUI communication mentioned here or program-to-program communication, is routed through the dispatcher.

Each work process consists of a task handler that activates, on demand, the ABAP/4 processor, the dialog interpreter, or the interface to the database. It also manages the loading and unloading of the user context at the beginning and end of a dialog step, called roll-in and roll-out, respectively. However, when the processes need the same data across different dialog steps, such data is held in shared memory areas or caches. Before SAP release 3.0, which uses pointer operations instead of copy operations to address memory in the work processes, the work processes used to have only two kinds of caches, called roll area and paging area. The roll area retained copies of user and control information such as authorization across the dialog steps, whereas the paging area retained copies of application-related data such as internal tables.

There are several kinds of work processes. There are work processes for dialog processing, for posting of changed documents, for print spooling, and so forth. The number of various types of work processes, size of caches, and so on are all configurable by using the profile parameters for the concerned SAP instance.

Dialog Process

Considering that all processing of SAP revolves around interaction of the user with the system, the dialog processes that control all aspects of user interactions are the critical work processes.

The dialog process functions like the multiuser functionality provided by an operating system. A dialog work process executes only one dynpro at a time and switches to the next available dialog request from any user. This leads to a tremendous optimization of resources.

The load balancing required for distributing the dialog process is handled by the message handler. Whenever a user requests a logon to an application server, the corresponding presentation server refers the request to the concerned message handler. The message server has access to a database of latest performances of the various application servers and routes the logon request to the comparatively lightly loaded application server.

Batch Process

Batch processes are an important part of the daily operations in any company. They are especially useful for long-running programs that can be scheduled to run at suitable times during the day or night. In background processing, the dispatcher assigns one batch process to a background job until the end of the job. This is unlike the case of dialog processing, during which each LUW is assigned by the dispatcher to the next free dialog process.

Batch or background processing jobs normally use the same programs as online processing jobs. Batch processes are scheduled and managed by the Computer Center Management System discussed in "Computer Center Management System (CCMS)."

Update Process

An SAP transaction can affect a posting or an update to a database in two ways:

- Synchronously; that is, directly and in real time
- Asynchronously; that is, indirectly

In a direct posting, the update is effected by the dialog work process. In an indirect posting, the online phase and the update phases are executed separately. The dialog program creates a log record for the update of the database separately, subsequent to the completion of the online phase. This is beneficial because it frees the system immediately to proceed to the next dialog step, resulting in overall improvement in performance.

Again, to optimize resources and performance, based on the criticality of updates, the log record is partitioned into two components:

- Primary posting component
- Secondary posting component

Whereas the primary components correspond to updates that are related to real-time changes in business operations, such as stock positions, good receipts, and so on, the secondary components correspond to those updates that relate more to business-oriented measures of performances (MOPs) across a certain period. Thus, the primary components consist of high-priority updates and must be executed as soon as possible. The primary component updates must be completed before beginning the secondary component updates on the database.

Usually, because the preceding online phase has completed successfully, no application errors are expected to occur. But, in the case of technical errors occurring during the log record updates, the treatment of primary and secondary components is totally different. In case of an error of a primary component, all updates for that particular log record are reversed, the secondary updates are abandoned, and the concerned original online user is mailed accordingly. However, in the other case, only updates for the error-generating secondary component are reversed, and processing of the remaining secondary components in the log record is continued. Again, the concerned user is informed accordingly.

Enqueue Process

This is a process that is analogous to the lock management system in databases, but is much more sophisticated. Because the SAP transaction can update databases on several servers, each installation of SAP has a single centralized lock manager or *enqueue process* that maintains the integrity of the database locks across the whole of the system for every SAP LUW.

But, even on the same database server, the lock manager is required to permit multiple application servers to synchronize their access to the database and maintain data consistency. This becomes especially important when different dialog processes are handling an SAP transaction's dialog steps. Even while the dispatcher is switching the work processes, all processes should be able to retain the integrity of the assigned locks until either the end of the SAP LUW or when the locks are released explicitly by the application itself.

This integrity of locks across processes is also required for the asynchronous updates mentioned in the previous section. During the online phase of an SAP transaction, the application might have initiated locks on certain data objects; the following update phase must be guaranteed of no change in data in the time since the online phase was completed and the start of the update phase. Only after the update of the record is completed does the update program release all the locks set at the beginning of the corresponding SAP transaction.

Spool Process

A request for an output might be generated either by a dialog or batch process. The spool process prepares the data format for the selected kind of outputs, such as printer, fax, email, and so on, and stores in the TEMSE (temporary sequential) file. The spool process then directs the request to the host spool system.

Other Services

The work process running on the application servers use the message service to exchange data and messages.

The gateway service basically allows communication between the R/3 system and other external systems, including R/3 and R/2 systems. It primarily deals with the exchange of large volumes of application data. It utilizes the CPI-C protocol of communication.

Computer Center Management System (CCMS)

CCMS provides a centralized, graphic-oriented, easy-to-use, complete system administration and management tool for the R/3 system. It provides tools for handling system operations, control, monitoring, and optimization. It accomplishes this because it is integrated completely with not only the R/3 system, but also with the operating system, network management, and database management system. Figure 7.2 shows a screen of CCMS.

Control Panel

As the name suggests, the control panel is the central monitor with an overview of operations and activities of the complete R/3 system. It oversees all management functions of the SAP system. It also has the facilities to present different views for the display of buffers, monitors, alerts, error information, system logs, and so forth.

Some of the views available on the control panel are as follows:

- Standard View
- Server Status View
- Buffer Memory View
- Alert View

- Performance View
- Dispatcher View
- System Log View
- Memory Management

One of the items displayed by the control panel deals with starting and running SAP instances, which will we discuss next.

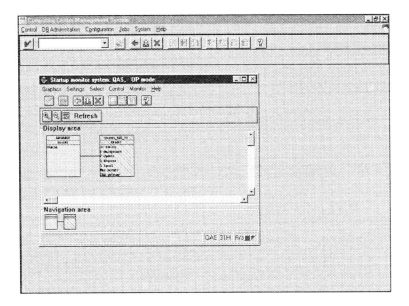

FIGURE 7.2

A Computer Center Management System dialog box.

The SAP Instance

An R/3 instance is a group of processes that provides the predefined set of SAP services mentioned earlier. Every instance has a dispatcher and a set of work processes. All instances are configured using an instance profile.

An instance profile specifies the following:

- The runtime resource requirement for the instance such as main memory, shared memory, and roll size
- Which work processes are invoked by this instance and their number
- The availability of other services, such as message server and so forth

Profiles are used while starting and stopping the system including all services that are made available by the corresponding instances.

Logon Groups

A logon group defines a group of instances. As mentioned earlier, when a user requests a logon, the message handler directs the request to the logical group that has the lowest load. This is referred as *logon load balancing*.

Operation Modes

Operation modes provide the flexibility to define instances to cater to the requirements of either more work processes or more resource-intensive dialog or batch processes at certain time periods.

System Monitoring

This function assists CCMS in monitoring the performance of the whole system and produces alerts whenever any of the concerned parameters cross a predefined value threshold. R/3 system monitors collect detailed information of all participating entities such as users, SAP R/3, operating system, network, and the database system. Using this collected data, the system monitor also provides detailed analysis and visual alerts on exception situations. Figure 7.3 shows a screen for Maintaining Alert Thresholds.

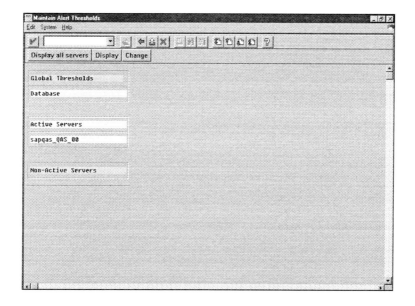

FIGURE 7.3
The Maintain Alert Thresholds dialog box.

SAP system alerts are mainly aimed at improving the availability of the SAP system by anticipating performance problems and signaling them online.

Alerts are of two kinds:

- Global alerts that are valid across all SAP instances
- Local alerts that are server specific

CCMS provides utilities for defining threshold values for several kind of alerts, corresponding to parameters related to the performance of the operating system, database, network, buffers, and system log.

CCMS also provides performance monitors for the following:

- Work process
- Operating system
- Buffer performance
- Database performance

Workbench Organizer and Transport System

The workbench organizer is actually part of the ABAP/4 Development Workbench, but I will discuss it here along with the closely related transport system. The workbench organizer provides an environment and tools for the ABAP development.

Because the workbench organizer is fully integrated with the ABAP/4 development workbench and the customizing tools, development objects could be any ABAP program, menu, screen, function module, table, domain, data element, documentation, print definition, and so forth.

The workbench organizer groups development projects into different tasks identified by unique development classes. Each development object has a development class associated with it. Development objects in a particular class are not available for changes by anyone other than members of its development class, except for "read-only" purposes. All changes to the development object within its class are immediately recorded in the tasks.

Furthermore, testing for the development projects are usually carried out in the test system. To guarantee the consistency of the objects, every development object has an original location and, therefore, an owner; changes can be made only to the original object in the original location. All these features have been incorporated to avoid accidental parallel development efforts. As a consequence, to perform an integration test of objects from several local systems, the individual objects would have to be first transported to a single integration system and then tested there. Corrections can be done in the development system and re-transported to the testing system for further testing.

A *change request* is a list of objects to be transported, information on the target system, and so on. Upon creation, the organizer automatically allocates a number to the change request. A change request is made up of one or more tasks corresponding to different developers. Only when all the tasks within a request are released can the change request be released from the workbench organizer screen and exported using the transport system. The objects could be transported to the test system within the group for integration testing and then subsequently to the production system.

The release of a task also automatically provides version control for all objects. The developers are also required by the organizer to write structured documentation for each request. Furthermore, when a change request is released, a transport log is automatically generated. The version control documentation, along with the transport logs, provides complete control over the development process.

The transport system is used for releasing development objects from one R/3 system to another system based on a valid change request. It also takes care of checking and monitoring the results of the transport request.

A transport process is constituted of two phases: export and import. Actually, from version 3.0 on, the export phase is executed automatically from the workbench organizer when users release the transportable change requests. The results of the export are logged. It also performs a test to simulate the export to the target system to detect any inconsistencies before actually exporting the objects. This enables you to take corrective measures before effecting the change request. Transported objects can optionally overwrite original repaired object or objects.

The import phase has to be performed manually by the system administrator at the operating system-level using the exported file, but the process and the results are recorded in the action and transport logs, respectively.

A summary of steps in using the workbench organizer and transport process follows:

1. Initialize the workbench organizer using transaction SE06.
2. Initialize the transport control program, tp.
3. Submit import background jobs.
4. Create a valid development class starting with Y or Z.
5. Create a new development object or modify the development object.
6. Release and export the transport request.
7. Import into the target system.
8. Monitor log files.

In addition to the workbench organizer, a customizing organizer (TA SE10) keeps track of the client-dependent customizing activities required to configure SAP during an implementation.

Other Administration Utilities

SAP also provides many other utilities and programs for performing various administrative tasks. They involve routine monitoring of the system, application servers, work processes, user sessions, update records, lock entries, short dumps, and trace facilities. Some of these are discussed in the following sections.

R/3 System Logs

All servers in an SAP system maintain extensive records or logs of all events occurring throughout the system. The system has facilities to provide extensive reporting on the logs depending on various selections such as SAP instance name, user ID, problem log code, transaction code, and even a particular work process or service. Figure 7.4 shows a screen for a System Log.

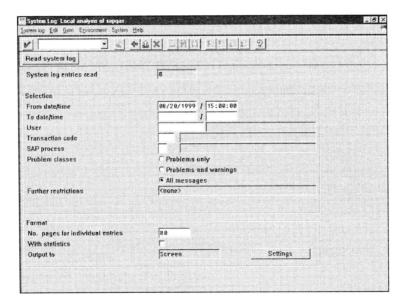

FIGURE 7.4

The System Log dialog box.

The system logs are of the following types:

- Local system log—Meant only for a local server
- Remote system logs—Meant for a particular remote server
- All remote system logs—Meant for all remote servers and instances
- Central system log—Meant for all servers

The local system log files are updated continuously in a circular fashion, whereas the central logs are configured for two separate log files for current and old logs, respectively. The logs are always updated in the current file until it is full, when it copies the current file to the old file (the old file is deleted first) and creates a new one for the current log records.

For doing more extensive troubleshooting, SAP also provides for a log analysis in an expert mode, wherein there is a provision for specifying more attributes or messages.

System Trace Utilities

The R/3 system provides many facilities for monitoring or tracking and debugging problematic situations. The problems could be related to the R/3 system, performance, and other issues.

The tracing utilities available are as follows:

- System traces
- Developer traces by SAP processes
- SQL traces by databases
- ABAP/4 program traces by ABAP Development Workbench

Figure 7.5 shows a screen for tracing SQL database requests.

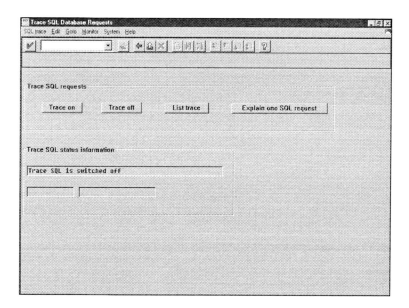

FIGURE 7.5
The Trace SQL Database Requests dialog box.

ABAP/4 Short Dumps

When an ABAP program terminates because of any programming error, the ABAP Development Workbench generates a short dump, which includes extensive information about possible causes of the error and possible solutions to resolve these problems.

Short dumps are kept in the database and are available for reference later.

Figure 7.6 shows a screen for ABAP/4 Dump Analysis.

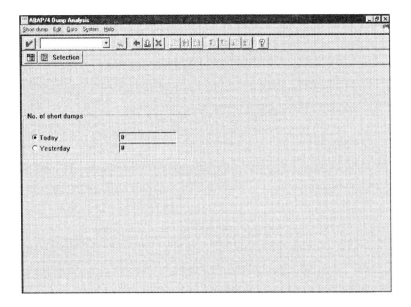

FIGURE 7.6

The ABAP/4 Dump Analysis dialog box.

Database Interface

The main task of the database interface is to convert the ABAP SQL statements to the underlying database's SQL statements.

Communication Interface

The R/3 Basis system supports all standard and de facto standard communication and networking protocols:

- At the operation system level, the protocol is TCP/IP.
- At the database level, the communication is through Remote SQL.
- At the application level, the communication is through CPIC, RFC, ALE, EDI, and so on.

With a Remote Function Call (RFC) interface, remote function calls are possible between two SAP systems or between SAP systems and other non-SAP systems like Microsoft Windows applications.

Presentation Interface

The presentation interface manages the function and appearance of the user interface. It ensures characteristics like:

- User specific customization
- Simple to learn and use
- Multi-lingual capability
- Portability

The presentation is constituted of two components: SAPGUI and the SAP Session Manager.

SAPGUI

Within a SAP system landscape, execution of a SAPGUI determines the system into which the user logs. SAPGUI has the same characteristics on each platform. This is achieved by exchanging only the data and logical information for the display between the application and presentation; the actual presentation is handled by the programs in the presentation layer using platform-specific resources.

SAPGUI corresponds to a single tasking environment. To perform multiple tasks in parallel, an additional SAPGUI session needs to be started.

SAP Session Manager

SAP Session Manager supports a multitasking environment; it can also support logging into multiple systems at the same time. The Session Manager enables the user to log on in parallel to multiple systems and work in these systems simultaneously in multiple SAPGUIs (that is, windows). It also supports individual configuration of the user interface in each of these windows.

Summary

In this chapter, I covered SAP's middleware layer, the Basis system. Integration of all business applications relies on the Basis system. In the next chapter, I look at the ABAP Development Workbench that is essential for custom development.

ABAP for Custom Development

IN THIS CHAPTER

ABAP Genesis

The programming language ABAP/4 originated in the '80s and continues to be enhanced and developed with every release of SAP R/3. All R/3 business applications are developed in ABAP/4. ABAP/4 has its origins in the report generation programming language developed for R/2 that enabled the creation of simple print lists. That language has expanded over time into a full-fledged development environment called the Advanced Business Application Programming (ABAP) language, which originally stood for Allgemeine Businessprozess Aufbereitungsprogramme.

ABAP/4 is highly reminiscent of the programming languages COBOL and Pascal, especially in its reporting aspects. However, ABAP/4 is quite different from typical third-generation languages (3GLs) and fourth-generation languages (4GLs) in that it is a language, as well as a full-featured client/server development environment, consisting of the ABAP/4 Development Workbench and R/3 Basis.

The essential characteristics of the ABAP/4 environment are

- It is a fourth-generation language based on structured programming methodologies; especially in its reporting aspects, it has a COBOL-like flavor.

- It is an event-driven language, especially in its dialog programming aspects, which are central to the R/3 system.

- It is an interpretative language; this makes possible prototyping of applications.

- It is an integrated, full-featured, development environment including a data dictionary, data modeling tools, program editors, screen and menu painters, testing and debugging tools, and so forth. It provides ready navigation between all these objects.

- It is open and portable because of the portability and open programming interfaces provided by the SAP system.

- It provides modularization by using reusable subroutines and function modules from a centrally managed library.

- It provides extensive data manipulation functions such as dates, strings, floating-point numbers, and so on.

- It supports multilingual text elements including labels, messages, and so on.

- It contains a set of standard SQL statements for transparent access to any of the underlying standard databases such as Oracle, DB2, Informix, and so on.

ABAP/4 Development Workbench is a full-fledged development environment for developing enterprise-wide client/server applications. It supports the entire software development life cycle (SDLC) from data definition, user interface design, processing logic, reporting, testing and debugging, and documentation to management of the work-in-process (WIP) programming effort. It provides a sophisticated metadata-management environment called ABAP/4 data dictionary, as well as a library of reusable executable functions. Above all, the programs developed in ABAP/4 can run without customization effort on any operating system, graphical user interface, database management system, network interface, and so forth, in both centralized and decentralized client/server environments.

Especially with the introduction of ABAP Objects, ABAP is no longer a fourth-generation language alone. It has many characteristics of an object-oriented environment. SAP already provides an object browser and class library that we will discuss later in this chapter. In the next section, we get familiarized with the concept of object-orientation and why it is significant for the future of all software application environments. We then look at the various components of the integrated ABAP/4 Development Workbench, before proceeding to an overview of various aspects of the ABAP programming.

Object Orientation

Before delving into the aspects of object-orientation of SAP R/3, we need to elaborate briefly on what object orientation means. The object-oriented paradigm is based on a new way of looking at the old dichotomy of data and computational procedures.

The Object-Oriented Paradigm

A *paradigm* is the totality of techniques, tools, attributes, and patterns of thinking or exemplars that constitute a world view. The '60s were characterized by the "algorithmic view," wherein the primary concern was to design and implement correct and efficient algorithms, which were related mostly to the performance issues of the numeric computations within the hardware constraints of main memory and offline storage memory. Subsequently, attendant problems of programming such as writing, debugging, modifying, and so on led to the progressive crystallization of the "procedural view." In the procedural view, algorithms were packaged into subprograms or procedures, and handled independently of the programs using them. This gradually led further to the "structural view" of the functional paradigm. In the functional paradigm, the focus is on the various functions and subfunctions that a system has to perform and the manner in which those functions have to be performed. The object-oriented view extends and couples this trend of abstractions not only to operations (such as subprograms and procedures), but also to the data.

The principal building blocks of the object-oriented paradigm are four in number: object, class, message, and method. They broadly correspond to the record, record type, procedure, and procedure call in traditional language systems. A set of methods is sometimes referred as an interface. SAP BAPIs are good examples of such interfaces (see Chapter 19's section "Business Applications Programming Interfaces (BAPI)").

An *object* is a thing that exists and has identity (that is, it occupies memory and is address-able). An object consists of data that is tightly coupled with all the operations that can act against it. The operations are referred to as *methods*, and the communication to the object triggering some method is the *message*. A collection of such messages defines the public interface of the object, and an object may be inspected or altered only through this predefined protocol of messages.

Because there is a considerable amount of commonality between the methods of several objects, objects with the same internal structure and methods are grouped into a class called the Class Defining Object (CDO), and are themselves called instances of this class. A class may have multiple instance classes; however, each instance has only one CDO and keeps reference to its CDO. Thus, a computation is performed by sending message to an object, which inherits or invokes a method of its CDO. This method in turn might invoke other objects by addressing to them and so on. This chain might terminate when a primitive object is invoked that either changes the instance variable or affects external entities such as the printer, hard disk, and so on. For instance, gasoline and diesel cars can be seen as the instance (sub-) classes of the four-wheeled vehicle object, which itself is an instance (sub-) class of the automobile class.

Inheritance and Encapsulation

A class is also a template from which newer objects can be quickly generated and used. This logically leads to many important characteristics of object-oriented environments, such as *inheritance* and *encapsulation*. Figure 8.1 shows the various sub-classes and instance classes of the Class Defining Object (CDO) called "Automobile."

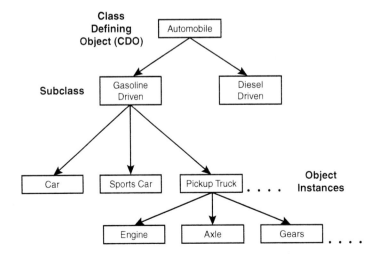

FIGURE 8.1

Sub-classes and instance classes of the Class Defining Objects (CDO) "Automobile."

In the automobile illustration, inheritance can be understood in terms of certain standard characteristics and components, such as the fuel, fuel tank, wheels, gears, axle, engine, and so on that can be presumed to be constituents of gasoline and diesel cars. These are properties as inherited from the four-wheeler class, and as inherited, in turn, from the automobile class. It is not difficult to imagine that this phenomenon of objectification can be carried out in either direction, from locomotion objects, down to the combustion engine parts, through the Bill of Materials (BOM). In fact, BOM itself is an example of a legitimate object! This results in a hierarchy or ladder at each level or step of classes and objects, not unlike the classification hierarchies of species in biology.

The second important characteristic of encapsulation refers to the transparency of any object within such a hierarchy of objects. That is, each object (for instance, X) merely performs a service, and queries as to how that service is accomplished or regarding the constituting objects of X, are immaterial. If one persists in getting answers to these queries, one might have to ascend or descend the ladder of inheriting objects for an appropriate answer.

Advantages of Object Orientation

Object orientation has gradually matured, and now it also subsumes activities of planning, analysis, and design of not only information systems, but also of enterprise modeling and engineering. Uses of the object model produces systems that are built upon stable intermediate forms, and thus, are more resilient to change. Object-oriented methodologies, when fully developed, can also provide a smooth and seamless transition across the various stages in the SDLC, such as the requirement definition, detailed specification, detailed design, and code generation stages. This also implies that such a system can be allowed to evolve over time, rather than being abandoned or completely redesigned when the first major change in requirements comes along.

Therefore, the basic advantages of the object-oriented paradigm are drastically increased opportunities for reuse of software components, the development methodology of rapid prototyping and incremental redesigning, and increased maintainability and environmental portability of finished applications. I am tempted to refer to the object-oriented approach as the re-engineered version of the traditional software engineering process!

Object Orientation and SAP

This completes the introductory framework necessary for us to tackle an object-oriented environment. Although there are a host of other related complex issues, such as composite objects, multiple inheritance, polymorphism, concurrency, persistence, and so on, this is sufficient for us to appreciate the object orientation of the SAP environment as a whole.

SAP R/3 is not an object-oriented environment per se, but SAP's architecture and design are highly influenced by that approach. The basic framework of SAP, including the ABAP/4 dictionary, event-driven programming, and event-driven business process chains, already implements a host of these concepts and may be reengineered into a full-featured object-oriented environment in the future. With SAP 3.0, a SAP workflow was introduced based completely on object-oriented architecture of business objects, methods, events, sub-classes, and so forth. In SAP R/3 4.0, ABAP Objects is a full-featured object extension to ABAP that is useful for providing and programming SAP on the Internet. However, for reaching the full potential of object-orientation, SAP basic architecture would have to be implemented in object-oriented fashion. Also, all SAP functional modules themselves would need to be developed, maintained, documented, and so on. in such an object-oriented environment. You will see the advantages of such an approach during our discussions throughout this chapter.

ABAP/4 Development Workbench

Figure 8.2 shows the initial screen of the ABAP/4 Development Workbench.

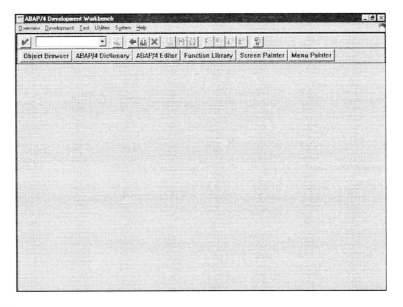

FIGURE 8.2

Opening window of the ABAP/4 Development Workbench.

All Workbench objects must be generated to become active in the runtime system.

All development objects of the ABAP/4 Development Workbench, such as data and process models, ABAP/4 dictionary, reports, dynpro, function module libraries, authorization objects, and so on are stored in the ABAP/4 repository.

The Repository Information System is fully integrated with the entire Development Workbench. The Repository Information System allows searching and sorting of various objects using various criteria. It also provides an extensive "whereused" list, giving all the points of use for a specified object. By default, it displays the different object types that are defined in the SAP system in hierarchical form.

As its name suggests, the application hierarchy contains the structure of the complete SAP standard business applications. For the customized version, SAP permits maintenance of the customer application hierarchy along with a development class defined for each node on the hierarchy.

ABAP/4 Dictionary

The ABAP/4 dictionary is the logical representation of the data stored in the underlying physical standard databases, such as Oracle, DB2, Informix, and so on. Figure 8.3 shows the initial screen of the dictionary.

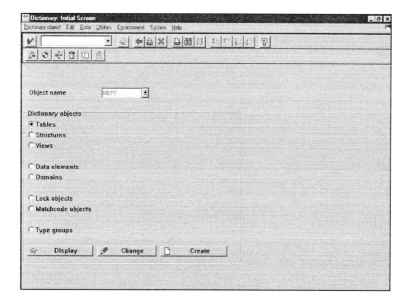

FIGURE 8.3
The initial screen of the dictionary.

The dictionary contains metadata about data that is stored in the application tables in the database. The metadata description in the dictionary involves two different levels: a syntactical or technical level and a semantic level. The first level corresponds to the domain object and the second level to the data element object.

Tables, structures, and composite objects are defined in terms of the data element objects, which in turn are modeled on the domain objects. This systemic hierarchy of domain, data element, field, and structure renders them reusable at all levels. This builds up tremendous flexibility and maintainability in the system. For instance, an increase in the size of the amount domain CDO instantly propagates the change to all data elements and fields, and therefore, to the tables, structures, and ultimately, database tables.

Because of the interpretive nature of R/3 runtime environment for ABAP/4 programs and dictionary, any changes made in the ABAP/4 dictionary are immediately propagated to all relevant application programs.

Domain

Domains specify technical attributes such as data type, length, value range, display characteristics, and so on. They are analogous to the class-defining objects (CDOs) mentioned earlier; generally speaking, they correspond to user-defined data types. Domain information recorded in the Dictionary includes short text, data type and size format, value table name, output sign, and output length.

Data Element

A field is semantically defined in terms of a data element, along with associated properties. These associated properties include key words, titles, description texts, and so on. A field in R/3 is always associated with a data element, which in turn is defined syntactically in terms of the domain. It truly corresponds to application-level data types. Data element information recorded in the data includes name, short text, domain name, and short, medium, and long field labels.

Table and Structure

All tables contain fields. The attributes of individual fields are described in terms of data elements and the corresponding domain. Figure 8.4 shows a sample screen of table structure for Material Document Header.

Tables have index tables defined on them, which are meant to reduce the access time when performing select operations on them. All tables, database indexes, views, and so on can be created from the dictionary without knowing the specifics of the underlying database.

Structures are like tables without any data records. They correspond to the field strings in the dictionary. Structure objects are useful for defining data in the interfaces from the module pools and screens. Structures exist only in the dictionary; they do not exist in the underlying database.

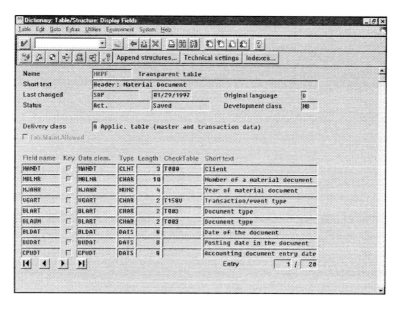

FIGURE 8.4

Sample table structure.

Moreover, structures can be embedded in the table definitions. Such substructures are analogous to include statements like the COPY statement in COBOL and the INCLUDE statements in C and Pascal. If any changes are made in the substructures, all tables and structures that include that substructure are changed automatically.

On the other hand, append structures are added to the standard table definitions of tables without changing the original definitions, and for that reason, could be used for extensions or custom development of the SAP system. Any future release upgrades by SAP will not overwrite such custom-developed append structures.

Composite Objects

Views are virtual tables formed by viewing jointly multiple tables. Views are used to link the information from several tables together or to give certain users a view of only selected fields.

Matchcode objects are used to locate records in a table based on knowledge of one of its constituent objects. It is a composite object that works as a special tool to help research for records in the tables. Matchcodes consist of two parts. The first part, called the matchcode ID, controls the actual search procedure. One or more of these matchcode IDs form a matchcode object that determines the table field to be searched for when it is executed. It determines which database fields can be used for the search. When a matchcode is used (it is simply mentioned in the attribute of the corresponding screen field), the matchcode ID display pops up a screen with its input fields in which the user can enter the search terms. Note that matchcodes have been replaced with search helps in version 4.0.

Lock objects are used to maintain the integrity of the object against inconsistent changes. They are used to lock and synchronize the access of the database tables. Lock objects are maintained independent of any specific application. For each menu command, the system uses the lock objects to define two function modules, which perform all the activities for locking or unlocking each table or data set.

Authorization in SAP is different from the implicit authorization checks employed in network and operating systems, which usually check only access to files using access privileges such as read, write, or delete. In contrast, SAP authorization also allows the protection of other objects like programs, reports, and so on. SAP maintains the authorizations as objects, which are created and maintained independent of the objects they protect.

An authorization is a complex object that contains several authorization fields (maximum: 10). The actual authorizations are multiple instances of authorization objects such as the CDO mentioned earlier. The authorization objects are combined into authorization classes. Logically related authorizations are combined into profiles and further into composite profiles meant for different application or task areas. All the authorization profiles that a user should have are entered in the user master record. Subsequent to the assignment of the composite profiles, profiles, and authorizations, the user gets the actual authorization fields with values. These and related topics on Authorizations are discussed in Chapter 11's section "User Administration."

Data Browser

The data browser allows navigation through and display of the ABAP/4 dictionary tables. It displays the table content along with the key fields, and it can also display foreign key relationships. It also permits new entries in case the specific table is set with the Maintenance Allowed check box within the dictionary.

Object Browser

This is the main navigation tool in the ABAP/4 Development Workbench. The object browser groups objects by development class. Figure 8.5 shows the initial screen for the Object Browser.

Program Editor

The ABAP/4 program editor enables you to edit programs, perform checking of syntax, provide online help, and so forth. Figure 8.6 shows the ABAP/4 Editor initial screen and Figure 8.7 shows a source code for a sample program: Note that the inline code is in German.

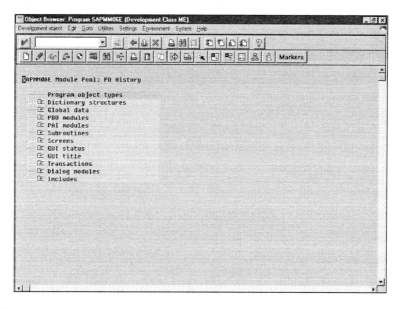

FIGURE 8.5

The Object Browser.

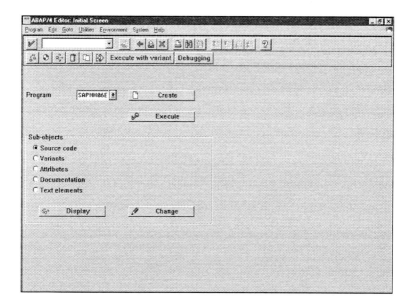

FIGURE 8.6

The ABAP/4 Editor.

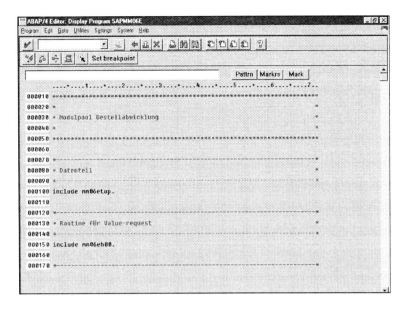

FIGURE **8.7**
Sample source code in the Editor.

This can be used to edit the source code of different development objects, such as

- ABAP/4 program source code for reports, interactive reports, module pools, and so on
- Flow logic for the screen painter
- Logical databases
- Function modules
- Maintenance of documentation and text elements

As a Workbench tool, the program editor also enables you to specify the attributes for ABAP/4 programs.

Screen Painter

Figure 8.8 shows the initial screen of the Screen Painter.

The screen painter enables you to define and design the screen, as well as the flow logic for dynamic programs (or dynpros). Supplementary control information includes the language used, the number of the follow-on dynpro, and so on. The screen is interpreted not by the ABAP/4 interpreter, but by a separate DYNPRO interpreter. It should be noted that DYNPRO is a full-fledged 4GL environment that enables you to develop prototypes quickly and then flesh out the full logic.

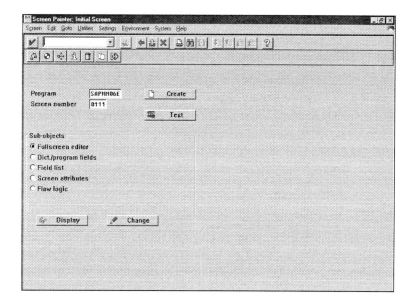

FIGURE 8.8

The Screen Painter.

The screen painter specifies the following:

- Screen program attributes such as screen number, screen type (normal, subscreen, dialog), and so on
- Screen layout, including field locations, labels, radio buttons, icons, check boxes, and element group
- Fields, including database field, cross validations, and so on
- Flow logic

For screen design, the screen painter has a graphical as well as an alphanumeric editor. Figure 8.9 shows details of a sample screen.

In the former, the field labels, positions, and so on can be changed or arranged directly on the screen. All text on the screen can also be represented by graphical icons. However, with the alphanumeric editor, screen design has to proceed only by selections from the menus of the screen painter.

Menu Painter

The Menu Painter is the ABAP/4 Development Workbench tool for developing user interfaces or more correctly, presentation interfaces (see Figure 8.10).

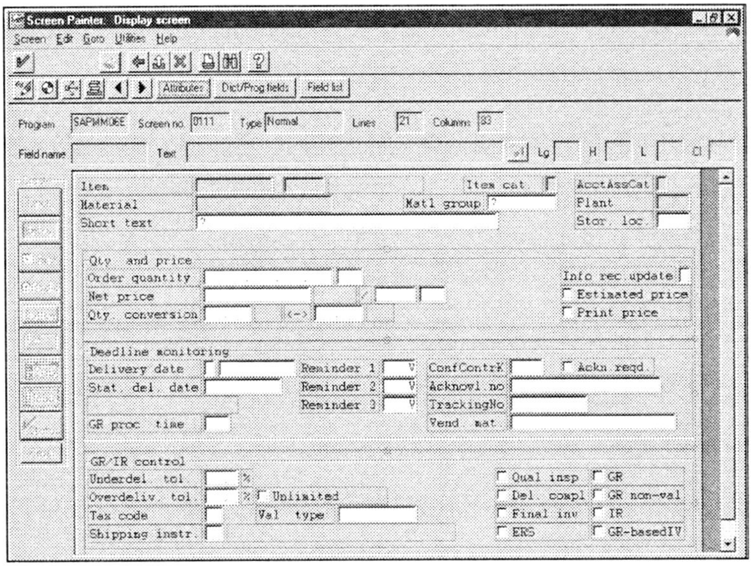

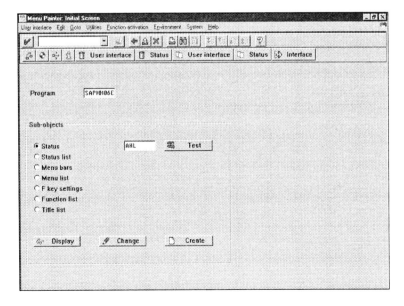

FIGURE 8.9
A Screen Painter detail window.

FIGURE 8.10

The Menu Painter.

It must be noted that these are not the customary user screens or menus, but only user interface standard frames that are used as a template for all SAP screens. They are not related to any screen generated by the screen painter. But they could become associated through the menu object called *GUI status,* which groups together the menu bar, standard toolbar, application toolbar, and the function keys that are usable in the presentation interfaces.

As mentioned in Chapter 4's section "History of SAP," the SAP system follows the Common User Access (CUA) standard defined within IBM's SAA framework. SAP uses a GUI system such as MS Windows or Motif on front-end computers as its front-end operating system (O/S) or presentation interface. This presentation interface provides the actual display window framework as well as several of the control elements; the use of the SAP system is relatively independent of this presentation interface. The association between the SAP system and the control elements is established through a direct mapping between them.

The toolbar allows communication with the R/3 Basis system. The icons trigger function codes, which control the running of the ABAP/4 application, and the icons are activated or deactivated by the ABAP/4 application. The function codes are either executed by the system or are dispatched to the ABAP/4 application for further processing. The command field is always input-ready for command execution by the SAP Basis system, which could be to call a transaction (see "SAP Transactions"), cancel a running program, create a new session, and so forth. The status bar at the bottom displays system-related information, including R/3 system information, messages, error messages (which can be double-clicked for detailed information on errors), and so on. The toolbar, the status bar, and the control elements of the front-end O/S cannot be edited directly.

The control elements provided by the front-end O/S are employed mainly for movement of the screen itself or for the movement of the display screen. A dialog program consists of several variants of the user interfaces, called the statuses. A status is defined by the following editable elements:

- Menu
- Pushbutton identifications
- Function key assignments
- Title bar

Figure 8.11 shows a sample status screen.

A main menu can consist of up to three levels, and each level can consist up to 15 entries. By using the menu painter, every menu item is mapped to an SAP transaction code. Important function codes are assigned to function keys for immediate access; this avoids the need to search through the menus for relevant functionality. Similarly, function codes can also be assigned to pushbuttons located below the toolbar. Again, it should be noted that these pushbuttons are not the same as those created by the screen painter; these pushbuttons can be defined only by the menu painter and can be mapped to SAP transactions (that is, ABAP/4 programs), but are not part of ABAP/4 applications directly.

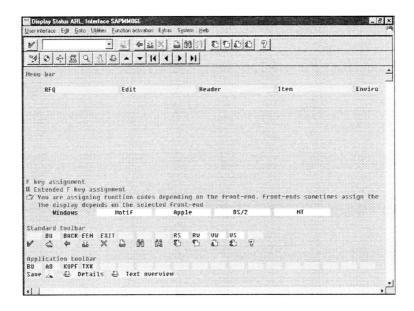

FIGURE 8.11

A status window.

This separation of the user interface and access—that is, the presentation interface and the SAP system—has been fortuitous because it enables SAP to use the latest Web browsers as front-ends without a major rehaul of their application architecture. In fact, SAP has adopted the strategy of replacing the front-end O/S, such as Microsoft Windows, with Microsoft Explorer. It is not only a change of presentation interface. The system that supports Web browsers has also helped SAP to launch a slew of services in the rapidly developing Internet-based services market (see the section in Chapter 4 entitled "MySAP.com").

Area Menus

Unlike normal menus, area menus are not related to any SAP transaction. Area menus are usually transactions that call other transactions. They are closer to the menus commonly found in traditional IT systems.

Function Library

The Function Library, which is also called Function Builder, is a tool for the maintenance and testing of function modules, which are usable from any program.

Figure 8.12 shows the initial screen of the ABAP/4 Function Library.

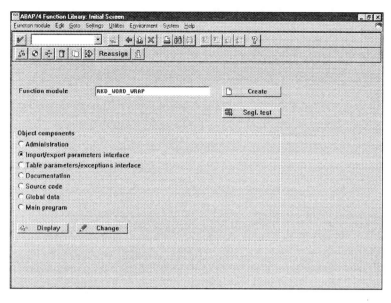

FIGURE 8.12
The ABAP/4 Function Library.

Testing and Performance Analysis

In this section, we look at some of the tools available in the Workbench for testing and performance analysis.

ABAP/4 Debugger

This is a tool available for testing ABAP/4 programs. It has facilities for setting breakpoints as well as step-by-step executions. Every time the program is stopped within a debugging session, the system has a provision for displaying or modifying the contents of the tables and fields. Breakpoints themselves can be static, dynamic, or watchpoints and specific to a keyword or an event.

The debugger can work in different display modes in terms of the program-related information the modes display. The default or preferred mode is V in which the contents of all data fields are displayed. The various display modes are as follows:

- V mode—Displays content of fields
- T modes—Displays content of internal tables
- F mode—Displays detailed information on a particular field, including content, every time a value is signed to that field
- O mode—Displays an overview of the current program with modules, events, and subroutines

- S mode—Displays the call sequence of various subroutines, function calls, and events

- P mode—Displays all programs that are required to execute the current program

In version 4.0 these display views do still exist, but without the modes (V, T, and so on).

Computer-Aided Test Tool (CATT)

This tool permits automated testing of business processes. It has facilities to describe and automate the testing of business processes; for example, by simulating the input screen dialogs. Because the test is automated, it can be repeated whenever required; the results of the test run and messages can be logged by CATT.

Runtime Analysis

This is a tool to aid diagnosis of performance problems in ABAP/4 transactions or programs. It provides information on the following:

- Executed instructions

- Chronological sequence of executed instructions

- Tables accessed and type of access

- Execution time

SQL Trace

This tool enables the analysis and display of the database calls made by reports and transactions written in ABAP/4. This assists in performance analysis, especially for batch programs.

Workbench Organizer

The Workbench organizer provides an environment and tools for the ABAP development (see Chapter 7's section "Workbench Organizer and Transport System").

Programming in ABAP/4

ABAP/4 is a full-featured 4GL that originated as a reporting language. Like any traditional computer language, ABAP/4's features can be described by broadly dividing them as follows:

- Data definition statements—These describe the data processed in an ABAP/4 program; for example, DATA, TYPES, and TABLES.

- Data query statements—These specify the attributes of the data record that must be retrieved and processed; for example, SELECT.

- Data manipulation statements—These render standard manipulation of data; for example, ADD, SUBTRACT, MOVE, and COMPUTE.

- Data control statements—These signal control structures such as loops, decisions, subroutines, and so forth; for example, DO, WHILE, IF, CASE, and PERFORM.

- Data event statements—These trigger the execution of certain routines depending on the occurrence of certain predefined events; for example, Pfnn, GET/ SET, END-OF-PAGE, AT USER-COMMAND, and AT LINE-SELECTION.

Data Types and Operations

ABAP/4 supports most of the standard data types. Based on those basic data types, ABAP/4 also enables you to develop complex data types or structures. It is in this area that the influence of languages such as COBOL is striking.

ABAP/4 also has all the standard language elements for manipulation of data such as assignment, comparison, computation, complex computation involving data of different types, and so on. It also provides extensive functions for processing textual data, including assignment, truncating or adding blank spaces, searching for a specific string, matching strings, concatenating strings, comparing strings, and so on. ABAP/4 also provides various operations for date calculations, such as calculating time periods in days, future dates, comparison of dates, and so on.

Data Table Processing

ABAP/4 permits access to data tables defined in the ABAP/4 dictionary as well as those in the underlying database. The former is achieved through SAP's OpenSQL and the latter through the native SQL specific to any of the standard databases, such as Oracle, DB2, Informix, and so on. To retain the independence of the R/3 system from the underlying databases, OpenSQL implements the barest set of SQL commands and features. The relational join operation, although not available in OpenSQL, can be used through views defined by ABAP/4 dictionary.

Internal Tables

These tables are temporary and exist only during the run of an ABAP/4 program. ABAP/4 provides various operations for processing internal tables such as sorting, searching, sequential access, and so on.

When a similar processing has to be done on a subset of records from the database tables, defining internal tables helps to simplify the programming effort by using control statements such as DO loops, CASE, and so on.

SAP Transactions

A transaction in SAP is like a program in normal computer languages, and is identified by a four-character transaction code. A transaction can be initiated directly from the command field on the presentation interface or from the corresponding menu option. There are two kinds of transactions: report and dialog transactions.

Report Transactions

Report transactions are SAP programs that collect selection parameters from the selection screen followed by the output called the *lists*.

Dialog Transactions

Dialog programs consist of more than one interactive screen called a *dynpro*. These transactions sometimes also need preselected information for triggering them, not unlike the explicit selection screens in report programs; these are called *parameter transactions*.

Subroutines

As in any other programming language, ABAP/4 allows subroutines for modularization of programs. This helps in reusability, and, therefore, in increased quality, productivity, maintainability, and documentation of the developed system. ABAP/4 provides for definition of subroutines using the FORM language element. Subroutines can be called by using PERFORM statements, and they can be called from within programs or from external programs.

Other characteristics of subroutines:

- Parameters of any type can be passed to subroutines
- Calls can be generated dynamically during the processing
- Calls can be nested, recursive, and so on

Functions

Functions, which are a special kind of subroutine, are very important for the modularization of ABAP/4 programs and applications. Function modules are available in a central library and can be called from there by any ABAP/4 program. Function modules are encapsulated objects, and have clearly defined interfaces with parameters such as import, export, and table parameters. Function modules have facilities for programming the handling of exceptional situations that occur during the processing of these functions.

Reporting

Reports access one or more tables and display their contents in the form of a list, which can be viewed either on the screen or on a printout. Report programs are very similar to the report programs in other languages, such as COBOL.

Logical Databases

For reporting data, reports might have to access several logically dependent tables. Consequently, the report program has to establish a connection with the concerned tables every time. Because many reports refer to the same set of tables, such requirements might be common across various reports. SAP provides a special category of program, called a logical database, that reads data from several databases and makes one data set available that can then be used by several reports at once. Each report then has to read only a single data set, analyze, and display it per specifications. This increases programming productivity, maintainability of the programs, and so on.

Selection Screens

Selection screens are presented before the execution of a report. Selection screens work as filters to limit the number of records included for analysis within a report. A selection screen is an automatically generated screen for every report. Selection screens can collect either a range of values or parameters for a field in a table.

Interactive Reporting

Interactive processing involves providing inputs or additional processing on report lists displayed onscreen. Additional processing, transactions, or reports can be triggered during the display of the report with the function keys. The latter case refers to the drill-down reporting that was mentioned in Chapter 4.

Dialog Programming

Dialog programming deals with the development of interactive applications in SAP. Dialog programming is based on the concept of a *dynamic program (dynpro)*, which is a combination of input screen and corresponding processing code. A dialog program consists of more than one dynpro.

A dialog program includes the following elements:

- One or more presentation interfaces
- One or more dynpro screens
    - Flow logic

The dynpro handles only the input elements and their behavior on the screen. As mentioned in section entitled, "Menu Painter," controls such as menus and pushbuttons are handled by the presentation interface.

A dialog program is called a *module pool*, which is a collection of processing modules. Figure 8.13 shows the list of modules for PO History.

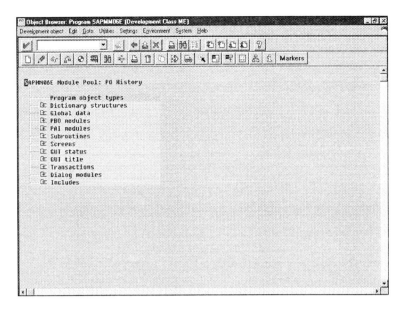

FIGURE 8.13

A module pool.

It is here that the object-oriented approach and the event-driven philosophy of SAP system become very clear. A dialog program is not a program per se, and there is nothing like sequential processing; all processing is dependent on the events resulting from the interaction of the user with the user interface of the system.

When a dialog program is started, it is the dynpro screens that are called and not the modules. It is the dynpro screens that implement the required business functionality by executing the individual modules from the module pool.

Dynpros

A dynpro consists of the following:

- Screen with field attributes such as formats, display characteristics, validations, next dynpro number, and so on
- Flow logic specifying the modules for processing

The dialog program begins execution with the specified initial dynpro. Because every dynpro screen also has the number of the next dynpro in the sequence, after the end of a dynpro, the next dynpro is called. This chain ends as soon as a dynpro with a 0 in the follow-on dynpro number is encountered. This is the standard and static way of calling the dynpros. There is also a provision for calling dynpros using SET SCREEN and CALL SCREEN in the flow logic.

Flow Logic

The flow logic calls modules from the module pool at the occurrence of predefined events.

The various modules are classified into groups as per the following events:

```
PROCESS BEFORE OUTPUT        PBO
PROCESS AFTER INPUT          PAI
```

Modules associated with the first event deal with issues such as initialization, default values, and so forth. The second module group handles processing after the end of data input by the user; these modules handle the validation and processing of data, database updates, and so on.

Two more module groups are available for providing help:

```
PROCESS ON VALUE-REQUEST     POV
PROCESS ON HELP-REQUEST      POH
```

ABAP/4 Query

End users can define simple reports through ABAP/4 query. Through a user-friendly interface, a user can specify the subject area of interest, the tables concerned, the desired fields, and also the list layout. The system automatically generates a selection screen not unlike produced in report programming, and asks for required inputs immediately.

Thereafter, the report is produced automatically. The output can also be routed optionally either to file storage or to a Microsoft Excel file or another file type.

SAPScripts

SAPscript is SAP's word processing program. Typical output produced by ABAP programs is devoid of any special fonts, size variations, and so on. SAPscripts enable SAP to produce professionally printed reports. It can also cater to the requirements for producing multilingual reports. SAPscripts define the layout set as well as other components such as paragraphs, text elements, and so on. Using the SAPscript function modules, layout sets can be called from ABAP programs; in reverse, ABAP subroutines can also be called from the layout sets.

Batch Data Communication and Interfaces

Before going live, a large amount of data needs to be uploaded into the system before it can be released into production. R/3 release 4.0 includes a utility to accomplish this called Legacy System Migration Workbench (LSM Workbench). This primarily works by mapping the source data structure onto the target data structures in R/3.

However, in the earlier systems there were three different methods for achieving the same:

- Batch Input: This approach was employed for importing large amounts of data from sequential files into the corresponding R/3 tables. The batch input program reads the data while executing and puts it into a *batch input session*, which essentially simulates the entering of the same data in the dialog mode on the corresponding transaction code screens. Different values are read from the sequential file records and are assigned to the corresponding screen fields as defined by the structure of the batch input session. This effectively enforces the integrity of data as rigorously as in the case of screen-based data entry because all validation checks as performed by the corresponding *dynpros*. SAP provides a library of standard batch input programs. This approach also enables the use of automatic logging facility.

- Direct Input: This approach skips the simulation of screen input in favor of direct input and validation using the function modules, which results in faster processing. SAP provides a library of standard function modules for data uploads that are typically required by most of the customers like material master and sales orders. This approach has a disadvantage because it does not provide automatically for logging and, therefore, in case of an error or interruption, the whole process may have to be started all over again.

- Fast Input: This approach is even faster because the data to be uploaded is first imported into internal tables with structures corresponding to the target transaction structures. The data is then transferred from the internal tables into R/3 using the CALL TRANSACTION statement in ABAP.

Future of ABAP/4 as a General-Purpose Programming Language

Programs developed in ABAP/4, and associate environments such as the ABAP/4 Development Workbench, Workbench Organizer, and R/3 Basis, are ready to run on any operating system, graphical user interface, database management system, network interfaces and so forth, in both centralized and decentralized client/server environments.

This portability coupled with the flexibility of changing data structures through object-oriented features such as the ABAP/4 dictionary lead to a very powerful software development environment.

Although the ABAP/4 language was developed mainly for the SAP system, it has a great deal of potential as a general-purpose development environment for non-SAP users as well. One of the best-kept secrets in the world of SAP is that COBOL programmers would feel quite at home here! Even in these times of object-orientation and the Internet, which have overturned the field of computers upside down, there is real hope for dear old COBOL programmers!

SAP R/3 Application Modules

IN THIS CHAPTER

This chapter presents the business functionality available in SAP R/3. Considering that SAP caters to all department functions within a company in various industries, it is not surprising that it is a huge and complex system. It is not easy to give an overview of an integrated system such as SAP. Hence, I have attempted to highlight the functionality that is made available by the major application modules of SAP.

Finance and Controlling (FI-CO)

Financial accounting is one area in which SAP, as an integrated system, has many advantages. SAP provides many features of internationalization that are of great significance; they include not only currencies and multiple languages, but also the flexibility to incorporate differing rules and regulations in different parts of the world. The modules can be configured readily to suit the different modes and rules of taxation, import/export rules and regulations, and so forth. The General Ledger module has a great flexibility to produce accounting reports either at the group level or at individual company level within the group. In costing, the benefits of the process-oriented view adopted in SAP become evident because it also allows costs to be allocated to business processes based on usage of resources, in addition to traditional cost center accounting. Figure 9.1 shows the Financial Accounting submenu.

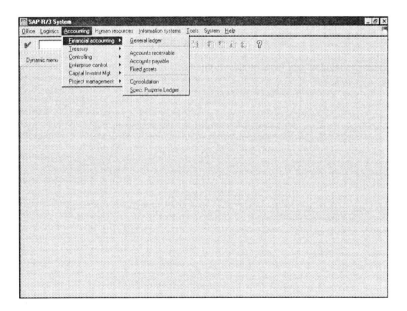

FIGURE 9.1

The Financial Accounting submenu.

Core Business Processes

In an integrated and real-time system such as SAP, every module posts transactions into the FI-CO module. It is virtually a repository of the operations within the organization, whereby every activity within the company is reflected and reposed here. As will be evident in this chapter, every other module in SAP, including SD, PP, MM, QM, PM, PS, SM, and so on, posts transactions into this module.

Finance (FI)

The various core processes that are available within SAP that companies may implement depending on their requirements are

- G/L accounting and closing
- Accounts receivable
- Accounts payable
- Asset Management
- Consolidation
- Special Purpose Ledgers

Controlling (CO)

The various core processes that are available within SAP that companies may implement depending on their requirements are

- Cost element accounting
- Cost center accounting
- Revenue element accounting
- Product costing
- Cost object accounting
- Profitability analysis
- Activity-based costing

Initial Configuration and Master Data

There are certain enterprisewide (client-independent as well as client-dependent) parameters that need to be defined initially depending on the business requirements of the company. Some of these prerequisite parameters are as follows:

- Client
- Company codes

- Business area
- Chart of accounts for each company code
- Controlling area
- Operating concern
- Bank data
- A/P reconciliation accounts
- A/R reconciliation accounts
- Currency
- Posting keys
- Number ranges
- Cost elements and cost element groups
- Cost center and cost center groups
- Activity types and activity type groups
- Statistical key figures and statistical key figure groups
- PA characteristics

Special Features

A list of some of the many features and facilities provided by the SAP FI-CO module includes the following:

- SAP provides facilities for manual posting into G/L accounts.
- SAP provides for posting outgoing and incoming invoices that are not processed through automated integration from the sales and procurement module.
- SAP allows manual reversal of financial entries; for this, only the posting number, author, date, or other details of the original entries are necessary.
- SAP has a facility to define and execute recurring transactions.
- SAP permits printing of various forms (for example, preprinted documents) such as letters, checks, and so forth.
- SAP provides for preparation of one-time invoices, one-time customer accounts, and payments between different locations of the company.
- SAP provides for intercompany transactions within a group of companies as well as for their reconciliation.
- SAP has a facility for defining an account hierarchy for the purpose of producing various reports with totals and so forth.

- SAP permits user-specified balance sheet versions.

- SAP provides special-purpose ledgers for addressing nonstandard requirements of users; for example, for producing US-GAAP-compliant financial statements, regulatory reporting by state for insurance companies, government reporting for public sector companies, and daily balance reporting for banks.

- SAP provides powerful features for the control of direct and indirect costs.

- SAP allows definition of the cost elements (primary and secondary) and cost element groups for identifying the nature of expenses or revenue of controlling transactions.

- SAP permits definition of cost centers, which are the lowest level of cost responsibility within the organization, and cost center groupings through the standard hierarchy.

- SAP has a provision for defining statistical key figures that can be used as the basis for periodic allocation of costs, such as the number of employees, time of usage, and so on.

- SAP has a powerful facility for producing variance reports for product costing.

- SAP provides for both accounts-based and costing-based profitability analysis through the definition of predefined characteristics.

- SAP provides for a close at month-end, year-end, or any other time, for that matter.

- SAP allows companies with multiple legal entities to create consolidated financial statements for statutory and management reporting purposes.

- SAP provides a facility for tracking transactions such as down payment requests and down payments.

- SAP provides hundreds of standard reports as well as flexible reporting tools such as the Report Painter, Report Writer, ABAP Query, and Drill-Down Reporting.

- SAP has an automatic payment program that is very versatile, allowing you to pay either by check or electronic payment and provides multiple features including the ability to automatically maximize early payment discounts.

- SAP can automatically generate different levels of dunning letters to remind customers of overdue accounts as soon as their balances become overdue and periodically until payment has been made.

- SAP includes detailed functionality on sales and use tax (both for purchases and sales), withholding taxes, GST and VAT taxes, and other tax processing.

- SAP provides a variety of depreciation methods and can simultaneously keep track of book depreciation, tax depreciation, depreciation for management accounting reporting, depreciation for group company consolidation, and so on.

Interface to Other Functions

In an integrated installation recommended in this book, the interfaces of this module with other modules are as given below:

- Sales and Distribution (SD)—Credit checking, material shipments, material returns, taxes and pricing, outstanding receivables, profitability analysis, dunning, down payments, goods on consignment, rebate payments
- Materials Management (MM)—Purchase orders, supplier invoices, payments to suppliers, inventory movements, quality inspection, stock inventory, physical inventory differences, payment program, freight and insurance charges, and so forth
- Production Planning (PP)—Production orders, production variances, finished goods, work-in-process, and so forth
- Human Resources (HR)—Salaries, allowances, travel expenses, advances and loans, benefits, and so forth

Sales and Distribution (SD)

The SAP SD module enables users to manage their sales and distribution activities effectively. The business process scenarios included in this module are for sales order, shipping, billing, sales information, and sales support. Figure 9.2 shows the Sales/Distribution submenu.

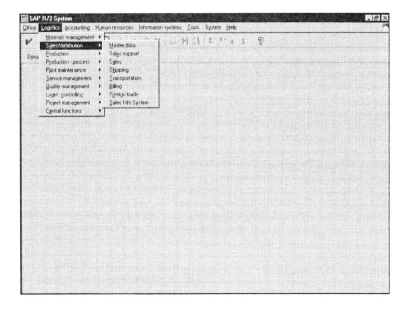

FIGURE 9.2
The Sales/Distribution submenu.

Core Business Processes

The various core processes that are available within SAP that companies may implement depending on their requirements are

- Customer RFQ processing and customer inquiries
- Customer quotation processing
- Order entry
- Scheduling deliveries
- Availability checking
- Pricing
- Credit checking
- Billing
- Packaging
- Shipping
- Customer payment
- Customer outstanding balances
- Customer marketing activities
- Picking lists and picking process
- Confirmation of picking
- Warehouse management processes
- Transportation processes
- Sales reporting

Initial Configuration and Master Data

There are certain enterprisewide (client-independent as well as client-dependent) parameters that need to be defined initially depending on the business requirements of the company. Some of these prerequisite parameters are as follows:

- Credit control area
- Sales organization
- Distribution channel
- Division
- Customer master: general, sales, and accounting data
- Pricing conditions

- Shipping points
- Customers
- Customer outline agreements and contracts
- Customer material information
- Material master
- Material determination (substitution)
- Pricing
- Discount/surcharges
- Freight
- Taxes

Special Features

A partial list of features and facilities provided by the SAP SD module is as follows:

- SAP provides for preparation of a customer RFQ with or without a customer query.
- SAP caters to all types of customer orders, ranging from standard orders to consignment orders. It also executes the credit control check for the customers.
- SAP provides for handling of customer contracts as well as schedule agreements.
- SAP also provides for handling of third-party orders.
- Proper integration of PP, IM, and SD for accurate availability checking or Available To Promise (ATP) information automatically. This could also be applied across plants.
- SAP provides the facility for a detailed view of the inventory and planned production and for manual inquiry of availability.
- SAP permits multiple ship-to addresses corresponding to a single sold-to party.
- SAP provides flexibility for providing essentially limitless entry space for special instructions on orders.
- SAP proposes delivery dates for each item in the order, depending on a set of established criteria. This automatically includes the manufacturing time as well as the time required for packing, shipping, and transportation and delivery of the product.
- SAP proposes deliveries in terms of schedule lines; all subsequent activities, such as transfer of requirements, shipping, profitability, and so on, can be done without regard to the schedule lines.
- SAP determines price by applying a set of conditions to different individual components of the pricing procedure. This enables the company to correctly discriminate price-oriented components from taxes and freight-oriented components, while applying discounts and

surcharges that are applicable only to the former. Thus, conditions can be applied both at the header and single-item levels.

- SAP permits mass changes to prices based on pricing conditions; the changes can also be made effective from specific dates.
- SAP provides online credit checking of customers; it provides for defining tolerance limits for exceeding these limits. Upon exceeding the tolerance limits, SAP enables the treatment of customers, individually or through customer grouping, in terms of measures such as holding orders or even blocking of the whole customer account altogether, depending on predefined criteria.
- SAP permits separate plant and shipping points for different schedule lines, even within one order.
- SAP permits the definition of billing blocks, depending on different criteria.
- SAP provides flexibility in defining items due for deliveries. It also permits the creation of delivery documents either singly or as an aggregate of due items.
- SAP permits delivery and subsequent processing of partial shipments.
- SAP provides flexibility in invoicing either singly or as an aggregate of shipped items to a customer; this can be processed online or as a batch process.
- SAP provides facilities for creating and delivering quality certificates along with delivered goods.
- SAP provides for real-time account postings; a goods issue reduces finished goods inventory, creates an accounting document that credits the finished goods inventory and debits the cost of goods sold account. Similarly, billing automatically creates an accounting document that credits sales revenue and debits customer account.
- SAP provides flexibility for the dunning process; that is, the preparation of notices on overdue invoices to customers depending on predefined criteria.
- SAP allows you to perform route planning, defining the zones for shipping locations and customer receiving locations.
- SAP allows for customer hierarchies for grouping related customers, allowing for more efficient pricing and reporting.
- SAP allows organization structures allowing for reporting by sales person, sales office, and sales areas or for other user-defined fields.
- SAP has flexible reporting tools such as the Sales Information System, which has standard reports. This tool allows for flexible reporting including Early Warning Systems, which can automatically send you messages (emails) or produce reports based on criteria you define—for example, when customer orders fall below trends or certain products are selling above forecasted values.

- SAP allows for different types of customers. For example, a customer may be the sold-to party but have different ship-to parties, bill-to parties, and a different customer paying the invoices. You can also have different agents, contact persons, and so on automatically assigned to your customer.

- SAP has functionality for back-order processing when goods are not available for delivery at the customer requested date.

- SAP allows the user to copy one sales document (inquiry, quotation, or order), delivery document, or billing document to another sales document, delivery document, or billing document. This copy functionality greatly reduces work in order entry and reduces errors.

- SAP provides functionality for payment by check, letter of credit, or credit card and can automatically validate information on letters of credit or authorization information on credit cards.

Interface to Other Functions

In an integrated installation recommended in this book, the interfaces of this module with other modules are as given below:

- Materials Management (MM)—Availability checking, scheduling deliveries, credit checking, material shipments, transfers of inventory between plants, material determination, material exclusion and material substitution, reorder points, and returns

- Production Planning (PP)—Availability checking, SOP forecasting, sales order requirements transfer to PP

- Finance (FI)—Credit checking, material shipments, material returns, billing, taxes and pricing, outstanding balances, profitability analysis

Materials Management (MM)

The SAP MM module functions with complete integration with other modules such as logistics and financial accounting. The MM module business processes include RFQs, POs, goods receipts and invoice verification, and supplier payments. MM is a multisite inventory management system and can handle consignment stocks as well as processing of subcontract orders. Figure 9.3 shows the Materials Management submenu.

Core Business Processes

The various core processes that are available within SAP that companies may implement depending on their requirements are

- Purchase requisition inquiry
- Request for quotation

- Quotation
- Purchase order
- Goods receipt
- Invoice verification
- Payments
- Outstanding payments
- Vendor evaluation
- Quality control

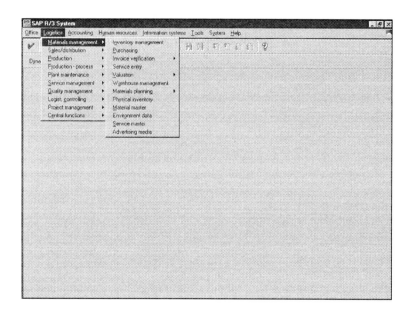

FIGURE 9.3
The Materials Management submenu.

Initial Configuration and Master Data

There are certain enterprisewide (client-independent as well as client-dependent) parameters that need to be defined initially depending on the business requirements of the company. Some of these prerequisite parameters are as follows:

- Purchasing organization
- Plant

- Storage location
- Conditions for pricing (gross, net, and effective price), taxes, discounts, surcharges, and so on
- Vendor master (general, purchasing, and accounting data)
- Vendor-material information records
- Material master (basic, purchasing, MRP, forecasting, storage, accounting, costing, job preparation, and quality management data)
- Quality information records
- Outline and scheduling agreements

Special Features

A partial list of features and facilities provided by the SAP MM modules is as follows:

- SAP provides for three major sources of requirements: production planned orders, purchase requisitions, and schedule lines. These sources arise from the stock requirement list prepared by MRP.
- SAP provides for international calendars, sizes, and UOM, as well as country-specific requirements such as taxes, postal codes, banks, currencies, and so on.
- SAP provides for defining various types of material, such as raw material, trading goods, finished product, nonvaluated material, and so on.
- SAP has facilities to handle vendor consignment stocks and subcontract orders, as well as processing of consumable materials.
- SAP provides multisite inventory management system
- SAP provides for MRP to release scheduling line against a long-term scheduling agreement with a vendor, without going through the requisition and purchase order process every time. SAP has provisions for maintaining a source list for such items for the MRP run to generate the scheduling lines automatically.
- SAP provides for maintenance of source list of vendors (including other plants), material vendor relationship information, and quota arrangements for allocation of purchases.
- SAP provides for creating purchase requisitions manually or automatically through MRP or PM module or from networks in the PS module. SAP also permits a flexible release strategy for approving purchase orders.
- SAP provides preparation of RFQs for items not having a source of supply, including a delivery schedule.
- SAP permits vendors responses to the RFQs to be stored as quotations along with specifics such as pricing.

- SAP provides for outline agreement for long-term agreements with vendors that could be either scheduling agreements, or quantity and value contract agreements that require a release order (that is, a PO) for every delivery.

- SAP provides for creation of POs, either manually or automatically, by using outstanding requisitions with exact delivery quantity and dates.

- SAP provides the facility to prepare the goods receipt on the basis of the corresponding PO. SAP provides for the goods to be received at different locations or directly as unrestricted stock, blocked stock, or stock in quality inspection if dictated by the corresponding PO.

- SAP permits for management of quality planning, execution and improvement activities resulting in the usage decision of acceptance in unrestricted stock, blocked stock, scrapped, return to vendor etc.

- SAP has a powerful facility for inventory movements, identified by the corresponding movement type, on account of goods receipts, goods issues, stock transfers, and transfer posting. The latter might occur after quality inspection, and so on.

- SAP enables each movement type to trigger a material document and, if required, an accounting document for reflecting the inventory and accounting impact of these movements. SAP achieves the latter through predefined automatic account determination for posting into the general ledger accounts, based on the movement type and the material type.

- SAP provides many facilities for tracking inventory involving monitoring stock levels and the status of materials at various locations.

- SAP provides different procedures for material valuation (FIFO, LIFO, and standard price).

- SAP provides facilities for ascertaining a physical inventory of goods to validate the accuracy of inventory data in the system through procedures such as periodic inventory, continuous inventory, inventory sampling, and cycle counting.

- SAP permits the definition of different cycle counts for different materials or groups of materials. SAP provides facilities for any reported differences in quantity and amount to be posted for updating stock, as well as the corresponding G/L account, respectively.

- SAP permits proper reflection of all deliveries by vendors, vendor invoices, and payments to vendors in the corresponding G/L accounts.

- SAP provides a powerful facility to set up a payment program for processing, as well as printing, the payments for open items selected into the program at the time the payment program is defined.

- SAP permits decentralized procurement and centralized inventory control simultaneously.

- SAP allows a three-way matching process whereby a payment is made only when the invoice received matches the price on the purchase order and the correct quantity in the goods receipt. SAP can also allow a two-way matching process or other business process based on your business requirements.

- SAP can be set up to allow different tolerances for quantity received against purchase order quantity, price invoiced against purchase order price, and so on.

- SAP has automatic update capabilities that immediately update previous documents when a new activity has occurred. For example, the purchase order will keep track of undelivered amounts and immediately be updated when a goods receipt has been made and when an invoice has been received.

- SAP has helpful information and warning messages that will inform you when a duplicate invoice has been received, or if a duplicate purchase order is being created.

Interface to Other Functions

In an integrated installation recommended in this book, the interfaces of this module with other modules are as given below:

- Finance and Controlling (FI-CO)—Purchase orders, supplier invoices, payments to suppliers, inventory movements, quality inspection, stock inventory, physical inventory differences, payment programs, and so forth

- Sales and Distribution (SD)—Availability checking, scheduling deliveries, credit checking, material shipments, transfers of inventory between plants, material determination, material exclusion, material substitution, reorder points, and returns

- Production Planning (PP)—Stock requirement list, MRP-run-generated schedule lines, backflushing via confirmation and production orders, and so forth

- Quality Management (QM)—Quality info records, usage decisions, and so forth

- Plant Maintenance (PM)—Purchase orders, external services management, and so forth

Production Planning (PP)

The SAP PP module provides real benefits of having an integrated, process-oriented, real-time, information-driven system such as SAP R/3. By accessing latest information from various functions, it streamlines and speeds up decisions and also increases productivity of the production logistics as a whole. SAP also reconciles the MRP II approach with the need to be customer oriented as well as to ensure quality. The customer requirements are translated into demand management, which is the input to the production plan. The MPS is balanced against the rough-cut capacity plan. The MRP run actually results in the automatic generation of production and requisition or orders for material procurements. The released production orders trigger actual production activities; at the end, the order is confirmed and closed. At every stage, accounting-related postings are executed in real-time in the finance and controlling modules. Figures 9.4 and 9.5 show the Production submenu's Master Data and Master Planning submenus.

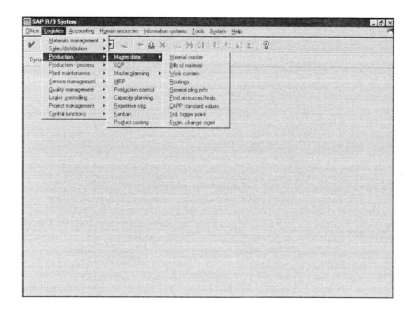

FIGURE 9.4

The Production submenu's Master Data submenu.

SAP covers all major logistics business processes; namely, continuous, repetitive, make-to-stock, and assemble-to-order. It can also handle variations of those processes, such as make-to-order as well as the complex category of engineer-to-order. The various categories of manufacturing processes are the following:

- Continuous—Continuous manufacturing is mainly driven by the production process infrastructure. Unlike the traditional MRP II systems, the MPS must be synchronized with the capacity plan from the beginning. Also, instead of the MRP, what is really produced is a materials flow plan (MFP); plant production infrastructure runs all the time. Other characteristic features include coproducts and byproducts, process manufacturing, formulation management, maintenance, and multiple units of measure. This type of manufacturing process typically is for the creation of interim raw materials required by other manufacturing plants within the same company or by other facilities; for example, manufacturing processes in the oil, gas, and petrochemicals industry.

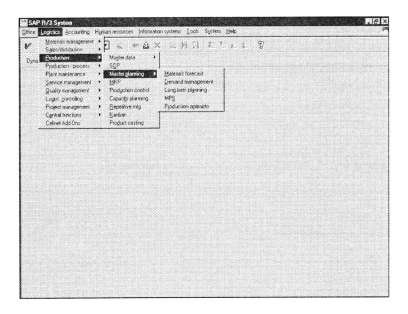

FIGURE 9.5

The Production submenu's Master Planning submenu.

- Repetitive—Repetitive manufacturing is involved with creating large volumes of standard product. The system tracks the material, quality, cost of material, and machinery across all stages of the system. Such systems typically backflush consumed materials from inventory or work-in-process. The amount of consumed materials is based on calculated average values rather than actual observed consumption of inventory. These systems also attempt to schedule runs and certain equipment for fixed intervals of time. For example, manufacturing processes in the consumer products industry.

- Make-to-stock—For this type of manufacturing, the volumes are not as large as those for repetitive manufacturing. Often these systems do not have very deep BOMs. They also use standard lot sizes, for which a standard cost can be determined and compared easily with the actual cost.

- Assemble-to-order—This is the only manufacturing process that is customized for the requirements of the customer at an optimal cost. The manufacturer or its representative dealers must store various assemblies, aggregates, and parts to quickly assemble an order in accordance with the specifications of the customer. Other characteristics include product configuration, contract manufacturing, shop-floor control and costing, sophisticated routing and tracking, distribution and inventory staging, multiplant scheduling, and interfacing with engineering and integration. Examples of this process are the manufacturing processes in automobile and personal computer and workstation industries.

- Engineer-to-order—The volume of the products in this type of manufacturing is low, but the complexity of the designs and the finished products tend to be very high. They are typically engineered and manufactured for a specific customer. Key characteristics required here are contract manufacturing, shop-floor control and costing, sophisticated routing and tracking, multiplant scheduling, computer-aided drawing and computer-aided manufacturing (CAD/CAM), and integration. Costs and turnaround times are quite high. Products falling into this category include specialized machine tools, power-plant machinery, airplanes, and defense products.

Core Business Processes

The various core processes that are available within SAP that companies may implement depending on their requirements are

- Sales and operations planning
- Rough-cut capacity planning
- Demand management
- Master Production Scheduling (MPS)
- Material Requirements Planning (MRP)
- Long-term planning
- Capacity planning
- Shop floor
- Plant maintenance

Initial Configuration and Master Data

There are certain enterprisewide (client-independent as well as client-dependent) parameters that need to be defined initially depending on the business requirements of the company. Some of these prerequisite parameters are as follows:

- Plants
- Storage locations
- Bill of Materials (engineering, production, and so on)
- Materials master
- Vendor master
- Production orders

Special Features

A partial list of features and facilities provided by the SAP PP module is as follows:

- Proper integration of SD, PP, QM, and PM for accurate sales forecasting and, therefore, production scheduling process.

- SAP provides for a planning table for a material or a product group.

- SAP allows the sales plan to be used as a basis for demand management.

- SAP permits the sales plan to be prepared manually, from the Sales Information System, from profitability analysis, or from a forecasting view of the material master. The last option can be done online, in batch, or on a periodic basis, depending on the forecasting time buckets, frequency of MPS and MRP runs, and so forth.

- SAP provides for planning in SOP by using flexible tables based on the projections for different consumption segments, as compared to the usual basis of historical consumption.

- SAP provides rough-cut capacity planning that ascertains the validity of the sales plan against key resource constraints and bottlenecks, thus making the production plan proactive. The requirements are backward scheduled from the day of the latest requirements.

- SAP provides for preparation of the demand program independently for each material in terms of quantity and corresponding dates. Demand management is the link between forecasting tool and the MRP, which is also split automatically or manually into finer time buckets for smoothing the MPS.

- SAP provides flexibility for planning at aggregate levels called *product groups*. Product groups can have different hierarchical structures and can be nested as well. SAP also permits a planning hierarchy to be based on different sales divisions, which permits the sales to be recorded in different consumption accounts.

- SAP permits production plans to be created manually, based on a sales plan, for zero-stock level, for a targeted stock level, or even for targeting a day's supply.

- SAP provides comprehensive feasible production schedules using the demand information, inventory status, production process characteristics, and so forth. MPS operates within only one level of BOM (usually the highest level of BOM), whereas MRP can be utilized throughout all the levels of BOM.

- SAP provides for both consumption-MRP as well as deterministic-MRP; the former is based on past or forecasted consumption, whereas the latter is based on the exact requirements based on BOM.

- SAP provides for MPS or MRP runs to be performed at any time, online or batch, and, even for individual materials. These can be configured to completely re-schedule all planned orders or only those that need to be modified using subsequent to the latest MPS/ MRP run.

- SAP permits MPS or MRP runs with options for retaining planning dates or for rescheduling based on lead time and routing data.

- SAP permits MPS and MRP to optionally create purchase requisitions as well as delivery schedules for externally procured materials. For in-house produced individual materials, planned orders are generated. SAP provides viewing these results through either the MRP list or the stock requirement list.

- SAP provides for MRP runs by any of the following means: create capacity load, dependent requirement, automatic purchase requisition, planned orders, automatically scheduled quantity, or automatic direct purchase requisition.

- SAP provides for any changes in the supply, demand, or inventory of materials to be reflected directly in the stock requirement list.

- SAP permits both 'firmed' or 'unfirmed' planned orders and also manual changes to the planned orders. SAP also provides for the firming of planned orders a specified number of days before the production schedule date.

- SAP provides for generating production orders—individually or collectively—from planned orders, corresponding BOM, routing master, and so forth. The order generation is based on a user-determined combination of criteria such as earliest or latest planned date, sales order numbers, material number, and so on. If required, SAP permits performing of a component-level availability check at this stage.

- SAP permits authorized users to change or delete production orders at any time. If required, the deleted orders can also be activated again.

- SAP provides for the release of production orders, individually or collectively, to trigger actual production on the shop floor. SAP also provides for a released order to trigger a component-level availability check. Each production or work order contains a list of all materials required (extracted from BOM) and a sequence of operations to be performed (extracted from the routing).

- SAP provides for capacity planning analysis of work centers depending on the category of the capacity of interest; for example, machine, labor, and so on. SAP provides facilities for handling overload situations by permitting manual leveling of capacity.

- SAP provides for the issue of materials to production order or work orders either manually, automatically (backflushing), or via electronic Kanban techniques.

- SAP permits confirmation—that is, declaring production at different levels—and provides for defining control keys such as printing, scheduling activities, and so on. Confirmation includes information on the number of goods manufactured, inspected, reworked, scrapped, and so on, as well as the activities performed. The latter records information such as labor time, setup time, machine time, an so on. SAP permits the definition of some of the confirmation levels as milestones, which then cannot be bypassed unless they are completed.

- SAP provides for a confirmation to trigger the recording of consumption of materials against a production order by backflushing based on the quantities consumed by an operation as defined in the BOM and the routing. This also transfers the corresponding material, labor, and other costs to the production order.

- SAP provides an option at the end of the manufacturing cycle to automatically or manually place the manufactured goods into the inventory, as well as to produce the corresponding goods receipt.

- SAP also provides a facility for a premature closure, called *technical completion*, of a production order that has to be abandoned for some reason.

- SAP permits the recording of attendance, working time, absence, leave, business trip, substitution, and so forth. This information is made available in different modules for related processing, such as production costs, employee records, travel expenses, payroll, and benefits.

Interface to Other Functions

In an integrated installation recommended in this book, the interfaces of this module with other modules are as given below:

- Finance and Controlling (FI-CO)—Production orders, production variances, finished goods, work-in-process, and so forth

- Sales and Distribution (SD)—Availability checking and SOP forecasting

- Materials Management (MM)—Stock requirement list, MRP run-generated schedule lines, backflushing via confirmation and production orders, and so forth

- Quality Management (QM)—In-process quality checks

- Plant Maintenance (PM)—Maintenance plan, scheduling, tools, gauges, and so forth

- Human Resources (HR)—Attendance, working time, incentive, wages, and so forth

Quality Management (QM)

Issues related to quality are involved with all processes within an organization. Companies have to furnish quality certificates or certificate of compliance along with order deliveries. They have to ascertain the quality of supplied goods, monitor quality performance for vendors, and also conduct in-process quality checks for production functions. The SAP QM module functions fully integrated with all these other modules. Figure 9.6 shows the Quality Management submenu.

Core Business Processes

The various core processes that are available within SAP that companies may implement depending on their requirements are

- Quality planning
- Quality execution
- Quality improvement
- Production in-process inspection
- Quality certificates for customers

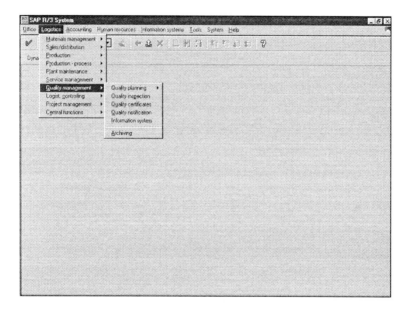

FIGURE 9.6

The Quality Management submenu.

Initial Configuration and Master Data

There are certain enterprisewide (client-independent as well as client-dependent) parameters that need to be defined initially depending on the business requirements of the company. Some of these prerequisite parameters are as follows:

- Plant
- Storage location

- Characteristics
- Controls for characteristics
- Catalogs
- Inventory movements
- Material master
- Material-vendor relationship information
- Vendor masters
- Quality information records

Special Features

A partial list of features and facilities provided by the SAP QM module is as follows:

- SAP permits different levels of inspection, such as during production, on goods receipt, before shipment, and so on.
- SAP provides facilities for quality planning of goods received, including defining quality inspection characteristics, quality reporting standards, inspection plans, inspection methods, dynamic sampling, and quality information records.
- SAP has facilities to define the various elements of a quality characteristic that must be measured and control parameters for each of those elements.
- SAP provides a facility to define catalogs that specify the valid range of allowable values for these elements.
- SAP provides for a quality plan for each material that indicates the list of quality tasks (and the related quality characteristics) necessary at the time goods are received. It also provides the status of the inspection at any moment of time.
- SAP permits the monitoring of vendor performance using the quality information records against predefined quality standards. Quality information records tie in a material with a vendor. It also permits, if required, to specify inspection at the source by the vendor that is checked against the quality certificate furnished with the goods.
- SAP permits definition of the quality sampling procedure and schemes, such as the sample size, dynamically based on dynamic modification rules maintained within the system.
- SAP provides for describing the inspection method to be applied for inspection of a characteristic.
- SAP permits recording of the inspection operations, inspection characteristics, and results of the inspection, depending on the corresponding control indicators in the inspection lots.

- SAP permits making the usage decision based on the results of the inspection to change it from quality inspection to unrestricted stock, scrapped, placed in blocked stock, placed in reserves, consumed as a sample, or returned to vendor.

- SAP provides many reports and SPC capabilities toward managing the quality improvement effort.

- SAP also provides for in-process inspection and inspection of tools and gauges for production.

Interface to Other Functions

In an integrated installation recommended in this book, the interfaces of this module with other modules are as given below:

•Sales and Distribution (SSD)—Quality certificates or certificate of compliance for customers

- Quality Management (QM)—Quality information records, usage decisions, inventory movements, and so forth

- Production Planning (PP)—In-process quality checks, tools and gauges, and so on

- Plant Maintenance (PM)—Production in-process quality result and so forth

Plant Maintenance (PM)

The SAP PM module has facilities for providing Total Productive Maintenance (TPM) for a company's plant and production equipment. It helps in various ways, such as

- Monitoring availability of resources, costs, materials, and personnel

- Optimizing use of resources and labor

- Reducing cost of inspections

- Reducing down time and outages

Figure 9.7 shows the Plant Maintenance submenu.

Core Business Processes

The various core processes that are available within SAP that companies may implement depending on their requirements are

- Preventive maintenance

- Service management

- Maintenance order management

- Plant maintenance information system

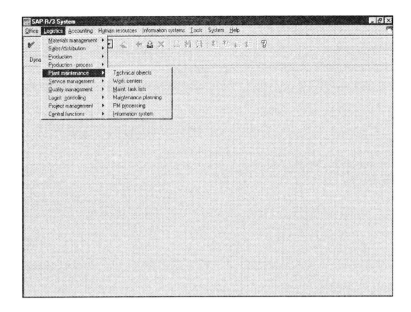

FIGURE 9.7
The Plant Maintenance submenu.

Initial Configuration and Master Data

There are certain enterprisewide (client-independent as well as client-dependent) parameters that need to be defined initially depending on the business requirements of the company. Some of these prerequisite parameters are as follows:

- Plant
- Counters
- Quality characteristics
- Controls
- Catalogs
- Maintenance plan
- Materials master
- Material-vendor relationship
- Vendor master

Special Features

A partial list of features and facilities provided by the SAP PM module is as follows:

- SAP provides for the creation and scheduling of both time-based maintenance plans for regular items and counter-based maintenance plans for production-critical items. Counters are usually based on usage, run times, mileage, and so on. SAP permits adjustment of the scheduling parameters. SAP also permits you to create multiple counter-based plans.

- SAP stores maintenance tasks as preventive maintenance strategies; within these strategies, the intervals of maintenance are defined as *packages*.

- SAP provides facility to assign one or more items to the maintenance plan.

- SAP processes the maintenance plans, which consist of maintenance items and a schedule that specifies the frequency, time, location, and order in which maintenance tasks must be carried out on identified equipment, assemblies, and so on.

- SAP permits the release of a preventive maintenance plan call either manually (based on notifications) or automatically, which makes it effective. For each maintenance item, one maintenance order is generated. The maintenance order contains details of the specific repair, the individual steps to be carried out, the tools and spare parts required, as well as the estimated time of performing the repair.

- SAP allows the release of the maintenance order for execution. The system checks for availability of the material, resources, tools, and so on.

- SAP provides, on completion of the order, rules for account assignment and settlement of the maintenance order.

- SAP also provides for generation of maintenance-related orders for procurement.

- SAP maintains and provides the maintenance history of any equipment, chronologically, in terms of repairs conducted, replacements done, costs, and so on.

Interface to Other Functions

In an integrated installation recommended in this book, the interfaces of this module with other modules are as given below:

•Materials Management (MM)—Purchase orders, external services management, and so forth

- Production Planning (PP)—Maintenance plan, scheduling, tools and gauges, and so forth

- Quality Management (QM)—Production in-process quality result and so forth

Human Resources (HR)

The SAP HR module permits optimum utilization of Human Resources throughout the organization. The HR functions handled range from organizational units, jobs and tasks, skill requirements, staffing and recruitment, personnel development, time management, salary and benefit management, and so on. The HR module assists an organization in recruiting, retaining, and upgrading its human resources. Figure 9.8 shows the Human Resources menu's Planning submenu.

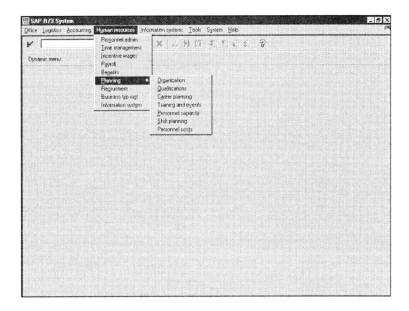

FIGURE 9.8
The Human Resources menu's Planning submenu.

Core Business Processes

The various core processes available within SAP that companies may implement depending on their requirements are

- Organization management
- Skills management
- Career and succession planning
- Events management
- Personnel capacity planning
- Personnel cost planning
- Maintaining personnel master data
- Personnel development
- Payroll accounting

- Statements
- Time management
- Travel expenses

Initial Configuration and Master Data

There are certain enterprisewide (client-independent as well as client-dependent) parameters that need to be defined initially depending on the business requirements of the company. Some of these prerequisite parameters are as follows:

- Client
- Company code
- Organizational structure
- Company objects (organizational units, jobs, positions, workplace, tasks, and so on)
- Object relationship
- Personnel department
- Personnel subarea
- Employee group
- Employee circle

Special Features

A partial list of features and facilities provided by the SAP HR module are as follows:

- SAP provides for maintaining detailed information on the organizational units, job descriptions, positions, and so on.
- SAP permits maintaining a full inventory of skill sets in the company.
- SAP permits defining career models, which can be helpful in career and succession planning.
- Personnel planning helps in monitoring costs, projecting costs, simulating effects of wage increases, taxes, deductions, and so forth.
- SAP provides extensive facilities for the management of events such as training sessions, programs, workshops, and so on. The management includes scheduling, organization, postponement, participation fees, feedback, and so on.
- SAP enables personnel capacity planning using the information on jobs, skills, and available manpower base.
- SAP helps in managing all aspects of the recruitment process starting from inquiries, applications, interviews, tests, selection, offers, correspondence, and so forth.

9

SAP R/3
APPLICATION
MODULES

- SAP provides for accounting for wages, taxes, deductions, benefits, travel expenses, advances, insurance deductions, and so forth.
- SAP provides for standard deductions from the salary every month.
- SAP has pre-configured payroll functionality for many countries in North and South America, Europe, and Asia. For the countries where this functionality is not provided, SAP has an international payroll functionality that can be copied and modified.
- SAP has hundreds of standard reports to meet the regulatory and information requirements of various companies. Where a new report is required, SAP provides flexible reporting tools to build the required reports.
- SAP allows you to produce all payroll reports and review them prior to posting the payroll for that month.
- SAP allows for retroactive payroll changes that can, for example, allow you to process a salary increase for a previous month and automatically calculate the correct payroll amounts.
- SAP has very detailed audit features that track each change to a employee master record, recording the original entry and the changed entry, the system time the change was made, and the user ID of the person making the change.

Interface to Other Functions

In an integrated installation recommended in this book, the interfaces of this module with other modules are as given below:

- Finance and Controlling (FI-CO)—Attendance, leave, payroll accounting, advances, travel expenses, training, and so forth
- Sales and Distribution (SD)—Events engagement, sales commission, and so on
- Production Planning (PP): Attendance, working time, incentive wages and so forth.

Industry-Specific (IS) Solutions

SAP recognized early that every industry has characteristic requirements that are specific to the companies operating in that industry. SAP provides a wide array of industry-specific vertical solutions that address such unique requirements through industry solutions (IS) that are complementary to the base R/3 solution. In 1998, SAP launched SAP Solution Maps for 19 industries and continues to upgrade these solutions as well as add more industry solutions on an ongoing basis.

The various IS solutions include

- IS-Automobile
- IS-Oil

- IS-Pharmaceuticals
- IS-Chemicals
- IS-Retail
- IS-Telecom
- IS-Utilities
- IS-Aerospace and Defense
- IS-Consumer Products
- IS-Engineering and Construction

Figure 9.9 shows a scheme of the important IS solutions.

FIGURE 9.9
Industry-specific (IS) solutions.

9

SAP R/3
APPLICATION
MODULES

SAP forms partnerships with customers, consulting companies, and other software developers to develop and enhance IS solutions at well established industry centers of expertise (ICOEs). These are now termed as strategic business units (SBUs).

SAP Solution Maps

SAP has developed a comprehensive initiative called SAP Solution Maps that describes the solutions needed for different industries and the corresponding technology and services that are necessary to support these solutions. The SAP Solutions Maps describe the required business functions of an industry. These are complemented by the SAP Business Technology Map, which describes the SAP technology infrastructure, and the SAP Services Map, which outlines the services that SAP and SAP Partners can offer in planning, configuring, implementing, and running the solution. Using common layouts and naming conventions, these solution maps help in easy evaluation and implementation of a compatible and comprehensive IT solutions.

Introduced in 1998, the Solution Maps, which provide a framework for managing the entire life-cycle of SAP Industry-Specific (SAP IS) solutions for more than 20 industries, consist of the following:

- SAP Solution Maps: These are comprehensive business blueprints, documenting all the key processes for a given industry.

- SAP Business Technology Maps: These describe the technology that is required to manage the entire life cycle of the SAP project including pre- and post-implementation as well as the production, maintenance and support phase. SAP Business Technology Map also includes information on how SAP and SAP Partner products work together to provide you a complete solution.

- SAP Services Maps: These identify key areas where SAP and SAP partners have service offerings that can value-add to a company's SAP implementation effort to ensure its completion on time and within budget. This could be at any stage of the ERP life cycle— right from evaluation and implementation to operations and continuous improvement. It addresses both business elements (including business process mapping through knowledge transfer) and technical elements (including infrastructure planning and implementation, help desk services, and technical support).

Each of these solution maps are available at two levels. Level 1 diagrams show the high level summary; whereas Level 2 diagrams show corresponding details for the various categories at Level 1.

Figures 9.10 through 9.12 show Level 1 maps, whereas the corresponding Level 2 maps are shown in Figures 9.13 through 9.18. These figures use the following icons:

● Product available

▶ Product available with future releases

◎ Future focus

Ⓟ Partner product available

▶ Partner product available with future releases

The second attribute identifies the available SAP or SAP Partner products as follows:

- Sn—SAP Product
- Pn—SAP Partner Product
- Vn—SAP Service
- Bn—SAP Partner Service

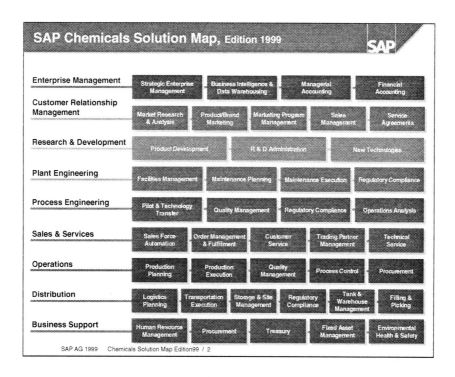

FIGURE 9.10

The SAP Chemicals Solution map.

9

SAP R/3
APPLICATION
MODULES

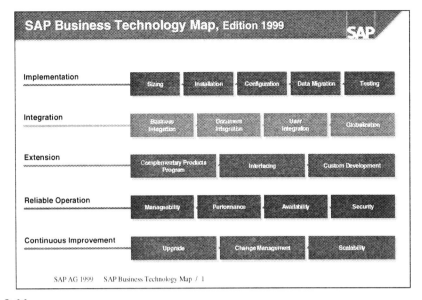

FIGURE 9.11

The SAP Business Technology map.

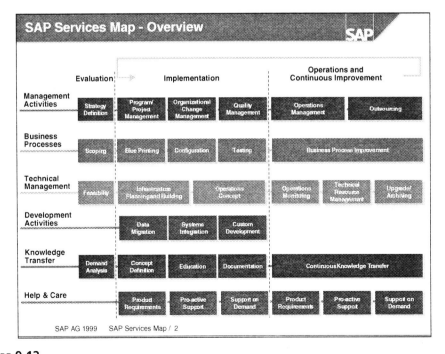

FIGURE 9.12

The SAP Services map.

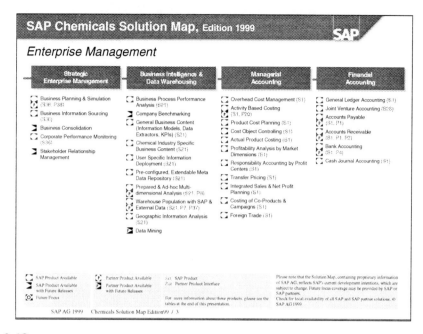

FIGURE 9.13

The SAP Chemicals solution map, Level 2.

Key	Component	Description
S1	FI	SAP R/3 Financials
S2	LO	SAP R/3 Logistics
S3	HR	SAP R/3 Human Resource Management
S20	APO	SAP Advanced Planner & Optimizer
S21	BW	SAP Business Information Warehouse
S22	B2B	SAP Business-to-Business Procurement
S25	EH&S	SAP Environmental Health & Safety
S26	JVA	SAP Joint Venture Accounting
S28	LES	SAP Logistics Execution System
S30	PP-MES	SAP Manufacturing Execution System (PP-PI and PFS)
S32	SAP Marketing	SAP Marketing
S33	SAP Sales	SAP Sales
S34	SAP Service	SAP Service
S36	SEM	SAP Strategic Enterprise Management
S37	MRM	SAP Treasury Market Risk Management
S38	TM	SAP Treasury Transaction Management
S240	IS-OIL	SAP Oil & Gas - Downstream

A variety of SAP products support the functions and processes in the SAP Solution Maps. The products that make up this SAP industry solution are listed in the table above and may require separate licensing. Please contact your local SAP office for more information.

SAP AG 1999   Chemical Solution Map Edition99 / 12

FIGURE 9.14

Solution Map Product Table, Level 2 diagram.

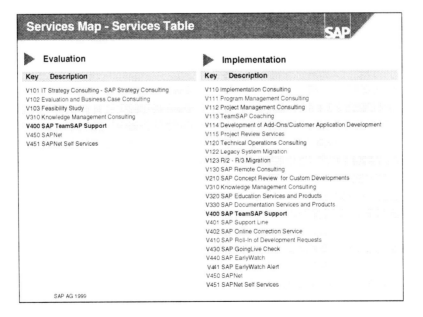

Solution Map Partner Interface Table   SAP

▶ **Application Specific Interfaces**

Key	Description	Key	Description
P1	Credit Management	P26	Quality Inspection, LIMS
P2	Sales and Use Tax	P27	Hydrocarbon Product Quantity Conversion
P3	Travel Expense Management	P28	SCADA, Process Control Systems
P4	Electronic Banking	P29	Maintenance, Repair and Operations (MRO)
P5	Optimization Algorithms	P30	Component and Supplier Management
P6	Process Engineering	P31	Product Data Management
P7	Data Migration	P32	External Project Systems
P8	Reporting Tools, OLAP	P33	Additional Printing of Labels
P9	Web Technology	P34	Point of Sale
P10	Health Insurance Settlement	P35	Shelf Space Management
P11	Time and Attendance	P36	Payment Card
P12	Vendor Management	P37	Decision Support
P13	Export Invoices	P38	ABC Modeling and Simulation
P14	R/F Devices, Mobile Data Recording	P39	Risk Management
P15	Warehouse Control	P40	Medical System
P16	Weighing Devices	P41	Technical Advertising Systems
P17	Transportation Optimization, Routing Planning	P42	Product Catalog
P18	Transportation Planning	P43	Merchandise Planning
P19	Activity Based Costing	P44	Terminal Automation System Interface
P20	Activity Based Costing Modeling	P45	Funds Transfer and Clearance
P21	Demand Planning	P46	Service Channel Management for Banks
P22	Demand Resource Planning	P47	Cashier / Teller Systems
P23	Production Orders	P48	Regulatory and Statutory Reporting for Banks
P24	Process Control Systems	P49	Outage Management
P25	Production Optimization	P50	Scheduling and Dispatching

SAP AG 1999   Telecommunications Solution Map Edition99 / 11

FIGURE 9.15

Services Map—Services Table, Level 2 diagram.

Services Map - Services Table   SAP

▶ **Evaluation**   ▶ **Implementation**

Key	Description
V101	IT Strategy Consulting - SAP Strategy Consulting
V102	Evaluation and Business Case Consulting
V103	Feasibility Study
V310	Knowledge Management Consulting
V400	**SAP TeamSAP Support**
V450	SAPNet
V451	SAPNet Self Services

Key	Description
V110	Implementation Consulting
V111	Program Management Consulting
V112	Project Management Consulting
V113	TeamSAP Coaching
V114	Development of Add-Ons/Customer Application Development
V115	Project Review Services
V120	Technical Operations Consulting
V122	Legacy System Migration
V123	R/2 - R/3 Migration
V130	SAP Remote Consulting
V210	SAP Concept Review for Custom Developments
V310	Knowledge Management Consulting
V320	SAP Education Services and Products
V330	SAP Documentation Services and Products
V400	**SAP TeamSAP Support**
V401	SAP Support Line
V402	SAP Online Correction Service
V410	SAP Roll-In of Development Requests
V430	SAP GoingLive Check
V440	SAP EarlyWatch
V441	SAP EarlyWatch Alert
V450	SAPNet
V451	SAPNet Self Services

SAP AG 1999

FIGURE 9.16

Services Map—Services Table, Level 2 diagram.

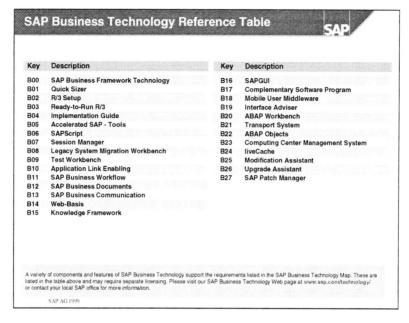

FIGURE 9.17

SAP Business Technology Reference Table, Level 2 diagram.

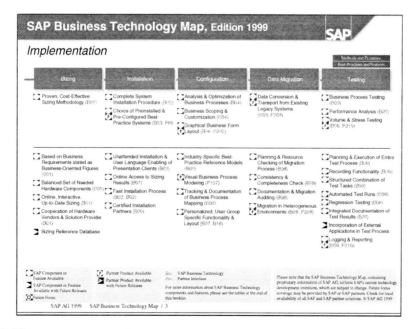

FIGURE 9.18

SAP Business Technology Map, Level 2 diagram.

9

SAP R/3
APPLICATION
MODULES

Summary

In this chapter, we saw the overview of the major modules that are available within SAP. For millennium enterprises, this book recommends that every company must implement the base modules of FI-CO, MM, SD, PP, and so on, depending on the company's industry and area of business. For the millennium enterprises, the approach I recommend is to adopt the big-bang approach whereby the company implements most of the standard suite of SAP modules along with any SAP industry-specific solution if available for its areas of business.

Only with the big-bang approach will the company start utilizing the information captured by the SAP system like any resource, such as manpower, materials, and money, rather than merely as a recording and reporting system. The traditional systems were hobbled into playing exactly such a role and were never able to deliver the productivity gains expected of them.

Now that you have become familiar with SAP as a product in this part, I will turn to the issues of the SAP implementation projects in the upcoming chapters.

The Pre-Implementation Stage

PART

III

IN THIS PART

Initiating the SAP Project

IN THIS CHAPTER

This chapter introduces the various issues that are prerequisites for initiating a SAP project. I will discuss the organizational structure recommended for managing a SAP implementation project. This chapter also details the constitution of the various committees and explains the various supporting issues of training and resource management. In the latter part of the chapter, it address the various kinds of risks that are associated with a SAP project and presents measures recommended by SAP to contain and even minimize their impact. The ground covered here would be covered from the point of view of ASAP methodology in Chapter 12, "Accelerated SAP (ASAP)," as well. The objective of dealing the same issues from two different views was to illustrate the importance of adapting a repository based integrated methodology like Accelerated SAP (ASAP).

SAP Executive Sponsor

The executive sponsor should be the executive with the power to make decisions with respect to processes, finances, and the project timeline. He should be a senior member of the organization and represent the business groups of the company. The executive sponsor should also provide resources/infrastructure support and report the project-related issues to the Managing Director (MD) on a regular basis.

SAP Project Executive Committee

Top management commitment is one of the key factors in a successful implementation of an enterprise resource planning (ERP) system. Hence, it is important that the top management of the company devote adequate time for planning and review of all the activities from the beginning of the project until it is completed. For the success of the project, it is also important that the commitment is visible to all the employees of the company and is exhibited through the direct involvement and actions of the top management.

An executive committee should consist of

- A CMD or CEO (Chief Executive Officer)
- An executive sponsor
- A project general manager
- A COO (Chief Operating Officer) or VP of business operations
- A CIO (Chief Information Officer) or VP of systems
- A Chairman and Managing Director's (CMD's) nominated consultant or any person that CMD may include

Executive committee meetings should be held approximately once every four weeks to review the overall progress.

SAP Project Steering Committee

The steering committee should consist of

- An executive sponsor
- A chief project officer
- A technical team leader
- All key user representatives
- All key consultants
- A technical support project leader
- Senior management representatives
- CMD's nominated consultant

Steering committee meetings should be held every two weeks to take stock of the event-based milestones and other project-related issues.

Roles of the Executive and Steering Committee Members

The roles and responsibilities of the executive and steering committee members should be to

- Provide direction for the entire project
- Approve and control the project scope and implementation strategy
- Approve identified risks and authorize measures to contain them
- Be responsible for milestone deliverables and project delays
- Authorize the staffing plan for the SAP project
- Authorize the training plan and budget for the SAP project
- Help resolve issues, if any, with the implementation partner, coordinate commercial matters, and approve payments on completed milestones
- Authorize and ensure infrastructural support (such as hardware, software, network, external software, office space, communication lines, OSS, and so on)
- Resolve the issues raised in business process finalization and standardization
- Resolve administrative issues faced by consultants from time to time

Mission and Objectives of the SAP Project

The mission of the SAP project should dovetail into the mission and objectives set forth by company for the following three to five years.

Deciding the Scope of the SAP Project

One of the most important responsibilities to be handled by the executive and steering committees is to decide on the scope of the SAP project. For the Millennium Enterprises under consideration, the approach being recommended here is to adopt the big bang approach, whereby the company implements most of the standard SAP modules and also any SAP industry-specific solutions if available for its areas of business.

Only in the big-bang approach does the company start utilizing the information captured by the SAP system as a resource like manpower, materials, and money, rather than merely as a recording and reporting system. The traditional systems have been hobbled into playing exactly such a role and have never been able to deliver the productivity gains expected of them.

The company must also decide the phases of implementation following the implementation at the pilot site. The true benefits of an integrated system can be reaped only when all sites and offices of the company are brought on board the SAP platform. Towards this objective, the pilot site team must be staffed by personnel from all future sites of implementations, and the functionality, as implemented at the pilot site, should be as comprehensive as possible, based on the available time frame and business know-how with the members of the team.

Starting the SAP Project

Initiating the SAP project primarily involves instituting the project management structure and appointing the chief project officer (CPO). The CPO would have to formulate and initiate the mechanism for the selection or nomination process for the members of the team.

The CPO would also have to formulate and get approval from the project's steering and executive committees on the project policies, guidelines, the strategies to be adopted for minimizing the identified risks, and the methods for reporting on the project's progress, budget, and resources.

SAP Project Management Structure

In this section we look at the organizational structure of an SAP project.

Chief Project Officer (CPO)

The Chief Project Officer (CPO) is also a member of the project's steering committee and has enough responsibility and authority to manage day-to-day operational project-related issues and meet all project-related resource requirements.

The company should appoint a senior manager as the full-time CPO. He or she should be familiar with the business environment and the functional and information technology (IT) to lead a team key users and technical consultants, who will also participate in the activities of the implementation process and be responsible for the successful implementation of the SAP R/3 system.

The CPO performs the following functions:

- Provide supervision of the entire project.
- Be responsible for milestone deliverables and project delays.
- Approve and control the project scope and implementation strategy.
- Prepare and get approval for the staffing plan, including the pilot site and the roll out sites.
- Prepare and get approval for the training plan of the project from the lead super-users and end-users at various stages of the project.
- Be responsible to get the relevant business users' time and attention at all relevant stages of the project.
- Accept deliverables and give sign-offs.
- Resolve the issues raised in business process finalization and standardization.
- Help resolve issues, if any, with the implementation partner, coordinate on commercial matters, and approve payments on completed milestones.
- Resolve administrative issues faced by consultants from time to time.
- Provide infrastructural support such as hardware, software, network, external software, office space, communication lines, online service system (OSS), and so on.
- Arrange steering and executive committee meetings and the decisions/clearances required from the committees.
- Provide guidance to SAP and its implementation partner on the company's specific business requirements.
- Provide all data for loading from the relevant business departments.

The CPO also guides the definition and maintenance of the project's implementation guide (IMG) for his or her company as a whole.

Site Project Managers

The site project managers (SPM) are responsible for the SAP implementation at various sites and work under the direct guidance of the CPO. They should be part of the SAP project team for the pilot site from the beginning. This will give them enough exposure and experience on how to handle the implementation at their own respective sites later.

The responsibilities of a SPM include the following:

- Supervise the entire project at their sites.
- Be responsible for milestone deliverables and project delays.
- Assemble the manpower and resources according to the staffing plan for the SAP project.
- Execute the training plan for the site, including training for the Functional and Technical team members, Super Users and end users at various stages of the project.
- Be responsible to get the relevant site business users' attention at all relevant stages of the project.
- Accept deliverables and give sign-offs.
- Resolve administrative issues faced by consultants from time to time.
- Ensure infrastructural support (such as H/W, S/W, external software, office space, communication lines, OSS, and so on) for the SAP project.
- Provide all data for loading from the relevant business departments.

The SPM is also responsible for maintaining the site project's IMG for their respective sites.

Module Leaders

The project team should include module leaders who are responsible for each of the major SAP modules to be implemented for the company. Module leaders should preferably have requisite prior experience in the concerned functional area and also have undergone adequate functional training in SAP, particularly in his/her module of responsibility.

Module leaders should be identified at the beginning of a project and should be part of the Business Blueprint and Realization phases. They should participate in identifying the processes and documenting them, their gap issues, and their resolutions not only for their modules, but also for other modules as well. This would enable them to later make a more effective contribution during the module-level and integration-level testing.

Resource Manager

The success of any SAP project is critically dependent on marshalling the right resources at the scheduled time and place. For an IT project with a similar scope and investments, SAP projects are usually of a much shorter duration. This requires a person, known as the resource manager, who has previously handled the purchasing and resourcing responsibilities in an IT project. He or she should be conversant with the purchase policies and procedures of the organization, as well as those for reporting on budgets in a SAP project.

In the beginning of the project, and at appropriate stages later, the resource manager could also be a member of the project steering committee. This would enable him or her to escalate issues quickly on resource approval delays, mobilization delays, deliveries, incomplete installations, pending training and support issues, and so on.

Training Manager

Unlike the traditional implementations, SAP implementations involve a much larger number of operational personnel who would be using SAP on a regular basis. The training manager should be able to execute training for the various groups of personnel as per the training plan at appointed sites.

A major responsibility of the training manager is to ensure the availability not only of the instructors, but also to release the various personnel from their normal functions at appropriate times so that they can participate in the scheduled training sessions. He or she must also work with the resource manager to complete the installation of the proper software licenses and authorize the training.

In the training of the functional and technical teams, IDES and InfoDB licenses can be obtained and installed with adequate infrastructural support of the PCs, networking, and so on. Similarly, before commencing training for the end users, the latest company-specific user documents for all requisite modules need to be complete and approved specifically for use in the training sessions.

Project Management Policies and Guidelines

The project management policies and guidelines should be finalized and communicated to all concerned at the earliest possible.

Project Strategy

As has been mentioned in Chapter 1's "Information as the New Resource," implementing SAP will benefit the company only when it starts using the information made available by a productive SAP system as a resource. For this, it is essential that all the base modules are implemented and go into production. Otherwise, the system will function merely as a system for recording and reporting on the past performance.

Project Planning and Monitoring

The issues of reporting the progress of the project can lead to contention among project members. Considering that SAP implementation projects are driven by the business managers, even decisions like whether to employ packaged software for the SAP project can become a major political issue.

Project Resources Requirements

For a successful SAP implementation, especially for the big bang approach recommended for the millennium enterprise, resources in adequate measures and at the right time are essential. These would be in terms of

- The allocation and disbursement of budget finances at appropriate stages.
- The acquisition and on-schedule installation of the server and PC hardware, the networking and communications hardware, the communications monitoring and network management software, O/S and office automation software at the servers and nodes, and, finally, the SAP R/3 software.
- Staffing by recruitment and subcontracting or deputation from the various departments for SAP functional teams, technical teams, resource administration, training and logistics teams, super-users, and, lastly, the end users for their orientation training and refresher training just before go-live phase.
- Data from the legacy system or other systems that are operational within the company or its key business partners. This loading of data could be a one-time exercise before the cut-over to the productive SAP system or on a regular basis at predetermined periods during the business cycle every month. The loading process could itself be in the batch mode or be a real-time interface that transfers data and updates between SAP and other systems on an ongoing basis.

Project Training Requirements

SAP implementation projects engender large training requirements. Traditional implementations, however, are closely administered by a centralized computer facility and are confined to smaller numbers of end users. Moreover, these end users are also not actually involved with the operations of the business; on the contrary, often they are usually personnel only responsible for transcribing transactions and other information into the system.

ERP, in the true sense of the word, brings computerization to the desktops of the operational people. Thus, the training requirements for a SAP project implementation would be huge and may easily involve 10 to 20 percent of the manpower of a company.

A company may have to undertake SAP-related training for three different groups of personnel:

- The select group of managerial personnel who are key members of their departments and have been nominated as the members of the functional team.
- The group of key users who form the core of the super-users to be entrusted with the task of life-scale testing the system and also training the end users.

- All other end users who would be using the system as part of their routine operational duties. As an important part of the strategy for post-implementation support, the third group is trained primarily by the members of the second group, the super-users.

The managerial personnel group will be trained with an overview of SAP and their module(s) of interest. The key user group will be trained with an overview of their module and all of the critical processes of interest. The end-users group will be trained only in the processes that are routinely used by them on a daily basis.

Risk Management in a SAP Project

Because the SAP project is an implementation of a standard package, the risks associated with a SAP project are different from those traditionally associated with software implementations. Traditional software projects' major risks are as follows:

- Lack of resources
- Lack of appropriate resources
- Lack of clarity, completeness, and certainty on the scope and functionality
- Requirements capture and analysis
- System design that is effective, efficient, and at the same time flexible for changes in the future
- Development of the system based on this design and testing using this design as a reference
- Training various group of users on the new system
- Interfacing real time with other application systems
- Loading all relevant and up-to-date data into the new system
- Parallel runs with the new system
- Switching to the new system
- Missing deadlines
- Disputes regarding roles, responsibilities, and performance criteria
- User disagreements or non-participation
- Software or infrastructure failures

In addition to the above risks, SAP projects have other risks including the following:

- Requirements capture and analysis
- Understanding what the SAP system can provide
- Evaluating and focusing on the gaps in functionality
- Configuring and customizing the SAP system correctly

- Integration testing of the SAP system
- Training all groups of users almost in tandem
- Loading all relevant and up-to-date data into the new system
- Switching directly to the new system without full parallel runs phase

The risks associated with the requirements capture and requirements analysis are no different than those with the traditional projects. Especially for future enterprises of the millennium, it is important to have shorter timelines for the project implementations.

A company implementing SAP can adopt several strategies for minimizing the risks inherent in the project. The most important one is to do away with the requirement analysis phase, but at the same time implement functionality that represents the optimal practices for the processes that are critical to business. This is effectively achieved by adopting SAP's recommended best-of-business practices that come bundled along with the system.

Selecting the Most Critical Processes

A company should evaluate and select the processes that are critical to its business and focus on implementing them effectively to add maximum value for optimal effort.

Implementing Best-of-Business Processes

SAP has a library of 800 of the best-of-business processes derived from companies throughout the world. The success of SAP in providing comprehensive functionality within a shorter time-frame compared with traditional implementations is based on the strategy of leveraging the commonality that is found in similar processes prevalent in companies within an industry.

Reusability has been a powerful concept in enhancing productivity and the quality of delivered software in the areas of traditional software development. SAP, in particular, extends this concept of reusability to the design of mission-critical systems. It packages such universal commonalties of functionality for rapid and successful implementations.

Before adding reusability to the library of the best-of-business processes, however, the company should document, rationalize, and standardize the company's select group of processes that are to be implemented using SAP.

Documentation of Processes

Documenting the various business processes permits the true comprehension of the characteristic structure and dynamics of the business environment within a company. This involves recording various details on the business processes like name, purpose, responsible function, process description, including inputs and outputs, and subprocesses. This also includes interfaces with other functions and systems, exceptional conditions, areas for improvement, impact analysis of suggested scenarios, and so on.

Rationalization of Processes

Many of the systems and procedures adopted by traditional systems were influenced by the architecture of the systems themselves. For instance, these earlier systems were designed to be used by IT-literate personnel managed and supported by a centralized IT function. In contrast, because of the end-user orientation of ERP packages like SAP as well as the online availability of data on all aspects of company operations, SAP permits the rationalizing of many processes. This could be in terms of eliminating sequential wait periods for approvals, acknowledgements prior to further processing, collating status updates from various departments before compiling the latest positions on inventory, and so on.

In enterprisewide integrated packages like SAP, many of these facilities and features become available automatically as a part of the architecture of the system. Thus, such process steps could be eliminated entirely from the business processes.

Standardization of Processes

Every plant or office site of a company develops its own character and culture, which is a result of the company's recommended corporate environment blending with the local situations. Such local practices have strong adherents and generate loyalty and pride. These factors often harm the progress of implementing a fairly uniform system, even if it's a computerized system like SAP, across the organization at all of its sites and offices.

The CPO must take ample measures to ensure the broad acceptance within the organization of standardized implementation. This can be ensured by

- The rapid implementation at the pilot site
- The rapid rollout of SAP at other company sites and offices
- The deputation of key personnel from all sites for the teams at the pilot sites, even at the risk of overstaffing these teams
- The judicious selection and documentation of functionalities for implementation at the pilot sites
- The democratic and transparent process of standardization based on the predefined criteria of value-addition in terms of customer friendliness, quality, timeliness, costs, and so on
- Configuring and customizing the maximum possible functionality at the pilot site, keeping in view the businesses and practices prevalent at all other sites and offices

Centralized Base Reference Configuration

A company can experience the real payoff of implementing an ERP like SAP only when it has implemented SAP at all of its plants, facilities, and offices. Traditional computerized systems have a much more difficult time implementing standardized processes across all locations of their organizations. Because a SAP project entails implementing both best-of business and standardized processes, it leads to fairly standard implementation solutions across all of its sites.

A company should plan to implement a fairly comprehensive functionality at its pilot site. This is termed as the centralized base reference configuration (CBRC). This can simply be transplanted at each of the rollout sites in the subsequent stages of the project. Such an approach engenders faster customization, training, integration testing, and, finally, go-live stages.

Accelerated SAP (ASAP) Methodology

The Accelerated SAP (ASAP) implementation methodology is the latest tool introduced by SAP for rapid implementation of the SAP system within an organization. ASAP is a structured implementation approach and can help you achieve a faster implementation with quicker user acceptance, well-defined roadmaps, and efficient documentation at various stages.

The key phases of ASAP methodology are

1. Project preparation
2. Business blueprint
3. Realization
4. Final preparation
5. Go live and support

By promoting the best-of-business practices for implementation, SAP does away with the time-consuming and tedious steps of requirements capture and analysis mentioned above.

The popularity, effectiveness, and reliability of such an approach was established by the great success achieved by a similar methodology adopted for the traditional software application development in the 1980s. The Structured Systems Analysis and Design (SSAD) methodology introduced by Gane and Sarson essentially skipped the then-popular practice of first analyzing the existing system and went directly to perform the analysis of the proposed system. The design of the proposed system was therefore a radically different interpretation of the future requirements of a company without being encumbered by the constraints, practices, and prejudices of the past systems and procedures prevalent within the organization.

With SAP, this process is taken a step further by optimizing the traditional design and development stages of the project life cycle by utilizing a library of best-of business, pre-implemented processes for any industry. I will be discussing all these phases of ASAP in detail later in Part IV of this book.

Change Management in a SAP Project

Initiating change and confronting change are the two most important issues facing companies today. The ability to change business processes contributes directly to your "innovation" bottom line. The traditional concept of change management is understood generally as a one-time event, but if an organization is looking for the ability to not only handle change management, but the management of changes on a continual basis, then SAP is a must. SAP provides a platform for such ongoing changes in the processes that are so critical to the success of a company's business.

As I have stated earlier, business processes that reside or are internalized within the minds of an organizations' employees are difficult to change, simply because we naturally find change difficult. However, processes that reside or are internalized within computerized systems are easy to change. Thus, SAP-supported processes are much more easier to change and execute than the conventional computerized system because SAP implements a model of the enterprise that is comprehensive and consistent.

Change management is essential because employees feel

- Fear of job reductions
- Fear of losing responsibility and control
- Anxiety arising out of a perceived inadequacy of their background
- Fear of failure
- Loss in the sense of ownership
- Sheer inertia for changing and learning new systems

The issues become further aggravated because of lack of clarity in terms of these questions:

- Why changes are needed?
- What changes are needed?
- Who is accountable for what?
- How will the performance and progress be measured?

The issues arising because of changes resulting from the implementation of SAP can be resolved by

- Demonstrated support from senior management
- Wide and rapid information dissemination on the SAP project
- Adequate training and refresher programs
- Accelerated progress and effectiveness with the SAP system
- Rotation of job responsibilities or replacement

Roles of the SAP Project Team Members

In the following sections, I discuss the roles and responsibilities for the members of the SAP team.

SAP Project Team

The SAP project team has the following responsibilities:

- Be responsible for studying and streamlining the business processes.
- Standardize the business processes across all offices.
- Study the system and configure it to suit the business processes with the help of the module consultant.
- Generate necessary documentation.
- Prepare a training manual.
- Identification of the roles and responsibilities and required authorizations in the SAP system.
- Setting up the authorizations.
- Training users.
- Complete tasks according to the implementation plan.
- Work on data collection and the purification of uploads to the system.
- Support the users after going live.
- Implementation at rollout sites.

Functional Consultants Team

The SAP team of consultants has the following responsibilities:

- Train the SAP team members in respective modules.
- Help the team map processes in the system.
- Find solutions for the gaps observed after mapping.
- Guide the team during the integration test.
- Be responsible for meeting the milestone deadlines of the module.
- Provide necessary input for programming.
- Help the team during discussions with users in case of any problems.

SAP Technical Team

The SAP technical team has the following responsibilities:

- Identifying the list of customizations using user exits, new reports using and so on
- Preparing the project SAP programming and documentation standards
- Writing ABAP programs, user exits, and reports using tools such as Report Painter, Report Writer, ABAP Query, Drill-Down Reporting, or ABAP programming
- Identification of interfaces and data to be uploaded into the SAP system from legacy and non-SAP systems
- Specification of the interfaces and data uploads
- Programming the interfaces and data upload programs
- Unit testing and integration testing

SAP Administration Team

The members of the SAP administration team will have to be skilled in three different areas: Basis system administration, database administration, and operating system administration.

The various tasks involved with the SAP Basis area are as follows:

- Starting and stopping the R/3 system
- Daily administration using Computer Center Management System (CCMS)
- Performing daily checks
- Monitoring system logs
- Monitoring R/3 system/database alerts
- Analyzing Advanced Business Applications Programming (ABAP/4) dumps and taking corrective actions
- Process monitoring
- Update monitoring
- Batch input monitoring
- Monitoring lock entries
- Managing user and system background jobs
- Print administration
- TemSe (Temporary Sequential) spool file administration for printing
- Spool administration and tuning

- Managing user information, authorization, and profiles
- Importing transport requests
- Error analysis and troubleshooting using logs, traces, and program dumps
- Managing operations and use of the Online Service System (OSS)
- Planning and managing the disaster recover site

The database related tasks are as follows:

- Performing regular R/3 database backups per the backup strategy
- Performing SAP database administration (SAPDBA) activities using utilities like BRBACKUP for backup and BRARCHIVE for archiving logs
- Performing regular archive log backups
- Monitoring and managing table spaces, indices, index extent sizes, and so on

Other operating system- and network-related tasks are as follows:

- Installing upgrades
- Coordinating with the H/W and other vendors for follow-ups on reported problems
- Monitoring network loads and identifying bottlenecks

Summary

In this chapter we looked at various aspects preparatory to launching the SAP project. We covered issues dealing with the planning, organization and managing of SAP projects. I also discussed the various elements of risks that may jeopardize the success of the project as well as measures to mitigate them. In the next chapter we look into the infrastructure planning and preparation for the SAP implementation project.

Installing and Administering SAP

IN THIS CHAPTER

This chapter tackles the last stage in the preparatory phase for launching an SAP project. We look at the infrastructure planning followed by the installation and landscape planning of the SAP system. In the later half of the chapter we look at several sub-functions constituting the SAP administration function including administration of the SAP clients, jobs, SAP users, printers and database administration.

Preparing the SAP Infrastructure Plan

The objectives of an infrastructure plan are ensuring the minimal downtime and optimal response-time for achieving optimal operational productivity at optimum costs. Due to the three-tier architecture of SAP, one can concentrate mainly on the central processing unit (CPU), memory, and data storage requirements of the R/3 database and application servers.

The performance of an end-user-oriented system like SAP can be gauged in terms of the performance of online and processing functions. The former is related to the number of basic online dialog steps that are to be executed for achieving a functional task; the latter is related to the number of computations, but primarily to the number of posting updates that are done to the underlying database tables. Thus, the performance of the SAP system can be calibrated broadly in terms of basic units of work, such as

- The estimated number of dialog steps per hour
- The estimated number of finance-like (FI) transactions per hour

The methodology of planning for the SAP infrastructure generally involves the following items:

- **General requirement parameters**: these parameters relate to information on the average number of working hours every day, week, or month for online and batch-oriented processing and the average distribution of processing loads between the online retrieval of document, reporting, and batch jobs. These are primarily used as the scaling or weighing factors to fine-tune the numbers generated by the remaining three estimates as a percentage of the normal online activity. For instance, sizing for the development, quality assurance, training, and testing systems is usually worked out as a percentage of the envisaged production system.

- **Estimating the number of users and their usage**: this relates to information on average number of users using each module and their categories in terms of the degree of activity (high, medium, and low).

- **Estimating the number of transactions and their intensity**: this relates to information on the average number users of both online and batch transactions in every module. Additionally, estimates are made of the average peak loads expected, based on the volume of the company's business activity and the future growth potential.

Installing and Administering SAP

CHAPTER **11**

245

11

INSTALLING AND
ADMINISTERING
SAP

- **Estimating the disk space size of database tables**: this relates to information on the table-wise average number of records per table expected in the database, along with the respective retention periods. SAP's Disk-Sizer tool provides the list of tables and record lengths for most disk space-intensive tables in SAP.

It must be noted that in line with the three-tier architecture of SAP, which permits one database server and multiple application servers, the performance of the database server is the key element for the overall performance of the SAP system. Additional disk space sizing may have to be considered for business warehousing, logistics information systems (LIS, EIS, and so on), industry solutions (IS-Oil, IS Retail, and so on), Workflow, interfaces to other systems, the work spaces required by these other systems, print spool files, operating system (OS)-dependent or database-specific organization, reorganization, maintenance, and so forth. This disk space sizing will have to be adjusted for the corresponding retention periods and envisaged growth.

The infrastructure is configured in terms of the amount of CPUs, memory, and disk space based on this collected information. An additional infrastructure may be needed to cater to specialized requirements like high-availability (i.e. with minimum down-time) and disaster recovery facilities. Judgement needs to be exercised in terms of balancing the need for a costly high-end system to tide over the shorter-duration peak loads against the need for a cheaper system that is primarily geared to handle extended periods of normal activity.

To assist in the infrastructure-planning exercise, SAP provides a Quick-Sizer tool that calculates CPU, disk, and memory resources based on the inputted information mentioned earlier. Similarly, for comparing the suitability of hardware from different vendors, SAP provides certified benchmark test results that help in optimizing price, performance, reliability, future growth, and upgrade capabilities.

The results are published by the SAP Benchmark Council that designs standard run-scripts consisting of a predefined set of SAP Sales & Distribution (SD) functions, specifies the system setup parameters for the runs, and defines corresponding threshold response times. The SD benchmark is considered a standard for determining hardware scalability because the time-critical performance requirements for the majority of the customers is best represented by the functionality in the SD module.

The SD module incorporates such time-critical processes as sales orders, delivery notes, scheduling, and invoicing. For example, entering a sales order invokes an inventory check, schedules production, creates delivery schedules, checks and updates credit, creates an invoice, updates accounts receivables, and finally creates journal entries for the cost of goods sold and so forth. As a measure of complexity, compared to an FI transaction that has only four dialog steps (initiation of transaction, display of transaction, update of transaction, and execution of the transaction and result status), an SD transaction can easily have 15 or more dialog steps.

Installing the Hardware and Operating Systems

SAP provides a checklist that acts as a guide for the requirements of the OS and the relational database management system (RDBMS) for a selected hardware platform. For instance, in R/3 Release 4.0A, the central instance of SAP needs approximately 15 GB of disk space.

Installing LAN and WAN Solutions

For every SAP implementation project, the network infrastructure must be planned not only to take care of the immediate needs, but also for the expansion anticipated in the future. The network should be planned with the following two objectives in mind:

- High network availability
- Ease of network administration

In every SAP R/3 production system, the presentation layer, application layer, and database layer services usually run on different computers. The front-end SAPGUIs are connected to the application servers through a local area network (LAN) or a wide area network (WAN). The application servers in turn, because of the high traffic, are connected to the database servers through a LAN. The application servers are separated on different servers for reasons of security etc.

Server Network

The server network connects all of the application servers to the database servers. For each dialog step, the amount of data that is exchanged between the database server and the application server is about 20 KB.

Front-end Network

The front-end network connects the user's workstations to the SAP applications servers. The required bandwidth for this network essentially depends on the number of users. The amount of data that is transmitted across the network between the SAP Graphical User Interface (SAPGUI) and the application server corresponding to each change of the screen is about 2 KB.

SAP Installation

Since R/3 Release 4.0, the installation program R3Setup is guided by a generic program, InstGUI, that transparently guides R3Setup for installation on different OSs like UNIX or NT and different RDBMSs like Oracle, Informix, and so on.

The installation usually proceeds from the database layer to the presentation layer. First, the relational database management system (RDBMS) and the database are installed on the database server; then the central instance is installed on the application server (which could also be same as the database server), followed finally by the installation of the front end (the installation program needs to be executed separately for each application server).

As a final step, a SAP license key needs to be obtained from SAP for using the installed software.

SAP System Landscape Planning and Management

The nature of the SAP development and runtime environments dictates that we cannot have a one-system landscape at any installation. The simple reason is as follows. Recall that all information is stored in the R/3 repository and any changes to the same immediately trigger a change in the runtime environment. The work process interprets a runtime object, which is always generated from the Advanced Business Applications Programming (ABAP) program source code. Every time the source code of an ABAP program is changed, runtime objects are regenerated before they are executed again. This would imply that in a one-system landscape either we cannot make any further developments after the system is in production or the production will be interrupted every time an ABAP/4 program changes, which may happen quite frequently in a development situation. Hence, we must have more than single system Landscape.

Two-system Landscape

The two-system landscape is relatively inexpensive and easier to manage (as compared with the three-system landscape) in terms of the administration of the system on a regular basis. In such a system, the roles of the two systems are as follows:

- System 1: Development and testing system.

  The customizations and ABAP development are done in the development client. Changed objects are released to the second client for testing.

  The customizations and ABAP programs are tested and validated in the quality assurance client. Only tested and approved changes are released to the production system.

- System 2: Production system.

  This system runs the released changes from the quality assurance client.

There are some disadvantages of the two-system landscape. For example, it's not possible to test client independent customizing or development, change repository objects before bringing them into production and so on. To avoid this, the only choice is to opt for the three-system landscape.

Three-system Landscape

Technically, this is the best option, but it is more expensive and requires additional administration duties compared to the two-system landscape.

- System 1: Development system. Customization and program development are done here.
- System 2: Quality assurance system. Testing and the validation of changes are done here.
- System 3: Production system. The changed programs are running here.

Client Administration

Client administration involves the copying of clients within one or across multiple systems, depending on the requirements or purpose of the utility. Some standard clients defined are

- Demonstration
- Development
- Customizing
- Testing
- Training/education
- Production

Before working on any of these clients, they need to be created first. The creation of a client is usually done by copying an existing client, which initially is usually standard client 000. Creating a client consists of first defining a client and then populating it with data, which could be both client-dependent or client-independent. Application data is mostly client-dependent data.

Three different options exist for creating a client:

- Copying a client within a system (also called local copy)
- Copying a client from another R/3 system (also called remote copy)
- Using a special transport request to transport a client from one system to another (also called client transport)

SAP System Administration

The general administration tasks that need to be performed on an ongoing basis include:

- Checking the system status
- Sending system messages
- Monitoring the system

- Displaying running processes
- Checking the system log
- Maintaining tables

Figure 11.1 shows the screen for system administration. Many of these activities are performed using CCMS, as described in Chapter 7's "Computer Center Management System," while some others are performed or assisted by the operating system.

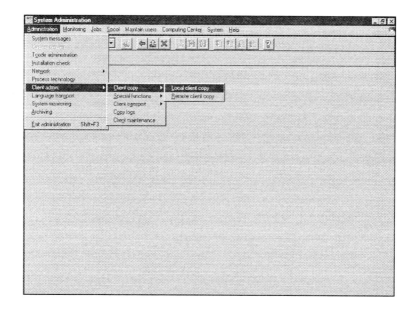

FIGURE 11.1
System Administration menu screen.

Job Administration

Job administration deals with the issues of defining, scheduling, executing, monitoring, and managing background jobs. Background jobs correspond to the batch processes that we discussed in Chapter 7's "Batch Process." Jobs can be triggered by schedulers that are active within the instances of SAP R/3 either at predefined times or when predefined events occur.

CCMS provides the facility to define jobs in terms of

- Job specification, which includes information like the job name, job priority, target computer, and so on

- Processing specification, which includes information on the various processing steps, such as the name of the ABAP program that is processed during a particular step

- Schedule specification, which includes information like the start time or prior triggering event

Figure 11.2 shows the screen for defining Background Jobs.

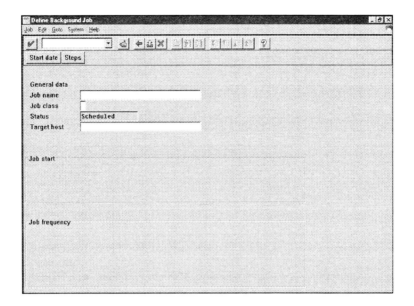

FIGURE 11.2
Screen for defining Background Jobs.

CCMS also provides the facility for monitoring jobs based on various criteria like job status, time period, and user. Particular selected jobs can also be drilled-down to reveal job logs. Figure 11.3 shows the selection screen for Background Jobs.

Certain jobs are required to be performed at regular times like those for maintenance and back-ups. Processing such jobs can also be dependent on the operation mode switch in SAP (see Chapter 7's sub-section, "The SAP Instance").

Installing and Administering SAP

CHAPTER 11

251

11

INSTALLING AND
ADMINISTERING
SAP

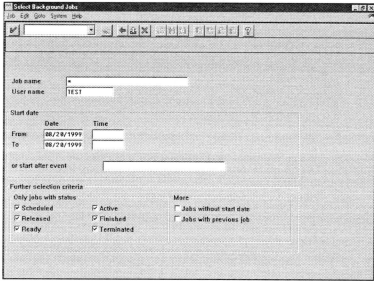

FIGURE 11.3
Screen for selecting Background Jobs.

User Administration

Subsequent to the installation of SAP and setting up the landscape, the next logical step is to define the users of the system. The SAP system provides a comprehensive and flexible method for making the data and transactions secure within the system. The concept of a user in SAP is a vehicle for implementing security in SAP. A user is defined and maintained in the user master records, and the security is defined and maintained in the corresponding profiles and authorizations. In SAP, the extent of authorization ranges from complete access to the SAP system (except for select exceptions like salary details) to highly restricted access confined to specific work-related tasks. Typically, users will be allowed to perform almost all functions in the development and test systems, but in the production system the access would evidently be much more restrictive depending on the job requirements of a particular user.

User Master Records

User master records are dependent on the SAP client. A user master record contains all the information that is necessary to validate the user when he or she logs on to the system. A user master record is also necessary when allocating access rights to the user in terms of the corresponding passwords and authorization profiles. This includes not only standard information on user contact and address, but also system-related information like the default logon-screen, user type, default printer, and so on.

The user master record contains the following information:

- The initial password, which can be changed daily by the user or the administrator at any time in accordance with the password requirements and restrictions

- The user type, which can be the default dialog user, the batch input-processing batch data communication (BDC) user, the batch processing (background jobs) user, the Common Programming Interface–Communication (CPI-C) user (for external communication interfaces), and the Internet user

- Valid from and until dates

- The account number for analyzing usage, activity, and so on could be used at the individual level or at the level of work areas

- The activity group, which is the name of a pre-existing activity group to which a particular user should be allocated

- Profiles that define the functions that are accessible by the user and are usually customizable pre-defined profiles available in SAP

- An address that contains all contact-related information

- Default values for the start-up menu, transaction, logon language, default printer, formats for date and amounts, and so on

- Default values for user parameters. Depending on the job-related requirements, this enables defining default values for fields frequently used by a particular user. This is mainly provided as a facility for speeding up the entry of data. For defining any parameter, the system only needs the corresponding field's PID number and the user-given value for this field. Thereafter, for this user, every appearance of this field on any screen in the system will default to the value specified here for that file. This can be defined and updated by the users themselves at any time.

R/3 Super-users

A standard SAP installation creates special users in each of the system clients 000, 001, and 066. These users are SAP*, DDIC, and EARLYWATCH, respectively.

As recommended by SAP, an SAP* user may not have a corresponding user master record, but when created, it may have the following authorization profiles: SAP_ALL and SAP_NEW. It has the default initial password 06071992 and has unlimited access rights. When a new client is created by copying SAP*, it has a password PASS.

Installing and Administering SAP

CHAPTER **11**

253

11

INSTALLING AND
ADMINISTERING
SAP

A DDIC user is always created with the initial password 19920706 and a user master record with authorization profiles SAP_ALL and SAP_NEW. This user has special authorizations for installation, software logistics, and the ABAP/4 dictionary, and is required to upgrade to the new R/3 release. A DDIC user, however, can only use the correction and transport system in display mode, and hence cannot do any custom development in the system.

An EARLYWATCH user only has authorization for access to performance-monitoring functions and display access to technical data that is required for the EARLYWATCH and GoingLive Check services when SAP consultants log on to your system through a remote connection. EARLYWATCH has the initial password SUPPORT and the user master record gets created with an authorization profile called S_TOOLS_EX_A.

It is advised that after installation all these special users should be made secure by changing their default passwords.

Activity Groups

Activity groups are groups of users having either common functional activities or activities common to a business process. These groups are based on the analysis of the job-role matrices for the users within the company. An activity group defines the transactions and activities involved with a job and identifies the users responsible for doing this job. Activity groups are also client-dependent.

Authorizations for Users

This broadly relates to all facilities in SAP deployed to grant access privileges to users for performing particular functions and activities. Such authorizations are given to the users by assigning them specific profiles and authorizations in their user master records. As we will see in the following subsections, giving access privileges to users in SAP is an elaborate exercise.

In tune with SAP's philosophy of reusability at all levels, SAP provides a large selection of predefined, frequently used authorization profiles to ease the job of the administrator. A user can easily be given a predefined profile from this collection or a standard authorization can be reused as a template to create new customized authorizations (standard authorizations should not be changed). When new profiles are created, they must be activated before they can become available within the system.

Authorization Fields

This is the lowest-level element of the authorization system. Authorization fields are the components of authorization objects and are associated with data elements in the ABAP/4 data dictionary. These fields could be a development class, a user group, or an application area or could identify the *activity*, that is, the operations on the elements that are protected by the system's access tests. The activity could be of following kinds: create, change, display, print, lock, delete, post, activate, display change documents, and so on.

Authorizations Objects

Authorizations objects are the elements or objects within the SAP system that need to be protected. An authorization object contains up to 10 authorization fields. Users are allowed to perform a system function only when access tests for all authorization fields have been complied successfully.

For better manageability, all authorization objects are grouped into authorization classes depending on the areas of application. Figure 11.4 shows the Maintain Authorizations screen.

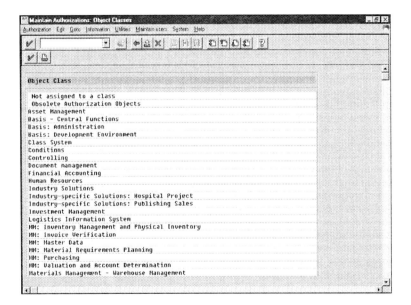

FIGURE 11.4

Screen for maintaining Authorizations.

Authorizations

Authorizations define the permitted values of authorization fields on company codes, application areas, user groups, and so on. An authorization can also consist of many valid values or ranges of values for the corresponding authorization filed. An authorization value of "*" authorizes for all values; a blank authorization value signifies a denial of authorization.

Authorizations are applicable to the authorization profiles with the corresponding authorization objects. Whenever any authorization is altered, it affects all profiles that include that authorization.

Authorization and Composite Profiles

An authorization profile consists of many authorization objects. A composite profile is made up of a set of authorization profiles. This is useful if users need multiple authorization profiles for their jobs. This is the highest level that authorizations can be specified for any user in the user master record. Figure 11.5 shows the initial screen for profiles.

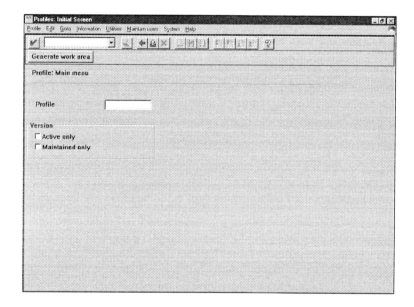

FIGURE 11.5

First screen for user authorization profiles.

Any changes in the profiles affect the corresponding users only when they are activated; the changes become effective only when the user logs on the next time after the change.

The authorization profile SAP_ALL indicates all authorizations within the system, including both technical- and application-specific functions. The SAP_NEW profile indicates that all authorization objects added in any R/3 upgrade for existing functions are also included.

Administering Authorizations

Although a single super-user can perform all user-related administration and maintenance tasks, SAP recommends subdividing the responsibility of maintaining users masters and authorizations among three administrators for ensuring optimal security as well as simplifying this procedure.

The three administrators are

- **User administrators**: these users can oversee all the user groups or only select user groups. User administrators define and maintain the user master records and assign the users to one or more activity groups.

- **Authorization profile administrators**: these users can define or modify authorizations and profiles, but they cannot maintain users or activity groups.

- **Activity group administrators**: these users create the activity group and define the associated R/3 transactions, but they do not maintain authorization profiles or users.

Tracing Authorizations

Tracing authorizations is useful when a user has a problem accessing certain essential functions or ascertaining the authorization checks performed by a transaction. Authorizations can be checked by two methods:

- **Authorization analysis transaction**: this is a fast method meant specifically for authorization analysis, but it is used for current user sessions only. Upon getting an error, a user can launch this method from any screen by selecting System, Utilities, Display authorization check (or use transaction code SU53) to display the authorization object along with its corresponding values.

- **System trace**: this is a general purpose tool that we have seen in Chapter 7's subsection "System Trace Utilities" and provides as one of its options an authorization check. The trace can be activated and the session can be conducted for any transaction or screen of interest. The output of the trace can also be directed to the disk for later scrutiny.

Profile Generator

SAP introduced Profile Generator to assign authorizations to users automatically. It is based on the concepts of authorizations, authorization objects, and authorization profiles, defined earlier. SAP delivers a large library of standard authorizations for different areas of activity.

Profile Generator works with the structure of the activity groups. As we have seen previously, activity groups can be defined for particular functional areas. The activity groups are authorized to use subtrees of the enterprise menu. Profile Generator generates the necessary profiles for the activity groups, which are then assigned by the user administrators to individual users. One user can be assigned to multiple activity groups.

Print Administration

Printers in SAP are administered with the spool system. A printer must be connected to one of the application servers and the instance profile specifies which application server formats the data for the print output. Figure 11.6 shows the Spool Administration screen. The spool system stores the output documents in the database or in files on the OS. Figure 11.7 shows the related screen for Temporary Sequential (TemSe) file.

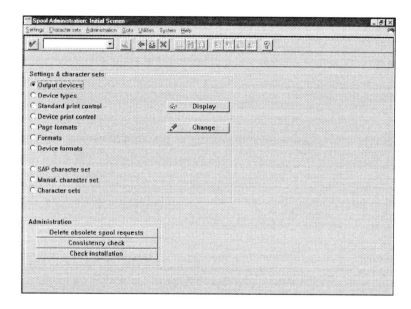

FIGURE 11.6

Initial screen for spool administration.

The objectives of a print infrastructure should be to

- group printers for easy administration
- differentiate printers to be used for high-volume, critical, or special print jobs
- ensure high availability as well as balanced print loads among printers

Printing jobs could be grouped in classes such as the following:

- High-volume prints: For lists and ledgers
- Time-critical prints: For dispatch and shipping documents

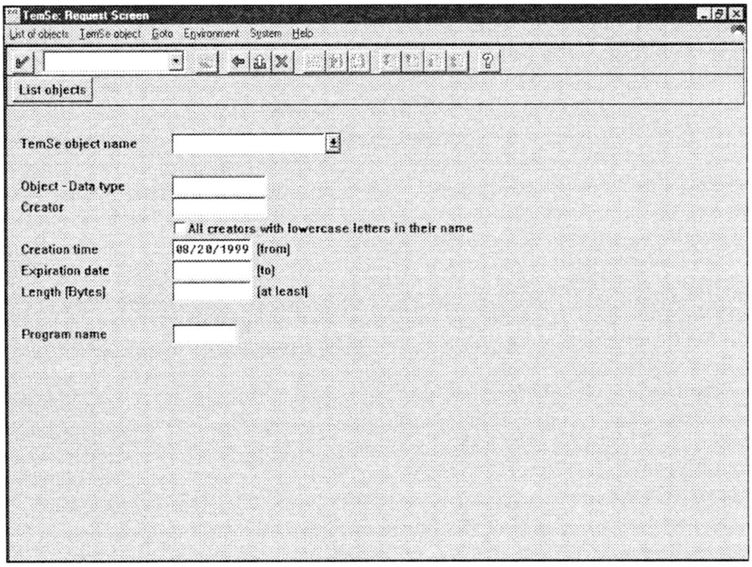

FIGURE 11.7

Request screen for a temporary sequential file.

- Normal prints: For short reports and letters
- Special prints: For bar codes and text with optical character recognition (OCR) fonts

Accordingly, printers could be grouped into

- High-volume printers
- Production printers
- Desktop printers

For this, they should have appropriate access modes from the following list:

- C - Local printer on a Windows NT or AS/400
- L – Local printer on a UNIX machine
- S – Remote printer at LPDHOST through SAP protocol
- U – Remote printer at LPDHOST through Berkley protocol
- F – Printer on front-end
- E – External output management system (OMS)
- P – Local or remote device pool
- I – Archiver (for example, ArchiveLink)

- X – SAPcomm (for example, a fax machine)
- Z – IBM AFP (for example, an IBM mainframe S/390)

Access methods are broadly the format or protocols used to transfer data for the output request from the spool server to the host printer.

Printers in SAP are not connected to the spool servers directly, but through a layer of logical servers. The advantages of having an in-between layer logical servers are as follows:

- Flexibility in moving a printer group to any other spool server
- Flexibility in the print landscape being independent of a particular R/3 system
- Effectively increases availability; any failed spool server can be replaced transparently by another manually or automatically

SAP also provides for the integration of a SAP R/3 system with an existing legacy printer landscape. Again, the printers in an OMS can be grouped into a logical OMS (LOMS), which in turn can link to a real (ROMS) that can connect to third-party product through the eXternal Output Management (XOM) interface.

Database Administration

The database administration involves the administration and management of the underlying database. Figure 11.8 shows the display of the database administration (DBA) operations. The tasks are RDBMS-specific but generally involve issues of

- Database table definition and maintenance
- Database integrity
- Database security
- Database performance
- Database reorganizations
- Database backups
- Database recovery

SAP provides a family of integrated database administration tools:

- **SAPDBA**: this is a menu-driven tool for managing all database administrative tasks, including calling and running the other three utilities.
- **BRBACKUP**: this tool enables online and offline backups of application data, control data, and redo logs. Figure 11.9 shows the Overview of Backup Status screen.

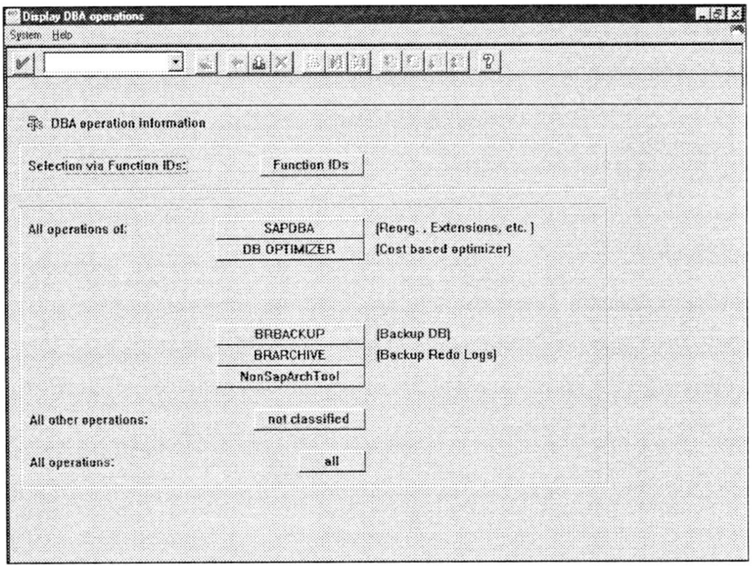

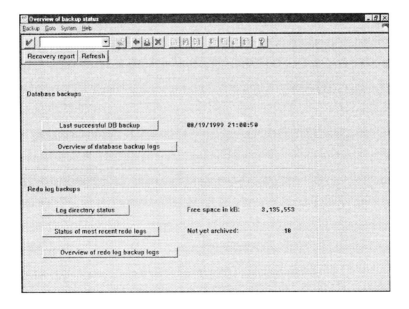

FIGURE 11.8

Display screen for DBA operations.

FIGURE 11.9

Display screen for an overview of backup status.

- **BRRESTORE**: this tool restores backed-up application data, control data, and redo logs.
- **BRARCHIVE**: this tool archives offline redo logs.

Summary

In this chapter we described the various aspects related to the infrastructure planning and installation of the SAP system. In the later half of the chapter we looked at several activities related with SAP administration. The following Chapters 12 through 17 of Part IV detail SAP's rapid implementation methodology called ASAP.

The Implementation Stage

IN THIS PART

AcceleratedSAP (ASAP)

IN THIS CHAPTER

This chapter introduces the novel implementation methodology devised by SAP to achieve successful implementations in shorter time periods, as compared with the R/3 procedural model methodology (see Chapter 5's "SAP Implementation Methodologies"). This is specifically targeted for customers from small and medium enterprises (SMEs).

Reusability has been the cornerstone of SAP's philosophy. As discussed in the first chapter, this can be seen in the library of 800 best-of-business scenarios or processes provided with each SAP license. Notwithstanding the comprehensiveness and flexibility of SAP to address requirements of diverse industries, implementing SAP in a reasonable time frame has become one of the most important issues for companies while evaluating SAP R/3 for their organization. Furthermore, as the high end of the market has become saturated, it is evident that SAP's potential for growth in the late '90s is in the SME market. These are the customers who do not have the resources and time to survive enterprise resource planning (ERP) implementation projects extending for periods ranging from two to three years.

In 1996, SAP introduced the AcceleratedSAP (ASAP) implementation methodology with the objective of speeding up the SAP implementation projects. ASAP enabled new customers to utilize the experience and expertise gleaned from thousands of implementations worldwide. This chapter introduces the concept and practice of the ASAP methodology for implementation of SAP R/3.

Why Are SAP Implementations So Complex?

The prime reason for the longer duration of SAP implementation projects is due to the peculiar complexity of the product. The contradictory demands of comprehensibility and flexibility are satisfactorily addressable in SAP, because of its repository-oriented architecture (in this chapter, we will mainly focus on the functionality aspects of this repository, rather than the technical ones, which also are substantial). Fundamentally, this is not much different from the trend of parameterized packages that have been gaining ground among application software packages since the '80s. The main difference is the extent or degree of parameterization: SAP is parameterized to an extreme. It is this property that enables it to be flexible enough to be configurable to the requirements of several industries.

The difficulty in implementing SAP arises from the fact that the success of the implementation project depends on correctly mapping all of the company's business process into the SAP system. This entails the correct configuration of all the required process right at the beginning or at the initial stages of the project. As we have seen earlier, SAP addresses the problem of providing usable application software systems by effectively short-circuiting the problematic requirements analysis phase, which is the bane of the traditional software development life cycle (SDLC) (see Chapter's section "Concept of Enterprise Resources Planning (ERP) systems"). Because of the demand for correct configuration right at the beginning, however, we are back confronting essentially the same problem.

The majority of the risks for the ultimate success of the project is also dependent on this initial mapping being completed correctly consistently and completely. Unlike the SDLC, where the end-users are expected to know only their requirements thoroughly, in the new dispensation, they have the additional burden of being required to become quite familiar with the functionality provided by SAP. Thus, SAP is very flexible, but in order to configure it correctly, not only is one required to know the business process requirements of the company, but one must be well acquainted with the SAP functionality even before starting on the configuration. In typical SAP projects, this is right at the initial stages of the project. This is the root cause for the large amount of effort and time required for completing the mapping and configuration of the base SAP system in all SAP projects. Although all the required the functionality may have been available in SAP all along, it takes everyone a long time to discover and use it correctly.

Configuration through the Implementation Guide (IMG)

Like in SAP's older implementation methodology called the procedure model, all configuration in ASAP is also done through an environment called the Implementation Guide (IMG). The IMG is not unlike the initialization modules of the traditional computerized systems, except that it is very large by comparison. SAP has more than 8,000 configuration tables. All the business processes of the company can be mapped into the SAP system's functionality by configuring the parameters in the IMG. When implementing any process, one must identify the parameters that have to be defined before this process can become operational in the system. For example, when creating of an invoice document, it is important to identify tax parameters and define them first through the IMG. The whole process of specifying the parameters suitable for the specific requirements of a company is also known as *customization*, which is accomplished using the IMG. However, the essential problem is that in an integrated system like SAP, there is no systematic way to identify all the relevant parameters quickly and completely for implementing these processes.

As we will see in "Implementation Guide (IMG)" the IMG is structured in a manner that reflects the sequence in which these parameters have to be defined, but for the most part, this is not adequate for customizing SAP quickly. For typical SAP implementation teams, locating hundreds of these parameters correctly, in a proper sequence, and also in a timely manner is an intractable problem. Rather than a systematic process, it is more of an experience in discovery, and the number of parameters to be identified and defined is simply overwhelming. To be on the safe side, typical project teams are always on the defensive, invariably confirming and reconfirming every small aspect (although this does not guarantee avoiding missing something) before proceeding further in the effort, and all this simply adds to a large timeframe for completing the project. Along the way, the benefit of using the departmental store model of computerization is being lost completely (see Chapter 1's "Concept of Enterprise Resources Planning (ERP) Systems").

The obvious remedy is to address the following two issues for achieving faster SAP implementations:

- Bridge the gap between the know-how of the to-be-mapped company processes and/or requirements on one hand and the functionality provided by SAP or what is configurable in SAP through IMG on the other

- The quick transfer of expertise and experience to newer implementation teams gained from numerous earlier implementations

As seen earlier in the book, repository-oriented systems like SAP *continue the tradition of computer-aided software engineering (CASE) environments.* By the same token, the second point above truly corresponds to a computer-aided software implementation (CASI) environment, which we consider next.

Computer-Aided Software Implementation (CASI)

ASAP is a classic illustration of a CASI environment that assists in speeding up the implementation effort based on the experiences of past SAP implementation projects and that continues the same in the future to improve its performance further. There are two aspects to a CASI; one is CASE and the other is intelligent assistance. In the next few paragraphs we quickly acquaint ourselves with the contexts of CASE and Expert System environments to see their essential continuity into the latest environments like ERP and ASAP.

Right from the inception of the computerization activity, there have been efforts towards employing computerized systems to aid in the software development effort at different stages. Among these program generators, screen painters, report painters, and prototyping and automated/assisted testing tools have been the most common ones. Many of these environments also embody the corresponding methodologies for speeding up the effort of respective phases of the SDLC. Some of these environments or accelerators have also become generic, making them adaptable to any methodology deployed for a particular project, rather than being confined to specific methodologies for analysis, system design, data modeling, database design, and so forth. As we will see further in this and following chapters, ASAP also uses accelerators in the form of questionnaire, guidelines, etc. to speed-up the process of implementation.

SAP as a Populated CASE Environment

In their most developed form in the later part of the last century, CASE technology was composed of the following components:

- Methods
- Tools environment

The CASE environment is a set of integrated tools that are designed to work together and to assist or possibly automate all phases of the SDLC.

SAP environments like the Basis system, the R/3 Repository (including advanced tools like the ABAP/4 dictionary, the ABAP/4 Development Workbench, CATT, Workbench organizer, and so on) and the Business Engineer (including the R/3 Reference Model, the Business Navigator, and the Procedure Model) form a state-of-the-art CASE environment.

However, as discussed in Chapter 1, "The Millennium Enterprise," SAP is not only one the best of the CASE environments; it is also a populated CASE, in that its repository is populated with the details of the most comprehensive application system. For example, SAP R/3 consists of financials, logistics and human resources systems.

SAP Implementations and Expert Systems

Expert systems (ES) are environments that extend the realm of reusability into the areas of design and operations of computerized systems. These knowledge-base-driven systems apply inferences to a knowledge base containing data and business or decision rules that mature depending on the veracity of the produced results.

In their most advanced form during the late '80s, ES technology was composed of the following components:

- A knowledge base
- An inference engine that "learned" and fine-tuned its performance based on some predefined criteria with reference to the usefulness of the inferred results. This learning could be in terms of generating new rules or modifying the strengths of the current rules or even updating the knowledge base itself.

ASAP is not an expert system in the traditional sense, but it does have the basic ingredients of a knowledge base and inferences or suggested actions. In fact, in certain cases, it affects these actions automatically in the SAP system (see Chapter 14's, "Initialize IMG"). The knowledge base of ASAP keeps on getting upgraded, based on the latest reported experiences and expertise gleaned from SAP implementations. Presently, this is not an online, dynamic, and automatic update like some of the other services provided by SAP, such as the GoingLive Check or EarlyWatch Alert services. SAP releases periodic upgrades of this knowledge base through CD-ROMs. It is easy to imagine, however, that ASAP may become an online service like GoingLive Check in near future. It may also become a full-featured expert system with its characteristic features and user interfaces.

What Is ASAP?

Launched in 1996, ASAP is SAP's rapid implementation and ongoing optimization methodology. ASAP consists of a methodology called the *Roadmap* that is linked to the configuration tools like IMG in the R/3 system. ASAP has been specifically designed for SMEs that undertake implementations on a tight schedule.

As mentioned earlier, reusability is one of the key aspects of ASAP. Like the 800 best-of-business processes, ASAP is a repository of the best experiences and recommendations from countless SAP R/3 projects carried out in the last five years. Further, as stated in Chapter 1's "Information as the New Resource," information provided by ERP acts as a tangible resource that drives the operational processes faster, without expending more conventional resources. Because ASAP represents the accumulated know-how from past projects, ASAP can also be seen to use all of this relevant information to speed up the process of implementing itself!

ASAP consists of a wealth of checklists, spreadsheets, questionnaires, answers, document templates, recommendations, and so on. It also provides white papers on important issues and includes guidebooks, learning tools, and accelerators on more technical issues related to the SAP infrastructure, installation, and operations. The various reviews and checklists available from ASAP verify not only the implementation project itself, but also the stability and integrity of the system along each phase of the project.

The Roadmap also includes change management tasks and accelerators that will be necessary for handling the changes in the organization resulting from the deployment of SAP. The Roadmap suggests measures that will raise the awareness of the impact of SAP implementation and provide insight and guidance on how to manage this change. ASAP represents a totality of all the experience and wisdom gained by SAP, its implementation partners, and its customers. Figure 12.1 shows the home page screen of ASAP for Release 4.0B.

ASAP supports the entire life cycle of the SAP installation; it is not confined to the implementation phase alone. ASAP also provides support for ongoing improvements as well as for efforts during SAP upgrades.

ASAP integrates the following three components that work in tandem to support the rapid and efficient implementation of the R/3 system:

- **ASAP Roadmap**: this is a step-by-step methodology for a successful SAP implementation project.
- **ASAP tools**: these include project management tools, questionnaires for business process consultants, and numerous guidebooks and checklists
- **R/3 services, support, and training**: this includes all consulting, training, and support services such as GoingLive Check, remote upgrades or archives, and so on.

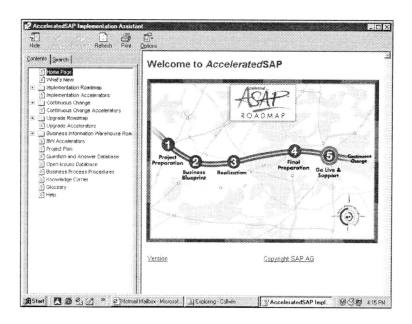

FIGURE 12.1

The ASAP home page.

Each of these will be discussed in the remaining subsections.

The characteristics of the ASAP methodology are as follows:

- It is a proven methodology, having been used successfully in hundreds of projects initially in the U.S. and subsequently all across the world.

- It is the process component of TeamSAP (the other component being the people and products).

- It is a comprehensive and seamless methodology with integration across the various phases of the project.

- It skips over the as-is problematic phase in the traditional methodologies to directly target the analysis and documentation of the to-be business processes.

- It promotes three distinct roles to guarantee full attention to all aspects of a rapidly moving project: project management, application consulting, and technical implementation.

- The input from the business blueprint phase is used as a direct input for configuration in the realization phase.

- Worldwide, there are more than 10,000 ASAP-certified consultants.

ASAP Roadmap

SAP provides a process-oriented, clear, and concise implementation roadmap for individual implementation projects. This Roadmap acts as a project guide that specifies steps, identifies milestones, and generally sets the pace for the entire project to deliver a live system at top speed and quality utilizing the optimal budget and resources. The ASAP Roadmap consists of the following phases: project preparation, business blueprint, realization, final preparation, and go live and support.

Project Preparation

The project preparation phase deals with setting up the project organization, including the teams, roles, and responsibilities. In this phase, the aims and objectives of the implementation are decided. The strategy and draft project plan is prepared. The project infrastructure, including the hardware and networking issues, are determined and finalized. Sizing and benchmarking the envisaged installation are performed and the acquisition of the SAP system is initiated. The project starts officially with a kick-off meeting attended by members of the executive and steering committees, project team members, and SAP consultants.

Business Blueprint

The business blueprint phase deals mainly with the documentation and finalization of the requirements. The team members and consultants conduct interviews and workshops in different activity areas to ascertain the requirements of various business processes. The functionality provided by the R/3 is demonstrated using the Information and Design Education (IDES) and is supported by questionnaires and process diagrams from R/3 Business Engineer. Any gap in addressing functional requirements is identified and appropriate solutions are explored and devised. The final outcome of this phase is the Business Blueprint document, which details the TO BE processes, including written and pictorial representations of the company's structure and business processes. Once this has been approved, the blueprint is the basis for all subsequent phases.

Realization

The goal of realization is to configure the baseline system using the IMG based on the Business Blueprint document. To do so, the business processes are divided into cycles of related business processes. The system is documented using the R/3 Business Engineer. The baseline system prepared here is the basis for the production system.

The SAP team undergoes Level 3 training. The system is presented to a team of power-users who also undergo requisite training in their respective areas of operations. The baseline system is fine-tuned by the validation done by the power-users, who employ an iterative approach. The technical team sets up the system administration and plans interfaces and data transfers. The interfaces, conversion programs, enhancements, reports, end-user documentation, testing scenarios, and user security profiles are defined and tested for effectiveness. The final deliverable is a fully configured and tested SAP system that meets that the company's requirements.

Final Preparation

The final preparation phase is aimed at readying the system and the company for the SAP implementation. It consolidates all the activities of the previous phases. Any exceptions and out-of-turn situations are addressed and resolved. The super-users under the supervision of the SAP team members conduct end-user training. The conversion and interface programs are all checked, volume and stress tests are performed, and user acceptance tests are conducted. This is followed with the migration of data to the new system.

Go Live and Support

The go live and support phase addresses the issues of putting the SAP system in production. The GoingLive check is also performed and completed. This involves solving issues of day-to-day operations including problems and security-related issues reported by end-users. SAP is also monitored for possible optimizations. This phase also involves verifying that milestones like day-end processing, first-month end, first-quarter end, and first- year end processes work correctly. It also involves completing any processes or parameters left uncompleted or undefined by oversight. Lastly, the business benefits of the new system are measured to monitor the return on investment (ROI) for the project, which may trigger further iterations of the implementation cycle in order to improve the business processes. A formal close of the implementation project is also performed.

ASAP Toolkit

ASAP provides tools for project management, functional consulting, and technical implementation including the following:

- Project plan document
- Project progress report
- Issues database
- QuickSizer
- System administration guide
- International Demo and Education System (IDES) tool
- Question and answer database
- R/3 Reference Model
- R/3 Structure Model
- R/3 Report Model

- Business Process Master List (BPML)
- Implementation Guide (IMG)
- Customizing wizards
- Business Process Procedures (BPP)
- Legacy System Migration (LSM) Workbench
- Initial Data Transfer Made Easy guide
- Data Transfer Workbench
- Authorization Made Easy guide
- Profile generator
- Interface advisor

ASAP Services, Support, and Training

SAP provides services including consulting, training, and support services that help in standardizing tasks and procedures like

- Onsite consulting
- Remote consulting
- Advanced training solutions/Information Database (InfoDB)
- GoingLive Check
- EarlyWatch Check

Advantages of ASAP

Adopting the ASAP methodology which entails using the standard checklists, questionnaires, document templates, guidelines and recommendations provided by SAP, has many advantages like

- Rapid implementation
- Optimal utilization of resources and budget
- Enhanced quality

ASAP, BPR, and Change Management

When a company adopts ASAP methodology for implementing SAP, their success depends on how quickly the company can implement changes in its business processes that are in line with the best-of-business processes in SAP. While using ASAP, it is advisable that the company should avoid undertaking a Business Process Re-engineering (BPR) effort in conjunction with the SAP implementation. It is recommended that the company should implement a vanilla SAP functionality initially. Once the implementation stabilizes, then custom functionalities could be introduced later judiciously. The vanilla approach cuts down on maintenance, as well as speeds the time to production and benefits of the new system.

ASAP for Application Consultants

For an advanced methodology like ASAP, which can still be considered fairly new, the role played by ASAP application consultants is critical. They have to ensure that the ASAP processes and tools are utilized effectively and to their fullest potential for the customer to succeed in realizing the gains of ASAP's approach. The ASAP application consultants must understand exactly what is expected at each stage during the project; otherwise, any tendency to lose focus and drift into an exploratory kind of activity may dissipate the basic advantage to be gained from this novel approach.

Since this book is primarily targeted to the implementation team as a whole, we will not dwell on the specific responsibilities of the ASAP application consultants. All these processes and tools will be discussed in the next five chapters without specific references to the responsibilities of the application consultants. For quick reference, however, the critical tasks that application consultants are expected to perform are listed below:

- Define the scope of the implementation in different areas of activity.
- Define the organization's structure.
- Complete the business process questionnaire.
- Complete the Customer Input (CI) template questionnaire.
- Generate the Business Blueprint document.
- Compile the business process transaction list.
- Prepare the BPP documents.
- Generate the BPML.
- Apply the project scope from Question & Answer database (Q&Adb) to the R/3 system's IMG.
- Produce the system and end-user documentation.

Preconfigured Industry Systems

This philosophy of re-using commonality has been extended further to devise industry-specific solutions. Notwithstanding the extent to which a package can be parameterized to address a large range of requirements, there is a limit to the variability that can possibly be configured and delivered within such a framework. The business processes within different industries are arguably quite dissimilar. No amount of rationalization and standardization can enable one to mold them into variations on a few hundred basic processes. Industrial processes can range from engineer-to-order to a continuous process in nature (see Chapter 9's section on "Production Planning"). The way that the processes are implemented, monitored, controlled, and managed is completely different. SAP provides preconfigured systems for certain industries to address all such issues (see closely related generic pre-configured SAP R/3 system called SAP RRR in Chapter 4's, "Recent SAP Strategic Initiatives").

These preconfigured systems contain the industry know-how for typical business structures in a given industry, but they go much further than the standard ASAP, in that the system is delivered even with the relevant default values for all basic parameters also predefined. Thus, the industry-specific ASAP being referred to here is the illustration of an advanced, populated CASE product (see "SAP as Populated CASE Environment"). This results in not only reduced implementation times, but also a more stable SAP implementation.

SAP has adopted the strategy of complementing its fairly comprehensive, generic functionality solutions with industry-specific predefined functionalities. During the implementation, the industry-specific customizing settings need to be altered to the requirements of the particular company. The preconfigured system is configured on a copy of Client 000 and can be transported using a transport request. The industry-specific structures, scenarios, and processes can be found in ASAP in the Q&A database and in the R/3 system using the Business Navigator or by using any compatible modeling tool.

Pre-configured industry systems are available for the following industries:

- Automotive
- Chemical
- Pharmaceutical
- Paper trade and production
- Metal trade and production
- Banking
- Consumer products
- Engineering
- High-tech
- Retail food and textile
- Aerospace and defense

Implementation Guide (IMG)

The SAP R/3 IMG plays a critical role in the customization of SAP R/3 to the specific require-ments of the customer. This is achieved through the configuration of the SAP software without modifying the base SAP software. As we have seen in Chapter 5's "Implementation Environ-ment," SAP provides the implementation environment called Business Engineer, which man-ages and assists this effort for the SAP configuration. This contains tools like the Business Navigator, IMG, Business Workflow, IDES, and so forth. Before proceeding further with the details of the various phases of ASAP in the following chapters, it is important to take a closer look at the IMG.

As mentioned in "Configuration Through the Implementation Guide (IMG)," the IMG tool is similar to the initialization modules of the traditional systems, except that, in comparison, the number of parameters that is definable here is very large. In fact, it is the most vital tool for successfully configuring SAP to meet the specific requirements of different companies. The IMG exists in the following versions:

- Reference IMG
- Enterprise IMG
- Project(s) IMG

The Reference IMG is the initial IMG with a base set of configuration options from which all SAP functionality can be derived, per specific requirements. It is the most generic version of the system available and all other IMGs are derived from this basic version.

In contrast, the Enterprise IMG is a subset of the Reference IMG that represents only the func-tionality that is needed by a particular enterprise implementing the system. Configuration options related to these excluded modules get filtered out at the time of generation of the Enterprise IMG.

Further down, since SAP implementations can be undertaken in phases, the Enterprise IMG is specified for each of these projects separately, resulting in the corresponding Project IMG for each of these projects. All configurations for a particular project are executed on the corre-sponding Project IMG. Access to Reference IMG and Enterprise IMG is restricted in order to avoid inadvertent changes being made to them. Whenever required, the scope of the Project IMG can be increased at any time and hence such architecture, rather than being a hindrance, is helpful in the management of the customization effort. We will refer only to the Project IMG for the rest of this section.

Features of Project IMG

A Project IMG contains multiple *configuration transactions*. Configuration transactions are the means for configuring the various processes or the functionality delivered by the SAP system. A particular business process can be configured in terms of more than one configuration transaction. In conventional terms, each configuration transaction is one of 8,000 parameter tables existing within SAP. They could be parameters like company codes, G/L accounts, ranges of account numbers, A/P and A/R control account codes, posting codes, location codes, vendor or customer categories, tax codes, fiscal calendars, currencies and conversion factors to the base currency, accounting transaction number ranges, and so forth.

For each configuration transaction, the *configuration help text* provides an explanation on a particular configuration transaction, why it is needed, and how it affects the functionality for a particular process.

The *configuration status* can be maintained at every level of the Project IMG hierarchy. It helps in the visual tracking of the customizing effort. The status flag can be configured to represent user-defined statuses. SAP provides standard status values like complete and in-process. Statuses have to be maintained manually.

The *configuration documentation* provides the facility for recording annotations, issues, and problems on the various configuration settings for each configuration transaction. This documentation is usually done in free-form text but could be standardized, based on the requirements of different projects.

Using Project IMG for Customizing SAP

The basic structure of Project IMG is hierarchical. The various configuration transactions are grouped in a hierarchy of folders that are broadly arranged in the order that the customizations are undertaken within a SAP module. Among the various SAP modules, the IMG folders are arranged in the order that the modules get implemented in real life. However, some parameters or configuration transactions are independent of any specific modules and are relevant to all modules and functionalities of the system. All such configuration transactions are arranged within the top-most IMG folder and are termed as *global settings*. Obviously, farther down the hierarchy, it becomes fairly difficult to maintain the order in which the transactions may be required to be configured. Therefore, this ordering is only a general guide; otherwise, it could degenerate into a huge list of configuration transactions at a single level, which would certainly become unmanageable.

Thus, the hierarchy of the folders in Project IMG is shown in Figure 12.2.

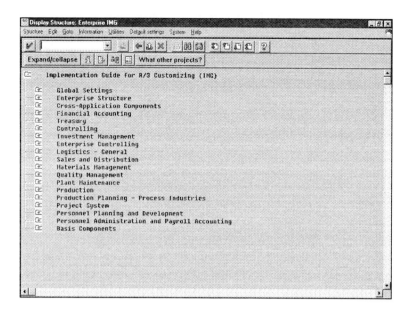

FIGURE 12.2

Top-level structure of Enterprise IMG.

For any SAP implementation, a small selection of the initial parameters or configuration transactions that need to be defined is as follows:

- **Client**: The highest organizational level in SAP R/3, not to be confused with a customer
  or client as defined in the SAP Basis environment.

- **Company code**: The lowest legal entity for external reporting purposes of the balance
  sheet, P/L statement, and so on. There can be multiple company codes for a client, but
  not the other way around.

- **Chart of accounts**: This is useful for legal reporting. Every client has only one chart of
  accounts; all company codes within one client must use only this chart of accounts.

- **Credit control area**: An organization structure used for credit control management and
  reporting.

- **Business areas**: Business areas are useful for flexible financial reporting. They are normally used when a separate balance sheet and profit-and-loss statement are required for a
  business segment. Business areas are often used in the U.S.

- **Controlling area**: The highest entity for internal reporting and accounting purposes. One
  or more company codes can be assigned to a controlling area.

- **Operating concern**: There is only one operating concern for each controlling area. It is used if the profitability analysis module is implemented (this module is not implemented by all SAP customers). Controlling areas are assigned to an operating concern.

- **Plant**: A unit where inventories are stored, accounted, processed, or manufactured. There can be multiple plants for a company code as well as a purchasing organization.

- **Sales organization**: The highest level for managing and reporting sales.

- **Sales distribution channel**: This characterizes different modes of supplying end-customers (retail sales, distribution agents, factory outlets, Internet sales, and so on). There can be multiple distribution channels for a sales organization

- **Sales division**: This is useful for the management and reporting of a group of products. There can be multiple product divisions for multiple sales organizations as well as distribution channels.

- **Sales area**: This is useful for flexible management and reporting. It is a combination of a sales organization, distribution channel, and division.

- **Purchasing organization**: This is an organizational unit for purchasing activities and the generation of purchase orders.

- **Storage locations**: The physical location where a company's inventory is stored. There can be multiple storage locations for multiple plants.

- **General Ledger (G/L) account**: G/L accounts are used for legal, external reporting through the chart of accounts.

- **House Bank and Bank Account**: These organization structures reflect a company's banking institutions and their individual bank accounts.

- **Vendor Master**: This contains important information on the company's vendors. For example, a vendor's name, address, telephone number, fax number, contact person, purchasing information, bank information, and accounting information is stored in the vendor master data. This information saves on transaction entries; when a transaction is made with the vendor, the vendor master data can automatically be used by default in the transaction.

- **Customer Master**: Similar to the vendor master data, the customer master data contains important information on the company's customers. Information such as a customer's name, address, buying habits, marketing information, and accounting information are stored here. When a transaction is made with a customer, the customer master data can automatically be used by default in the transaction.

Figures 12.3 through 12.11 show the screens for defining some of these parameters.

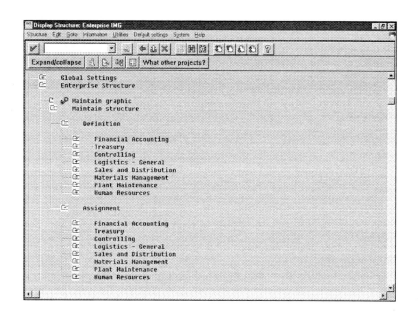

FIGURE 12.3

Customizing enterprise structure within IMG.

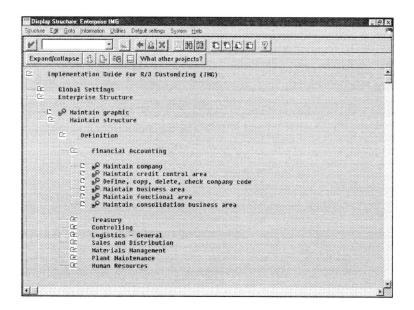

FIGURE 12.4

Defining financial accounting-related parameters in IMG.

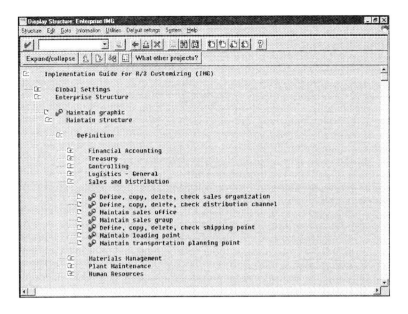

FIGURE 12.5

Defining sales and distribution-related parameters in IMG.

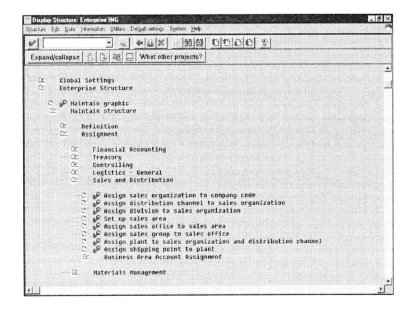

FIGURE 12.6

Assigning sales and distribution-related parameters in IMG.

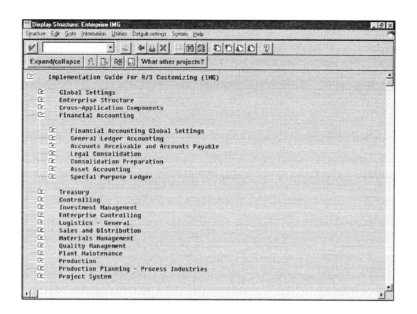

FIGURE 12.7

Customizing financial accounting within IMG.

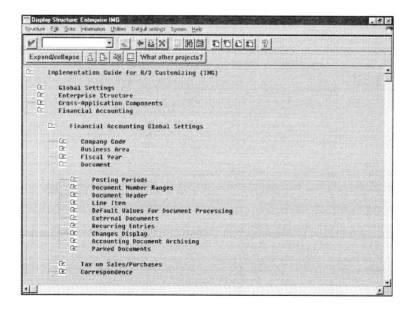

FIGURE 12.8

Customizing SAP document-related parameters in IMG.

12

ACCELERATEDSAP

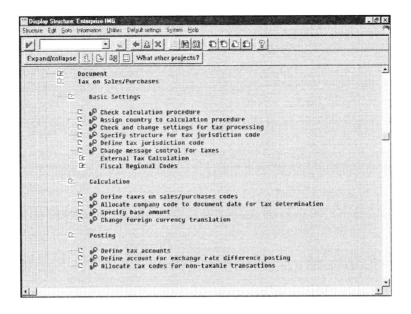

FIGURE 12.9

Defining tax-related parameters in IMG.

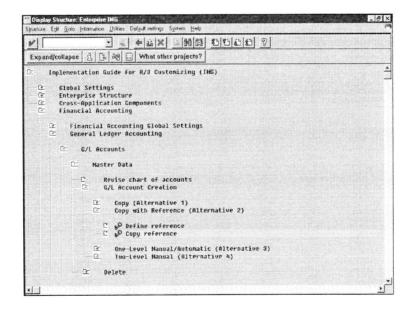

FIGURE 12.10

Defining G/L accounts in IMG.

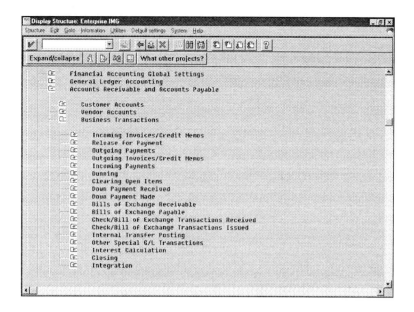

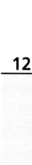

FIGURE 12.11

Customizing transaction-related parameters in IMG.

Summary

SAP is especially targeted for the Small and Medium Enterprise (SME) customers that have annual revenues between $50 million to $1 billion. Beginning with understanding why SAP projects tend to be complex, this chapter discussed the background and context of SAP's rapid implementation methodology for SAP implementation: AcceleratedSAP or ASAP. We also presented an overview of the various phases of the ASAP implementation cycle. In the remaining chapters of Part IV, we discuss each of these phases in detail.

Project Preparation

IN THIS CHAPTER

We discussed various aspects of initiating the SAP project in Chapter 10, "Initiating the SAP Project." In this chapter, we discuss the first phase of the ASAP methodology, which covers similar ground. The objective of dealing with the same issues from two different views is to illustrate the importance of adapting a repository-based, integrated methodology such as AcceleratedSAP. In this chapter, we see SAP's view on preparing for a rapid implementation project. This chapter is based on ASAP documentation published by SAP.

NOTE

The importance of referring to the original SAP AcceleratedSAP documentation CD cannot be overemphasized. What I have presented in this chapter are the essential details of the Project Preparation phase of the ASAP methodology. However, this chapter is not intended as a replacement for the colossal amount of instructive documentation, guidelines, checklists, templates, samples, questionnaires, and so forth provided and recommended for use by SAP. Those are well-proven instruments, and for an actual project, it is highly recommended that you procure the version of ASAP corresponding to the version of your SAP installation and use it in conjunction with the implementation project.

In this chapter, we discuss setting up the right context for the SAP project. The discussion addresses the issues of goals, objectives, scope, strategies, and plans for the SAP project. This establishes a framework for all subsequent phases, activities, and tasks performed as a part of the implementation project. This phase deals with instituting the project organization, including the teams, roles, and responsibilities. The project infrastructure, including hardware and networking issues, is determined and finalized. Sizing and benchmarking of the envisaged installation are performed and the acquisition of the SAP system is initiated. At the end of the preparatory phase, the project starts officially with a kick-off meeting attended by the members of the executive and steering committees, project team members, and SAP consultants.

Project Planning

This task deals with the preparation and finalization of the project charter, implementation strategy, and establishment of the project organization, as well as plans for various activities of the project, such as the budget, schedule, resources, and so forth.

Prepare Project Charter

The project charter establishes the success-defining criteria for the project. In light of the major investments of time, money, and resources to be expended in the envisaged project, the first step is to seek the business drivers that the SAP implementation aims to assist after it goes in production. These aims could be knowledgeable responses to customer queries, quick turn-around times, minimization of errors in registering requirements for products and services, making the best pricing available to a valued customer, up-to-the-minute tabs on delivery schedules, error-free dispatches of goods and invoices, proper follow-up on payables, and so forth. Consequently, there is a need to define how the performances will be measured and to define a threshold of performances. It is important to realize that SAP implementation is not an end in itself, but a means toward the achievement of the business objectives of the company, which is not unlike any other similar major effort undertaken within the company.

Project Mission
This helps in orienting company-wide effort toward the success of the implementation as well as ensuring focus on the most significant aspects of the project.

Project Benchmarks
This lays down the thresholds of performance that the SAP implementation project must deliver in the envisaged timeframe. These include benchmarks for the implementation project itself, including milestones for achieving the various phases, and so on, but they also include business benchmarks on the post-implementation business processes in terms of predefined measures in tune with the goals and the objectives of the project.

Change Charter
SAP puts a great deal of emphasis on the change-related aspects of SAP and the issues of change management arising from them. SAP implementation entails many changes in the general operations of the company.

ASAP does not engender BPR in the conventional sense; the actual business processes do not undergo major changes in design *per se*. But SAP by its very nature (refer to Chapters 1, "The Millennium Enterprise," and 4, "The SAP Solution") triggers major changes in the operational procedures of the company because of

- Single-point entry of business transactions
- Comprehensive and automatic audit trails
- Single integrated database
- Real-time operations
- Immediate update and postings of transaction
- Immediate access to up-to-the-minute information, queries, reports, and so on to all authorized users.

Therefore ASAP, which targets to achieve SAP implementation in extremely reduced time-frames, has necessarily to address the issue of change management.

Define Implementation Strategy

This addresses the issues of the approach to implementing various functional modules at various sites.

Implementation Strategy

The options of implementing are either as a big bang or in waves. In the former, all relevant SAP modules are implemented at the same time. In this book, I am recommending this approach. The other approach is to implement various modules in succeeding waves of implementations, one after the other.

Roll-Out Strategy

This deals with the approach to be adopted for implementation at sites other than the pilot site chosen for the implementation project. Usually a base configuration set at the pilot site is rolled out at other places with requisite changes in the master data and so on.

Implementation of Pre-Configured Systems (PCS)

As we have seen in Chapter 12's section "AcceleratedSAP for Application Consultants," these are SAP R/3 licenses that come preconfigured for requirements of specific industries, including global parameters, process parameters, reports, and so forth. This option, if it provides satisfactory functionality that is acceptable to the company, can greatly accelerate the implementation.

Define Project Organization

This task is related to structure and constituents of the project team. It ensures proper allocation, monitoring and managing of resources, and resource utilization, as well as work accomplished by the various subteams.

Define Roles

ASAP has identified precise roles for people with the requisite background for ensuring the success of the project. ASAP documentation defines the following roles in detail:

> Project Sponsor
>
> Steering Committee Member
>
> SAP Project Manager
>
> Customer Project Manager
>
> Business Process Team Leader
>
> Business Process Team Member
>
> SAP Consulting Manager
>
> Technical Consulting Manager
>
> Quality Auditor

Application Consultant

Change Team Leader

Change Team Member

Business Process Owner

Power User

Documentation Developer

End User Trainer

Help Desk Manager

Internal Auditor

Technical Team Leader

Development Manager

ABAP Developer

Layout Developer

Cross Application Developer

SAP System Administrator

Database Administrator

Network Administrator

Operating System Administrator

Authorization Administrator

Technical Consultant

Project Engineer

The change management team has the responsibility to assess the project and organizational risks involved, and to devise and drive the communications, sponsorship, skill development, knowledge transfer, and process optimization processes defined by SAP for addressing these risks.

Organizing the Team

This task involves identifying, interviewing, and allocating people to the various roles identified earlier. This also includes arranging for the requisite project infrastructure and administrative support personnel.

Prepare Project Plan

The aim of this task is to prepare a project plan in light of the goals, objectives, strategies, resources, and budgets allocated for the project. This includes a resource utilization plan and a budget plan, as well as a schedule for achieving the project milestones. Obviously, this is not a static plan but a dynamic plan that is fine-tuned as the project progresses through the various predefined milestones.

Project Work Plan

It is vital to create a detailed plan of schedules, tasks, and activities that aids in keeping control of the project effort. A clearly defined and disseminated plan also helps in orienting and focusing everyone concerned toward the achievement of the agreed objectives.

The work plan addresses key variables such as activities and related tasks, milestones and deliverables, periods and deadlines, and dependencies of tasks, as well as the responsibility centers for these tasks.

Project Budget Plan

A proper plan delineating all envisaged expenses can help in arrangement of proper funding and also for management of the project. The expenses budgeted cover consultancy fees, hardware, software, training, travelling, and so on.

Project Resource Plan

The project resource plan deals with the allocation of manpower in required numbers and with requisite background at the various stages of the project. Although SAP implementation is very critical to the future strategy of the company, all necessary personnel cannot be allocated to the project on a full-time basis. The reason is simply that the company must run its business in the meantime! The size of the core team, with its contingent of full-time members, is rather small. Therefore, it has to be supplemented with members from the concerned departments and functions during the project. The SAP resource plan enables proper planning and resourcing at the level of the company as a whole. The SAP resource plan dovetails into the human resources plan for the company.

Prepare Training Plan

This task ensures that all members of the core and extended teams undergo proper training that might have been identified as an essential prerequisite for their roles on the team. It is also essential to ensure that members are trained in their areas of responsibility and in keeping with the role at right junctures; otherwise, too wide a gap between training and the actual delivery of learned skills might deteriorate the performance. In case of the latter occurrence, the plan must have provisions for refresher courses to ensure meaningful participation of all members in the project effort.

The training programs could be conducted in-house, at SAP training centers, or at a partner's training facilities. The courses will vary, depending on the scope and the background of the various members of the team.

Project Standards and Procedures

The objective of this task is to lay the ground rules that will be adapted for the project work. A uniform method of working, recording, and reporting permits consistency, avoids redundant effort, and helps in clear communication.

The SAP project must establish two kinds of standards: those applicable directly to the project work and those that deal with communication with various concerned parties regarding the status and progress of the project.

Define Project Management Standards and Procedures

This addresses the task of establishing various standards to be adapted for the SAP project, which includes project communications, recording project activities and milestones, system documentation, application-related quality standards, and issues on change management, team building, and so on.

Project Communications

This subtask deals with the scheduling of planned and ad hoc meetings, norms for agendas and recording of minutes, conducting meetings, and reporting on the issues, actions, and statuses, as well as communication with concerned people outside the project team.

Project Planning and Monitoring

This relates to the method of recording the effort expended by various consultants, project reporting, task start and end dates, quality reviews and feedback, maintenance of schedules, planning or rescheduling, approval procedures for new schedules, and so forth.

Project planning is based on ASAP Roadmap, IMG Customizing activities, and ASAP Implementation Assistant, using a project management tool such as MS Project.

This helps in maintaining the project schedule as per the project work, budget, and the resource plan.

Project Documentation Standards

This task relates not only to the project work documentation, but also to business processes, configuration and customization settings, company-specific enhancements, end-user documentation, and SAP services reports and inputs.

Scope Management Plan

These tasks relate to maintenance of the scope of the SAP implementation project, request for changes, justification for requested changes, assessment of the impact of changes, pending requests, and records of implemented changes. The scope management plan also helps in managing the approval processes for the numerous requests received during the course of the project. This is a very important activity because it is customary to get numerous requests for increases in scope of the functionality, which has a direct effect on the resource requirements, overall schedule, and budgets.

Issues Management Plan

This task relates to recording and follow-up on ongoing issues. It is very useful in the review, and status on suggested actions and resolutions, as well as follow-up on open issues.

Organizational Change Management Plan

Organizational change is a very critical issue for the ASAP implementation methodology and works in tandem with the SAP project plan. This task seeks to account for the various risks that influence the successful outcome of the SAP project at the levels of the organization, team, and individual members of the company. This plan acts as the framework for the various initiatives that are launched during the Business Blueprint phase, such as impact analysis, assessment of baseline risks, sponsorship strategy, strategy for communications, skills development, and knowledge transfer, as well as the organizational optimization process.

The plan identifies the activities, methods, deliverables, deadlines, and reporting processes for status on the change management program within the company.

Team Building Plan

This task relates to all measures and plans undertaken for building a cohesive team, which is critical for the success of the team. It helps in arranging team events and programs for recognizing outstanding performance and contributions to successful completion of project tasks and also celebrations on achievement of major milestones. It helps in making the arrangements, scheduling these events, keeping tab on the expenses, and so on.

Strategy of Using R/3 Services

SAP provides many services at different phases of the project that provide specialized expertise for accomplishing the related tasks and activities in the optimal way.

The various R/3 services available from SAP are the following:

Customer Competence Center (CCC) Program

Quick Sizing Service

Review Services

Training Services

Conversion Services

EarlyWatch Service

Remote Consulting

Onsite Consulting

Remote Upgrade

Remote Archiving

GoingLive Check

Quality Assurance Plan

This task deals with planned or on-demand reviews of the level of quality of various project tasks and activities, and, therefore, assessment of the risk and corrective measures or recommendations. It also deals with third-party audits and follow-up on their feedback and recommendations.

Define Implementation Project Standards and Procedures

The purpose of this task to establish standards and procedures for both the functional and technical aspects of the SAP project. It relates to the standards applicable in areas of system configuration, testing, authorizations, enhancements, and productive operations.

Implementation Project Review Standards

This deals with the issue of presenting a review of the project status at various stages. It includes updates on the milestones crossed, the status of various planned tasks, influencing or impacting factors, position of resource availability and utilization, infrastructure issues, performance issues, identified delays and corrective measures, and so forth. A standardized approach to review presentation makes it easier for comparison and assessment of progress across a period, as well as background references to the decisions made and supporting data for them.

System Configuration Standard

This task establishes the norms for undertaking and managing customizing-related activity though IMG. This task defines standards for the authorizations for access to IMG, documentation on the customization and changes, and release and transportation of the customization to the QA and, eventually, to the productive system.

If the customer opts for Ready-to-Run R/3 (RRR) along with PCS, this task would relate to the maintenance of all configuration settings and customizing for the specific preconfigured industry system.

End-User Documentation Standards

This relates to the standards for the documentation and training programs and materials for the training of end users. These programs are mainly individual performance-oriented training programs compared to the traditional classroom-oriented training. The documentation should be designed so it is easy for a person to follow and perform on his or her job. This training is critical in both the pre- and post-Go Live phases.

Testing Standards

ASAP primarily follows an iterative approach to testing in which the same areas and functionality may be visited at more and more focused levels. The testing might start at the level of the configuration, proceed to the business process level, and go further to the user-acceptance level.

This task defines the overall strategy throughout the life cycle of the implementation project. The testing is done at the following levels of granularity:

Unit testing

System testing

Integration testing

User acceptance testing

Stress and volume testing

And, later,

Release upgrade testing

ASAP's Implementation Assistant recommends at least the following testing milestones:

Baseline configuration testing

Final configuration testing

Final integration testing

Stress and volume testing

Post-Implementation Services and Support Standards

This task deals with planning the strategy for handling the post-implementation phase in terms of

SAP Support

SAP Help Desk

In this case, the customer is an SAP value contract customer who has contracted with the Customer Competency Center (CCC) (see Chapter 18's section "Customer Competency Centers (CCCs) Program"). This task dovetails into the general strategy of SAP support of the post-implementation phase.

System Authorizations Standards

This task deals with defining the policies, standards, and procedures for maintaining the user master, activity groups, and authorization profiles. It also decides the method of administrating the authorizations by coordinating with

User administrators

Authorization profile administrators

Activity group administrators

Change management team

ABAP development team

System Problems Reporting and Error Handling Standards

This task primarily aims to set a project-wide system for addressing reported problems and their resolutions. This task addresses the issue of establishing a system that can transition smoothly to the help desk system envisaged in the post-implementation phase.

Considering the technical components of the SAP operational environment, the following service areas are handled separately, with respective standards and procedures for turnaround on the solutions for the reported problems:

Desktop level

Server level

Network level

In each case, the system will entail registering and identifying the problem, identifying the reporter of the problem, estimating a time for responding, actual response, analysis of both open and closed issues, and so on.

Change Control Management Standards

In an SAP implementation, despite the proclaimed "No Change" policy for the SAP system, there will many occasions for admitting changes in the system that are in the nature of extensions or modifications of the SAP software. As is customary, any such enhancements and modifications should always leave the vanilla SAP untouched (see Chapter 5's section "SAP Implementation Methodologies").

This task deals with laying down the rules for requesting and justifying changes, specifying the changes, changing system documentation, testing and QA of the changes, and so on.

ABAP Programming Standards

This relates to the specification, development, testing and implementation of ABAP programs including reports, dynpros, and so on. It is advisable to maintain SAP-recommended standards for ABAP programming, naming conventions, company-specific tables, screen layout style guides, repository objects, and so on.

Define System Landscape Strategy

The system landscape strategy involves defining the systems that will be part of the installation including their purpose and identification. It should deal with the set up and maintenance of the systems and clients, during both the pre- and post-implementation periods. The strategy should also define the release and transport strategy for the distribution of the customizations and development across the landscape to the desired system.

While defining the landscape, the strategy should take into consideration whether the customer intends to use Ready-to-Run R/3 system or a preconfigured system.

Determine and Identify Required Systems

Usually, SAP recommends three system landscapes comprised of the following:

> Development system
>
> Quality system
>
> Production system

Many customers may also have a Sandbox or Play system where new ideas and customization can be tested before performing customization in the development system. This is a highly recommended safe approach.

Depending on the requirements, a landscape can have a larger number of systems as well; however, the administration and maintenance of the systems becomes that much more complicated. While planning, a proper balance must be achieved between the requirements and the subsequent load of administrating this landscape.

NOTE ——————————————————————————————

As we have seen in Chapter 11's section "SAP System Landscape Planning and Management," a landscape consisting of only a single system is a practical impossibility in the SAP environment unless the company simultaneously adopts the policy of *no* enhancements or modifications to the licensed system.

Every system is allocated a system ID or SID.

As we have noted in Chapter 4's section "SAP Ready-to-Run R/3 (RRR)," RRR is delivered with a preconfigured, two-system landscape in which the quality assurance also takes place in the development client. The predefined system IDs of the two systems are R3T (development system) and R3P (production system), respectively.

Client Deployment Strategy

A *client* is an organizationally independent unit within the R/3 system. Each client requires its own setup and maintenance effort, and, therefore, the setup of a system landscape necessitates a well-defined strategy.

Within a single R/3 system, every client is uniquely identified with a three-digit number. We are already familiar with the default standard Client 000 and the Client 066 meant for the EarlyWatch Service. Clients meant for the same purposes, but on different systems, should be identified by the same number in each system. This measure helps while transporting changes, in that changes from the source system are transported by default to the same client number in the target system.

Each client has its own data environment, which includes

- Customizing settings (global as well as client-specific)
- Repository objects
- Application data (master and transactional)
- User master records

Depending on the purpose, the clients could of the following types:

> Development client
> Testing client
> Quality assurance client
> Training client
> Production client
> Sandbox client
> Preproduction

SAP provides facilities for defining the attributes of a client to provide that client with desired properties, including change capabilities or restrictions on making changes.

Release Strategy

This task deals with upgrading the SAP R/3 system depending on the correction or functionality release upgrades of the R/3 system made available by SAP. ASAP primarily recommends deferring functionality releases to the post-implementation phase.

Transport System Strategy

This task establishes a mechanism for the release and transport of the customizations and changes from the development system on to the quality assurance system for verification and finally into the production system. This task primarily establishes the norms for the issue of change requests, import into the quality assurance system, import into the production system of only tested and signed-off objects from the QA system, and so forth.

Project Kick-Off

This task signals the formal initiation of the SAP project. The occasion should be graced by the presence of all the senior management, steering committee members, SAP project managers, SAP team members, SAP consultants, and partner representatives, as well as the change management team and members. This is the platform in which to elaborate the project charter, the implementation strategy, the project organization, and the overall project plan. It also presents the key roles, requisite skills, timeframes, and responsibilities of the various members of the team. The meeting should especially emphasize the change management goals and objectives. In the final analysis, it is basically a forum for get the immediate team motivated and excited about the successful completion of the SAP project in time and on budget.

This meeting also implies the corporatewide adaptation of the declared goals and objectives, defined strategies and plans, and established standards and procedures by not only the members of the SAP team, but also by the company as a whole. The kick-off meeting is followed by a team standards meeting to adopt all the relevant standards as well as to provide wide dissemination of the project-related details throughout the organization.

Infrastructure Requirements Planning

This task targets gathering company-specific data to define the requirements of the infrastructure, including size, and to benchmark the hardware and related infrastructure, as well as to procure the hardware, keeping in line with the overall timeframe of the project.

Define Infrastructure Requirements

The hardware and related infrastructure requirements are estimated by using the technical questionnaire in the Quick Sizer tool or by contracting SAP's Quick Sizing services.

Benchmark Hardware

The infrastructure must be benchmarked for different profiles of tasks at the following levels:

Desktops

Network

System (application and database servers)

Procure Initial Hardware

This task follows the review of the sizing of the hardware and deciding on the hardware configuration. The agreement with the hardware vendors must especially include a service level agreement for support during and after the project separately.

Order Remote Connection

This task also involves ordering for the remote connection to the nearest SAP servers in that part of the world. This connection acts as the lifeline for specific services provided by SAP at various stages of the project, such as OSS, GoingLive service, and EarlyWatch service. This lifeline might become extremely critical at times of unforeseen problems or emergencies.

Quality Check Project Preparation Phase

This is the final verification of the completion of all tasks involved with the Project Preparation phase.

The SAP recommended checklist for the Project Preparation phase is as follows:

1. Review project charter and verify completeness.
2. Verify that an implementation strategy has been chosen.
3. Ensure that the project team room has all components.
4. Verify that all needed team roles have been filled.
5. Review the project plan component for completeness.
6. Review the change management plan.
7. Review the project team training plan.
8. Validate that all project management standards and procedures are created.
9. Validate that all implementation standards and procedures are created.
10. Make sure the project kick-off has occurred, or is scheduled.
11. Verify that the system landscape strategy is agreed.
12. Validate that the initial system is installed and remote connection is ordered.

Signoff Project Preparation Phase

This task is concerned with obtaining the final signoff from the project management and approval to proceed to the next phase.

The signoff on the Project Preparation phase signals the end of the first phase of the ASAP methodology, which is also the preparatory phase of the SAP project.

Business Blueprint

IN THIS CHAPTER

The purpose of this phase is to primarily prepare the Business Blueprint document of the SAP implementation. The Business Blueprint documents the business process-related requirements of the company. The team members and consultants conduct interviews and workshops in different areas of activity to ascertain the requirements of various business processes. The functionality provided by the R/3 is demonstrated using the International Demo and Education System (IDES) and is supported by questionnaires and process diagrams from the R/3 Business Engineer; any gap in addressing functional requirements is identified and appropriate solutions are explored and devised.

NOTE

The importance of referring to the original AcceleratedSAP (ASAP) documentation CD-ROM cannot be overemphasized. What I have presented below are the essential details of the business blueprint phase of the ASAP methodology; however, this is not intended as a replacement for the colossal amount of instructive documentation, guidelines, checklists, templates, samples, and questionnaires provided and recommended by SAP. These are well-proven instruments, and for an actual project, it is highly recommended that the reader procure the version of ASAP corresponding to the version of their SAP installation and use it in conjunction with the progress of his or her implementation project.

Some of the material in this and following chapters might seem repetitious. However, on closer scrutiny you will note that activities like project management, organizational change management, risk assessment, sponsorship and communication strategies, skills development, and know-how are common throughout all the phases of the project, and are referred to in the beginning of each phase. Similarly, because many activities go through the stages of planning and execution, I refer to all such activities through their different stages during the various phases of the project. They are not being repeated; they are only part of the ASAP process checklist recommended by SAP.

The final outcome of this phase is the Business Blueprint document, which details the TO BE processes, including the written and pictorial representations of the company's structure and business processes. When this has been approved, the blueprint is taken as the basis for all subsequent phases.

This phase also deals with the other central issue addressed by the ASAP methodology for implementing SAP: the change management process. This is related to the organizational and human resources issues that influence the momentum of the R/3 implementation project. The objective of the change management process is to facilitate the timely implementation of SAP within the planned budget and resources.

Project Management of the Business Blueprint Phase

The project management task deals with managing and monitoring the business blueprint phase. Following the findings on the requirements of the new organizational structure and the business processes, you can identify where the changes in the relationship between the business processes and the organizational structure need to be managed. These serve as major factors in refining the implementation plan.

Review Project Preparation

This task deals with analyzing the potential risks that have been identified during the project preparation phase. This review project preparation drives the various tasks that are launched during this phase, such as the impact analysis, the assessment of baseline risks, the sponsorship strategy, the communications strategy, skills development, knowledge transfer, and the organizational optimization process.

Conduct Project Team Status Meetings

This task deals with ascertaining the status of the various project teams, such as the

- Business process team
- Change management team
- Technical team

These meetings help in collating all this information to form the overall status of the implementation project. Any negative variances observed with reference to the planned schedule are corrected by deciding the appropriate actions for the various teams. The action items are also followed up later. This has a direct bearing on the schedule, resources, and budget of the project, as well as the final go-live date. The project plan is updated and revised on an ongoing basis.

Conduct Steering Committee Meetings

This task deals with convening the steering committee to update the latest status of the project as well as to make quick decisions on project issues that cannot be handled at the project management level. These include

- Additional resources
- Changing the timeline
- Increasing the scope

In steering committee meetings, the decisions for resolving the various issues are recorded as well as the periodic follow-ups.

Preparing for the Business Blueprint Phase

This task deals with the building up of effective process design teams. It is also concerned with defining the end-user skills, roles, and responsibilities that are essential for the successful outcome of the various tasks and activities of this phase.

Organizational Change Management

Apart from the tasks related directly to the deliverables of the SAP project, ASAP puts a major focus on the change management issue related to the implementation of SAP. As discussed in Chapter 13's "Prepare Project Charter," SAP implementation has a fundamental and far-reaching effect on the organizational and human resources aspects of the company, although not in the conventional sense of a corporate-wide business process reengineering (BPR) effort.

This organizational change management task deals with a series of change processes that facilitates diagnosing and managing change issues in order to optimize the organizational processes for sustaining the momentum required by the ASAP methodology. To contain the attendant risks, ASAP has devised a full array of processes like impact analysis, the assessment of baseline risks, the sponsorship strategy, the communications strategy, skills development, knowledge transfer, and the organizational optimization process. We visit each of these aspects of the change management process next.

Create Business Impact Map

This task is the starting point of the change management process and its aim is to determine the potential impact of the envisaged SAP implementation. The business impact map helps greatly in assessing the scope, degree, and priority of the anticipated changes.

The business impact map is prepared based on the following inputs:

- The divisions and units expected to be impacted by the envisaged SAP implementation, and hence the planned change management process
- The perception of the senior personnel on the expected changes both within their own and other units
- The timing, magnitude, and relative importance of the various changes

Based on these inputs, the change team compiles a matrix of business units versus the degree of anticipated change. An effective and comprehensive change management strategy can be devised based on the critical areas highlighted by the resulting business impact map. This enables the change team to develop the organizational change management plan that is in tune with the overall SAP implementation plan and at the same time is aligned with the perceptions and concerns of the individual departments.

Complete the Baseline Risk Assessment

This task assesses the degree to which the company's environment facilitates or inhibits the rapid implementation of SAP. The results of the assessments provide the critical inputs to the change management process.

The risk assessment exercise is performed in three different contexts:

- Leadership
- Team
- Organization

In each of these cases, the change team first devises an appropriate tool that is administered to a select group of people. The findings are used to generate a risk profile that in turn leads to conducting assessment workshops. These workshops basically come up with recommendations that are used to shape the communications and sponsorship programs and other change processes. The risk assessment process identifies the key messages that should be disseminated throughout the organization and that are also suitably tailored to the conditions of the individual organizational units.

Develop Risk Assessment Tool

This tool gauges the initial support for the SAP implementation project. Furthermore, the assessment tool also reveals the factors that may adversely effect the control and management of the project.

SAP has provided detailed risk assessment tool guidelines, which should be referred to when developing a tool suitable to a particular company.

Administer the Risk Assessment Tool

The results of this exercise enable the change team to identify the risks associated with the envisaged changes, the potential implications of these risks, and possible remedial actions.

While administering the organization risk assessments, the change team focuses on the following three groups in the same chronological order:

- Those whose jobs and responsibilities will be changed appreciably during the implementation
- Those whose jobs and responsibilities will change appreciably as a result of the implementation

- Those whose jobs and responsibilities are affected by the work done by the other two groups

Create a Risk Profile

This is the overall risk profile at the levels where the risk assessment exercise is carried out: the leadership, team, and organization levels (see Chapter 10's "Risk Management in a SAP Project)."

Conduct Risk Workshop

This subtask primarily acts as the incubator for devising strategies that can counter the adverse effects of the risks identified earlier. It also leads to identifying responsibilities and timeframes for the envisaged measures.

Implement Results of the Risk Workshop

The identified measures for risk mitigation are implemented and the results are monitored for their effectiveness.

It must be noted that the risk assessment process is not a one-time exercise, but an ongoing one. Periodic assessments will need to be performed during the implementation and after the implementation for effective risk mitigation.

Develop a Sponsorship Strategy

The project leadership is the most critical element of a comprehensive change program. There is a need to assess the positive and the negative factors inherent in the leadership itself that can directly accelerate or undermine the momentum of the implementation project. The baseline leadership risk assessment is essential to the sponsorship process. The *sponsor point* is a senior executive champion of change who by his or her actions and communications helps in maintaining project credibility, momentum, and committed support throughout the company.

The leadership risk assessment tool enables the change team to do the following:

- Get a measure of the risks associated with the envisaged SAP implementation.
- Uncover the potential implication of these risks on the SAP project.
- Identify the actions for mitigating these risks to acceptable levels.

The change management team needs to work closely with the project and site sponsors as well as the communication point person to consistently address the key negatives and reinforce the potential benefits of implementing SAP. Periodic administration of the risk assessment process, described earlier, helps in ascertaining the effectiveness of the sponsorship process. Any perceived deviation towards increasing the risks should be countered immediately by specifically targeted communications and credible actions.

A consistent message on the organization's demonstrative commitment and focus to see the R/3 implementation through to a favorable end is a powerful means of sustaining the right context for achieving the successful completion of the project.

Establish the Communications Framework

This task handles the design of the framework for sharing project-related information and statuses throughout the organization. While doing so, it incorporates the results of the latest risk assessment processes to address the members' genuine concerns and apprehensions about the SAP implementation and its perceived impact at the organizational and individual levels. This could come about through direct communication via formal channels like project and site sponsors or indirectly through the active involvement and participation of company members during project-related events, risk assessment processes, or focus group sessions.

This involves identifying the communication point person, who works closely with both the change management team and the key site sponsors to fine-tune the message and its medium, depending on the audience, the criticality of the stage, and the status of the SAP project effort. It is important to ensure that the messages are also customized to the different sites in order to discuss how SAP would change jobs, skills, roles, responsibilities, and standards. Tailoring communications on an organizational unit level also provides the opportunity to enlist the support of the unit-level management or even the line management.

This task also includes ascertaining the effectiveness of the communications strategy through

- Informal feedback from focus groups and/or "opinion leaders" or "thought leaders"
- Formal feedback through the periodic risk assessment processes, wherein specific questions regarding the project communications process can be presented

Establish the Skills Development Process

This task is concerned with forming the skills development team, identifying the important constituencies of the SAP project effort, compiling the skills inventory, analyzing the gaps in skills, assessing the training needs, and arranging for the content and logistics of the skills development training program. The various constituencies are all members of the SAP core and the extended team, including senior executives, project and site-level sponsors, project team members, SAP consultants, site-level executives, managers, supervisors, and workers.

The type of training required for the various constituencies is as follows:

- SAP implementation project impact training
- Business process-related training
- Technical and functional training in SAP

- SAP skills training

The skills development team would decide on the following:

- Content, such as the prototype, IDES, tutorial, workshop, case study, R/3 testing, or Quality Assurance (QA) client.
- The delivery mechanism for the different kinds of skills training, such as instructor-led or CBTs (Computer-Based Training programs).
- The delivery system for imparting this training like SAP training partners

The skills development team must also set the procedures for assessing the effectiveness of the training given to members covering their identified roles in the SAP project.

Implement the Know-how Transfer Process

I have spoken about the tacit (or implicit) and explicit knowledge in Chapter 1's "Knowledge as the New Capital" and how SAP acts as a medium for converting the tacit knowledge of a company into a valuable resource. Further, in Chapter 1's "Information as the New Resource," I also discussed how information acts as a tangible resource that drives the operational processes faster without expending more conventional resources. ASAP does for the SAP implementation process exactly what productive SAP R/3 does for the company as a whole: it uses all of this relevant information to drive the very process of SAP implementation itself faster.

Implementing the know-how transfer process is related to the achievement of the following objectives:

- Converting and codifying the tacit knowledge scattered across the organization into a coherent and integrated body of knowledge for driving the accelerated implementation of SAP within the organization.
- Preventing history from repeating itself in the case of problems occurring during a SAP implementation by codifying and disseminating the knowledge generated during a SAP implementation to all the concerned stakeholders. It can also be useful for other organizations to benefit from the experience and expertise gained from past implementations.

The valuable experience and insights gained by all members of the SAP team should not be lost to other members in the company. All this know-how is an asset and the organization needs to capitalize on the same. The ASAP know-how transfer process taps the information and experience found both outside and inside the organization. It builds and leverages on the knowledge base that accelerates the SAP implementation by helping the SAP project team and the extended team make correct decisions and enact them quickly.

ASAP defines the know-how transfer process to consist of the following aspects:

- **Knowledge drivers,** which relate to the research, collection, authentication, rationalization, standardization, and benchmarking of the information, know-how, and technology

- **Knowledge delivery** process, which relates to the storing, presentation, sharing, and application of the project knowledge

The know-how transfer process is administered and managed by the change team.

Project Team Training

The purpose of this task is to plan and conduct training for the SAP team members. This enables them to combine the business process requirements of the company and the R/3 functionality in order to prepare the Business Blueprint document. These are primarily Level 1 and Level 2 courses.

SAP now also allows its clients to attend the five-week Partner Academy courses that provide in-depth instruction in one topic area, either FI, CO, SD, MM, PP, HR, ABAP, or Basis.

Establish Development System Environment

The objective of this task is to install and configure the sandbox client and development system.

Create Technical Design

SAP recommends the documentation of the technical infrastructure using its template, *IT Infrastructure Document.* This task involves the following:

- Prepare system layout and distribution

- Prepare print infrastructure

- Prepare network topology

- Prepare interface topology

- Prepare change request management

- Prepare release management strategy

- Prepare desktop management strategy

Set up Development Environment

The objective of this task is to use the technical design to set up the development and sandbox client system. This involves

- Installing the initial hardware

- Prepare the initial system landscape

- Configure and test the transport system

- Install desktop components for project members
- Prepare user master records and secure the system
- Install the initial printing services
- Set up a remote connection to SAP

Maintain the System Administration System

This task deals with defining, testing, and establishing the system administration procedures for the development system. It involves the following:

- Conduct Basis and the system administration workshop
- Define the system administration for the development system
- Configure the CCMS based on the earlier definition
- Define the backup strategy

Initialize the IMG

The purpose of this task is to create the IMG. The IMG has been discussed in Chapter 12's section "Implementation Guide (IMG)."

The Reference IMG is used as a reference at the later stages of the business process definition.

Create the Enterprise IMG

Select allEnterprise IMGs application components of interest and generate the Enterprise IMG. It should be noted that by selecting a component, all hierarchy levels lower than this selected level also get selected automatically. However, if the company intends to use the ASAP IMG link, all functions, that is, components of the Enterprise IMG, should be selected for generation of the Enterprise IMG.

The Enterprise Process Area Scope document can be produced from the Questions and Answers database (Q&Adb) (see Figures 14.1 and 14.2).

Create Project Header and Generate the Project IMG

Broadly speaking, there should be as many Project IMGs as the number of go-live dates. In other words, the Project IMG provides a specific set of configuration activities for components that go live at the same time. A Project IMG should be created by furnishing all relevant details like project name, person responsible, start and end data, and so on. It helps in planning and controlling the business blueprint-related tasks.

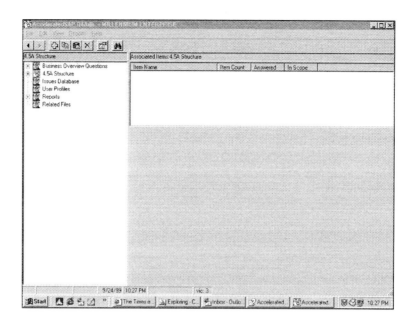

FIGURE 14.1

Main screen of the AcceleratedSAP questions and answers database (Q&Adb).

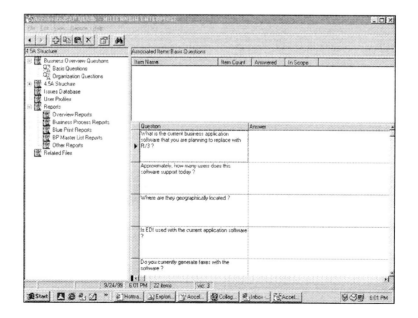

FIGURE 14.2

Recording basic information regarding the company.

The possible values for status keys used for IMG administrative purposes are as follows:

- In process
- Completed
- Quality check done
- Review planned
- Not relevant
- Out of scope

A Project IMG can be created in two ways:

- The traditional manual generation of the Project IMG.
- The recently introduced automatic generation of the Project IMG from ASAP. This new facility transfers the scope settings within an ASAP Q&Adb automatically into one corresponding Project IMG.

If the ASAP methodology is used completely, the second approach is highly recommended.

Define the Business Organization Structure

Defining the business organization structure deals with the concept of the organization's structure, as defined in SAP using SAP organizational units like the client, company code, controlling area, business area, purchasing organization, sales organization, and so on. This structure defined in SAP structures the processes of the financial and logistics areas of SAP and, consequently, of the human resources area within SAP.

This task produces the business organizational structure of the company within SAP, based on R/3 system organization rules. ASAP provides the Structure Modeler documentation and a corresponding Visio template to help a company in completing this task. Defining the business organization structure is accomplished by arranging a workshop involving the project sponsor, the SAP project manager, the business process team leader, and key team members. The workshop might have separate sessions for financial and logistics processes, followed by a session integrating the findings and conclusions of the individual sessions.

ASAP provides an organization structure questionnaire that is used as a basic input for the workshop. The questions related to the organizational structure are available in the Q&Adb under "Business Overview Questions" (see Figures 14.2 and 14.3) and under each process area of the company. Additional related information is available under "Enterprise Modeling Consultant's Handbook" on the SAP R/3 Online Documentation CD-ROM.

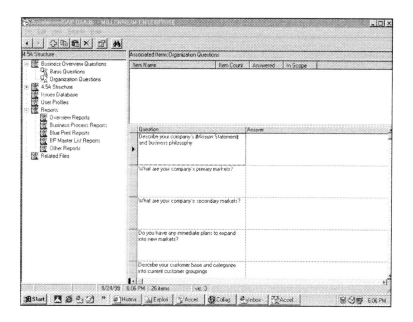

Figure 14.3

Recording responses to organization-related questions about the company.

The workshop achieves the following:

- Helps identify the existing business organizational structure, including the major business processes and reporting structures by using the business impact map.

- Clarifies organization structures in SAP.

- Maps the company's organizational structure requirements, including future requirements, in terms of organizational elements provided in SAP, as shown in Figure 14.4.

- Performs a cost-benefit analysis and gap analysis of the newly defined organizational structure in SAP.

- Iterates and fine-tunes the SAP organizational structure.

- Documents the SAP organizational structure.

As a final step, the company approves and accepts the proposed organizational structure across the company.

14

BUSINESS BLUEPRINT

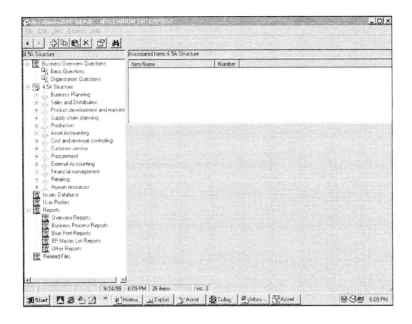

FIGURE **14.4**

Recording the organizational structure of the company.

Business Process Definition

After defining the organization structure comes the task of defining the company's business processes with reference to the business processes supported by SAP. This significant input goes on to the creation of the Business Blueprint document. In the following subsections, I discuss the various subtasks of this important step.

Prepare for Business Process Workshops

In preparing for the workshop, the following prerequisites must be completed:

- Confirm that the business processes are within the project's scope.
- Determine the business process owners within the team as well as identify the power users from the respective operational areas.
- Update the Q&Adb using the latest version of the enterprise process scope document.
- Schedule the participation of the power-users.

It is also important to assign the business process owners to particular business process areas and the corresponding areas within the Q&Adb.

Conduct General Requirements Workshop

This task deals primarily with the global parameters and standards that have enterprisewide applicability, which is a significant factor for a company that has worldwide operations.

In the IMG, this is relevant to the global settings:

- Chart of accounts
- Enterprise organizational structure, discussed earlier
- Balance sheet and profitability analyses
- Central and local master data maintenance
- Countries
- Currencies
- Units of measurement
- Calendar maintenance
- Document number ranges

Conduct Business Process Workshops

Here you are responsible for conducting workshops for gathering business process requirements with all the related requirements, as discussed below. The information gathered here eventually becomes the Business Blueprint document.

Determine Business Process Requirements

This task is conducted using

- An enterprise process area scope document
- The Q&Adb
- Customer Input (CI) template forms

ASAP provides a business process questionnaire that is used as basic input for the workshop. The questions related to the organizational structure are available in the Q&Adb under "Business Process Questions," shown in Figure 14.5.

This questionnaire is followed by details on business processes by answering the CI template questions that consist of 15 generic questions on each of the processes (see Figure 14.6). The topics covered are as follows:

- Requirement expectations
- General expectations
- Explanation of functions and events

- Special organizational considerations
- Business model
- Changes to the existing organization
- Descriptions of improvements
- Descriptions of functional deficits
- Approaches to covering deficits
- Notes on further improvements
- System configuration considerations
- Interface considerations
- File conversion considerations
- Reporting considerations
- Authorization considerations

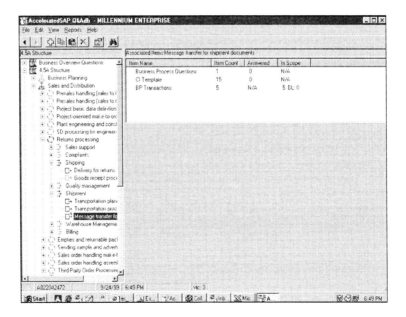

FIGURE **14.5**

Business process questions.

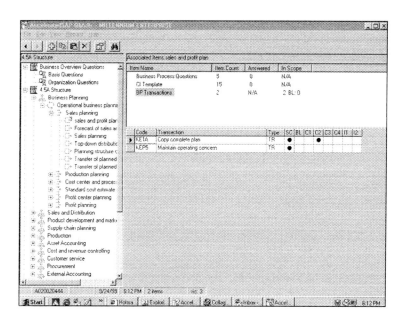

FIGURE 14.6

Business process transaction-related questions.

Determine Reporting Requirements

SAP provides thousands of standard delivered reports. Many of the reports delivered in the system are flexible enough to replace multiple existing legacy system reports in one SAP report. Any requirement for reports should be confirmed for its availability within the system through the general reporting tree. For reports that are not available within the system, SAP provides a *report specification form*. SAP provides many options for catering to non-standard reporting requirements including Report Writer/Report Painter, ABAP Query, ABAP Reporting, and so on.

Determine Required Interfaces

The aim of this subtask is to identify the utilization of special functionalities and facilities provided by the SAP system like Internet Application Components (IACs), SAP Workflow, SAP Business Warehouse, Application Link Enabling (ALE), and so forth. These functionalities cannot be used in the initial implementation phase.

Determine Conversion Requirements

Here you gather information on the volume and frequency of data, requirements for validating data, source table structures, and mapping data into relevant SAP tables.

Determine Enhancement Requirements

This deals with deficiencies that can be remedied by modifications or enhancements to the SAP system. SAP provides for the preparation of a modification approval form. This subtask also identifies if the enhancement can be achieved via a user exit, future release, or an interface to a third-party product.

Determine Gap Areas

This subtask identifies any gaps in functionality delivered by the current version of SAP.

Revise Business Process Descriptions and Models

Any changes to a business process arising due to SAP's approach to the implementation of the business process should be documented here. This task also integrates all of the information gathered during the workshops and reviews all aspects of the requirements from this macro view for locating inconsistencies, gaps, or even solutions for earlier defined gaps.

Conduct Detailed Process Workshops

These workshops are conducted to complete the following tasks:

- Clarify requirements using business process (BP) and CI information.
- Clarify and analyze the SAP business process implementations to determine, for example, a more efficient or flexible version of the same process.
- Research deficient areas and gaps for possible solutions.
- Revise business process requirements in terms of processing optimizations, authorization requirements, and so on.

Prepare Business Blueprint

The Business Blueprint document details the business process requirements and serves as the reference document for subsequent customization and development activities.

As a part of preparing the Business Blueprint, the following subtasks are also performed.

Perform Organizational Optimization Analysis

Here you fine-tune the organizational relationships and coordinations resulting from the information gathered in the detailed process workshops. This information is used further to update and prepare the latest

- Business impact maps
- Process impact maps

Revise Project Organization and Roles

This task deals with refining the project organization roles in light of the information gathered for the Business Blueprint. This information is fed to the change management process. It is also a useful input in the preparation of the

- Training plan
- Authorization profiles

Compile the Business Blueprint

This task involves consolidation of all the compiled Q&Adbs into a central database and generating the Business Blueprint.

The Business Blueprint should consist of the following:

- Executive summary
- Enterprise process area scope document
- Organization structure
- Completed business processes questionnaires and CI templates
- Justifications for enhancements, conversions, and interfaces
- Completed technical questionnaire

On business processes, the Business Blueprint includes the CI input based on the 15 generic questions referred to earlier.

Business Process Master List (BPML)

The objective of this task is to identify the detailed scope that should be implemented during the realization phase. The Business Process Master List (BPML) is the R/3 system representation of the total scope of the implementation project. The configuration effort is divided into two parts: baseline and final configuration (see Figures 14.7 and 14.8).

ASAP recommends that the baseline scope should cover about 80 percent of the company's requirements (see Figures 14.9, 14.10, and 14.11). It should include those scenarios, processes, and functions that are priority requirements of the company. All scenarios and business processes that are not included in the baseline scope are handled during the final configuration. To make the final configuration effort easier, ASAP recommends the formation of a series of configuration cycles consisting of a selected set of business processes, depending on their importance.

14

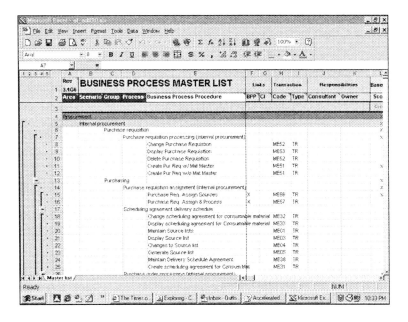

FIGURE 14.7

Preparing the business process master list.

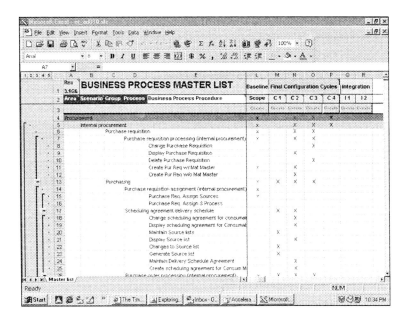

FIGURE 14.8

Additional information captured on the business process master list.

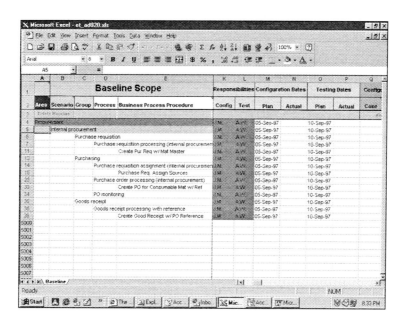

FIGURE **14.9**
Schedule information captured on the baseline scope document.

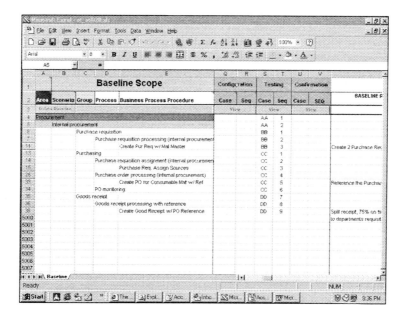

14

BUSINESS
BLUEPRINT

FIGURE **14.10**
Testing-related information captured on the baseline scope document.

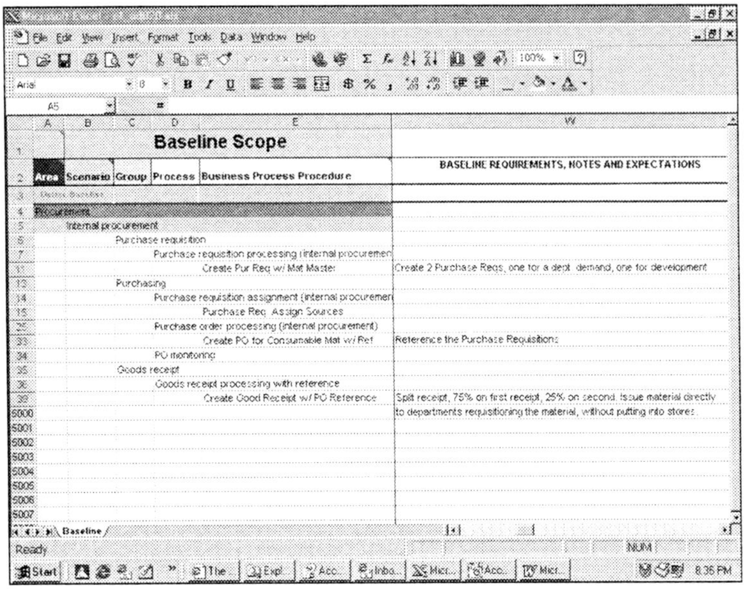

FIGURE 14.11

Additional information captured on the baseline scope document.

In the Q&Adb, when selecting the business process transactions for any business process, the associated transactions for this particular process are displayed. One or more of the eight columns displayed are selected to indicate that they should be included in the configuring and integration cycles used during the realization phase. The eight column indicators are (refer to Figure 14.6 and Figure 14.8 earlier)

- SC - In scope
- BL - Included in the baseline configuration
- C1 – Included in Configuration Cycle 1
- C2 – Included in Configuration Cycle 2
- C3 – Included in Configuration Cycle 3
- C4 – Included in Configuration Cycle 4
- L1 – Included in Integration Cycle 1
- L2 – Included in Integration Cycle 2

To generate the BPML, go to the Q&Adb, find *Report*, select *BP Master List*, and then choose *Generate*. In the BPML, the Links column provides access to the CI template for that process as well as to the corresponding Business Process Procedure (BPP) documents. The BPML also contains information collected from each of the BP transactions described above, or it can be entered in the BPML itself.

Review and Approve the Business Blueprint

This task requires a final review of the Business Blueprint that includes

- Reviewing the enterprise process area scope document
- Reviewing the Business Blueprint
- Reviewing baseline scope

NOTE

In ASAP, this task is the second important milestone of the project.

The project manager, business process owners, and the steering committee finally approve the Business Blueprint.

Prepare End-User Training and Documentation Plans

The objective of this task is to prepare end-user training and documentation plans based on input from the Business Blueprint. These plans act as a reference for any future changes that the project decisions have on the schedule of the user training and documentation effort.

These plans include:

- End-user analysis, that is, the number of end users and their job functions
- The type of end-user documentation and training materials
- Preparation of end-user documentation and training materials
- Resources required
- Training schedule

The system and end-user documentation is based on the BPP documents. Around 700 such documents are predefined and made available by SAP. The customer can tailor these BPP documents to meet their own specific requirements, expanding on the business process descriptions and adding system screen prints. The list of BPP procedures available in ASAP is as follows:

- Enterprise planning
- Sales

- Product development and marketing
- Supply-chain planning
- Production
- Asset management
- Human resources
- Revenue and cost controlling
- Customer service
- Procurement
- External accounting
- Finance management
- Retailing
- ALE distribution model

Quality Check Business Blueprint Phase

This is the final verification of the completion of the project's business blueprint phase. The SAP-recommended checklist for the business blueprint phase is as follows:

1. Validate that the project team status and steering committee meetings(s) have occurred.
2. Confirm that successful project team training has been accomplished.
3. Verify that a team building activity has taken place.
4. Ensure that user roles and responsibilities are defined.
5. Confirm the development of a technical design.
6. Validate the setup of the development environment and development environment system landscape.
7. Verify that the proper systems administration functions have been set up.
8. Validate the IMG initialization.
9. Validate the completion and sign off the business blueprint and baseline scope.

The business blueprint phase ensures that everyone has an accurate understanding of the final scope regarding organizational structure, business processes, and the technical system environment.

Signing off the Business Blueprint Phase

At this final stage, you are concerned with obtaining the final signoff from the project management and the approval to proceed to the next phase. It is extremely important to get project management signoff before proceeding to the next phase. The Business Blueprint phase contains the basic building blocks of the SAP implementation and it is important to have a common understanding of the scope and direction of the project before continuing with the next phase of the project.

Signing off the business blueprint phase signals the end of the second phase of the ASAP methodology that is also the conceptual design phase of the SAP project.

Realization

IN THIS CHAPTER

The goal of this phase is to configure the baseline system using the Business Blueprint document. For this, the business processes are divided into cycles of related business processes, and the SAP team undergoes Level 3 training. The baseline system prepared here is the basis for the production system. The system is presented to a team of power-users who also undergo requisite training in their respective areas of operations. The baseline system is fine-tuned by the validation of the power-users by employing an iterative approach.

> **NOTE**
>
> The importance of referring to SAP's original Accelerated SAP (ASAP) documentation CD-ROM cannot be overemphasized. What I have presented below are the essential details of the realization phase of the ASAP methodology; however, this is not intended as a replacement for the colossal amount of instructive documentation, guidelines, checklists, templates, samples, and questionnaires provided and recommended by SAP. These are well-proven instruments, and for an actual project, it is highly recommended that the reader procure the version of ASAP corresponding to their SAP installation's version and use it in conjunction with the progress of the implementation project.
>
> Some of the material in this and the following chapters might seem repetitious. However, on closer scrutiny you will note that activities like project management, organizational change management, risk assessment, sponsorship and communication strategy, skills development and know-how transfers process and so on are common throughout all the phases of the project, and are referred to in the beginning of each phase. Similarly, because many activities go through the stages of planning and execution, I refer to all such activities through their different stages during the various phases of the project. They are not being repeated; they are only part of the ASAP process checklist recommended by SAP.

In parallel, the technical team sets up the system administration and plans interfaces and data transfers. The interfaces, conversion programs, enhancements, reports, end-user documentation, testing scenarios, and user security profiles are defined and tested. The final integration test is also conducted. The final deliverable is a fully configured and tested SAP system that meets the company's requirements.

Project Management Realization Phase

The project management task is similar to the other phases in that it deals with managing and monitoring the realization phase. Using the study on the requirements of the new organizational structure and the business processes enables you to identify where the changes in the relationship between the business processes and the organizational structure need to be managed. This study acts as a major factor in refining the implementation plan.

Review Business Blueprint

This task deals with analyzing the potential risks that have been identified during the project preparation phase. This analysis drives the various initiatives that are continued during the realization phase, such as the organizational change management process based on the periodic risk assessment at the team and organizational levels.

The purpose of this task is to ascertain the progress of the implementation towards its final goal. The review covers issues like

- Project management
- Technical project management
- Information technology (IT) infrastructure
- Change management process
- Member commitment

Conduct Project Team Status Meetings

This task deals with ascertaining the status of the various project teams:

- Business process team
- Change management team
- Technical team

This helps in collating all this information to form the overall status of the implementation project. Any negative variances observed with reference to the planned schedule are corrected by deciding the appropriate action for the various teams. The action items are also followed up later. This has a direct bearing on the schedule, resource, and budgets of the project as well as the final go-live date. The project plan is updated and refined on an ongoing basis.

Conduct Steering Committee Meetings

This task deals with convening the steering committee meetings for updating the latest status of the project and obtaining quick decisions on project issues that cannot be handled at the project management level, including

- Additional resources
- Changing the timeline
- Increasing the project's scope

Here actions to resolve the various issues are recorded as well as periodic follow-ups on the same.

Initial Planning for Production Support and Cutover

ASAP recommends that the company should plan early for the post-implementation phase. The cutover planning subtask ensures that all preparatory activities leading to the cutover are completed in a proper sequence with the right resources and people. This includes plans for the following:

- Setting up and initializing the production environment
- The data conversion effort and schedule
- Organizing the cutover team
- Shutting down the legacy systems that are being replaced with SAP
- A contingency plan to revert back to the legacy system in case of problems
- Testing the operation of the new system
- A checklist of all activities leading to the cutover

The production support planning subtask addresses the requirements of the support environment after the go-live phase. It includes plans for the following:

- Finalizing the technical configuration
- Procuring hardware
- Determining the go-live production team
- Determining the regular production support team
- Defining the help desk procedures and facilities
- Staffing the help desk
- Staffing the production support team
- Creating the disaster recovery plan, procedures, and facilities

Conduct Team-Building Activities

The objective of this task is to arrange events and activities that help in building team spirit. These measures help in making the team more cohesive, motivated, and able to work in tandem with other teams and members towards the achievement of project milestones and the final goal of completing the project successfully.

The project management could arrange for any of these several events:

- Team lunches or dinners
- Small gifts

- Celebrations
- Outings
- Project newsletter

Preparing for the Realization Phase

The objective of this task is to review the plan for the realization phase and anticipate any risks that would hinder the achievement of the objective of this phase. This serves as input to the ongoing change management process.

Sustaining the Organization Change Management Process

As you have seen in the last chapter, this tasks deals with a series of processes that help the change team diagnose and manage change issues to optimize the organizational processes for sustaining the momentum required by the ASAP methodology to the end of the project. In order to contain the attendant risks, ASAP advises continuing with the full array of processes, such as risk assessment, the sponsorship strategy, the communications strategy, skill development, knowledge transfer, and the organizational optimization process. Sustaining the organization change management process enables the change team to manage organizational risks, accelerate the R/3 implementation, and optimize the organizational processes.

Periodic Risk Assessments and Workshops

Every couple of months, this task assesses the degree to which the company's operational environment facilitates or inhibits the rapid implementation of SAP on an ongoing basis. The results of the assessments provide the critical inputs to the change management process.

The risk assessment exercise is performed in three different contexts:

- Leadership
- Team
- Organization

In each of these cases, the change team first devises an appropriate tool that is administered to a select group of people. The findings are used to generate a risk profile that in turn leads to conducting assessment workshops, which basically come up with recommendations that are used to shape the communications and sponsorship programs and other change processes. The risk assessment process identifies the key messages that should be disseminated throughout the organization and that are also tailored to the conditions of the individual organizational units.

It is important to document the type and degree of the risks covered by the ongoing risk assessment workshops, because these directly reflect of the pace and progress of the project. Moreover, these records can also be used as testimony to the effectiveness of the change management measures taken previously and enable suitable alterations to the actions planned for the future.

Create and Provide Feedback to the Line Managers

The feedback report to the line managers can include key actions, milestones, deliverables, and so on.

Conduct Risk Management Meetings with Key Constituencies

This subtask is concerned with updating the members of the team and the extended team on the latest status and findings of the risk assessment workshops. The data gathered and analysis is also shared to ensure that the concerned team members are appraised of the latest trends as they manage their process areas.

Deliver Key Project Communications

Risk assessment results are used to modify key project communications to maintain their relevance to the changing circumstances as the project progresses through the remaining phases.

Manage the Ongoing Project Sponsorship Process

The purpose of this subtask is to sustain the effectiveness of the sponsorship process initiated in the business blueprint phase.

Manage the Ongoing Skills Development Process

This subtask sustains the momentum of the skills development process initiated during the business blueprint phase.

Manage the Knowledge-Transfer Team and Process

The knowledge-transfer team continues to support the change management process during the realization phase.

Renewal of the Change Management Team

This subtask ensures that new members inducted into the team get familiarized with the creation and administration of the assessment tools. They should also become acquainted with the change management process history of the project.

Conduct Project Team Training

The purpose of this task is to plan and conduct training for the SAP team members. This enables them to configure and test the business process documented in the Business Blueprint. These are primarily Level 3 courses.

System Management

The purpose of this task is to prepare the system environment for production. This includes establishing the infrastructure requirements, the performance levels, the system administration activities, and finally setting up the production environment.

Establish Level Commitments

This task determines the service-level commitments that are essential for the development system and achieves those commitments.

Determine Failure Scenarios

The aim of this task is to determine the scenarios that could partially or completely disrupt the operations of the R/3 system, such as

- Hardware failure scenarios
- Network failure scenarios
- Desktop failure scenarios
- Application server failure scenarios
- Database server failure scenarios
- R/3 transport failure scenarios
- Security failure scenarios
- Computer center security failure scenarios

Using these scenarios, corrective measures can be drawn up that minimize the impact of these failures or prevent them altogether. In the case of an actual failure, these measures should also include procedures for reporting, managing, and escalation.

Establish Disaster Recovery Procedures

This task establishes the disaster recovery procedures, which are based on a detailed analysis of the downtime scenarios that can be tolerated by the various applications for quickly being able to transition back to regular operations. It also helps in anticipating disaster risks, so plan to cover them as far as possible through maintenance- and service-level commitments with concerned vendors.

The disaster recovery procedures involves the following:

- Analysis of downtime tolerance
- Disaster recovery procedure scripts
- Service- and maintenance-level vendor agreements
- Escalation procedures and communication paths
- Transitional operations
- Restart procedures
- Disaster recovery success criteria
- Transition to regular operations

Establish Commitment on Service Levels

Here you establish quantifiable and measurable service-level criteria from the various vendors, including those that are mutually dependent on each other. This includes not only vendors of hardware, operating system (OS), network, and peripherals, but also SAP.

Develop System Test Plans

The purpose of this task is to define the test plans for the final preparation phase. The included tests are discussed in the following subsections.

Develop Failure Test Plan

This subtask develops a test plan for the simulating component failure in order to assess the impact, dependencies, expected results, troubleshooting, error-fixing procedures, training, and so on.

Develop Volume Test Plan

This subtask develops a volume test plan for the final integration test. The qualification of this test ensures requisite throughput and performances for entering, querying, or reporting critical business transactions.

Develop Stress Test Plan

This subtask primarily addresses the system's load-bearing capability to handle increases in the number of the users. This task plans for the stress test parameters, backup, support, the monitoring of results, and enforcing recommended reconfigurations or upgrades to the system configuration.

Develop a System Administration Test Plan

This subtask simulates the daily system administration activities to ascertain their adequacy and completeness.

Develop a Printer Test Plan

This subtask confirms the correctness and performance of time-critical printing, restart procedures, switches between alternate printers, high-volume printing, and so on.

Establish System Administration Functions

This task aims at verifying the use of system administration tools and utilities provided in SAP.

Establish Client Copy Procedures

This deals with using the client copy utilities, including reversing client copies.

Establish Daily Check Procedures

This task ensures familiarity with daily checks, including

- The system log
- The spool management system
- Job scheduling
- Dump analysis
- Computer Center Management System (CCMS) monitors, their settings, and testing
- Trace setting and analysis

Establish Transport Procedures

The purpose of this task is to ascertain the functions of the transport system, such as the following:

- The release of change requests
- Imports into Quality Assurance (QA) and production systems
- Code freezes and QA-testing procedures
- QA and production sign-off procedures

Establish Backup and Recovery Procedures

This involves testing the database backup and recovery procedures by backing up database and log files, restoring them, and verifying the correctness of recovery.

Set Up the Quality Assurance (QA) System Environment

The QA system is used for the final integration tests. The purpose of this activity is to install and configure the QA system.

Install Hardware

This subtask deals with the installation of hardware, operating system (O/S), and so on that meets the requirements of the current R/3 release, including obtaining the Online Service System (OSS) connection.

Install a QA System

The purpose of this subtask is to install R/3 and follow these steps:

- Start the R3SETUP program.
- Install the central instance.
- Perform the database installation.
- Install the presentation server software on the application servers and on the central instance.
- Review the R3SETUP.log for any reported problems.
- Verify everything by installing and using SAP graphic user interface (SAPGUI) and online documentation.

Set Up Master Records

This task deals with setting up user master records and profiles for enabling the QA system users to carry out testing-related activities. Consequently, the access profiles in the QA system are a subset of what is available in the development DEV (Development) system.

Secure the QA System

This primarily concerns securing access to the OS and database in order to prevent accidental or intentional changes to the QA environment. This access is only available for a restricted number of technical members through a well-defined procedure for obtaining such access.

Set Up the Printing System

This task installs, configures, and tests the printers used by the project team.

Set Up the Client Management and Transport Systems

The purpose of this task is to install and configure the system clients, including client roles, cross-clients, and automatic transports.

Establish the Production System Management

The purpose of this task is to define and document the system administration tasks for the production system. These include the roles and responsibilities for the following tasks:

- Establishing the production system security procedures
- Establishing the production operating procedures
- Establishing the production system administration procedures
- Establishing the production system printer environment
- Establishing the production database administration procedures
- Preparing the SAP system operation manual

Set Up the Production Environment

The purpose of this activity is to install and configure the system that will be used subsequently for the production environment. Refer to the SAP Advanced Installation Guide for installing R/3. The constituent subtasks are as follows:

- Install the production hardware
- Install the production system
- Install and configure the network environment
- Install and configure the desktop hardware and components
- Secure the OS and Database
- Set Up the printing system

Baseline Configuration and Confirmation

The Business Process Master List (BPML) is the R/3 system representation of the total scope of the implementation project. The configuration effort is divided into two parts: the baseline and final configurations.

This configuration task relates to the configuration and confirmation of the settings for the baseline scope. The baseline scope includes those scenarios, processes, and functions that are priority requirements of the company. The remaining 20 percent of the scenarios and processes are considered during the final configuration and confirmation.

ASAP recommends that a company should initially consider processes for the baseline configuration that can be configured without modifying the system. This involves the following subtasks:

Revise the Baseline Scope Document

Revise the baseline scope document prepared during the business blueprint phase.

Create the Baseline Configuration Plan

The baseline configuration plan for the baseline is created by doing the following:

1. Choose the BPML and select the baseline worksheet.
2. Add global settings to the beginning of the BPML.
3. Add configuration tasks to the organizational structure after the global settings.
4. Enter the planned schedule date in the Plan subcolumn within Configuration.
5. Add sequencing information for dependent processes; this can be done by entering a case number and a sequence number to a group of related processes in the subcolumns of Configuration: Case and Sequence No.

   Note that clicking the View cell under the Configuration column sorts the processes in the order of case number/sequence number.

6. Save this information as the Baseline Configuration Plan document in the MS Excel workbook.

Create Test Cases

Create test cases by doing the following:

1. Choose the Baseline Configuration Plan document and select the Baseline worksheet modified above.
2. This includes the default test cases you can adopt for the project.
3. Set up the test and sequencing information for dependent processes; this can be done by entering a case number and a sequence number to a group of related processes in the subcolumns of Testing: Case and Sequence No.
4. Add testing information to the baseline requirements, notes, and expectations.
5. For more detailed information on test procedures, select Test Procedure and add details.
6. Save your work.

Create a Test Plan

Create a test plan for the baseline configuration by doing the following:

1. Choose the Baseline Configuration Plan document and select the Baseline worksheet, modified by step 3 above.
2. Enter the planned schedule date in the Plan subcolumn within Testing.
3. Save your work.

Allocate Resources

Allocate the resources for the baseline configuration and test them by doing the following:

1. Choose the Baseline Configuration Plan document and select the baseline worksheet modified earlier.

2. Determine the skills set needed, confirm its availability, and allocate responsibility to process owners, team members, and power users.

3. Enter the initials of the team member in the subcolumns of Responsibilities: Configuration and Testing.

4. Save your work.

Approve the Baseline Configuration Plan Document by the Process Owners

Here the IMG is modified to record the information on the resources and assignments. This can be done either manually in the IMG or automatically in case the company is using the ASAP IMG link (see Chapter 14's "Initialize IMG").

Configure the Initial Settings and Organizational Structure

This task refers to the configuration of the global settings and organizational structure that is a prerequisite of the baseline and final configuration.

Configure the Global Settings

This corresponds to the information that was gathered during the general requirements workshop of the business blueprint phase (see Chapter 14's "Conduct General Requirements Workshop"). This includes parameters like countries, currencies, units of measurement, calendars, and so forth.

In the IMG, update the status information for each configuration task and enter the documentation using IMG Notes. Similarly, also update the Baseline Configuration Plan document with the configuration's actual date and status.

Configure Organizational Structure

This step corresponds to the decisions taken and the documentation prepared during the business organization structure task of the business blueprint phase (see Chapter 14, "Define Business Organization Structure").

15

Create and configure the organizational units by reference or by using the copy facility. Also update the information and documentation for this activity in the IMG as well as in the Baseline Configuration Plan document.

Configure the Predefined Settings

If the company is using the predefined configured system (PCS), use the predefined settings provided by the predefined client (PCC). These settings can be verified and changed if necessary. Again, update the information and documentation for this activity in both the IMG as well as the Baseline Configuration Plan document.

Configure and Validate the Baseline

This is the heart of the realization phase that corresponds to changing the configuration settings for the baseline scenarios and processes. The completed settings are migrated to the QA environment for testing using the test plans and test cases prepared earlier. The information gathered during this task also helps in revising the Baseline Configuration document as well as the Business Blueprint.

Configure the Process and Functions

This task deals with changing the configuration settings in conformity with the Baseline Configuration Plan document. Again, update the information and documentation for this activity in the IMG and the Baseline Configuration Plan document.

Transport to the QA System

Transport the baseline configuration objects to the QA system.

Test the Baseline

Test the baseline configuration using the test cases and plans from the Baseline Configuration Plan document. Document the setup and test data for each test case. This is useful later during the confirmation task that is considered later.

Document and Resolve Issues

This task deals with recording discrepancies or issues and resolving them quickly. The issues are recorded using the issues database within the Q&A database (Q&Adb). If the issue relates to a configuration within the preview of the final configuration task, it should be scheduled for the appropriate cycle (see "Perform Final Configuration and Confirmation"). Pending issues must be reported and escalated rapidly.

Revise the Business Blueprint

Based on the results of the configuration and validation of the scenarios and business processes, revise the Business Blueprint to reflect the current information of the process.

Verify the Completeness of the Baseline Configuration

In the Baseline Configuration Plan document, scrutinize the planned and actual configuration dates to confirm that all the scenarios and processes have been configured and tested for correctness or are subject to resolution in the issues database of the Q&Adb. This can also be confirmed from the IMG by performing project analyses from the Customization menu.

Perform Baseline Confirmation

Here you are responsible for formulating the confirmation scenarios that verify the successful configuration of the system. This involves the following subtasks:

- Compile confirmation scenarios.
- Perform the baseline confirmation session.
- Prepare the confirmation scenarios agenda by the cross-functional process owners and assign participants.
- Review and sign off the baseline confirmation.

NOTE

In ASAP, this task is the third important milestone of the project.

Confirmation Scenarios

A confirmation scenario (or process group) corresponds to a complete business or an end-to-end scenario. It can be subdivided into business cases that make it easier to confirm the complete scenario in incremental steps. A business case includes the critical information flow, associated conditions, and exceptions.

Compiling a confirmation scenario involves the following:

1. Choose the Baseline Confirmation Plan document and select the baseline worksheet.
2. Set the confirmation and sequencing information for dependent processes by entering a case number and a sequence number to a group of related processes in the subcolumns of Confirmation: Case and Sequence No.
3. Add information on confirmation procedures by selecting the case procedure form and adding details.
4. Save your work.

Perform the Final Configuration and Confirmation

As referred to at the beginning of Section," Baseline Configuration and Confirmation," all scenarios and business processes that are not included in the baseline scope are handled during this task.

To make the configuration effort easier, ASAP methodology recommends the formation of a series of configuration cycles consisting of a selected set of business processes, depending on the degree of their importance. These are the configuration cycles that were mentioned in Chapter 14. The cycles are configured sequentially until all issues are resolved and the configured system is ready to be delivered for final integration tests.

Each cycle represents an iterative process that systematizes the final configuration effort. The cycles are defined based on the following guidelines:

- **Cycle 1**: The purpose of this cycle is to tune the configuration of the business processes for the master data and high-priority transactions.
- **Cycle 2**: Here you tune the configuration of the remaining master data and basic transactions.
- **Cycle 3**: Here you tune the configuration and master data by running high-priority business processes.
- **Cycle 4**: Here you tune the configuration by running the business processes that include exceptions, transactions, reports, user profiles, and so forth.

The final configuration and confirmation process is similar to that adopted for the baseline scope, except that in the BPML only those processes that are set to indicate Cycle 1, 2, 3, or 4 are selected. The subtasks involved are listed below:

- Revise the final scope.
- Create the configuration plan for the final scope.
- Prepare the test cases.
- Prepare the test plan for the final scope.
- Assign the resources.
- Approve plans for the final scope configuration.

Configure and Validate the Final Scope (Cycle 1 to n)

This step involves changing the configuration settings for the final scenarios and processes. The completed settings are migrated to the QA environment for testing using the test plans and test cases prepared earlier. The information gathered during this task also helps in revising the BPML configuration document as well as the Business Blueprint.

NOTE	

Note: The reference to the number of cycles in the parentheses earlier (and later in this section) refers to the number of configuration cycles decided by the company.

The task, which is similar to that undertaken for the baseline scope, as explained earlier, consists of the following subtasks:

- Configure the processes and functions.
- Transport the objects to the QA system.
- Test the final configuration.
- Establish the final configuration.

Establish the Final Confirmation (Cycle 1 to n)

The task here is to formulate the confirmation scenarios that could be enacted to verify the successful configuration of the system. Again, this is similar to the approach used for the baseline confirmation, except that this is conducted in iterative cycles.

This involves the following subtasks:

- Prepare the final confirmation scenarios.
- Perform the final confirmation scenarios.

Perform ABAP/4 Development

The purpose of this task is to ready the environment for ABAP development. You have seen an overview of the Workbench Organizer and transport system in Chapter 7. However, every development team member must be registered as a legitimate development user by doing the following:

1. Create a development user ID for each member of the team.
2. Register the development user through the SAP Software Change Registration (SCCR) in the OSS and transfer the access key to your development system.
3. Create a change request for each Advanced Business Application Programming (ABAP) development project. All development users belonging to this project will be assigned to this change request.
4. Create a change request for all ABAP objects that are common across all projects.

5. Group the repository objects into a hierarchy of application objects, wherein each node in the hierarchy is assigned to a development class.

The ABAP development broadly encompasses the development of forms, reports, data conversion programs, interface programs, and functional enhancement modules. In the remaining part of this subsection, we consider each of them in turn.

Develop Forms

The purpose of this task is to undertake company-specific requirements of forms, as detailed in the Business Blueprint. The subtasks involved in this are described below:

- Specify forms by defining the layout sets and the technical specifications. Then update the information for the concerned business processes in the BPML.

- Develop forms. If the standard forms available in the system are useful, they can be reused as a base template.

- Prepare the test procedures for forms by defining the functions and sequence of testing as well as the test data to be used.

- Test, review, and approve the results.

- Transport the forms to the QA system for final integration testing.

Develop Reports

The purpose of this task is to undertake company-specific requirements of reports, as detailed in the Business Blueprint. The subtasks involved in this are described below:

- Identify processes that have requirements for reporting and analyses that cannot be satisfied by the standard reports available within the system. Determine the frequency of the report, the content of the required report, the source of the data, and so on.

- Define the report specifications and update the information in the corresponding business processes in the BPML.

- Develop reports by using the appropriate tool most suitable to the concerned report, such as ABAP/4 Query, SAP Report Writer/Painter, ABAP Reporting, and so on. Use any standard reports if they are reusable as templates. Special attention should be paid to performance issues.

  When creating reports, the proper reporting tools should be utilized for the report. Reports should be analyzed to ensure they are efficiently created using the proper indexes and accessing the correct tables. Creation of inefficient reports can increase the usage of system resources and dramatically affect system performance.

- Prepare the test procedures for the reports. Define the functions and sequence of testing as well as the test data to be used.
- Test, review, and approve the results.
- Transport reports to the QA system's final integration testing.

Develop Conversion Programs

This task deals with the development of programs and manual procedures that are related to the transfer of data from the company's legacy systems to SAP. When developing conversion programs, you must consider the following details:

- Which data objects are required to be transferred to SAP from legacy systems.
- The method of transfer: SAP standard data transfer programs, manual data entry using online transactions, or batch input (BI) programs.
- The amount of data and the quality of data available in the legacy systems.
- The availability of a standard R/3 data transfer program, which requires data to be in a certain file/record format as well as a certain sequence of data records. The required data structure format can generate the related flat file with the details of each field.
- Map the legacy data fields to the fields of the flat file corresponding to the R/3 data transfer program.

If there is no standard data transfer program, a custom batch input BI program might have to be developed to transfer the data to the R/3 system. SAP provides a Data Transfer Made Easy Guidebook for providing guidelines on undertaking the data conversion and transfer effort from the legacy systems.

Thus, a data transfer/conversion program specifies the following:

- Data is read in a flat file format from the legacy system.
- The data from the various fields of the data record are assigned to the corresponding data fields in R/3.
- The data records assembled by the conversion program are stored in another flat file that is used by the SAP BI or the direct input (DI) program.

In case of a custom-developed program, subsequent to the development of the conversion program, the following remaining tasks are performed:

- Prepare the conversion test procedures.
- Test, review, and approve the results.
- Transport conversion programs to QA final integration testing.

15

REALIZATION

Develop Application Interface Programs

This deals with the development of programs that interface with the R/3 system.

For accomplishing this task, the following needs to be considered:

- The data that needs to be interfaced
- The system that drives the interface
- The various alternatives available for devising the interface
- The various optional techniques available for designing the interface
- Manual interfaces
- The possible impact on other applications

Like the case of conversion programs or when integrating different applications in the R/3 system, predefined SAP interfaces should be used whenever possible. Predefined interfaces are based on business scenarios meant for the import of data into the SAP R/3 system or for exporting data through the application exits. The business scenarios are well defined in terms of affected business objects and are easy to implement and maintain. As an alternative, those third-party products that are already qualified for interfacing with SAP through complementary software programs (CSP) should be evaluated.

Only as a last resort should a company consider developing its own solution for interfacing with SAP and satisfying the requirements that have been justified in the Business Blueprint. Based on the business' needs, a company can select two basic methods of transferring data.

The first is a file-based transfer wherein data is first transferred into a flat file. The file is then uploaded into the other system or used in a shared mode by one or more of the other systems. This store-and-forward method is a batch method, allowing only synchronous transfers of data. The various techniques available for implementing batch interfaces are as follows:

- Batch input (BI)
- Call transaction (CT)
- Intermediate Document (IDoc)
- Business Applications Programming Interface (BAPI)
- Direct input (DI)

The second is program-to-program communication, which requires an interface program for each interfacing system. The connection is established by a system seeking a transfer of data to the other interfacing system. This method enables only synchronous data transfers and the processing of data. The various techniques available for implementing online interfaces are as follows:

- Remote Function Call (RFC)
- Common Programming Interface for Communication (CPI-C)
- OLE/ActiveX components technology
- GUILIB/Graphic User Interface (GUI) components
- IDoc interface for an Electronic Data Interchange (EDI)
- IDoc interface for Application Link Enabling (ALE)
- SAP Business Workflow
- Business Application Programming Interface (BAPI)
- Internet Transaction Server (ITS)/Internet Application Components (IAC)

In case of a custom-developed interface, subsequent to the development of the conversion program, the following remaining tasks are performed:

- Prepare the interface test procedures.
- Test, review, and approve the results.
- Transport the interface programs to the QA final integration testing.

NOTE

Enhancements and interfaces to SAP including SAP Workflow, Business Information Warehouse, SAP Business Framework, BAPIs, IDoc, ALE and ITS/IACs are considered in detail in Chapter 19.

Develop Enhancements

The objective of this task is to develop modifications, enhancements, and extensions to the SAP system, as proposed in the Business Blueprint. Enhancements include

- Use of the R/3-designed user exits
- Custom modifications of standard R/3 objects
- The development of custom programs, preferably in ABAP/4

All modifications and enhancements need to be registered using the SAP Software Change Registration (SSCR). It must be noted that with the modification of SAP sources and dictionary objects, the warranty obligation of SAP is invalidated.

As before, the following steps are performed:

- Specify the enhancements.
- Develop the enhancements.

15

- Prepare the enhancement test procedures.

- Test, review, and approve the results.

- Transport the enhancements to the QA final integration test.

Establish the Authorization Concept

The authorization concept defines the various functions that can be performed by users in different organizational units. As you have seen in Chapter 11's "User Administration," the authorization concept maintains a balance between managing access security and assigning privileges to perform jobs on the system, as well as the effort expended for administrating this system itself. The aim of this task is to establish an authorization concept or framework that satisfies all these requirements.

Customers should be aware that SAP authorizations could be substantially different than authorizations in legacy systems. User roles and job tasks could be different in SAP than in the legacy systems, processes may become more decentralized, steps in the process may be eliminated, and access to integrated data may be necessary. SAP has a concept of open information access, integration, and reporting. This could result in some difficult change management issues with regards to authorization and open information access.

In the Business Blueprint, the responsibilities of various processes and functions are defined. These responsibility definitions are used to establish the authorization concept or framework. SAP provides the R/3 System Authorizations Made Easy Guide as a reference for helping with implementing and validating this framework.

Compile the Authorization Concept's Detailed Design

The objective of this subtask is to provide a framework for controlling the use of individual functions through profiles and authorizations. The authorization concept primarily consists of the following:

- Compile the department-wise DO Some/All and SEE Some/All matrix to portray the security risk profile of the company in close consultation with the process owners, data owners, and HR department. The four quadrants of this two-dimensional matrix correspond to the following:

  End users execute only a selected set of transactions (DO Some) and have access to only specific data (SEE Some) across the organization.

  End users execute all relevant transactions (DO All) and have access to only specific data (SEE Some) across the organization.

End users execute only a selected set of transactions (DO Some) and have access to all data (SEE All) across the organization.

End users execute all relevant transactions (DO All) and have access to all data (SEE All) across the organization

- Prepare the job role matrix in close consultation with the process owners, data owners, and HR department for each user, along with details of the various functions and activities handled by each user.

- Map the R/3 transactions (and menu options) to these job functions, activities, and corresponding data. The Business Blueprint furnishes information on these associations.

- Define the activity groups, which are selections of activities grouped together.

- Define the authorization profiles.

- Define the user master data for each user (see Chapter 11 "User Administration").

- Assign activity groups and authorizations to users.

- Generate user profiles with the help of the profile generator, which uses the predefined activity groups and authorizations supplied by SAP.

Certain activity groups are defined only for general authorizations like printing, faxing, and using SAPOffice that are assigned to all users. But generally speaking, the more risk that a company assumes, the more restrictive the DO transaction and SEE access privileges will be and, consequently, the easier it will be to implement the security environment.

Management of the Authorization Environment

This subtask deals with the implementation of the authorization system. SAP recommends subdividing the responsibility of maintaining user master data and authorizations among three administrators for ensuring optimal security and simplifying the procedure. The three administrators are

- **User administrators**: they define and maintain the user master records and assign the users to one or more activity groups.

- **Authorization profile administrators**: they can define or modify authorizations and profiles, but they cannot define the activity groups or users.

- **Activity group administrators**: these users create the activity group and define the associated R/3 transactions, but they cannot maintain authorization profiles or users.

Validate the Authorization Concept

This subtask deals with validating each user to perform the required processes, transactions, and reports. This includes verifying associated business processes for job functions, resolving discrepancies, and revising the authorization concept in light of the same. The authorizations are signed off by the business process owners and data owners.

Establish the Archiving Management

This task deals with establishing and creating an archival management system. Data that is not needed online in the system should be removed. Large data not only make database administration difficult, but it also affects performance. It includes these subtasks:

- Design the archiving management system. The archiving system aims at maintaining the balance between increasing the data volume (because of the daily transactions and processing) and reducing the data volume (because of archiving) to ensure optimal performance. The business process owners assist in fine-tuning the archiving cycle for a company.
- Prepare the archiving procedures.
- Implement the archiving procedures.
- Validate the archiving procedures.

Conduct the Final Integration Test

The purpose of this task is to plan and execute the final integration test. Conducting the final integration test simulates, in the Quality system, the live operations for a functional verification of the productive system.

Define the Scope of Integration Test

The scope of the test is based on the process design for the business areas and the corresponding business areas defined in the Business Blueprint. Like the final configuration and confirmation tasks, the final integration test is also process-oriented. The plan includes the following:

- Test scope
- Test scenarios
- Test processes
- Resources

A test scenario (or process group) corresponds to a complete business or an end-to-end scenario. It can be subdivided into test processes that make it easier to confirm the complete scenario in incremental steps. A business case includes the critical information flow, associated conditions, and exceptions. This is handled in a manner similar to the approach adopted for final scope configuration and confirmation.

To make the testing effort easier, ASAP methodology recommends the formation of a series of integration-testing cycles consisting of a selected set of business processes, depending on the degree of their importance. These are the integration testing cycles L1 and L2 that were mentioned in Chapter 14's subsection "Prepare Business Blueprint." The cycles are tested sequentially until all issues are resolved and the tested system is ready to be delivered for final preparation before going into the productive phase.

Each cycle represents an iterative process that systematizes the final testing effort. The cycles are defined based on the following guidelines:

- **Cycle 1**: The purpose of this cycle is to tune the business processes for the master data and high-priority transactions, followed by testing the high-priority business processes.
- **Cycle 2**: The purpose of this cycle is to test the business processes that include exceptions, transactions, reports, user profiles, and so forth.

The final integration process is similar to that adopted for the final configuration, except that in the BPML only those processes are selected that indicate integration testing cycle 1 or 2.

If one cannot schedule to test everything, the test cases can be prioritized based on

- The frequency of the process
- The failure impact of the process or dependencies of the process
- The probability that the test case will occur

ASAP provides a formula to calculate the test priority for test cases. As the test priority increases, the need to include the test case in the integration testing becomes greater.

Prepare the Final Integration Test Plan

The purpose of this task is to prepare a detailed integration test plan that must include all processes and components, such as

- Business processes
- Reports
- Interfaces
- Conversions
- Enhancements
- Printer/fax outputs

The scope of the test is based on the process design for the business area and the business processes, as defined in the Business Blueprint. The test plan identifies necessary dependencies and ensures that everything in the blueprint is tested. Again, ASAP provides a list of predefined test procedures to help in accelerating this step.

Transport All Objects to QA and Freeze the System

The purpose of this task is to freeze the system settings to protect the completed system from changes until the full cycle of integration testing is completed. This includes

- Configuration settings
- Client settings
- Application data
- Repository objects

Conduct the Final Integration Tests

The purpose of this task is to conduct the final integration test, based on the final integration test plan. This involves usual steps like entering the initial setup data, running test cases, recording the results, comparing them to the expected results, evaluating the results, recording the issues, resolving them, and, finally, completing each of the test cases one after another. The final integration test is conducted by the team of process owners and power users. The importance of integration tests should not be underestimated. Because of the integrated nature of SAP, customization across modules can become complex and changes in one area might have profound impacts in other areas. Integration testing should be thorough, checking in detail each possible scenario in a business process.

NOTE

In ASAP, this task is the fourth important milestone of the project.

Approve the Final Integration Test Results and Finalize the System

The purpose of this task is to resolve all outstanding issues from the final integration testing of the system to ensure that the configured system satisfies all business requirements before going into production.

Prepare End-User Documentation and Training Material

The purpose of this task is to define the necessary training to be undertaken by the end users before the go-live Phase.

Define the End-User Documentation Plan

The objective of this task is to

- Identify the end users and their training requirements by using the Job Role matrix.
- Identify the user documentation requirements.
- Identify the responsibilities and schedule for completing the documentation.

This is based on the documentation plan prepared in the business blueprint phase.

Compile the End-User Documentation

SAP provides end-user procedure (EUP) templates for help in accelerating this task. The EUPs are prepared based on more than 600 predefined BPPs that are made available by SAP (see Chapter 16's "Prepare End User Training and Documentation Plan").

Prepare the End-User Training Plan

End-user training is critical for the acceptance and success of the go-live phase. The end-user training tasks are linked to the end-user documentation. These tasks include

- Identifying the methods and material required for training
- Identifying the responsibilities and schedules for preparing the training material
- Identifying the responsibilities and schedules for preparing the instructor material
- Identifying the responsibilities and schedules for conducting training
- Arranging for notification and enrollment of the identified end users

Role-based training is available through the Information Database (InfoDB). The role-based courses list helps in identifying the necessary courses.

Prepare the End-User Training Instructor Material

This includes preparation of the training slides, screen prints, exercises, handouts, and so on.

Prepare the End-User Training Material

This task provides additional notes, hints, FAQs, and so on for the end-user training.

Quality Check Realization Phase

This is the final verification of the realization phase. The SAP-recommended checklist for the realization phase is as follows:

- Verify the completion of project statuses and steering committee meetings.
- Validate the completion of the cutover plans.
- Ensure a team-building activity has been undertaken or is scheduled.
- Validate the completion of the project team training.
- Ensure that system test plans are developed and that service-level commitment is defined.
- Validate the configuration of the global settings, organizational structure, and baseline scope.
- Review the baseline confirmation approval and signoff.
- Confirm the setup of the QA system.
- Confirm the setup of the production system.
- Validate the configuration of the final scope and the signoff of the final confirmation.
- Verify the migration of tested conversions, application interfaces, enhancements, reports, and layout sets.
- Validate the creation of authorizations, and review the signoff of the authorization design.
- Confirm the creation of archiving management.
- Verify the existence of a integration-tested and finalized system.
- Ensure the creation of user documentation and training materials.
- Validate the preparation for user training.

This quality check verifies that the final configuration of the R/3 system meets the business requirements specified in the Business Blueprint.

Sign Off the Business Blueprint Phase

Here you obtain the final signoff from the project management and gain the approval to proceed to the next phase. Signing off the realization phase signals the end of the third phase of the ASAP methodology, which is also the development and testing phase of the SAP project.

Final Preparation

IN THIS CHAPTER

This phase is aimed at readying the system and the company for the SAP implementation. It consolidates all the activities of the previous phases to prepare for the go-live phase, including end-user training, system testing, stabilizing system management, and starting the cutover activities. Any exceptional or rare situations are also addressed and resolved.

> **NOTE**
>
> The importance of referring to SAP's original AcceleratedSAP (ASAP) documentation CD-ROM cannot be overemphasized. What I have presented below are the essential details of the final preparation phase of the ASAP methodology; however, this is not intended as a replacement for the colossal amount of instructive documentation, guidelines, checklists, templates, samples, and questionnaires provided and recommended by SAP. These are well-proven instruments, and for an actual project, it is highly recommended that the reader procure the version of ASAP corresponding to their SAP installation's version and use it in conjunction with the progress of the implementation project.
>
> Some of the material in this and following chapters might seem repetitious. However, on closer scrutiny you will note that activities like project management, organizational change management, risk assessment, sponsorship and communication strategies, skills development, and know-how are common throughout all the phases of the project, and are referred to in the beginning of each phase. Similarly, because many activities go through the stages of planning and execution, I refer to all such activities through their different stages during the various phases of the project. They are not being repeated; they are only part of the ASAP process checklist recommended by SAP.

The conversion and interface programs are all checked, volume and stress tests are performed, and user acceptance tests are conducted. This is followed by the migration of data to the new system, and the super-users under the supervision of the SAP team members conduct end-user training. This phase also contains strategies for the next phase, including the routine, periodic uploading of data from non-SAP systems, internal audit procedures, and organizing the help-desk support activity.

Project Management of the Final Preparation Phase

The project management task is similar to that of the other phases. The objective is to maintain the momentum as well as focus the effort throughout the company on completing the remaining phases on schedule. It is also important to maintain the motivational level within the

FINAL
PREPARATION

organization, especially among the end users, who play a critical role during the cutover phase and, especially, in the post-implementation phase.

Review the Final Preparation Phase

This task deals with analyzing the potential risks that are likely to pose problems in achieving the project goals. The review covers issues related to

- Project management
- Technical project management
- Information technology (IT) infrastructure
- Change management process
- Member commitment

This review assesses various risks and drives the various initiatives that are continued during the final preparation phase to ensure that deadlines are met. This includes programs like organizational change management processes based on specific risk assessments both at the team and organizational levels.

Conduct Project Team Status Meetings

This task deals with coordinating and integrating the status of the various project teams such as

- Business process team
- Change management team
- Technical team

This helps in collating all this information to form the overall status of the implementation project and decide on coordinated actions in case of observed deficiencies or if slowing the pace of the project is necessary. The project management decides on the measures that are essential for maintaining the project schedules; these could be additional resources to augment the basic teams or even additional budget changes for completing the end-user training on time.

Conduct Steering Committee Meetings

This task deals with convening the steering committee meetings for updating the latest status and obtaining quick decisions for all project issues that cannot be handled at the project management level. The project management should present the following:

- The project status
- The plan for the next phase
- Planned versus actual completion dates

- Planned versus actual costs
- The percentage of work completed
- Pending and remaining work to be completed
- Negative and positive variations
- Corresponding measures taken
- Remaining deliverables
- Timelines and milestones
- Issues needing decisions
- Adjustments in resources needed for achieving critical activities

Continue Team-Building Activity

These measures help in making the team more cohesive, motivated, and better able to work in tandem with other teams and members toward the final goal of SAP going live successfully.

Continuing the Organization Change Management Process

As seen in the earlier phases, this task deals with a series of processes that help the change team diagnose and manage change issues in order to optimize the organizational processes for sustaining the momentum required by the ASAP methodology until the end of the project.

This task continues with the full array of processes like risk assessment, the sponsorship strategy, the communications strategy, skill development, knowledge transfer, and the organizational optimization process that were initiated in the business blueprint phase. There is an additional importance to these efforts in this phase because this phase initiates the exercise of scaling the SAP implementation to the enterprise as a whole. This task ensures that skill development, the transfer of knowledge, and the communication processes are all geared towards taking on the increased number of participants in the last stages of the project as well as in the post-implementation phase.

End-User Training

This task ensures that all end users undergo the requisite SAP training prior to the go-live phase. It should be in line with the plan and schedule prepared during the realization phase.

The basic input for this plan is the business process master list (BPML) compiled during the business blueprint phase and the job role matrix prepared during the realization phase. Consequently, the training plan ensures adequate coverage of all types of end users, but at the same time it avoids redundant training. The latter is not only a drain of resources, but it can also lead to losing precious time on a project, which might be under a tight schedule by this stage of the project.

The end users can be broadly classified into

- Transaction users
- Query and analysis users
- Information users

The various subtasks involved in completing this task are as follows.

Prepare for End-user Training

This task deals with arranging the general logistics and also the SAP environment for training. This includes transporting and freezing the training client, as well as loading the company-specific training data into the training environment.

Conduct End-user Training

The purpose of this subtask is to conduct end-user training. After completing this training, the end users should be able to handle their routine tasks on the SAP system confidently.

Review and Assess Post-training Skills

The purpose of this task is to assess the effectiveness of the training in making the end users comfortable with SAP for their operational requirements. The feedback and suggestions should be used to suitably modify the future cycle of training courses. This assessment can also lead to identifying the requirement of all users to go through additional courses to enhance their use of the SAP system. These courses could focus on specific areas of interest like reporting or querying information.

System Management

The objective of this task is to ready the technical infrastructure and establish the system administration for the production system.

Establish Production System Administration

This subtask aims at establishing the system administration for the production system and this entails installation of the Computer Center Management System (CCMS). The right kind of infrastructure, coupled with a matching system administration setup, contributes toward high performance of the system and maximizes the availability of the system.

Configure CCMS for the Production Environment

The purpose of this subtask is to configure the CCMS for the production and post-production phase in order to comply with the approach defined during the realization phase. As referred to in Chapter 7, configuring the CCMS involves

- **Configuring the logon groups**: this logical grouping enables planning for balancing the response time requirements of the users and also ensuring the proper response times for time-sensitive transactions.
- **Configuring the system profiles**: this is essential for setting up suitable operation modes.
- **Configuring the operation modes**: this is to ensure suitable resources during a particular period of operations, like providing additional dialog or background processes.
- **Configuring the job scheduling system**: this is to ensure the correct execution of background jobs at suitable times during the daily operations.
- **Configuring the alert monitors**: this sets up the threshold values for different alert monitors available within the system.
- **Configuring the back-up schedule**: this sets up the schedule for the regular and periodic back-ups.

Configure the Production System Printing and Spool Administration

This task refers to the setting up of procedures and policies to ensure the efficient administration of spooling and printing processes. The scheduling of the print processes should comply with both the decisions and the corresponding print infrastructure from the realization phase. The logic of the print infrastructure has been dealt with in Chapter 11's section "Print Administration."

Train System Administration Staff

The members of the technical team might not be members of the system administration team for the production system. Therefore, it is important for the system administration and management policies and procedures to be explained and demonstrated to the envisaged team.

The system administration team training workshops should cover the following:

- Introduction to the SAP system
- System navigation
- System monitoring
- System backup
- Print management

Conduct System Tests

The purpose of this task is to test and validate the configuration of the system infrastructure as well as the system administration procedures devised for managing the system.

System Administration Tests

The purpose of these tests is to ensure the correctness and completeness of all the system administration processes and procedures listed in the SAP Operations Manual. They verify the comprehensiveness of the manual against the roles and responsibilities actually performed by the administrators during this phase of the system.

Conduct Volume Tests

The purpose of these tests is to validate that the current configured system is able to perform satisfactorily with the full load of transactions and other data anticipated in the production system. The test results can identify potential improvements to the system performance.

Conduct Stress Tests

The purpose of these tests is to validate that the current configured system is able to perform satisfactorily with the full load of business operations, transaction processing, postings, and printing in the production system. The test results can identify potential improvements to the system performance.

Conduct Printing and Fax Tests

The purpose of these tests is to verify the proper functioning of all printing and faxing programs. The tests should confirm printing efficiency and correctness for all types and volumes of print jobs.

Conduct Backup and Restore Procedure Tests

The purpose of these tests is to validate the correctness and completeness of the database backup and restore procedures. These procedures are dependent on the database as well as the underlying operating and hardware systems. They should also confirm the tolerance of downtime under differing data corruption and loss scenarios.

Conduct Disaster Recovery Tests

The purpose of these tests is to validate the correctness and completeness of the disaster recovery processes and procedures. The tests should cover all components of the technical infrastructure, including the storage disks, networks, databases, user authorizations, and so forth. The tests should also verify the tolerance for downtime, the adequacy of service- and maintenance-level vendor agreements, the effectiveness of escalation procedures and communication paths, the completeness of the transitional operations, the restart procedures, and the final transition to regular operations.

Conduct GoingLive Check

The purpose of this test is to check system configuration and performance before transitioning to the go-live and support phase.

The GoingLive service provided by SAP measures the following aspects of the envisaged production system:

- Server
- Database
- Applications
- System load
- Configurations

As a part of the service, SAP provides a report on the results and recommendations for improving the performance of the envisaged production system.

Refine the Cutover and Production Support Plan

The objective of this task is to refine the cutover and support plan devised during the realization phase.

> **NOTE**
>
> In ASAP, this task is the fifth important milestone of the project.

Prepare a Detailed Cutover Plan

The purpose of this activity is to ascertain the readiness of the system and the company to go into production. As pointed out earlier, SAP implementation does not have any phase analogous to the traditional phase of "parallel runs." Therefore, it is important to confirm the readiness of the SAP system to go live in terms of not only the SAP system and system administration, but also in terms of the timely conversion and uploading of data into the SAP system.

Compile the Conversion Checklist

The subtask is connected with compiling a detailed checklist of all processes and procedures that are essential for the successful conversion of data into the SAP system. This includes a review of

- Data to be converted
- Specifications of the data conversion

- Conversion programs
- Conversion program test data
- Conversion program test results both in terms of performance and converted data
- Manual conversion processes and procedures

For this to go through successfully, the checklist should also contain an exhaustive list of all the changes to the production system, which might include

- Configurations of various functional modules like Finance (FI), Controlling (CO), Sales & Distribution (SD), Production Planning (PP), Materials Management (MM), and so on
- New tables, screens, Advanced Business Application Programming (ABAP) programs, and SAPScript programs
- User profiles

Determine Production Readiness

The purpose of this task is to verify the production readiness of the system.

ASAP suggests the following checklist for determining the readiness of the system for production:

- CCMS is configured for the production environment.
- The operating system and database is secured.
- All tables, programs, configurations, and data have been converted.
- The database is ready for production.
- The network is ready for production.
- User security is in place.
- Printing is configured for production.
- Background jobs are scheduled.
- The database backup and restore strategy is operational.
- The disaster recovery plan is operational.

Approval for Cutover

The purpose of this task is to report the readiness of the system to go live to senior management and obtain the approval to initiate the cutover process.

Prepare the Production Support Plan

Here you refine the production support plan prepared during the realization phase in terms of the processes and procedures as well as the roles and responsibilities of the personnel that man the help desk.

Define Help Desk Procedures

This subtask deals essentially with defining the various kinds of communication processes that are essential for the functioning of a help desk:

- Reporting and recording problems
- Handling, solving, and tracking problem messages
- Escalating unsolved problem messages
- Escalating pending problem messages to SAP
- Delivering information on solutions
- Demonstrating the solution

Establish the Help Desk Facility

This task involves organizing and installing the help desk facility, including

- Installing the office infrastructure
- Installing the technical infrastructure
- Allocating personnel and resources to the help desk
- Training workshops for the help desk personnel
- Creating OSS users for the corresponding help desk personnel

Organize Help Desk Resources and Staff

This subtask deals with the allocation and training of help desk personnel. The roles and responsibilities of the help desk personnel are defined and circulated to all end users throughout the organization.

Long-term Production Support Strategy

Here you define a long-term strategy for supporting the SAP system to address the issues of

- The post-implementation system changes
- Subsequent release upgrades
- The increase in scope resulting from the growth of business
- Training new employees resulting from the employee turnover

Cutover to the Production System

The purpose of this task is to perform the cutover to the production system.

This involves executing the following tasks:

1. Transport all the customizing settings and repository objects to the production environment.

2. Perform conversions of all master and transaction data.

3. Manually enter the legacy data that is small in volume or is not easily amenable to data conversion because of the complexity of its structure.

Final Approval for Going Live

The purpose of this task is to make the final decision on the readiness of the system to go live into production. The decision is based on completion of the following requirements:

*   End-user documentation is complete.
*   End-user training is complete.
*   The R/3 system administration is in place.
*   The technical setup is complete.
*   The conversion of customization settings, master data, and transaction data is complete.
*   The production cutover and support plan is in place.

The system goes live into production after

*   Obtaining the approval from management
*   Verifying that the users are ready
*   The security system is made fully operational

Quality Check of the Final Preparation Phase

This is the final verification of the final preparation phase. The SAP-recommended checklist for the final preparation phase is as follows:

1. Verify that the project team status and steering committee meetings took place.

2. Confirm that a team-building activity has occurred or is scheduled.

3. Verify that the user training was completed successfully.

4. Confirm the administration of the productive system.

5. Ensure that the various R/3 system tests yield the required results.

6. Review the production support plan and verify its completeness.

7. Verify that the cutover was performed successfully.

Sign off the Final Preparation Phase

This task is concerned with obtaining the final signoff from the project management and gaining the approval to proceed to the final phase. Signing off the final preparation phase signals the end of the fourth phase of the ASAP methodology, which is also the cutover phase of the SAP project.

Go Live and Support

IN THIS CHAPTER

This phase addresses the issues of the SAP system in production. The GoingLive check is performed and completed. It involves solving issues of day-to-day operations including problems and security-related issues reported by end users. The SAP system and transactions are also monitored for possible optimizations.

NOTE

The importance of referring to the original SAP Accelerated SAP (ASAP) documentation CD cannot be overemphasized. What I have presented in this chapter are the essential details of the Go Live & Support Phase of the ASAP methodology. However, this chapter is not intended as a replacement for the colossal amount of instructive documentation, guidelines, checklists, templates, samples, questionnaires, and so forth provided and recommended for use by SAP. These are well-proven instruments, and for an actual project, it is highly recommended that you procure the version of ASAP corresponding to the version of your SAP installation and use it in conjunction with the progress of implementation project.

The business benefits of the new system are measured to monitor the return on investment for the project. This might be a trigger for further iterations of the implementation cycle for improving the business processes. A formal close of the implementation project is also performed.

Production Support

The objective of this task is to provide support to SAP system users and maintain optimal system performance. The support issue is very critical, especially in the first few weeks of the live operation.

Go Live and Support Review

This task deals with analysis of the potential risks that are likely to pose problems in achieving the successful completion of the project.

The review covers issues related to

- Project management
- Technical project management
- IT infrastructure
- Change management process
- Member commitment

It assesses various risks that could affect the successful close of the project.

Implement Go Live

The system goes into production.

Provide Production Support

The purpose of this activity is to support SAP users. The production support plan devised during the Final Preparation phase is set into operation. The functioning of the help desk itself is monitored and fine-tuned, depending on feedback from users as well as analysis of documented problems and their resolutions.

Power users are also trained to use SAP's Online Support System (OSS).

Validate Live Business Process Results

The purpose of this task is to confirm that the live SAP system is performing correctly. It confirms the correctness of customizing settings and master data.

It also monitors the business transactions to ascertain their correctness.

This task involves the following:

- Monitor daily transactions
- Resolve issues, ensuring that the issue has been resolved, and corrective actions have been taken and verified

The corrective action could be any of the following:

- Altering the business process
- Modifying the ABAP code
- Modifying the configurations
- Refresher training
- Training on additional modules or functionality

Finally, the task addresses obtaining approval for the production environment. This is the official approval of the live system.

Project End

The purpose of this task is to officially close the project. Any open issues still pending resolution are reviewed and closed.

Project Review

This task commences the exercise of measuring the business benefits for the SAP implementation:

1. Review and close all open issues—All issues in the issues database are identified, reviewed, resolved, and closed.

2. Review business benefits—The results of the SAP implementation are compared to the goals and objectives that were set for the implementation project. This also leads to the establishment of an evaluation procedure that can monitor benefits on an ongoing basis.

3. Evaluate the knowledge transfer process—The key lessons or conclusions of the project are reviewed and documented. This is done with the help of the information gathered during the course of the project in the Questions & Answers Database (Q&Adb) because that information reflects the distillation of the true insight into the functioning of the organization.

4. Complete organizational change management process—The key gains of the organizational change management process are evaluated. Any remaining organizational change management issues are resolved and closed.

Project Sign-Off

The purpose of this task is to obtain the formal approval for the close of the project.

Success Patterns for SAP Implementation Projects

The concept of patterns was introduced by Christopher Alexander in late-70's in the field of architecture. A pattern describes a commonly occurring solution that generates decidedly successful outcomes.

It is logical at this stage to summarize the lessons learned from the past SAP implementation projects in form of a checklist that can be referred easily. It should be noted that these patterns are applicable for SAP implementations envisaged for the Millennium Enterprises: by which I mean companies that are considered as Small and Medium Enterprises (SME) that have annual revenues between $50 million to $1 billion

The following is a checklist of patterns of successful SAP implementation projects:

- *Success Pattern 1:* Direct involvement of the top management throughout the project
- *Success Pattern 2:* Clear project organization structure and strong project management
- *Success Pattern 3*: Proper visibility and communication throughout the project
- *Success Pattern 4:* A company-wide Change Management plan

- *Success Pattern 5:* Allocation of appropriate budget and resources

- *Success Pattern 6:* Deputation of experienced achievers and key managers on the project and not by people who can be spared from the department

- *Success Pattern 7:* Project driven by the user departments rather than the IT-department; and implements only user-driven functionality

- *Success Pattern 8:* Implementation of the pilot site followed by the roll-out sites

- *Success Pattern 9:* Big Bang implementation of at least the base modules

- *Success Pattern 10*: Clear scope and control on functional creep during the project

- *Success Pattern 11:* Comprehensive training of SAP team members

- *Success Pattern 12*: Standardizing business processes and preferably implementing SAP standard functionality

- *Success Pattern 13:* External consultants used mainly to train the core team and not for executing the project

- *Success Pattern 14:* Plan, monitor and manage the project schedule throughout the project.

- *Success Pattern 15*: Interface with existing or legacy systems for specialized or low-priority functionality

- *Success Pattern 16:* Ready support infrastructure and systems as per project schedule

- *Success Pattern 17:* Support and manage infrastructure throughout the project for high availability

- *Success Pattern 18*: Train all concerned end-users close to GoLive

17

GO LIVE AND SUPPORT

The Post-Implementation Stage

IN THIS PART

Supporting SAP

IN THIS CHAPTER

In this chapter, we look at post-implementation support of SAP R/3 within an organization. In traditional application software systems, ongoing maintenance is known to account for more than 50 percent of the total cost of any system. SAP R/3 simplifies ongoing changes in the delivered functionality of a system because of

- Comprehensive functionality
- Inherent flexibility
- A comprehensive upgrade strategy

In this short chapter, we highlight some of these aspects that are related to supporting and enhancing the performance of the SAP implementation, and hence its return on investment (ROI). We end this chapter by looking at the issue of building up consultants and teams for sustaining the momentum and effectiveness of the SAP implementation, and then retaining them for maximizing the advantages to the company.

SAP Deployment

One of the major issues after completing the pilot site implementation of SAP is the its implementation at a company's other plant sites and office locations. As touched upon in Chapter 5, "The SAP Implementation Project Cycle," and Chapter 10, "Initiating the SAP Project," SAP deployment at other sites is simplified by adopting the following measures during the pilot site implementation:

- Rationalizing the processes
- Standardizing the processes
- A comprehensive set of processes relevant to all businesses and locations
- The inclusion of members in the implementation from the other sites and offices

The deployment effort involves the following steps:

1. **SAP installation**: this involves the installation of the infrastructure and SAP licenses based on the experience gained from the first-site implementation.
2. **Uploading base configuration**: this involves importing the base configuration prepared, implemented, and stabilized to all other sites.
3. **Uploading data**: this corresponds to the loading of basic data that is common to the operations of the company at all locations. This basic customization data may differ at each site to the extent that the facility addresses different industries, market segments, and so on. This may be reflected in the fact that supplier community may be different at each of these facilities. There may also be differences because of differing rules and regulations at different sites.

4. **Integrated training**: this involves conducting an integrated and tightly scheduled training session conducted for SAP support personnel, power-users, and end-users at the respective sites. Unlike the case of the pilot site, this training for the rollout sites can be done on the company-specific implementation, an opportunity that is unavailable for the pilot sites.

5. **Integration testing**: this involves conducting integrated and tightly scheduled integration testing using the test scripts that were prepared for the pilot site as the base. This approach makes this exercise highly focused and efficient.

The above applies to cases in which every plant or pilot site has exactly the same configuration. In reality this may not be the case. Correspondingly, you may have another step for customizing SAP for the specific requirements of the rollout sites. This customization may involve the configuration of new organization structures such as sales offices or purchasing departments; it may involve configuration of new business processes specific to the new sites; new authorizations may need to be set up to accommodate differing roles or requirements of the rollout sites; and it may involve setting up new reports, new forms, and additional interfaces to the legacy systems of the plant or pilot site. If the pilot site or plant is in a different country (Canada, for example), there will be significant changes due to different tax regulations, reporting requirements, and other country-specific requirements.

Continuous Change

This activity deals with ongoing changes that may be adopted in order to enhance the efficiency and effectiveness of the SAP system. This may consist of

- Ongoing training
- Performance monitoring and fine-tuning
- SAP Release upgrades management

This change activity also provides the opportunity to address some of the aspects that were decided to be out of the project's scope for the base implementation. It must be noted that we are not referring to any extensions or enhancements to the functionality provided by SAP per se, but to the functional modules and processes that may not have been implemented during the first wave. Thus, ancillary modules like Plant Management (PM), Quality Management (QM), Projects System (PS), and even important functionality like HR may get implemented in the second wave of implementation. SAP's Accelerated SAP (ASAP) methodology provides a separate component to address this phase of the life cycle of the SAP implementation.

This activity may also deal with the implementation of functionalities or systems that add value by overlaying on the base modules:

- SAP Workflow
- Document management systems
- SAP Business Information Warehouse
- SAP system on the Internet
- Automatic Data Collection (ADC) systems
- Mobile data capture systems
- Supply-chain Management (SCM) systems
- Customer Relationship Management (CRM) systems
- Enterprise Integration Applications (EAIs)
- Strategic Enterprise Management (SEM) systems

We will visit some of these systems in the remaining chapters of the book.

SAP R/3 Upgrades

This deals with the effort that needs to be undertaken to implement the periodic release upgrades provided by SAP. SAP provides upgrades in two categories:

- **Correction release upgrades**: these are smaller patches released by SAP for rectifying problems that have been reported in the system.
- **Functional release upgrades**: these primarily extend the functionality of SAP in the concerned areas.

The SAP upgrade effort involves

- Assessing and planning the projected technical downtime
- Upgrading all the systems within the system landscape
- Planning and executing the post-upgrade activities
- Skills planning and resourcing for an upgrade

An upgrade is not just a technical procedure. It may involve significant effort and resources of the company. When SAP does an upgrade, it may change the table structures, it may add additional functionality or change the functionality of existing business processes, code may change, and the look of the system may change. When performing an upgrade, additional steps would include:

- Integration testing of business processes, reports, interfaces
- Identification and resolution of issues with regards to changes required to reports, interfaces, ABAP programs, authorization, changes and modifications required as a result of the upgrade

- Configuration and testing of new functionality released in the upgrade
- User documentation and user training as a result of the upgrade (this would be required as a result of a major upgrade where the user's daily tasks would be changed as a result of the upgrade).

The ASAP methodology provides a separate component to address this phase of the SAP implementation life cycle. SAP also provides additional tools like SAP Software Logistics.

Customer Competency Centers (CCCs) Program

Under this customer competency centers (CCCs) program, SAP supports setting up the CCC at the value contract customer's site. This provides a direct interface between the company and SAP.

The CCC undertakes the following tasks in the company:

- Help desk support
- Training
- Information services
- Project implementation and support
- Coordination of development requests
- Business support
- Technical support
- SAP contract administration
- Internal marketing for promotion and better acceptance of SAP

Help Desk

The success of a SAP implementation is dependent to a great extent on the deployment of an enterprise-wide and properly resourced help desk. This is especially critical during and immediately after the go-live period, because this is when the system is used by a large number of users for whom the system is new, unfamiliar, and even disorienting. For companies that do not have a history of computerization, this may be a very trying period.

The majority of the problems reported during this period may be due to a lack of knowledge, human errors, system bugs, or technical problems with printers, network connections, and so on.

Some of the issues involved with instituting a help desk include:

- Defining the standards for identifying problems
- Defining and establishing the method for registering problems
- Defining the standards and procedures for problem diagnosis and resolutions

- Defining and establishing the service levels and response times for problem resolution
- Defining the standards and procedures for communicating the solution
- Defining the standards and procedures for tracking unresolved and pending problems
- Defining the procedure for escalating overdue, unresolved problems
- Establishing help desk logistics
- Implementing a help desk application system
- Defining the help desk team organization and the corresponding requisite skills and resources
- Appointing and training the help desk team

All unresolved problems are finally referred to SAP support services, such as the Online Service System (OSS).

Retaining and Retraining SAP Consultants

Until the recent past, SAP implementations were essentially considered complete after implementing the modules of interest to the organization. However, with the growing importance of virtual corporations or extended enterprises enabled by the Internet, companies are undertaking numerous development efforts. These involve various enhancements and interfacing SAP with supply-chain management systems and customer-facing applications, including sales force automation, call center applications, and so on. Thus, retaining the SAP implementation team may be critical for the organization to maintain the momentum of implementing satellite systems that interface with SAP or overlay the operational systems of SAP R/3.

The Retention Horizon

If one recalls that companies are advised to nominate their key performers to work as part of the SAP implementation in order to ensure its success, the effect of SAP-trained employees quitting the organization in search of better opportunities is doubly damaging. In such cases, the company not only loses SAP experts who are familiar with the specifics of their implementation, but it may also be deprived of some of its best performers. It is critical for a company to retain its implementation team members at least for twice the period of implementation.

Even if the retention of the core team is achieved at a cost that may double the budgeted figures, it will enable a company to extend its competitiveness further by rapidly implementing additional systems that overlay or interface with SAP. These systems include

- The Web-enabling of SAP functionality
- Workflow systems
- SCM systems

- CRM systems

- EAI systems

- Performance-enhancement programs like BPR, activity-based management, Balance Scorecard, and so on

Extending the Boundaries of Expertise

Apart from an increase in remuneration and compensations, training in advanced features and functionalities of SAP and other enterprise applications can be a powerful method of retaining SAP talent within your organization. An Advanced Business Applications Programming (ABAP) developer's skills could be upgraded by

- Training in Application Link Enabling (ALE)/IDoc and Electronic Data Interchange (EDI) systems like Mercator.

- Training in implementing Internet-enabled SAP functionality through the SAP Internet Transaction Server (ITS)/Internet Application Components (IAC) environment

- Training in Web-based application development projects in HTML, XML, ASP, EJB, Java, JavaScript, VisualBasicScript, and so on

- Training and participation in EAI systems like computerized telephone integration, barcodes, security and access systems, data capture systems, and computer recognition systems

- Training in data warehousing projects using the SAP Business Information Warehouse solution or even non-SAP solutions that use data from the SAP system

- Training in Workflow for participating in workflow, imaging, and document management projects to be undertaken by the company

- Training in functional modules, depending on background and aptitude

A Basis consultant's skills could be upgraded by

- Training in ABAP development and further opportunities available in that activity

- Training and participation in enterprise infrastructure upgrade projects

- Training and participation in Web infrastructure projects

- Training and participation in enterprise infrastructure management projects including Web-enabled systems management, network management, and performance monitoring systems

A functional consultant's skills could be upgraded by

- Cross-training in different modules. MM and PP consultants could be cross-trained in either module as well as other related modules like QM, PM, PS, and SM. Similarly, FI and CO consultants could be cross-trained in either module as well as other related modules like AM, TR, FM, IM, CCA, PA, and EIS

- SCM systems
- CRM systems
- Performance enhancement programs like BPR, activity-based management, and Balance Scorecard

Summary

In this chapter we looked at the post-implementation period in the cycle of an SAP implementation. We visited aspects of SAP deployment, configuration changes and enhancements, SAP release upgrades and Help Desk. In the last section we looked at measures for ensuring the longevity of the SAP team member's association with the company.

Enhancements and Interfaces to SAP

IN THIS CHAPTER

As mentioned in Chapter 1's sub-section "ERP Fundamentally Models a Process-Oriented Enterprise," enterprise resource plans (ERPs), including SAP, still perpetuate the legacy of the data-oriented view of the enterprise, which is essentially foreign to the basic nature of organizations and their operations. Organizations do not operate merely as a collection of data structures interacting with each other to change their states. Such a view is devoid of any reason for the organizations to exist or to produce anything of value whatsoever. A collection of interacting data structures basically lacks the element that gives a direction and motivation to all levels of the organizations; without such a direction, despite all the effort and interactions, the tangible outcome produced by the organization might as well be a zero. A workflow that corresponds to the company's business processes is an example of an organizational characteristic that is not portrayed directly by the current information systems, including ERPs like SAP.

Moreover, the really unique and competitive advantage of an organization is not in its data structures, but in the way it operates and differentiates itself from other players in the market. Thus, the real differentiator is the manner in which an organization can change its strategies and operations, depending on the changing market conditions. This differentiator arises not because of the way it is structured, but mainly because of the way it operates and cooperates inside and outside the company. In a world where every company operates on ERPs like SAP, using the best business practices, a company needs elements to differentiate itself from similar companies in the market.

In this chapter, I discuss the elements of an organization or, rather, their computerized versions that contribute to this essential uniqueness. These could be divided into two main parts: elements that generally operate within the boundaries of the organization and elements that operate outside of it or interface with external systems. Not surprisingly, SAP itself provides computerized versions of many of these elements; for others, it provides standardized interfaces that enable the organization to extend its reach and visibility much farther than the physical boundaries of the organization. SAP Business Workflow is a good example of the former, while SAP on the Internet is a prime example of the latter.

SAP R/3's architecture was the basis of its success in the '90s; now its architecture and the openness of its interfaces provide the solid foundation required for delivering the functionality and enhancements essential not only for the rapidly emerging e-commerce businesses, but also for the functions of e-businesses in general. In the next section, I discuss SAP's business framework that offers a framework for the integrated use of business functions that permits the company to go beyond the customary constraints of the inward-facing ERP systems.

As seen in Chapter 1's sub-section "ERP Transforms an Enterprise into a Information-driven Enterprise," the nature of organizations has changed drastically from being a collection of independent units with the command and control structures of the industrial era to collaborating units with flatter hierarchical structures, cross-functional teams, and empowered members of the information era. Consequently, this has resulted in a new type of non-hierarchical network organization with distributed intelligence and decentralized decision-making powers. This entails a demand for constant communication among the various teams or functional groups. SAP R/3 essentially provides such an enabling environment through its modules like SAP Office, SAP Workflow, and SAP Business Warehouse.

SAP Business Workflow

SAP Business Workflow enables mapping business processes in the R/3 System and processes them under the control of the workflow system. Like any other workflow management system, SAP Business Workflow can process and monitor well-structured processes that contain a sequence of activities involving coordination between several people and which recurs regularly.

Office and administrative systems have often been plagued by many problems, including

- Large in-transit times
- Inwarding or receipt processing
- The tedious recording of information at various stages
- Error-prone duplicate transcriptions of information at various places
- Backward queries
- The tracking of documents
- Locating misplaced documents
- Slowing down of the decision process because of serialization
- The effort to keep the work task progress though the various stages of the business process

Workflow management systems support the various business processes within a company. They permit close coordination, cooperation, and collaboration between the various members of an organization, meeting the essential needs of post-modern organizations of the '90s. They are the best illustration of how technology can be an enabler for corporate-wide process re-engineering (see Chapter 1's "Enterprise Change Management"). Workflow management systems automate a predefined set of related work steps and provide a tool for processing a sequence of steps in an organized manner, with user interaction for obtaining any decisions at various steps.

Workflow management systems have many advantages like

- Closely mirror the business processes and its various steps
- Direct support of business processes
- Quick access to relevant information

- The completion of individual work steps is monitored

- In the case of a bottleneck, escalation procedures are initiated

- Throughput times are dramatically reduced

- In-transit and wait times are minimized

Workflow management systems support the execution of the various business processes and can accelerate them considerably. They are the best illustration of how technology can enable corporate-wide process reengineering (see Chapter 1's "Enterprise Change Management"). Workflow management systems automate a predefined set of related work steps and provide a tool for processing a sequence of steps in an organized manner, with user interaction capabilities for obtaining any decision at various steps.

Thus, workflow management systems provide the following:

- Work list definition and management

- Event management

- Control and monitoring of the workflows

SAP Business Workflow Concept

The SAP Business Workflow does not replace the functionality of standard SAP. It functions at a level above the transaction level of SAP R/3. The SAP Business Workflow also permits individual process steps to be assigned to organizational agents and as such it corresponds to the control aspect necessary for the functioning of an organization. The SAP Business Workflow has been available since R/3 Release 3.0.

The SAP Business Workflow was the first application to use business objects. The R/3 Business Objects Repository handles the management of the business objects. Examples of business objects are purchase orders, vendor or customer records, and invoices. After its creation in the system, the Business Object is processed in a workflow through several steps by various members of the organization. An example of a workflow is the verification and passing of an invoice for releasing corresponding payment to the supplier or vendor. A workflow consists of individual steps that are linked together. Each step corresponds to an activity, which refers to a single-step or multiple-step task. SAP provides a catalog of standard tasks that are easy to extend and adapt to customer requirements.

The various basic concepts of the SAP Business Workflow are as follows.

The Object Model defines the following components of a business object:

- Object identification

- Object name

- Hierarchical relationship
- Subtype
- Constraints
- Business rules
- Methods
- Attributes
- Input events
- Output events

The process model defines the workflow steps of the business process. The simplest and most prevalent workflow step is the activity step; a set of which constitute a workflow. Technically, workflow steps are usually methods of the business objects like conditions, events, control commands, user decisions, and wait steps.

The organization model defines all the organizational elements of the company and the corresponding associated tasks.

SAP Business Workflow Environment

The SAP Business Workflow is constituted of three parts, as shown in Figure 19.1.

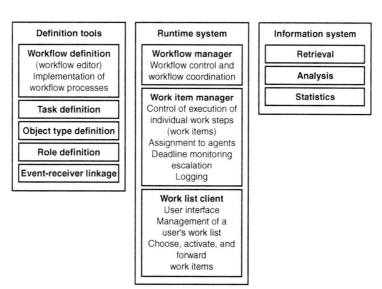

FIGURE 19.1

Components of the SAP Business Workflow.

Definition Tools

This part has components for the following tasks:

- Defining Workflow into its constituting steps.

- Defining single-step tasks, including their assignments to related persons or groups.

- Defining Workflow object types in the Business Object Repository. Workflow tasks basically operate on Workflow objects, which are runtime instances of object types. Workflow objects are defined in terms of the corresponding object types, methods, attributes, and events.

- Defining roles of the agents to whom the workflow tasks are assigned.

- Defining the events that are recognized and responded to by a predefined set of activities, depending on the status changes in the Workflow objects.

Runtime System

The runtime system has the following components:

- A Workflow manager that controls and coordinates the status of the workflow

- A work item manager that controls the execution of individual work tasks, including assignments to agents and the completion of the mandatory processing in the scheduled time for this work step or task

- An event manager that detects the occurrence of an event and triggers the corresponding response function(s)

Information System

The information system has the following components:

- An overview of the running and completed work processes at any time; all relevant data on the processes, such as the status, time required, sequence, and concerned user, can be logged and reported for analysis.

- Components for displaying and managing a users work list.

- Monitoring, error detection, and diagnosis in individual workflows.

SAP Business Information Warehouse

As you have seen in Chapter 1's "Knowledge as the New Capital," real-time information that is collated and analyzed in the proper context is the most important asset of the organizations in this century; it is also a tremendous competitive advantage to a company. A company can enhance its effectiveness and the efficiency of its management processes by gaining the ability to quickly extract mission-critical information from a flood of data made available by its operational systems. For achieving this, on one hand, companies need solutions that can provide immediate access to information that is relevant for decision making as well as the ability to analyze it flexibly. On the other hand, these solutions also need to be integrated with the existing operational systems for easy and fast access to this essential information.

The traditional solution for meeting such divergent goals is known as *data warehousing*. A data warehouse is a separate application environment with a dedicated database that draws on diverse data sources and is designed to support sophisticated query and analysis.

The SAP Business Information Warehouse (BW) is a state-of-the-art, end-to-end data warehouse solution that gives company members rapid access to data in any desired combination, aggregation, or level of detail from SAP systems, non-SAP systems, and even from external applications. It is a comprehensive solution that includes a relational online analytical processing (OLAP) engine, automated data extractor and population tools, a preconfigured metadata repository, a user-friendly, front-end tool with powerful reporting and analysis facilities, and an administrator's workbench to manage this whole environment. BW includes a number of components that permit it to perform many of its tasks with a high degree of automation and to complete a fast implementation with minimal ongoing maintenance.

Compared to the traditional data warehousing solutions, the SAP BW has a tremendous advantage because it can benefit from the simple fact that SAP R/3 itself is a repository-based application environment. Usual data warehouse solutions are designed to extract and map at the level of the individual database fields because they do not recognize the context of the data. This information on the context and meaning of data has to be established as a separate exercise. BW is based on the R/3 business processes. Making use of R/3's integration and metadata concepts, BW extracts, loads, and aggregates data in accordance with the enterprisewide business processes and presents them in a flexible and user-friendly manner customized to the needs of the user.

Also, because of the fundamental integration of BW with SAP R/3, the results of the BW analysis can also be immediately integrated into the SAP system, which is the powerful "second loop" learning that I spoke about in Chapter 1's "The Learning Organization." It represents the capability of institutional learning that gives a tremendous advantage to companies in these times of rapidly changing markets. Additionally, SAP, being a highly secure and auditable environment, is also a source of correct, clean, and reliable data, all of which are major concerns for normal data warehousing projects.

SAP BW projects can be implemented easily, quickly, and cost-effectively. Many time-consuming and painstaking stages of the traditional data warehousing projects are either eliminated completely or are taken care of automatically by the SAP BW. Some of these stages are as follows:

- Building departmental-level data marts leading to the enterprise-wide data warehouse
- Providing complete, correct, and reliable data

- Compiling an integrated enterprise-wide, business-driven view of data

- Discovering, defining, and building metadata models

- Mapping from R/3 data stores to the metadata of the data warehouse

- Populating the data warehouse from the R/3 data stores

SAP BW is also able to take advantage of

- Integrating an enterprisewide business processes view of data

- Extensive reporting functions within SAP R/3

- SAP's numerous open system solutions for interfacing to differing external systems

- SAP's leading-edge Basis technology with its three-tier architecture and concomitant benefits like security, integrity, scalability, high availability, and interoperability with a uniform environment

SAP BW is a comprehensive solution that takes advantage of the capabilities of R/3, but is not limited to R/3 alone.

Characteristic Features of SAP BW

The salient features of SAP BW are as follows:

- Data is gathered automatically from SAP systems and via open interfaces from non-SAP applications and external resources.

- SAP BW makes use of business processes and metadata already supported in a SAP system.

- Preconfigured information models and reporting templates help users generate reports quickly and easily.

- BW supports predefined standard reports and ad hoc analysis; both enable drill-down and multidimensional views.

- BW displays reports in MS Excel, allowing the rapid customization of reports per the need of the user.

- Users can group their own collections of preferred reports for frequent use.

- BW provides load and access monitoring for better fine-tuning of configuration and performance.

- BW accepts data from any source or system, including legacy and third-party applications.

- BW includes a proven enterprise model for the application of business rules to data.

- BW provides all the advantages of the standardized R/3 Basis technology, such as scalability, high availability, security, integrity, and interoperability.

Components of SAP BW

The main components of the BW architecture, shown in Figure 19.2, are described in the following sections. Figure 19.3 shows the corresponding Solution Maps.

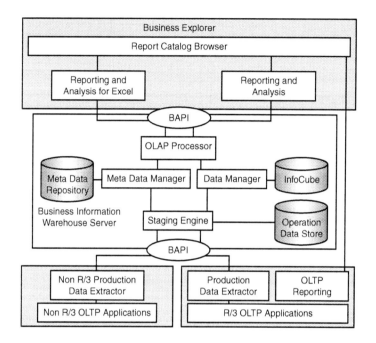

FIGURE 19.2

Components of the SAP BW.

System Administration

BW utilizes the SAP Basis environment to ensure the best performance for its functions. This includes the monitoring of data load batches and defining access at all levels of users. The Scheduler maintains the recurring extract and load jobs.

Data Administration

The Administrator Workbench provides for the management and maintenance of all key aspects of the data warehouse. This is greatly aided by the SAP repository that is common to both environments. Companies can also define and maintain departmental-level data marts. A schema designer enables users to create InfoCubes, InfoSources, and mapping and transformation rules for mapping BW operational data stores into the InfoCubes. (The following sections describe InfoCubes and InfoSources in more detail.)

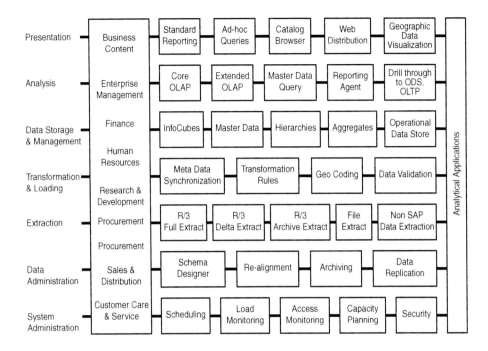

FIGURE 19.3

The SAP BW solution map.

When the source and target structures and mapping rules are established, the administrator uses the Scheduler, the Data Load monitor, and the Data Access monitor to control and manage the ongoing operations of the BW. The Data Load monitor supervises the load, transformation, and population processes and provides statistics on current, completed, or aborted jobs, along with the reasons for the same. The Data Access monitor provides statistics on the usage of BW, such as the frequency of query execution or access to the summary levels.

Data Extraction

The SAP BW, being preconfigured for the R/3 environment, extracts data from R/3 easily, based on some selection criteria. Data can also be extracted from legacy systems, archives, or external data sources. The extracted data is stored into transfer structures called InfoSources. The BW includes extract programs for all major applications, including financials, logistics, and human resources.

The extracted data represent a consistent snapshot of OLTP data from all of these standard SAP application modules. During the initial population or build stage of implementing the BW, the BW transfers all of the required OLTP data. Unlike some of the usual data warehouses, however, only the incremental changes in data need to be transferred to the BW. This significantly reduces the volume of data that needs to be transferred during ongoing operations.

Data Transformation and Loading

These tasks correspond to the actual process of mapping and transforming the data that is driven by the metadata. Transformation refers to suitably transforming the code structures from the source to those defined for the target BW. This might be necessary, especially for data being loaded from legacy or other external systems. Based on the R/3 metadata models, extracted data is validated before being loaded into the InfoCubes. The data undergoes a series of condensing, mapping, and transformation before it is stored in the InfoCubes.

Data Storage and Representation

The BW uses a combination of InfoCubes and master data to provide a robust platform for the analysis, reporting, and exploration of data. InfoCubes are multidimensional data matrices that provide multidimensional views of data; evidently, the multidimensional data matrix is simulated via the two-dimensional tables of the actual database. For instance, these dimensional characteristics include information on year, month, geographic regions, and product and key figures include such things as actual values or quantities. This permits, for instance, sales analysis by year, by geographic region, and by product. InfoCubes also provide the means for aggregating data per user requirements.

An InfoCube is a set of relational tables arranged according to the star schema with one large fact table at the center, surrounded by several dimensional tables. The fact table stores the key figures mentioned earlier at the lowest level of aggregation, whereas the dimensional tables store the characteristics that are used for reporting and analyzing these key figures. Usually, dimensions are assumed to be mutually independent of each other; their only link is through the key figures in the fact table. Master data consists of non-volatile information on customers, suppliers, and products, which is easily loaded from R/3. BW also permits defining hierarchical relationships between the dimensional characteristics. These relationships are separate from the InfoCubes, which are mainly used for querying and reporting the relevant data at different levels of aggregation.

The BW does not have to define and build the metadata repository that holds the descriptions of the data residing in the InfoCubes, InfoSources, and BW operational stores. This is because the SAP R/3 system already has a basic environment for this purpose: the R/3 repository. This ensures a uniform data model across all the subsystems of the BW as well as the OLTP sources in the R/3 system.

The BW maintains the various classes of metadata in the form of catalogs as listed here:

- **InfoObject catalog**: this provides a uniform definition of all characteristics and key figures used in the InfoSources and InfoCubes. It also maintains definitions of the derived key figures that are calculated based on the basic key figures at the time of reporting.

- **InfoSource catalog**: this contains the description of each InfoSource in terms of the InfoObjects as well as their mapping to the InfoCubes.

- **InfoCube catalog**: this contains the definitions of each InfoCube in terms of the constituting characteristics and key figures.

- **Report catalog**: this stores all the basic information regarding the reports in terms of the layout of the report, the applicable InfoCube, and the business analysis functions that need to be applied to the concerned data before being added to the report.

The simplest category of data is in the BW operational data stores. These are the intermediate stores where data from SAP and non-SAP is compiled, cleansed, and prepared for its load into the InfoSources and subsequently into the InfoCubes. They also provide the capability to drill-down to a singular transaction without leaving the BW environment. The only limitation is that often the BW operational store may not contain all data fields that are available in the corresponding SAP OLTP system.

Business Analysis

The BW provides a full-featured OLAP engine that supports several types of analysis. The OLAP engine or processor analyzes the data in the InfoCubes and presents different views on the basic data as well as the analyzed data through the Business Explorer.

The OLAP processor performs various slice and dice operations on the InfoCube data that are cross-sectional views of InfoCubes from different directions. The slice operation corresponds to the more finer levels of aggregation, whereas the dice operation corresponds to taking an alternate view at the same level of aggregation. For instance, slicing would imply drilling-down to individual orders contributing to sales, whereas dicing would change focus from territory-wise sales to product-wise sales. The slice and dice operations are made possible because of the fundamental multidimensional nature of the InfoCubes. The OLAP processor uses the characteristics stored in the InfoCubes to present different views of the key figures or derived key figures per the needs of the user.

The OLAP engine also provides powerful functions for analyzing the data contained in the InfoCubes. These functions are useful in analyzing the data that makes the OLAP engine more meaningful in the business sense. The various functions provided are as follows:

- **Aggregate functions**: these are functions for summing, finding minimum and maximum figures, averages, and averages over period sums.

- **Comparison functions**: these are functions for calculating deviations, variances, correlations, and so on.

- **Sequence functions**: these are functions for performing sorts, quartiles, cumulative sums, ABC analysis, and so on.

- **Exception conditions**: these are functions for defining threshold limits, values, top/last $n\%$ in sales, and so on.

• **Financial functions**: these are functions for currency conversions, calculation of financial ratios, and so on.

Business Reporting

The BW provides Business Explorer as the reporting environment for performing not only standardized reporting, but also ad hoc analysis and the data in the InfoCubes. Reports are created in the following steps:

• The relevant characteristics and key figures are selected and derived, and key figures are calculated.

• The results are displayed per user requirements either in standard layout structures or in predefined report layout templates.

In the standard layout structure, the characteristics are displayed as row headers and selected key figures as the columns or vice versa. Templates are predefined and customized report layouts can be used thereafter as a boilerplate for any report. Templates permit reports to be easily produced, displaying information such as budget versus actual costs, planned versus actual deadlines, balance sheets, and so on. All facilities of business analysis are usable within these reports. The system also provides seamless movement between the R/3 application and back.

The BW also provides a report catalog browser that supports report catalogs in a form of nested folders. The folders are nested according to the reports used by the company as a whole, those used by a group of users, and those used by individual users. Using the catalog, the end-user can select and execute any authorized report. The Administrator Workbench defines and maintains the catalogs, catalog reports, and access rights.

Presentation

The BW's user interface Business Explorer outputs results to MS Excel, permitting the use of Excel's powerful formatting and layout features. As mentioned earlier, a variety of predefined reports are provided. The system also permits ad hoc views of the data residing in the data warehouse.

BW's Business Explorer helps users in organizing the information according to his or her own requirements. A user can group together frequently used reports for quick access.

SAP Business Framework

SAP's Business Framework provides an all-encompassing framework that enables it to integrate and function with other R/3 systems and non-SAP systems. It enables maximum interoperability, the flexibility to incorporate rapid changes in interfacing products and technologies, and ongoing maintenance of the different Framework components without disrupting the activities of the environment as a whole. The Business Framework extends the object orientation of the SAP development environment also to the business functions (see Chapter 8's "Object-orientation in SAP"). The SAP R/3 Business Framework provides a structure for R/3 functionality based on business application components and business objects. SAP introduced object-oriented technology by making R/3 processes and data available in the form of SAP Business Objects. All external applications can access these objects through standardized and platform-independent interfaces called BAPIs.

The Business Framework is composed of a hierarchy of such components and that we will discuss in the following sub-sections. The advantages of the Business Framework include the following:

- Available functional components can be combined, depending on requirements
- Components from different vendors can be combined
- The development, introduction, and maintenance of components without interrupting normal usage
- The choice of deployment centrally or decentrally
- Components can be developed or enhanced selectively for industry-specific and company-specific requirements

Business Components

These business components are semi-autonomous components addressing major areas of the business requirements. They provide predefined and standard interfaces to the functionality and data that are encapsulated within the components. This encapsulation permits these business components to be enhanced and upgraded without disrupting the structure and functions of the other business components constituting the complete system. These components also have their separate kernels, like the SAP HR system.

Progressively, SAP envisages converting its singular application kernel into business components like financials, logistics, industry-specific solutions, and so on, each having their own separate kernels. This unbundling also would enable a company to implement only some of the SAP modules with solutions or modules from other companies.

Business Objects

These are unique units of business functionalities that represent traditionally identifiable, closely-associated enterprise activities corresponding to sales orders, purchase orders, invoices, and so forth. The SAP definition of these as separately identifiable business objects enables them to be defined, managed, and maintained in a semi-autonomous fashion without affecting the operations of any other functions or objects. SAP R/3 3.0 had more than 200 BAPIs.

Like any other typical instance object, a Business Object is characterized by its object type (or CDO), methods (BAPIs), attributes, and so on. As discussed in Chapter 1's sub-section "Object-orientation in SAP," the main benefit of object-orientation is in re-usability of software as well as the delivered functionality. The reuse of software manifests itself in terms of deriving new objects from the existing ones: the derived object is called the *subtype* and the existing object is called the *supertype*. A *sub-type* inherits all attributes and methods of the *supertype*; although it can also have additional attributes and methods of its own. In the example of the Automobile discussed in the earlier referred section, the sub-type Pick-up Truck inherits all properties from the supertype Automobile.

SAP business objects encapsulate R/3 data and business processes while hiding the structure and implementation details of the underlying data. This is achieved by creating SAP Business Objects entities as layered structures consisting of

- Kernel layer: this core layer represents the object's inherent data.
- Integrity layer: this layer represents the business logic of the object; this consists of business rules as well as constraints on values and domains that are applicable to the SAP Business Objects.
- Interface layer: this layer provides a platform independent description of the implementation of the SAP Business Object for the external systems. This is achieved via BAPIs.
- Access layer: this layer identifies and defines the technologies that can enable external system to access the kernel layer, that is, the object's data. These technologies could be COM/DCOM, RFC, and so on.

Figure 19.4 shows the different layers of a Business Object.

Business Programming Interfaces (BAPI)

BAPIs are methods or procedures that are assigned to a business object. They are encapsulations of the various operations that can be performed on the corresponding business objects. For instance, in case of customer invoices, different BAPIs provide functionalities for performing validations; verifying calculations of taxes, freight, and so on; identifying pending or overdue invoices; and verifying payments received, aging analysis, and so on. The SAP standard license already has a library of more than 200 BAPIs and it continues to add more BAPIs to this library on a regular basis.

The Business Object Repository (BOR) stores and manages business objects along with their corresponding BAPIs as singular units. This is the practical manifestation of the business components at the lowest level of functionality. The SAP already has a library of more than 200 BAPIs and it continues to add more BAPIs to this library on a regular basis. The BAPIs are currently implemented as function modules that are created and managed in the Function Builder. The BAPIs have the following characteristics:

- they are associated with a SAP Business Object
- they support the RFC protocol for communicating with external systems
- they get executed without returning any screen dialogs to the calling programs

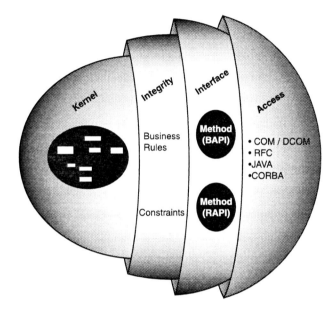

FIGURE 19.4

The Architecture of a Business Object.

BAPIs primarily provide the best advantages of object orientation, such as

- Development and implementation in any computer language
- Support for standard interfaces
- Compatibility with different communication technologies
- It is enhanced and maintained autonomously

The business objects, along with the corresponding BAPIs, clearly indicate the direction of the future enhancements in the SAP system.

Application Link Enabling (ALE)

There is an increasing trend for the various units of an organization to function like semi-autonomous units within the company. The intra-company relationships are modeled along the same lines as customer-vendor relationships. On the other hand, there is also an increased integration of enterprisewide processes like purchasing, sales and distribution, and even production and accounting. Thus, the modern enterprises have a simultaneous need for the following:

- A high degree of integration between the various application systems
- A set of decoupled systems that can be implemented independently

Application Link Enabling (ALE) is a fundamental component of the SAP Business Framework that enables software components from SAP and other vendors to communicate and be integrated with each other. The standard SAP license provides pre-configured ALE business processes along with tools for developing and testing ALE applications.

Typical distribution scenarios that are required to be handled are as follows:

- Centralized sales and production planning and decentralized Material Requirements Planning (MRP)
- Centralized vendor contracting with decentralized procurement
- Centralized logistics with decentralized warehouse management
- A centralized financial system with a decentralized logistics system
- Centralized sales with decentralized dispatch or vice versa
- Centralized profitability analysis with decentralized cost determination

The traditional solutions for satisfying these requirements are not adequate. Even more centralization of systems merely aggravates the problem of throughput, response times, maintenance, and upgrades, as well as cost effectiveness. The other conventional solution of using distributed databases is confronted with problems of security and integrity (such as for replication) and tremendous overheads of communications and processing (such as for two-phase commits).

Application Link Enabling (ALE), which became available with R/3 Release 3.0, introduced the concept of operations and management of *both* distributed applications and databases. ALE permits the implementation of loosely coupled clusters of applications that run semi-autonomously and have their own separate databases. This is made possible by the controlled exchange of data messages while ensuring consistency across these loosely coupled application installations. The integration of the various applications is achieved by using synchronous and asynchronous communication, rather than by a central database.

Essential advantages of ALE are

- Integration across semi-autonomous systems
- Better inbound interfaces compared to batch data communications (BDC) and call transactions (CT).
- It enables communications between different releases of SAP

19

ENHANCEMENTS
AND INTERFACES
TO SAP

- Release independence of individual applications
- It connects non-SAP applications without disrupting the consistency of the business functions and data
- Asynchronous integration of Business Framework components, including business components, business objects, and BAPIs

Architecture of ALE

The basic principle behind ALE is the guarantee of a distributed yet fully integrated R/3 installation. Each application is autonomous and exists in the distributed environment with its own set of data. The use of autonomous systems implies a certain degree of data redundancy; this implies that data has to be both distributed and synchronized across the entire system. This is achieved through asynchronous communication. The message-based architecture of ALE consists of three layers.

Application Services

This layer provides ALE with an interface to R/3 to generate or receive messages containing data to or from other R/3 or external systems. These messages contain information like the identity of the recipient, the type of transmission, and the type of processing.

Distribution Services

This layer truly enables the coupling of the business applications, including

- Determination of the recipients on the basis of the distribution model
- Filtering and conversion of messages
- Compression of messages for reduced volume of messages

Communications Services

ALE messages are exchanged either by using the asynchronous remote function call (RFC) or electronic data interchange (EDI). For information retrieval purposes alone, even synchronous RFC can be used.

Components of ALE

The various components of ALE, many of which are also common for the EDI interface discussed in the next section, are as follows.

Logical System

A logical representation of the entire system needs to be constructed before the distributed and integrated system can be implemented in its entirety in a company. This logical model, which is conceived as if it were a single SAP instance, specifies which applications should be run on which systems and how the various systems should exchange data.

SAP supplies a distribution reference model that provides all possible, feasible scenarios for the distribution of applications. A company can develop its own customer distribution model by using this library of scenarios as a reference.

Message Type

This represents the application message exchanged between the various systems. The message type identifies the message and relates to the intermediate document (IDoc) type. MATMAS, for example, is the standard message type for the material master. ALE supports over 200 message types.

IDoc Type and IDocs

IDoc type represents the structure and format of data for a message type. An IDoc consists of the following records:

- **Control records**: These identify an IDoc uniquely in terms of the IDoc type, the message type, the sender, and the receiver; an IDoc is an instance of the IDoc type.

- **Data records**: These contain the application data. Every record contains a key portion that describes the content of the data. An IDoc can consist of one or more data records and the data portion is redefined for every occurrence, based on the structure of the segment in the key portion identifying the segment name, sequence, and hierarchy. In outbound processing, ALE/EDI function modules populate these segments with application data. In in-bound processing, the application modules populate these segments with application data.

- **Status records**: These keeps track of the processing stage that the IDoc has gone through at any moment. It also stores information regarding the time and date stamp of the corresponding status. An IDoc can have one or more status records.

Customer Distribution Model

This is applicable only for ALE and describes how the applications are actually distributed. It describes the message flow between the distributed logical systems. It also specifies the criteria for deciding which is a correct partner for a specific message. The customer distribution model is distributed from the central system to all of the concerned systems.

Filter Object Type and Filter Objects

A filter object type is used to impose selection criteria on the message type flowing to a logical system. In the case of a customer master message type, the filter object could be company code. Multiple filter objects with different values for the same message type can be associated with the same logical system.

Listings

Listings are another type of filter object based on the SAP classification system and are applicable only to material, customer, and vendor master data. After a list is created, it is used to create a filter object for a message type associated with a logical system.

Change Pointers

ALE has the powerful facility to capture changes occurring to the master data and to distribute them via the IDoc interface. This is the feature that is used to keep two or more distributed systems synchronized with respect to the master data.

Ports

This is a logical representation of a communication that is used by ALE (for example, R/2, tRFC, File, and Internet) to send IDocs. EDI uses mostly file-based ports.

Message Control and Output Type

This determines how documents are output in terms of number, type, time, and medium. Message control and output type use the condition technique to determine if a particular application document qualifies for output through search strategies using predefined output type, access sequences, and requirement conditions.

Process Codes

These are used both in ALE and EDI to identify the application modules that will process the outbound (corresponding to the message control) or inbound IDoc.

Partner Profile

A partner profile identifies a system used to communicate messages. Four kinds of partner profiles exist: KU for customer, LI for vendor, B for bank, and LS for logical system. Only LS is used for ALE; the rest are used for EDI interfaces. Partner profiles contain all vital parameters like message types, IDoc types, partner functions, process codes, application identifiers, message functions, output types, and ports.

Scenarios of ALE

The permanent exchange of data between the distributed systems ensures that they are all synchronized. The data that can be communicated is as follows:

- **Control data**: This includes the R/3 IMG customization data, IMG distribution scenarios control data, and customer distribution model control data.

- **Master data**: This includes information on the material, customer, vendor, General Ledger (G/L) account, cost center, cost element, activity type, corresponding Unit of Measure (UOM), and the corresponding activity price.

- **Transaction data**: Here you will find the invoice, customer order, purchase order, shipping notification, and so on.

As an example, we consider the ALE scenario of distributing master data across multiple R/3 systems, as shown in Figure 19.5. For instance, the head office (HO) maintains centralized responsibility for the material master data. This is distributed to systems at two different plants, 5001 and 6001. ALE provides the capability to filter and distribute only relevant data to the respective systems. The filter object type used for message MATMAS (material master) is WERKS (plant). As mentioned earlier, the full material master is transmitted from the HO to the respective systems, but thereafter only the changes need to be captured and communicated to the respective plant systems.

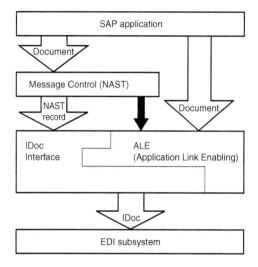

FIGURE 19.5

Transmission of an IDoc using ALE.

Electronic Data Interchange (EDI)

Companies work closely with their customers and vendors. For many large companies, this relationship that is more in the nature of partnership entails a close association between their respective computerized systems. EDI is a system that was devised for the automatic transmission of business documents. EDI could also be seen as a BPR of inter-company processes that, unlike traditional BPR, is not confined to a particular company but extends beyond the boundaries of the company. According to this view, apart from reducing effort in terms of avoiding inward and outward processing and reconciliations at the respective ends, inter-company processes reengineered by the use of incorporating EDI primarily reduce the non-value-added wait times dramatically.

EDI Architecture

The EDI architecture consists of the EDI-enabled application, the IDoc interface, and the EDI subsystem. An EDI-enabled application has the capability to process business transactions received through EDI, like SAP R/3. The IDoc interface provides an interface between the application and the EDI subsystem. The EDI subsystem converts the EDI messages from international standards like EDIFACT or X.12 into IDoc and vice versa and transmits them typically via the VAN's network. The EDI subsystem, which are typically third-party products, also performs many other functions like

- Performing the transmission and receipt of EDI messages
- Status checking and reporting
- Performing functional and receipt acknowledgements
- Performing retransmissions in case of interruptions
- Mapping EDI messages to IDocs and vice versa
- Translating EDI messages to IDocs and vice versa
- Performing Partner specific processing
- Maintaining Partner profiles
- Exchanging IDocs received with the R/3 system

Data Flow in Outbound Processing

As stated in the section on ALE, the communication of IDoc is quite similar both in the case of ALE and EDI. The scenario of sending the EDI messages via the IDoc interface involves the following steps (see Figure 19.6):

1. Connect the IDoc interface to an EDI subsystem.
2. Define the port.
3. Prepare the partner profile.
4. In case of logistics applications, defaulting the source of the message to be either the application module or the Message Control. In case of the latter, all parameters of the Message Control should be defined.
5. Set and schedule the RSNAST00 program.
6. As soon as a new purchase order (PO) is created, this PO will be scheduled for communication, depending on the settings in the Message Control.

7. The RASNASTED program is executed for preparing the EDI message.

8. RASNASTED reads the partner profile, determines the process code, and calls the application's selection module and selects the record for generating the IDoc.

9. The IDoc is now located in the SAP database; depending on the selected output mode, the IDoc is written, either alone or collectively, to a file that has already been specified while defining the port.

10. Depending on the specification of the output mode in the partner profile, the IDoc is sent out.

11. Using the IDoc number as the identifier, the EDI system sends the corresponding acknowledgement messages to the IDoc interface.

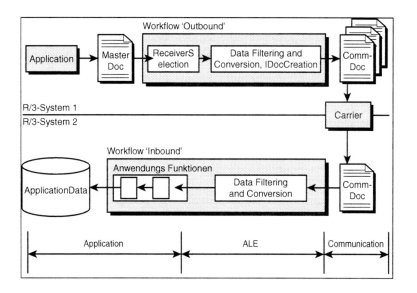

FIGURE 19.6

Data flow in outbound processing.

SAP R/3 System on the Internet

The importance of the Internet system does not lie in the fact that it increases the reach and flexibility of the enterprise. Rather, it lies in the fact that the Internet has become the most important component of the market environment itself and all global enterprises need to be able to integrate with this new state of the market environment. The intelligent use of Internet technology for business operations has already become a critical success factor for many enterprises. The same is true for all ERPs like SAP R/3.

Web-enablement of SAP R/3 has proved comparatively easy because of the following reasons:

- The Internet and SAP's client/server computing use an identical transfer protocol (TCP/IP).
- The browser technology of the Internet greatly corresponds to SAP's thin client version of the implementation of the three-tier client/server architecture. SAP's division between the application and presentation layers fits neatly with the separation of the presentation, as HTML is combined with the R/3 function operating in the SAP system.
- The Internet, like SAP, also operates completely independent of hardware and the underlying software on which the Web server provides the requested services.

Generally speaking, the principles on which the Internet works do not differ significantly from those used in the SAP R/3 system. In the R/3 system, the application server functions as the server and the SAP graphic user interface (SAPGUI) acts as a client. Similarly, in the case of Internet, the browser functions as the client and the Web server functions as the server that provides all the documents and services requested by the Web browser client.

Connecting to SAP Through the Internet

Two distinct approaches exist for connecting to the SAP system using the Internet: outside-in and inside-out. The former corresponds to the case where the application logic lies in the external system, whereas in the later the application logic remains within the SAP system. Each one has its advantages, depending on the requirement of the application system. The outside-in approach is suitable for applications that do not specifically require the use of SAP services or need to interface with many heterogeneous sources and systems. Both approaches access and use BAPIs provided by the SAP system, the only difference being that in the case of the outside-in approach the BAPIs are controlled by the application logic of the external system.

Outside-in

Outside-in has the major advantage of being able to use a wide variety of programming languages, development and integration environments, runtime environments, and presentation environments. However, unlike the inside-out approach, the external application has to provide the functionality for enforcing security, transaction management, data integrity, and so on.

This approach normally uses the RFC for calling SAP functions via RFC APIs. However, to access data through RFC, the user has to program in ABAP/4.

A variation on this approach is to use SAP automation that permits direct use of the SAPGUI functions from external programs. Additionally, this does not demand knowledge of ABAP/4, but SAP automation is useful for accessing existing SAP transactions only.

It must be noted that writing your own data access programs is required only if no BAPI is available. Also, plain RFC calls are a thing of the past; SAP allows you to call the BAPIs via DCOM connector very efficiently.

Inside-out

The Internet transaction server (ITS) became available for the first time with Release 3.1 of SAP R/3 and is SAP's recommended solution for accessing SAP on the Internet. ITS provides access to the functions of the R/3 system while also serving as a gateway for the conversion of HTML and as the interface to the Web server (for details see later in this chapter "SAP System on the Internet" section). The ITS primarily simulates the SAPGUI expected by the R/3 system; the communication channel of the SAPGUI affects the actual connection to the R/3 application server. The Dynamic Information and Action Gateway (DIAG) interface at the level of the SAPGUI enables transparent to-and-from exchanges of data with the SAP system, thus enabling it to process several Internet transactions simultaneously.

In this inside-out approach, all the application logic resides within the SAP system, the BAPIs are under the control of the corresponding SAP transaction, and the ITS automatically uses functionality available within the system for enforcing security, transaction management and integrity, scalability, session management, and so forth.

NOTE ───

> I discuss the ITS in the next section, but it must be noted that another advantage of the R/3's four-tier architecture is that it completely separates the design and development of ABAP/4-based R/3 Internet applications from the design of the user interface for the Web front-end. The latter is essentially a different type of skill and is best handled by expert visualizers and ergonomists.

SAP Internet Transaction Server (ITS)

The R/3 system and the Internet use different communication protocols and data formats. This is because of the lack of status (or statelessness) on the Web, unlike the case of a session- and transaction-oriented system like SAP. The ITS provides an interface between the Internet and the R/3 system for accessing the R/3 system from a Web browser or an HTTP server program.

When the HTTP server receives a user request, it invokes the ITS program to convert the field contents of the HTML pages to R/3 screen data. This data is exchanged between the ITS and R/3 system by using the DIAG interface, which makes ITS function like a normal SAPGUI when communicating with the R/3 system. This triggers a transaction in the R/3 system; the screen data provided by the SAP system is converted back into an HTML page by ITS, which is then transferred via the HTTP server to the Web browser where it is displayed. The transaction running in R/3 completes another step, depending on each additional action taken by the user; the data required to control this comes from the input by the user on the HTML page.

Apart from acting as the gateway between the HTTP server and the R/3 system, the ITS also performs other functions like administrating Web users, system resources, and Web transactions.

Using this approach to interface between the HTTP server and the R/3 system has the following advantages:

- A Web transaction can basically be developed and tested in the R/3 system.
- Connections use only the standardized and tested R/3 interfaces.
- All transaction components can be stored in the R/3 system, including those used by the ITS outside of the R/3 system during runtime.
- The different components of Web transactions can be included in the Workbench Organizer. Like other transactions, Web transactions can first be developed in a test system and then transported to the production system.
- Language-dependent HTML pages can be created at runtime using the multilingual features provided by SAP.
- R/3 transaction security can also be enforced on the Web applications.
- R/3 availability and scalability can also become available for the Web transactions.
- The R/3 system can provide dynamically retrieved or current, latest information to the Web applications.
- Support for all leading Web browsers.
- Support for integration with all leading Web servers like Microsoft IIS, Netscape Enterprise server, or any other common gateway interface (CGI) server.

By choosing to use the SAP R/3 application server as the development platform for Web applications, SAP is able to take advantage of many benefits of its proven environment such as

- The ABAP/4 development workbench
- The user management and authorization concept
- The change and transport system
- Workflow
- Lock management
- Database buffering
- Update task management
- Multilingual capabilities

- Platform and database independence
- Scalability

ITS enables the ready conversion of R/3 transactions to Web transactions. Most of SAP's standard business applications use HTML 4 and its capabilities like Cascading Style Sheets (CSS).

ITS Architecture

ITS is constituted of two separate components: Web Gateway (WGate) and Application Gateway (AGate) that communicate over TCP/IP. This makes it possible for them to be run on different computers, which is advisable for reasons of security and scalability.

WGate provides the interface to the Web server and is available to be loaded as a DLL (Dynamic Link Library) at runtime for Windows NT 4.0 only on the MS IIS and Netscape Enterprise server. This can also reside on the Web server as well.

AGate provides the interface to the R/3 applications using the DIAG protocol and is currently available for Windows NT 4.0. Several Web servers and the corresponding WGates can communicate with a single AGate. The first call of a new session on Web server creates a new session in ITS. During the data transfer, the system stores the data in the context data structures of the AGate, which is useful for making ITS accessible to the R/3 transactions as well as to control the ITS session.

AGate is responsible for the session management, including the mapping of R/3 screens or function modules to HTML, Web session time-out handling, R/3 connection management, and generation of the HTML pages. A connection breaks only because of a user logging off or because of the time-out. The session state enables the resynchronization of the situation on the Web and the corresponding R/3 transaction.

The AGate is implemented with a highly optimized thread and memory management model that enables fast context switching between different sessions. Like the dispatcher process of the application server, the AGate dispatcher organizes the queries from the Web and the work threads of the WGate. A thread is in use for one request/response cycle (see the last section of this chapter "An ITS Request/ Response Cycle") and not for a complete user session that enables many Web user sessions to reuse the threads.

ITS Files

Outside of R/3, an R/3 transaction is identified not by a transaction code, but as an Internet application or service identified by a service name. The following service description files are important while creating the Internet application components (IACs) and are called at the time of starting the IACs:

- **Global service**: this service file provides information, such as the system name, that is independent of the specific service. The global service descriptions are applicable to all

Web transactions executed via the ITS. Thus, for each SAP ITS, there is only one global service description.

- **Specific service**: there is one specific service file for each called R/3 transaction; the information of the specific service file overwrites those of the global service. This file contains information like the mandatory name of the transaction; the name of the corresponding R/3 application server; and optional information on login, password, client, language, and so on. Services are created through SAP@Web Studio.

- **HTML templates**: ITS uses a multistep process for generation of the final HTML pages by utilizing predefined HTML templates made available by ITS. Again, like services, HTML templates can be of two types: system and specific. The HTML templates contain placeholders for the corresponding fields on the R/3 screens, and this enables the AGate to allocate information from the HTML to the screen fields and vice versa. System HTML templates that are not recognizable or not relevant to the R/3 transaction cause error messages in the Web browser to be displayed.

Business HTML

Business HTML consists of ITS-specific statements contained within the HTML templates. These statements are not part of the standard HTML and are not recognized by the Web browsers. These statements only control the interface of the ITS with the R/3 system.

HTML templates are created through SAP@Web Studio; each HTML template corresponds to only one R/3 transaction and is assigned to exactly one theme of a service. They can also contain the URL for binary objects like graphics and sound files that are used by the Web server, although they are transparent to ITS functions. The HTML templates do not contain any business logic, only the visual elements for the input and output from the R/3 transactions; all logic continues to remain within the R/3 system.

- **Language Resources**: An HTML template can contain placeholders for text elements that can be filled by text from a language resource file in accordance with the language chosen at the time of the logon. The translation is done by specifying keys in the template and storing the mapping from the key to the actual string in the language resource. The language resources can be created through SAP@Web Studio for each service or for each theme in a service. Each service can contain one or more language resource files to accommodate different languages available for a specific Web transaction.

- **Theme**: this allows a service to have a different look and feel through usage of different themes.

ITS Tools

SAP@Web Studio is used for creating the transactions for the Web; it enables the creation and maintenance of the various service files described previously that are essential for starting the Internet applications IACs.

ITS Debugger enables a parallel connection between a Web transaction and the corresponding R/3 transaction via the SAPGUI simultaneously. This makes it possible to switch between transactions that are visible in both environments, which aids tremendously in debugging.

Internet Application Component (IAC)

IACs are Internet applications that consist of ABAP transactions and the corresponding HTML templates discussed earlier. IACs also include the service descriptions mentioned earlier. They implement business processes by using BAPIs, although they can also use traditional functional modules. However, the object-oriented nature of BAPIs makes IACs easy to maintain and ensures their release independence.

However, ITS cannot use the standard R/3 transactions without any modifications. The characteristics of the Web disallow the use of the following screen characteristics in a normal R/3 transaction:

- Menu bar
- Toolbar
- Pop-ups (for error messages, warnings, and so on)
- F1 Help and F4 for matchcodes and selection help
- Table widgets

IACs can be developed using one of three programming models: transactions, function modules, and reports. R/3 transactions, which are stateful applications, are basically screen-based applications. An application is divided into individual screens with a dialog flow that connects each of the screens. The R/3 applications maintain extensive user contexts in the memory until such time that the object is finally committed to the database. Transactions are more suitable as the programming model when the user is not meant to browse or jump arbitrarily between screens.

ITS can also call function modules using SAP's RFC interface. The programming model based on the RFCs is called the WebRFC, which calls a function module for every HTML page. This model is useful for applications where the corresponding Web user does not have to follow a strict dialog flow. Examples of such applications would be browsing a list of sources or shopping for items, catalogs, and so on. The WebRFC enables the development of both stateful and stateless applications. It enables an RFC-based interface without the need to program access to the Web in languages like C or C++.

Reports enable one to display reports in an HTML browser and also to automatically generate the HTML page corresponding to the selection screen. It also provides for a Web reporting browser for providing selections of reports available within the system.

An ITS Request/Response Cycle

An ITS request/response cycle, as shown in Figure 19.7, works as follows:

1. A user selects an HTML page corresponding to an IAC on the Web browser.

2. The WGate establishes a connection with the AGate. AGate loads the corresponding service and interprets the service descriptions, with the more specific settings overriding the more general settings.

3. AGate opens a SAPGUI connection to the R/3 system and starts the R/3 transaction identified in the service file on the R/3 system.

4. The system transmits the first screen to the AGate via the DAIG interface. The AGate stores the required context fields in the ITS.

5. AGate finds the HTML template file corresponding to this screen and allocates the screen data into the correct placeholders by using the HTML business statements as well as the context information.

6. The AGate transmits the completed HTML page to the WGate, which returns the page to the user's browser via the Web server.

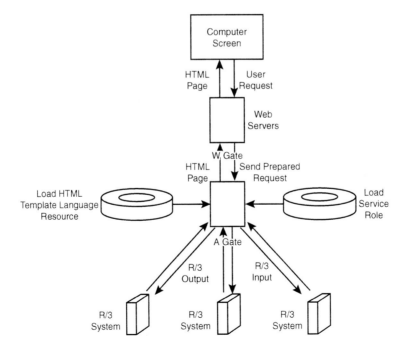

FIGURE 19.7

An ITS request/response cycle.

Summary

In this chapter, I discussed the enhancement and interfaces provided by SAP to extend its reach both within and outside the organization. In the first part of the chapter, I discussed SAP intra-company solutions like SAP Business Workflow, SAP Business Information Warehouse (BW) and the SAP Business Framework; while in the later part of the chapter, we looked at application communication solutions like Application Link Enabling (ALE), Electronic Data Interchange (EDI) and SAP ITS/ IACs. However, there is a business need to extend the application functionality itself to incorporate your partners and even customers. In the last chapter of this book, we look at the different types of solutions that are required for such an extended collaborative enterprise (ECE), and the corresponding strategy and solutions provided by SAP.

SAP Implementation and Beyond

IN THIS PART

Valuing the Millennium Enterprise

IN THIS CHAPTER

Chapter 1 of this book, "The Millennium Enterprise," deals at length on the collaborative nature of today's enterprises. In the subsequent chapters, you have seen various aspects of SAP R/3 that enable an enterprise to operate as an integrated, enterprisewide, process-oriented, information-driven, real-time enterprise. You have also seen that as organizational and environmental conditions have become more complex, globalized, and therefore competitive, processes provide a framework for dealing effectively with the issues of performance improvement, capability development, and adaptation to the changing environment.

In turn, continued value addition along every business process has become an essential prerequisite for viability of not only a particular process, but also for that of the organization as a whole. Here is the fundamental rationale for measuring and valuing an enterprise in terms of the value determinants that are relevant to all stakeholders of an organization. These include not only the traditionally known stakeholders of a company, like the company's investors and customers, but also the suppliers, managers, and employees of the company as well.

An enterprisewide solution like SAP, which embodies the process-oriented view of the organization, must provide the means for evaluating and maximizing the value delivered by the enterprise to all of its stakeholders. The first half of this chapter provides a fairly detailed introduction to such a perspective on the value created by an enterprise. It also discusses the now-popular Balance Scorecard (BSC) approach for valuation of an enterprise or the enterprise of a company. It suggests an interpretation of the scorecard in terms of the value to the five primary stakeholders of an enterprise: customers, vendors, investors, managers, and employees. In the latter half of the chapter, I present SAP's strategic enterprise management (SEM) solution that enables companies to pilot the execution and implementation of their corporate strategies.

Enterprise Stakeholders

An organization is defined by a constellation of collaborations. All collaborative relationships are truly stakeholder relationships; thus, a company is truly a continuum of collaborative stakeholder relationships. A corporation is embedded in a network of interdependent stakeholder relationships that are defined mutually and dynamically. The competitive response of an organization is the result of all such stakeholder relationships or collaborations. One of the earliest proponents of what is known as stakeholder theory is R. E. Freeman, who wrote "Strategic Management: A Stakeholder Approach." The stakeholders are investors, owners, management, political groups, customers, community, employees, trade associations, suppliers, alliance partners, government, competitors, and so forth.

Two kinds of stakeholders exist: primary and secondary. Primary stakeholders are those entities that are effected directly by the success or decline of a company like investors, financial institutions, customers, suppliers/vendors, employees, and so on. Secondary stakeholders like the media, government, and regulatory agencies are affected only indirectly by the varying fortunes of the company, but they definitely exercise influence on the functioning of the company. Sometimes this influence might not only exceed the influence of the primary stakeholders, but might also prove to be decisive for the enterprise.

For the value created by an enterprise, the five stakeholders of primary importance are

- Customer
- Investors
- Vendors
- Managers
- Employees

Collaborations are characterized by contracts that can range from explicit to the implicit. These contracts specify or allude to what the company can expect from each stakeholder in achieving its objectives and what each stakeholder can expect in return from the organization. For instance, explicit contracts are contracts whereby a customer pays a predetermined amount of money for availing of the company's products or services. Similarly, implicit contracts are contracts whereby an employee gets a promotion, depending upon the performance with reference to the expectations set at the beginning of the concerned period.

It is with reference to these contracts, whether implicit or explicit, that every stakeholder invests capital in the continued and envisaged future success of the company; this capital could be financial, managerial, intellectual, environmental, social, and so forth. The continued involvement, interest, and commitment of the stakeholders are dependent on the stakeholders getting a reasonable *return on investment (ROI)*. This ROI could be different for different stakeholders. For the customers, it could be in terms of assured competitive products, services, support, and upgrades in the future. For the vendors, it could be in terms of assured supply contracts on favorable terms. For the investors, it could be in terms of an assured dividend in the future. For the managers, it could be in terms of an assured rise up the corporate ladder and for the employees of the company, it could be in terms of assured security, professional development, and career growth.

Aspects of Enterprise Value

From the perspective of the collaborative enterprise, it is evident that a single stakeholder cannot sustain an appreciable ROI for itself at the cost of the other stakeholders. For instance, shareholder value cannot be maximized indefinitely by reducing product quality or customer service, negotiating arbitrarily lower rates from suppliers/vendors, or by cutting down remuneration of the employees. An ROI for different stakeholders is not in opposition to each one, it is not a "zero-sum game." You have already seen concrete proof of this in the last century when manufacturing quality and cost were mistakenly believed to be in opposition to each other. As it has been shown in the '90s, an enterprise can achieve excellent quality *at reduced costs.*

Although all companies focus on creating value for all constituencies, these efforts do not or are not able to address all the constituencies simultaneously. An enterprise does not usually have the capabilities to track the information that is essential for maintaining a cross-functional view of the impact of efforts for

- improving value addition activities at local activity centers.
- minimizing the non-value addition activities at local activity centers.

The apparent improvement in value addition or non-addition activities needs to be tracked enterprisewide across all functions and constituencies. This is because value addition or non-value addition at a local level may not be so for the company as whole. It has been well accepted by now that output of the organization as a whole cannot be maximized only by max-imizing the output of each constituting organizational unit or activity. For overall efficiency and effectiveness, a unit might often have to undertake activities that are essentially non-value–added at the operational level of the unit. SAP R/3 provides such a system that gener-ates, retains, analyzes, and reports on parameters that can track activity-level measures of per-formance, revenues, and expenditures. More importantly, SAP highlights cross-functional dependencies of activities across the enterprise.

Value to Customers

Value to customers is one of the most important values that is created by the company. Customers value the product and services not only in terms of the its innate use, but also in terms of its price relative to the competition. This in turn leads to other satellite criteria that ulti-mately lead to customers' continued patronage of the company's products. Customers look for

- Price
- Quality
- Flexibility
- Utility
- Variability, or the range of options
- Responsiveness
- Reliability
- Standardized interfaces and auxiliary systems
- Durability
- Maintainability

- Upgradability
- Support
- Service
- Innovation

Some of these properties characterizing a product/service might be in opposition to each other; the constellation of values that become applicable might vary from one product to another. Moreover, over the course of time, even the values for one particular product or closely related products might undergo changes. As you have seen in Chapter 6's section "Value-Added View of Business Processes," the value shifts might happen because of competitive products, changes in technology, or changes in the regulatory conditions. In fact, in the absence of other causes, value shifts might also occur merely because of the customer's illusive urge for innovation and the need for more than ordinary experiences. Added to this is the complication arising from the fact that the customer base itself is not static and keeps on changing dynamically, depending on the shift in critical value determinants (CVDs).

The customary way to determine the relative importance of value determinants is through customer satisfaction surveys and subsequent customer value analysis to generate normalized customer satisfaction indices. These indices might differ, depending on the objectives of the customer value analysis.

Value to Shareholders

Shareholders expect a reasonable ROI in the long term. It must be mentioned that whereas none can deny that higher returns are the basic motives for any investment, shareholders also value their contribution in the creation of wealth and job opportunities for their community. They derive immense satisfaction by sharing the created wealth with the community through the employees of the company. If a company demonstrates that it is utilizing its capital competitively and has a viable strategy that will sustain this rate of return or better it in the future, they will continue to maintain their financial interests in the company.

From the traditional earnings point of view, for industrial enterprises geared to mass production strategies, the investors look for Return-on-Capital-Employed (ROCE), Earnings per Share (E/S), Return on Assets (ROA), and so on in terms of integrity and quality of accounting information like

- Relevance
- Reliability
- Neutrality
- Fidelity

- Verifiability
- Comparability
- Consistency

However, the earnings point of view has not proven to be a reliable indicator of the value of a company. It is primarily oriented towards existing and past values and is not geared to address its arc in the future. Earnings is a static concept that uses linear projections based on the figures of the last accounting year. The underlying assumption in the traditional approach is that a company's value can be forecast based on its reported earnings. That this is erroneous has been established beyond doubt by the fact that market values of successful companies have always been greater than twice their book value.

On the other hand, the cash flow perspective sees value as a function of the expected future cash flows, which reflects the company's value in the long term and makes due allowance for the attendant risks. Unlike the accounting approach, in the cash flow approach, a strong correlation has been found to exist between the market price per share and predicted value per share based on cash flow forecasts.

According to the cash flow perspective, the investors look for

- Increased future surplus cash flows
- Assured future cash dividends
- Share price appreciation

For a company with relatively small capital, the earnings and cash flow perspective may not produce appreciably different results, but, even in such cases when we factor in accounts payable and inventories, the two approaches may provide highly divergent views.

Value to Managers

By convention, in the discussions on stakeholders, senior managers are usually grouped with owner/investors, which is incorrect. Managers with their responsibilities for driving the growth and profitability of the company have a different perspective of the values that are important to them vis-à-vis the owner/investors.

Senior managers look for the following:

- The freedom to articulate the vision of the organization and translate the same into objectives for the organization
- The latitude to focus on a select set of strategies and tactics
- The latitude to form the management team that believes in this vision and gels with this approach

- The facility to define the measures of performances for the organization as a whole as well as the individual business and operational managers
- The authority to allocate and deploy systems and resources for executing the plans
- The authority to institute and implement systems for measuring and reporting on the measures of performance for different functions and levels of the organization at predefined time periods or on ad hoc basis
- The latitude to mold the policies and procedures in line with the company's vision
- The latitude to commit research and development (R&D) efforts on technological and managerial issues that they perceive to be of importance for the future
- Remuneration that is commensurate with risks and targeted tasks

With the increase in the pace and pulse of businesses, the leeway available for CEOs and other senior executives has been diminishing continuously. The window of tolerance for failing revenues or periods of executing corrective strategies is progressively becoming smaller. In such circumstances, the hard-driving managers become conscious of the value that is catalyzed by them for the enterprise and the returns that they accrue to themselves. It is a supreme irony of our times that, with their increasing power and prestige, the CEOs and members of a management team are also most vulnerable to being summarily replaced because of perceived nonperformance.

Value to Vendors

In recent times, vendors are getting increased recognition for the value that they add not only to the final output of an enterprise, but also to its profitability. Vendors play a major role in enhancing the overall performance of the organization be it in terms of quality, input costs, overheads, responsiveness to the changes in the market, and so forth. Increasingly, they are perceived more as enterprise partners, rather than as the traditional adversaries to be browbeaten to lower prices.

Vendors in turn look for the following values in the value-creating enterprise of a company:

- Steady order commitments
- Optimal lead-times
- Immediate information on deliveries, rejects, returns, and so on in terms of the quantity and control information (such as delivery note numbers and batch numbers)
- Systematic invoice verification
- Prompt payments for verified and accepted invoices
- Interfaces with an enterprisewide, implemented system like SAP

- Sharing changes in production schedules
- Sharing changes in the positions of inventories vis-à-vis the production orders and so on
- Sharing results and analysis of quality tests on supplied materials
- Participation in plans of new products, models, technologies, and production processes

As mentioned in Chapter 1's "The Virtual Organization," only mature enterprise resource plans (ERPs) like SAP R/3 can provide the backbone for holding together the virtual value chain across such collaborative relationships with vendors.

Value to Employees

As described in Section Chapter 1's section on "Management by Collaboration," the dynamic changes in the market and global competition being confronted by companies have resulted in more flexible organizations. These organizations are populated with empowered workers who are multi-skilled with enhanced responsibilities. No organization can sustain the generation of value at high levels for extended periods without a corresponding value-add to the employees of the company.

Employees value factors like the following:

- Opportunities for participating and contributing significantly to the activities of the enterprise
- Reasonable compensation
- Opportunities to learn, develop skills, and handle challenging roles
- Access to all relevant information and resources for making decisions and discharging their responsibilities creditably
- Opportunities for recognition and rewards
- Opportunities for advancement
- Opportunities for training

The integrated, real-time, and transparent access to relevant data provided by SAP empowers the traditionally deprived members of the organization to make timely decisions and derive the satisfaction of being involved meaningfully in ensuring the well-being of the company.

In many ways, the value for the employees is analogous to the value for the external customers. Like the customers of the company, the effectiveness of employee value is gauged through employee satisfaction surveys that are administered on a periodic basis.

Enhancement of Measures of Performances by SAP

It is important to define the right measures for assessing a company's performance and its progress towards its declared goals and objectives. SAP assists in monitoring and managing the measures of performances (MOPs) to enhance the company's operational performance. With its integrated and real-time availability of operational data, SAP has the enabling environment to create, monitor and manage enterprise value. SAP provides the empowered platform for SMEs to address the competitive demands of the rapidly changing marketplace and be successful in terms of:

- Improved customer relations and management
- Reduced cycle time
- Improved quality
- Increased sales volumes
- Improved margins
- Reduced product development time
- Reduced manpower for routine operations
- Improved market share

The process of monitoring the MOPs can be guided by the value determinants that have been identified for the company. The value determinants can then be prioritized as well as customized suitable for the different activities within the company. Additions and deletions to the selected measures will be likely, depending on the market situations or alterations in the emphasis and focus of the measures already implemented.

The following lists show some of the performance factors that could be considered for measuring the excellence of the processes in SAP.

The sales and distribution performance factors are as follows:

- The number of new customers
- The number of one-time customers
- The number of customers retained
- The number of repeat orders and type
- The customer order-to-delivery time
- The number of non-standard or customized orders
- The number of errors per order shipped
- The percentage of back orders as a percentage of total orders

- The percentage of on-time first delivery to customers
- The percentage of on-time complete deliveries to customers

The quality performance factors are as follows:

- The number of defects and their type
- The elapsed time for rework and its type
- The number of customer complaints and their type
- The elapsed time for the first response
- The elapsed time for the delivered resolution
- The average number of customer interactions between problem reporting and resolution, and the type of interactions

The financial performance factors are as follows:

- Return on capital employed (ROCE)
- Earnings per share
- Weighted average cost of capital (WACC)
- Return on assets
- Turnover growth rate
- Operating income
- Gross margin
- Cash flow
- Sales per employee
- Value added per employee
- Energy dollars used per end item unit of production

The accounting performance factors are as follows:

- The number of days to close the books at the end of the month or quarter
- The number of errors per line item billed
- The number of unverified items and their type
- The number of unreconciled items and their type

The vendors/suppliers performance factors are as follows:

- The supplier lead times and their type
- The percentage of certified vendors
- The percentage of late deliveries

- The number of long-term contracts with suppliers
- The percentage of orders processed by the electronic data interchange (EDI)

The materials management performance factors are as follows:

- Inventory turns and type
- The requisition-to-receipt time

The production performance factors are as follows:

- The setup time as a percentage of the production cycle time
- Preventive maintenance as a percentage of sales
- The mean time between failures and type
- The mean time of repair

The engineering performance factors are as follows:

- The product and process design lead time
- The product concept-to-volume production lead time
- The percentage of engineering changes

The human resources performance factors are as follows:

- The percentage of absenteeism and type
- The percentage of employee turnover and type
- The percentage of revenue spent on training

Given the multiplicity of dependencies and influencing factors, the selection of the right measures is a complex task. There is a need for a framework under which multiple measures are integrated and related to each other so that a set of measurements should not be perceived to be in opposition to others. Moreover, there is also a need to have the right balance between the financial and non-financial measures, which is the focus of the section on the Balance Scorecard.

Value-based Management

For delivering superior stakeholder value, especially shareholder value, a company's management must not only be able to formulate strategies, but should also be able to execute them. Value-based management (VBM) ensures the implementation of a corporate strategy by directly linking the strategy, finance, and operations within a company. By linking strategic objectives to resource allocation and performance management, the operational decision-making is focused fully on delivering the strategic objectives.

To be effective, VBM entails combining the internal, external, historic, and predicted views with the financial and non-financial drivers of the business. Leveraging VBM essentially involves the following four steps:

1. Understanding what factors drive value

2. Finding out where value is created or destroyed

3. Establishing value as the criterion for decision-making

4. Embedding value into the corporate culture

The financial-oriented VBMs currently in vogue are primarily aimed at operationalizing the VBM so that individual members of a company can perceive and identify with the shareholder value that is contributed by the various functions and activities within the organization. But, it must be noted that there is already recognition that a finance-oriented view needs to be supplemented with a value-added view of manufacturing directly. ERP systems basically perpetuate the philosophy of top-down, build-to-stock and supply-driven mass-producing manufacturing strategy. The value-add view of manufacturing is in line with the increasing emphasis on:

- demand pull reflected in order changes
- flow manufacturing entailing fast changeovers

Like the Corporate Performance Monitor (CPM) discussed later, it is possible to envisage a Manufacturing Performance Monitor (MPM) that monitors in real-time manufacturing processes in terms of the various technical and economic value drivers.

Balance Scorecard (BSC)

The BSC is a VBM system based on four distinct perspectives for evaluating the performance of a company: financial, customer, internal, and learning. The BSC aims to provide a balance between the external and internal measures of performance, between short- and long-term objectives, between financial and non-financial measures, and between lagging and leading indicators. It is not limited to being merely a measurement and control system, but has actually developed over the course of time into a full-featured management system for the successful implementation of a company's strategy.

As discussed in Chapter 1's "Knowledge as the New Capital," in this post-industrial and post-modern era of information, the focus of capital and investments has changed dramatically. In the industrial era, all measures and managerial assessments were geared towards the efficiency with which financial capital could be allocated for capturing as quickly as possible the economies of scale for maximizing the return on capital employed (ROCE). In this post-modern computerized era, however, a company's competitiveness resides primarily in the collaborative systems, processes, and people that enable it to be flexible and reconfigure rapidly in response to the changes in the marketplace.

It should be noted that a company's emphasis is not on the capability to ingest the latest technology per se, because that would continue to change in future too. The emphasis is related more to the capability to confront any changes in the market with a strategy that will not only make the customers continue to value the company's products and services, but also differentiate them effectively from those provided by the competitors. This is the subtle reason why a few years back General Motor's much known foray into highly automated manufacturing facilities to beat the Japanese on productivity and quality was not very successful.

Thus, a company needs a management system to assess and evaluate its strategy in terms of competitiveness and performance in the future. There is also the important need for the company to be able to dynamically monitor the progress and performance of the execution of these strategies, which will then enable the company to administer any corrections or adjustments based on the real-time operational feedback received from such a system. The BSC is precisely such a strategic management system that enables an enterprise to monitor and manage the execution of its value-adding and value-creating strategies effectively. Enterprises also need an information system that would empower them to implement the BSC. SAP's SEM is a solution for implementing BSC within an organization and is discussed later in "SAP Strategic Enterprise Management (SEM)."

BSC provides companies with a framework for translating the company's vision and strategy into a coherent set of performance measures. BSC derives the objectives and measures of the value determinants or the corresponding performance drivers based on the vision and strategy of the company. As shown in Figure 20.1, the BSC framework is constituted of the following four perspectives:

- Financial
- Customer
- Internal business processes
- Learning and growth

BSC retains the financial perspective of the company's performance that is essentially based on past performance and is valid for short-term performance in the immediate future. However, it supplements this traditional perspective with those of the customer and the internal system, process, and people that determine the company's value-generating potential and hence long-term financial performance in the future.

The customer's perspective ensures the continual relevance of the products and services provided by the company. The internal perspective of business processes and the people ensures that the company surpasses the customer's expectations on critical value determinants like quality, timeliness, innovation, and service. It is in this sense that the BSC represents a balance between the external value determinants of the customers and shareholders, and the corresponding internal value drivers of the critical systems, business processes, and people.

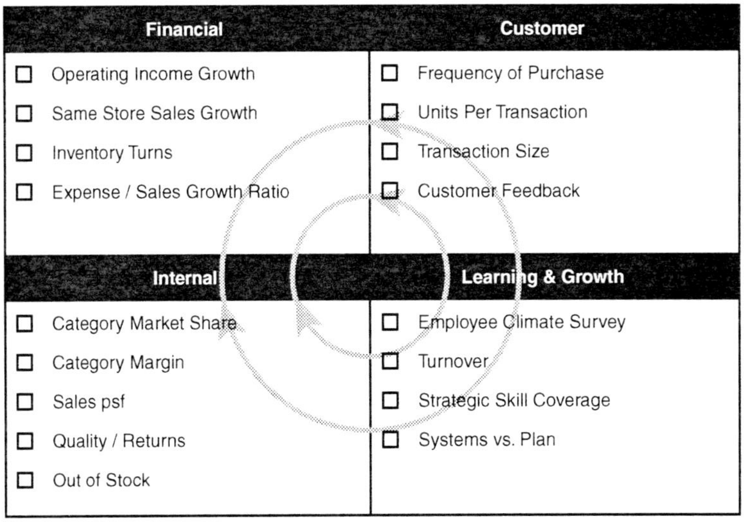

Financial	Customer
☐ Operating Income Growth	☐ Frequency of Purchase
☐ Same Store Sales Growth	☐ Units Per Transaction
☐ Inventory Turns	☐ Transaction Size
☐ Expense / Sales Growth Ratio	☐ Customer Feedback
Internal	**Learning & Growth**
☐ Category Market Share	☐ Employee Climate Survey
☐ Category Margin	☐ Turnover
☐ Sales psf	☐ Strategic Skill Coverage
☐ Quality / Returns	☐ Systems vs. Plan
☐ Out of Stock	

FIGURE 20.1

The Balance Scorecard framework.

Two kinds of value drivers exist: outcome and performance. Outcome drivers are lagging indicators like financial measures that are objective, quantifiable, and are past-facing. On the other hand, performance measures are leading indicators that link with the company's strategy and provide the rationale for achievements of the outcome drivers. Although performance drivers are future-facing, the impact and effectiveness of performance drivers on the outcome measures is highly subjective. This is compensated by the dynamic nature of the BSC system that treats evaluation and feedback as an important element of the framework. The value drivers are constantly under tests for continued relevance in the market and any deviations observed in the customer's value determinants are immediately cascaded in terms of the changes in the value drivers' measures or the value drivers themselves. This corresponds to the learning and growth perspective of the BSC framework. It represents the capability of institutional learning, which is the powerful concept of "double-loop" learning that I spoke about in Chapter 1's "The Learning Organization" that gives tremendous advantages to companies in these times of rapidly changing markets.

In fact, the whole BSC framework is based on a perceived cause-and-effect relationship between the various strategies, organizational elements, and processes of the enterprise. It is in the context of these assumptions that the BSC also incorporates the cause-and-effect relationships in terms of the relationships between the various outcome and performance drivers. For instance, the ROCE driver (in the financial perspective) is dependent on customer loyalty (in the customer perspective). Customer loyalty is dependent on the organization's product quality and responsiveness (in the internal business processes perspective), which in turn is dependent on the minimization of product defects, knowledge of the customer's prior transaction history, recorded preferences, and so on. (learning and growth perspective). It is because of this that the multiple objectives and measures of BSC do not entail complex trade-offs but can easily be integrated into a consistent framework of 20 to 25 value drivers that can help navigate the strategy of the company successfully through the turbulent marketplace. This aircraft analogy is not very far fetched; in "Business Consolidation and Sourcing (BCS)" I discuss the SAP management cockpit for the strategic management of enterprises that is based on a similar concept.

The strategic management of enterprises using BSC involves the following stages:

- Mapping the company strategy into the BSC framework in terms of the strategic objectives and drivers for BSC. This might also involve reconciling or prioritizing among various objectives or defining differing objectives and drivers for different divisions. This stage identifies all processes that are critical to the strategic performance of the enterprise. It must be noted that the BSC is a methodology for implementing a company strategy and not for formulating one. This is another reason why it is highly suitable for incorporating it into the SAP SEM solution.

- Communicating the link between the strategic objectives and measures throughout the organization at all levels. This might also involve operationalizing the defined set of measures to the specifics of the local circumstances for the various departmental and functional units of the company. BSCs are usually defined at the level of strategic business units (SBUs), but for a multi-divisional company, the defined BSC might incline more towards the financial perspective.

- Setting targets, devising aligned strategic initiatives, and planning/scheduling initiatives to achieve a breakthrough performance. This might also include financial planning and budgeting as an integrated part of the BSC. From the customer's perspective, this step should include requirements of both existing and potential customers.

- Enhancing performance through feedback and learning, based on operational data and reviews. This might entail reprioritizing or changing the performance thresholds or even the value drivers themselves. The latter might become necessary either because of the changes in the marketplace or because the selected set of value drivers might be ineffectual.

Figure 20.2 shows the BSC approach to create a strategy-focused organization.

In the BSC framework, the financial perspective enables a reality check of the strategic management activity of the enterprise. This is because all strategic initiatives meant for improving the quality, flexibility, and customer satisfaction might not necessarily translate into improved financial results. If the improved operational outcome as seen from the other three perspectives defined by the company does not end in improved financial results, it might be a powerful indicator of the need for reformulation of the strategy itself. All cause-and-effect relationships that knit a BSC program must eventually link to financial objectives. Therefore, the financial perspective is pre-eminent among all perspectives of the BSC framework.

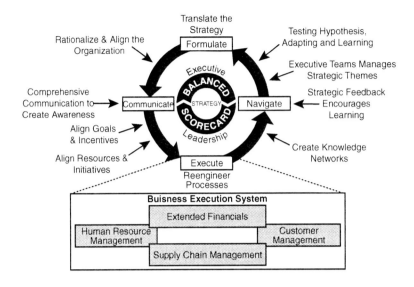

FIGURE 20.2

The Balance Scorecard approach to create a strategy-focused company.

The standard BSC framework talks of only four perspectives, but, if required, the framework can be supplemented with additional perspectives of stakeholders discussed in "Enterprise Stakeholders." In view of the increased importance of supply-chain management (SCM) for the extended collaborative enterprises of today, a prime candidate for addition would be the suppliers/vendors of the company. As I will discuss in the final chapter of the book, the suppliers will play as critical a role in the success of the enterprise as any of its constituent SBUs for the extended collaborative enterprises. In the remaining part of this section, we briefly look at the various perspectives of the standard BSC framework.

Financial Perspective

As mentioned above, the financial performance measures indicate whether a company's strategy, implementation, and execution are translating into bottom-line financial results. Depending on the business strategy, the financial objectives could be in terms of:

- ROCE, economic value add (EVA) or operating income, and maintaining the market share
- Rapid sales growth and increased market share
- Maximize the generation of cash flow

Customer Perspective

The customer perspective mainly addresses the customer- and market-oriented strategies that would deliver improved financial results. This involves the identification of the market segments of interest, the value propositions for each of these segments, and the measures that would help in ascertaining the performance of the company in the selected segments.

The basic outcome measures for this perspective could be

- Customer acquisition
- Customer satisfaction
- Customer retention
- Customer profitability

Internal Business Processes Perspective

The internal business processes perspective provides focus on the business processes that are critical to the success of the enterprise. These processes selected for improvement could be existing processes (as discussed in Chapter 6's "Selecting Business Processes for BPR") or they could also be entirely new processes conceived as a consequence of the strategy of the company. For instance, an excellent example of such a process could be a provision for a Web-based procurement of a company's goods and services.

SAP contributes directly to a company's performance in this perspective through its now-familiar library of best-of-business scenarios and processes as well as its ability to incorporate innovative processes or variations on the existing processes by means of rapid reconfiguration of the IMG.

Learning and Growth Perspective

The learning and growth perspective addresses the need to build and maintain an appropriate infrastructure for the long-term growth and success of the company. Contributions from the other perspectives, especially regarding envisaged shifts in customer value, might identify the technologies and products essential to the continued relevance of the company's offerings in the marketplace. These contributions might encompass the following:

- People's skills
- Information and support systems
- Organizational processes and procedures

This perspective comprehensively covers employee-related issues like employee satisfaction, employee training, advancement and promotion policies, employee-friendly policies and procedures, productivity-multiplying application environments, and so forth. SAP is an enabling environment for supporting the management of all these perspectives, an aspect that is tackled in the next section.

SAP Strategic Enterprise Management (SEM)

Launched at SAPPHIRE '98 in Madrid, SAP SEM is a comprehensive set of software functions and processes that enables a company to implement and operate a strategic management process. Based on the BSC concept, SAP SEM enables organizations to translate strategy into action faster and more efficiently. SAP SEM provides an integrated, real-time view of the corporate performance information across business structures, enabling the assessment and enhancement of the corporate value from the perspective of all the stakeholders. SEM is a part of the SAP Business Intelligence Initiative.

The SEM process involves the following:

- Analyzing stakeholder expectations
- The automatic sourcing of external and internal information
- Simulating and developing business strategies
- Planning and analyzing investment decisions
- Dedicating resources and integrating strategic, financial, and operational information
- Providing interpretation models like BSC, value trees, and so on
- Monitoring and managing performance
- Communicating the status of performance and manage relations with the stakeholders, especially the shareholders

Figure 20.3 shows the architecture of the SAP SEM.

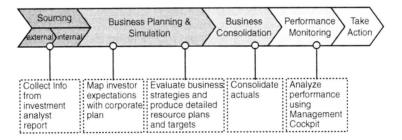

FIGURE 20.3

The SAP Strategic Enterprise Management (SEM) process.

SAP SEM enables executives to simulate, analyze, implement, monitor, optimize, and communicate the strategies at the operational level within the company. It supports the translation of the corporate strategy into measures of operational performance in terms of key performance indicators (KPIs). The system provides facilities for the simulation of alternative scenarios to predict the impact of the potential decisions on the KPIs to reach optimal decisions. The system ensures continuous feedback on KPIs from the business execution level via its close integration with SAP and non-SAP systems. Thus, the feedback can be used not only for managing the KPIs and making better decisions, but also for strategy optimization and learning.

The SAP SEM system is a set of five integrated analytical application components operating on the multi-dimensional SAP BW structures within SAP's business framework architecture. We discuss the five components in the remaining part of this section.

Thus, SAP SEM provides comprehensive functionality for supporting enterprise management, resulting in the following advantages:

- It provides end-to-end solutions for strategic enterprise management (modeling, planning, monitoring, reporting, and stakeholder relationship management).

- It supports various SEM methodologies like VBM, BSC, activity-based management (ABM), portfolio management, target costing, risk management, and so forth.

- It provides for generic and industry-specific SEM approaches.

- It supports integrated strategic management processes by linking strategies with operational measures of performance.

- It enables management of an enterprise on a day-to-day basis using value-based management principles.

- It supports integration with SAP R/3 but can also function with non-SAP systems or even in a standalone mode.

All SEM functions can operate with the SAP Business Information Warehouse (BW) and therefore can exchange data between the various components as well as use the full functionality for reporting available in BW.

Key Performance Indicators (KPIs)

KPIs are the various operational parameters that can be measured and benchmarked for assessing and evaluating the company's performance in strategic, financial, and operational areas. KPIs not only measure performance within the organization, but they have a much wider validity for the entire supply chain of an organization. These include measures like ROI, cash-to-cash cycles, customer satisfaction indices, employee satisfaction indices, material acquisition costs, order delivery times, production flexibility, production cycle times, and so on.

In SAP, all KPIs are primarily based on the supply-chain operations reference (SCOR) model and stored within the SAP BW repository. More than 250 KPIs are read across areas like

- Supply-chain costs
- Finance
- Delivery performance

- Production control
- Cycle/lead times
- Inventory control
- Supplier performance
- Human resources
- Scorecards

Business Planning and Simulation (BPS)

Business planning and simulation (BPS) enables comprehensive simulations and scenario analysis for modeling complex relationships between the company, its competitors, and the market. It integrates different levels of planning to permit building an integrated planning model right from the strategic level down to the resource allocation level.

BPS supports integrated strategic and operational business planning. These plans include the creation of dynamic and linear business models, scenario simulations, scenario evaluations, taking into account the business risks, carrying out the resource allocation, and forecast planning. BPS supports common planning strategies like top-down planning, bottom-up planning, interactive planning, automatic planning, and decentralized or distributed planning, as well as a combination of these planning strategies. BPS provides modeling and planning in classical areas like sales volume, price, cost, investment, balance sheet, and financial or headcount planning. Using these models, BPS simulates the effects of operational aspects like price changes, process optimizations, investments, and even reorganization on the KPIs or the total plan.

Through the ABM functionality, it also provides decision support for

- Management of costs
- Optimization of operational and strategic resources

The planning scenarios defined by BPS are the basis of the subsequent analysis within SEM. The planning scenarios generated by BPS are consolidated by the Business Consolidation and Sorting (BCS) component and are visualized, analyzed, and assessed by the Corporate Performance Monitoring (CPM) component.

Business Information Collection (BIC)

Business information collection (BIC) deals with the collection of structured or unstructured data from internal and external sources. BIC provides the infrastructure necessary for collecting the data required by SEM, including financial figures, statistical key figures, stock prices, financial reports, commercial databases, and so forth. This data could be collected from sources like SAP and non-SAP systems as well as from the Internet.

The major focus of the BIC component is to gather data available from the Internet that may be relevant for making informed decisions for the management of the company. The Web-based Editorial Workbench maintains information on the following:

- Areas of interest (investment reports, company/industry evaluations or analysis, press reports, and so on)
- Potential Web sources
- Corresponding recipients within the company

The Editorial Workbench, as an intelligent agent, filters out the most relevant information according to predefined requirements and provides the processed information to the internal decision-makers after linking it with the relevant internal information.

Business Consolidation and Sourcing (BCS)

The BCS component provides complete functionality for creating consolidated financial statements consisting of balance sheets, income statements, and cash flow statements both for the external as well as internal accounting purposes. It enables a company to carry out consolidations based on user-defined organizational units and hierarchies. Thus, one can perform consolidations for companies, divisions, business areas, or profit centers.

The BCS module uses local currencies for the organizational units and the respective group currencies for the consolidation groups; the system calculates and posts the translation differences automatically. The system accelerates the consolidation process by providing extensive automation of all these functionalities. The component permits further enhancement of the consolidation by defining various characteristics such as product group, geographical region, customer group, distribution channel, and so on.

Other features provided by BCS are as follows:

- It uses different charts of accounts like US-GAAP, IAS, and local GAAPs in parallel, depending on the requirements.
- It eliminates interunit payables and receivables, investment income, P/L in transferred assets/inventories, and so forth (with automatic translations and adjustments for currency differences).
- It maintains different versions of consolidation data like budgets, forecasts, simulations, models, and actual data.
- It defines different periods within a year for viewing financial data monthly, quarterly, semi-annually, or annually.
- It displays the overall status of consolidation using a graphics-based status monitor that also highlights exceptions visually using traffic-signal icons.

- It transfers data from a SAP system for consolidation with a company, business area, or profit center.
- It provides standard and ad hoc reports including drill-down capabilities to operational areas and transactions levels.
- It can interface with MS Excel and MS Access.

Corporate Performance Monitor (CPM)

The Corporate Performance Monitor (CPM) is a component that enables the monitoring and management of the company's performance. CPM uses industry-specific and customer-defined KPIs linked to the BSC to continuously monitor the performance against the predefined targets. These monitoring capabilities, coupled with the simulation capabilities provided by the BPS, enable a company to analyze and optimize strategic decisions to assess and improve corporate value. CPM provides a near-real-time, closed-loop feedback mechanism that enables the company to learn and optimize performances of the business processes critical for the continued financial success of the company.

Management Cockpit

The management cockpit is an innovative concept for the interpretation and visualization of critical management information that enables managers to quickly go beyond the details to see the big picture. Based on the BCS, it includes both financial and non-financial KPIs corresponding to different perspectives within the BCS. It also provides an environment for engendering collaborative intelligence that enables company executives to efficiently understand and resolve each other's issues as a team. This can be achieved by displaying KPIs and other related information graphically on the walls of an ergonomically designed meeting room. The management cockpit is a specially designed "war room" that resembles an airplane cockpit filled with visual displays. KPIs and information relating to the critical value determinants (CVDs) can be displayed graphically on the walls of the management cockpit.

The management cockpit was created by Patrick M. Georges of N.E.T. Research and is being developed further jointly by SAP and N.E.T. Research.

Stakeholder Relationship Management (SRM)

Stakeholder relationship management (SRM) primarily improves the communication with the stakeholders. It ensures that the stakeholders are informed regularly and systematically about the business strategy and its effect on the stakeholder value. It also provides for collecting feedback from the stakeholders as inputs to the BPS and CPM components of SEM.

SAP AG's ValueSAP Program

The ValueSAP program, launched at SAP users conference at Nice, France in mid-1999 (SAP-PHIRE '99 Nice), is a program designed to assist SAP customers in evaluating their investments in SAP solutions. The ValueSAP covers all stages of the SAP implementation, including evaluation, implementation, and ongoing improvements during the post-implementation period.

This program leads a customer through a programmed set of questionnaires to facilitate decision-making related to each stage of the implementation. The questions are classified into six key business areas:

- Management activities
- Business processes
- Technical management
- Development activities
- Knowledge transfer
- Help and care

The ValueSAP program recommends measures in conjunction with tools like SAP solution maps, SAP technology maps, SAP services solution maps, and ASAP for maximizing the value of the SAP implementation for the customer's business.

The first deliverable of the ValueSAP offering is continuous business improvement (CBI) services that help customers in identifying and adopting business practices to increase their profitability and competitiveness. This enables the customers to define benchmarks and ROI criteria for evaluating the success of the ERP implementation at various stages. The value gaps identified at various stages also provide pointers for possible areas of improvement.

The ValueSAP CBI services help customers to identify business opportunities through comparative assessments of KPIs, total cost of ownership (TCO), documented ROI studies against industry averages, and market leaders. Thus, ValueSAP extends the best-of-business practices to the process of implementing SAP itself. ValueSAP also incorporates the latest extension of SAP beyond the boundaries the company, such as mySAP.com. With SAP finally abandoning the monolithic approach to developing systems and embracing a more symbiotic strategy vis-à-vis other players in the market, mySAP.com marks a watershed in the history of SAP. In the last chapter of this book, we familiarize ourselves with this latest development in the universe of SAP.

Summary

This chapter introduces the perspectives on the value created by an enterprise from the point of view of its five major stakeholders: customers, investors, vendors, managers, and employees. This generated value can be monitored and managed in terms of the measures of performances characterizing the operations of the company. The measures of performances can be defined and managed strategically through the Balance Scorecard framework implemented by SAP Strategic Enterprise Management (SEM) solution. At the end of the chapter we looked at a sample list of improvements in measures of performances that have been achieved in various companies by the implementation of SAP R/3.

Beyond the Enterprise

IN THIS CHAPTER

In Chapter 1, "The Millennium Enterprise," I introduced management by collaboration (MBC) as a unifying framework in the context of the enterprise. The real power of this concept can be seen when we go beyond the boundaries of an enterprise. Here in the last chapter of this book, I look beyond the physical confines of an enterprise, which does not exit in isolation. It interacts with other entities like suppliers, dealers, traders, banks, courier and transport companies, and customers.

In this chapter, I consider various issues and aspects related to the extended collaborative enterprise (ECE). I also discuss SAP supply-chain management (SCM), customer relationship management (CRM), and other solutions addressing such inter-enterprise requirements in the context of ECEs. In light of the revolution being wrought by the rapidly burgeoning Internet-based applications, I end this chapter appropriately with an introduction to the mySAP.com Internet solutions recently delivered by SAP.

The Extended Collaborative Enterprise (ECE)

In the '90s, the enterprise resource plans (ERPs) focused attention on enhancing performance within the enterprise, yet more than 50 percent of the variable costs that affect the performance of an organization are driven by decisions outside the boundaries of the organization. After benefiting from streamlining and reengineering the internal processes, enterprises will address the potential for major gains obtainable from these cross-company processes. But why is supply chain considered important for the next quantum leap in organization performances? Enormous opportunities for enhanced efficiencies exist between supply-chain partners, as also the potential for a greater level of customer satisfaction.

Like the non-value-adding hand-offs within an organization, many of the interfaces and hand-offs between partners are non-value adding, efficiency-depleting, and time-wasting. The customer ends up paying for all these inefficiencies, regardless of how far removed or hidden he or she may be from the source. Similar to the inefficiencies associated with typical internal processes (before the implementation of enterprise-wide solutions like SAP), supply-chain inefficiencies can easily account up to 25 percent of the company's operating costs.

The future of ERP is closely related with the efforts to reengineer such inter-enterprise interfaces and foster closer collaborations across multiple enterprises, that is, the extended collaborative enterprise (ECE). This is in quite contrast to the traditional adversarial relationships that have been known to exist among the suppliers, manufacturers, and retailers. The true economies of production can only be gained by the economies of cooperation. The virtual organization that I referred to in Sub-Section 1.2.5 spans all such members of the traditional supply chain; the virtual value chain spans all such value-adding members of the supply chains. Thus, an ECE differs from a traditional supply chain in the extent to which a company can integrate with its partners. The ECE is truly embodied in the full-featured e-SCM systems to be described later in "The Electronic Supply-chain Management (e-SCM) Systems."

The supply chain encompasses all activities associated with transporting and transforming the raw materials from the suppliers into the finished products delivered to the customers. This includes order processing, sourcing and procurement, inventory management, production scheduling, production, packaging, transportation, warehousing, delivery, and customer service and support. The SCM is involved with integrating, coordinating, and collaborating all these activities into a seamless process that embraces and links all partners in the chain. These include not only the internal constituents, but also external partners like suppliers, wholesalers, carriers, third-party logistic companies (3PLs), warehousing companies, retailers, authorized service providers, and so forth. For companies seeking long-term advantages, the SCM system is a key platform needed to support rapidly burgeoning Web-based business models. Traditionally, SCM is concerned with having the right product in the right place, at the right price, at the right time, and in the right condition.

Three basic supply-chain architectures exist:

- **Direct Channel**: this can be compared to traditional grocery retail stores. At the expense of high inventory and thin margins, this channel provides good market reach and customer services.

- **Indirect Channel**: this corresponds to the sale of capital and electronic goods; at lower inventories and better margins, this channel has longer fulfillment times, depending on the geographic location.

- **Virtual Channel**: this corresponds to sales on the Internet; with medium margins, this channel has the convenience of being accessible from any PC anywhere.

The complexity of supply-chain operations is increasing because of intensifying competition resulting in

- Mass customization of products

- Shorter demand cycles

- Proliferation of products and stock-keeping units (SKUs)

- Implementation of agile manufacturing strategies like just-in-time (JIT) manufacturing and distribution

- Implementation of supply integration concepts

- Greater outsourcing of manufacturing operations

- Increased use of 3PL

- Implementation of co-managed inventory programs with customers (such as vendor-managed inventory (VMI), cross-docking, and so on) or suppliers (such as continuous Replenishment programs (CRP))

- Implementation of synchronized supply-chain strategies like efficient consumer response (ECR) leading to collaborative planning, forecasting, and replenishment (CPFR)

- Increased globalization of operations
- Increasing mergers, acquisitions, and consolidations

Supply-chain Management (SCM)

In this section, I will give an overview of the concepts involved with the SCM systems. This will be essential for you in order to prepare for the SAP SCM solution presented later in the "SAP Supply Chain Optimization, Planning, and Execution (SCOPE)" section. We will adopt the approach recommended by the Supply-Chain Council called the Supply-Chain Operations Reference (SCOR) model. The first version of SCOR, launched in 1996, was a result of the collaborative efforts of two Boston-based consulting firms, PRTM and AMR Research, along with approximately 70 top manufacturers in the U.S. SCOR enables companies to employ a standard approach to describe and analyze all supply-chain issues. It also enables companies to define standardized metrics for measuring the performances of supply chains and therefore define the best-of-class performance with wide acceptability.

The supply chain involves all resources and activities that are needed to source, create, and deliver products and services to the customers. According to SCOR, SCM involves the management of activities like coordinating, scheduling, procurement, production, packaging, distribution, transportation, warehousing, and delivery. SCM overlays and leverages ERPs like SAP, legacy, and other transaction-oriented operational systems. At the greatest level, SCOR addresses several aspects related to creating and delivering processes like

- Cash-to-cash cycle time
- Supply-chain response time
- Production flexibility
- Total supply-chain management cost
- Value-added productivity
- On-time delivery
- Warranty cost or returns processing costs
- Inventory days of supply
- Inventory turns
- Out-of-stock rates
- Order fulfillment performance

At the next level of detail, SCOR assists in the optimal configuration of the supply-chain infrastructure in terms of process elements, depending upon the strategic objectives set by the enterprise(s) driving the ECE. For instance, the configuration could be targeted at a make-to-stock, make-to-order, or even engineer-to-order production strategy. This could also involve different configurations of the supply chain for different products and services. An objective measurement of contribution by the various members of each of these supply chains would also enable a proper understanding for the sharing of ownership, costs, ongoing improvement efforts, benefits, and rewards.

In this context, it should be noted that particular decisions leading towards the optimal performance of the supply-chain community as a whole might not be locally optimal for particular members of the supply chain. Such members would have to be suitably rewarded and compensated for the benefit of the community as a whole. Similarly, because the model involves distributed data by a shared application, there might also be a need to agree on identifying ownership (along with its attendant costs) for the product/service at any moment. Such measures are critical for the maintenance of productive supply chains and sustenance of the corresponding partnering relationships. Only over time would all members be able to reduce inventory capital costs, reduce material shortage, and also become more responsive.

SCM systems address all these requirements for the management of supply chains in terms of providing functionality for supply-chain planning and optimization leading to the synchronization. I discuss these requirements in the following sub-sections, but it must be noted that the SCM systems need to balance between the flexibility and built-in functionalities provided by their applications. These characteristics have a direct impact on their applicability to a wider range of industries as well as the optimal effort and time required for their implementation. SAP, in line with its established repository-driven philosophy, tries to achieve both in the SAP Advanced Planning and Optimization (APO). In the future, the present general-purpose APO applications may be followed by SAP introducing several industry-specific APO solutions.

Supply-chain Planning

The supply-chain planning framework deals with the structure and optimization of the supply chain as a whole. The supply chain is usually represented as a network of nodes corresponding to the suppliers, production centers, distribution centers, and customers. The planning is carried out over the following three time horizons:

- **Strategic**: this is mainly concerned with the design of the supply-chain network based on various predefined parameters like the plant location, size of the facility, distribution center location, and the warehouse capacity.

- **Tactical**: this involves optimizing the flow of goods throughout the predetermined supply chain across a time horizon. It develops sourcing, production, deployment, and distribution plans. These are done either on a monthly or daily basis.

- **Operational**: this is primarily related to the production scheduling of plant resources like labor, equipment, and materials on a daily or even an hourly basis, depending on machine failures, material shortages, and changes in orders. It takes into account the lowest level of details like setup and changeover times, routings, BOMs (bill of materials), and so on.

Supply-chain Optimization

Supply-chain optimization deals with the decisions relating to the supply chain arising out of the constraints on resources like time, production capacity, modes of transportation, and so forth. This covers the following issues:

- Controllable variables like when and how to manufacture a product to a customer.
- Constraints like the limitation of raw materials, the production capacity, the handling capacity, the transportation capacity, and the time of transportation.
- Performance objectives, in terms of maximizing customer service, maximizing profits/margins, minimizing costs/cycle times, minimizing delays, maximizing production setup or overall throughput, and minimizing wastes/rework; this might also address the need for multiple objectives at the same time (with equal or different weights/ priorities).
- Optimizing models that represent the dependent relationships among the controllable variables, constraints, and performance objectives. These vary depending on the tractability of the problem, the availability of data, and the complexity of the model in terms of necessary computational resources and so forth. The models could be algorithmic, heuristics, genetic algorithms, or even exhaustive enumerations. The last category of models is only useful in simplified situations.

Subsequent to the formulation of the problem, the solver component calculates and determines the optimal solution that is in conformity with the context of the four issues given above. The solver can locate a working solution that satisfies all the constraints and is implementable immediately or it finds a partially optimized solution that meets part of the desired optimization criteria. In exceptional cases, the solver might actually discover the optimal solution that satisfies all the constraints and objectives.

This discovery helps in making the decisions on factors relating to the supply-chain performance, mentioned above. It should be noted that, like in the case of ERPs, the inventory and capacity of the supply chain are two important parameters that are of interest in any optimization exercise. For all practical purposes, as capacity is seldom changeable, it is the inventory that gets the maximum attention.

Supply-chain Synchronization

The synchronized supply chain is more in line with the emerging trend of customer-preferred "pull" environments on the Internet (environments driven by customer demand).

Synchronization eliminates costs associated with inefficient movements of goods, redundant processes, and excess inventory and promotes a dedicated collaboration among all members of the supply chain. Synchronization focuses on reducing the inefficiencies that are hidden at the boundaries within organizations.

The complexity of supply-chain synchronization can be considered across the earlier-mentioned time horizons: strategic, tactical, and operational. First, at the strategic level of supply-chain configuration, synchronization has become extremely relevant because of the capabilities and opportunities made available by the Internet. These vary from providing an alternate all-pervasive channel for sales, distribution, and delivery; customer segmentation; service station; and so on (see next sub-section).

Secondly, at the tactical level of supply-chain planning, synchronization entails reflecting changes in the downstream planning processes onto the upstream processes. In particular, the demand plan is cascaded into the distribution, manufacturing, and procurement plans. This is significant because of the increasing volatility and variety of demand in the market. In the future, this would also involve the reconfiguration of the logistics network for particular products. For achieving this, each individual plan is also synchronized at all planning hierarchical levels. This can be done sequentially or concurrently; concurrent and real-time planning is essential for more lean and responsive supply chains.

Lastly, at the operational level of supply-chain execution, synchronization has been enabled traditionally by technologies like EDI, Internet-based communications, and more recently by collaborative solutions like SAP's business-to-business solution. Synchronization is also made possible by a large number of products that can be generated from a smaller set of standard or generic products. In these cases, the supply-chain efficiency is increased tremendously by postponement of the point of product differentiation as close as possible to the point of demand by the customer. In other words, you customize the product required by a specific customer only at the last moment.

In this regard, SAP APO provides key capabilities like

- Setting up specific goals and objectives for the supply chain
- Rapid order configuration and order promising using the available-to-promise (ATP) component
- Sophisticated demand-based planning
- Sophisticated forecasting algorithms
- Optimization logic to plan supply-chain activities
- Planning around real-world constraints and priorities
- Concurrent planning of material, capacity, and distribution
- Interactive scenario-planning facilities

The Electronic Supply-chain Management (e-SCM) Systems

Unlike the problems that confronted the traditional SCM, today the issues extend beyond the conventional static and predefined individual supply chains. This is because of the dynamic reconfigurations that are possible by the Internet. The Internet enables the formation and dissolution of momentary supply chains, that is, e-supply-chain management (e-SCM) systems, even for individual customer transactions depending on the optimal combination of collaborations to deliver a product and/or service triggered by the customer. More than supply chains, these will be a network of suppliers and partners. The extended collaborative enterprise will be more like a community of enterprises guided by the major value-adding players within the communities.

Instead of the competitiveness of individual enterprises, the competition today will exist among different communities of enterprises, that is, extended collaborative enterprises (ECEs). The success of an enterprise will depend on the competitiveness of the corresponding supply chain or, more correctly, the supply network to which it belongs. Since the threat of substitution is available not only to the end-customers, but also to the other constituents of the ECE, it may become vital to become a valued member of a successful supply chain.

The Internet has altered forever the ways in which enterprises interact and work with their customers, suppliers, and even their own members. Companies might commence e-business activities initially via a Web presence that can later be augmented effectively by an e-commerce component. However, it is well accepted by now that mere e-commerce functionality does not lead a company to become a successful e-business. The e-commerce functionality needs to be integrated tightly with the back-end order fulfillment processes. Because companies no longer perform end-to-end in-house production, this quickly leads to the issues of e-SCM. Accommodating e-commerce introduces new levels of complexity, volatility, and opportunity that compel companies to share and manage information across the ECE at the pace of Internet-time.

The traditional approach to supplying products to the market is based upon optimizing production handling and transportation through computations of economic batch quantities. It is essentially a "push" system in which a product is produced ahead of demand based on a forecast and is then held awaiting orders. For manufacturers, this inventory-centric strategy entails building and maintaining safety stocks, while for distributors and retailers, it implies buying and holding inventory to ensure ready product availability.

On the other hand, with an e-SCM, the supply chain is effectively transformed into a demand chain whereby the product is produced in response to an actual customer order. An agile supply chain is market-sensitive and intelligent. This is significant because it senses and responds rapidly to the requirements of "'mass customization," that is, variety and changes in customer preferences. This is made possible by accessing the data as close as possible to the point of demand like the point-of-sales (POS) terminals or the point-of-use (POU) Web sites.

In conventional systems, the gap between the logistics lead time and the customer's order time is bridged by carrying inventory based upon a forecast. In the case of an agile supply chain or e-SCM, the increased responsiveness helps in narrowing the gap, thus reducing the burden of producing more and more accurate forecasts for maintaining inventory. These efforts have been found to quickly reach a point of diminishing returns. Only through Internet-based collaborations and real-time optimizations can companies deliver the mass customization required by the customers profitably.

In addition to the performance-enhancing KPIs stated in relation to the supply chains in "Supply Chain Management (SCM)" earlier, e-SCM would lead to the following advantages:

- Leaner supply chains by purging intermediaries down to the essential minimum
- Intelligent and agile supply chains
- Reduced inventory levels
- Greater customer loyalty
- Reduced cycle time
- JIT is enabled
- Reduced cost of sales
- Reduced costs of purchasing

All this is possible via the Internet only because the extended collaborative enterprises would adopt the same strategy that is identified for the ERPs in Chapter 1: the utilization of information as a resource. Like the case of ERPs, the e-SCMs would use information as a resource. The e-SCMs would gain agility and competitiveness by using information as a substitute for inventory, the movement of goods, the sampling and selection of goods, and so forth.

Instead of the goods, what would really traverse the chain would be the accurate information on products, specifications, customizations, additional options, design, components, BOMs, production schedules, inspections, quality certifications, delivery details, payment detail, and collections that is obtainable from operational ERP systems like SAP. The value of inventory is replaced by the value of information. Compared to the costs of a just-in-case (JIC) inventory, the costs associated with the generation and maintenance of accurate information *on inventory* are marginal. Members of the e-SCM would be integrated with each other transparently and can initiate business processes within each other's systems.

The e-SCM would also involve the reengineering and automation of routine inter-enterprise processes. It should be noted that these inter-enterprise processes will not remain fixed but will be configured dynamically and in real-time among the extended community of suppliers, depending on the configuration that is optimal for delivering a particular order. Like the end-customer, the Internet also empowers enterprises to manage the supply chain to maximize opportunities; the flexibility to change partners and processes would be an indispensable requirement of the Internet-based economy.

Moreover, because information is "non-material," it has no inertia; it can also travel faster than papers, documents, and inventories. This enhances the throughput of the supply chain as a whole; obviously, speeding up inventory would also produce bottom-line financial benefits. The assembly and manufacture of goods is postponed as far as possible to the last moment prior to the actual delivery and dispatch to the customer. Again, as in the case of ERP, because information can be shared infinitely and simultaneously without degradation, the economies of customization for such Internet-based, customer-triggered, extended, collaborative enterprises will be enormous.

All the characteristics and concepts of ERPs that we presented in Chapter 1 in the context of an enterprise are also valid for the e-SCMs of the extended collaborative enterprise or community. Thus, the e-SCMs today could accomplish the following tasks:

- Transform the traditional supply chain into an information-driven community.
- Fundamentally perceive an ECE as a global community.
- Reflect and mimic the integrated and dynamic nature of a community.
- Fundamentally model a dynamic process-driven community.
- Enable a real-time, reconfigured, agile, and concurrent community.
- Elevate a supply-chain-wide information technologies (IT) strategy as a part of the business strategy of the community.
- Engender channel-spanning performing measures that would be a major advance on the earlier supply-chain performance improvement approaches.
- Become a mass-user or even mass-consumer-oriented application environment.

SAP Supply-chain Optimization, Planning, and Execution (SCOPE)

SAP supply chain optimization, planning, and execution (SCOPE) is SAP's SCM initiative. It provides a framework for integrating supply-chain forecasting, planning, optimization, and execution with online transaction processing (OLTP) systems of SAP R/3, decision support systems from the SAP Business Information Warehouse (BW), and the envisaged sales force automation and customer relationship management (CRM) systems. It enables the integration of information and corresponding decisions across the entire supply chain into a seamless, automated, and optimized infrastructure.

Many components of SAP SCOPE are still under development, but the basic components of SCOPE are as follows:

- The SAP Advanced Planner and Optimizer (APO)
- The SAP business-to-business procurement (B2B)
- The SAP logistics execution system (LES)

Figure 21.1 shows the components of SAP's supply-chain management initiative. The following subsections give a brief overview of the above components.

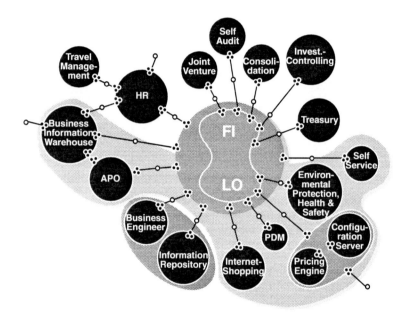

FIGURE 21.1
The SAP supply-chain management schema.

SAP's Advanced Planning and Optimization (APO) System

SAP APO is a complete suite of supply-chain tools for advanced planning and decision support. In line with the SAP repository-oriented philosophy, APO can also be configured to provide optimization, automated decisions, and real-time event notifications that are specific to an industry, company, or even particular tasks. SAP APO employs a library of advanced optimization algorithms and a memory-resident data processor, LiveCache, for delivering high-performance planning and optimization.

Figure 21.2 gives a schematic of the components of SAP APO, which are discussed in the following section. SAP APO can also work with legacy and non-SAP systems.

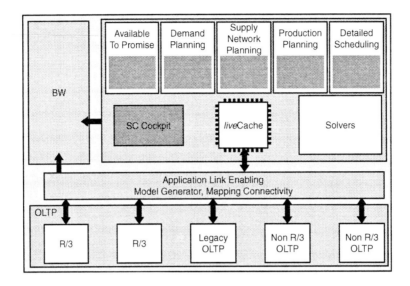

FIGURE 21.2
SAP APO overview.

Demand Planning

Demand planning is a toolkit of statistical forecasting techniques and demand-planning functionalities that enable a company to prepare accurate forecasts and plans based on these forecasts. Demand planning is integrated with the operational systems of SAP R/3 and SAP BW that enable the drill-down analysis of planned, operational, and historical data. It is also interfaced with the APO Alert Monitor to signal exceptions arising with reference to the planned scenarios.

Demand planning provides facilities for the following tasks:

- Performing collaborative forecasting
- Forecasting new product demands
- Managing product life cycles
- Planning product promotions
- Performing a causal analysis

Global Available-to-Promise (ATP)

Global ATP performs multilevel component and capacity checks in real time and also provides a simulation analysis to ensure that the company can match supply and demand for a particular product and/or service. It achieves this efficiently and effectively by using a rule-based strategy.

Global ATP also maintains access at all times to product availability along the supply chain to ensure delivery on commitments to end-customers. Global ATP has automatic features for performing

- Product substitutions for unavailable products
- Sourcing materials from alternate locations in case of shortages at particular sites
- Allocations of products or components based on predefined criteria

Supply Network Planning and Deployment

This supply network planning and deployment component enables a company to model, analyze, and synchronize its entire supply network along with its corresponding constraints. This component enables planning at both aggregate and detailed levels, primarily on a tactical planning horizon. It permits the synchronization of all the company's activities for purchasing, manufacturing, inventory, and transportation. Consequently, it helps in planning the flow of materials along the entire length of the supply chain.

The deployment component uses the current status of material inventory along the distribution network to dynamically balance and optimize the distribution network on a regular basis. Supply network planning and deployment provides the facilities for the following tasks:

- Determining the optimum distribution of supply
- Performing a what-if analysis
- Dynamically matching supply and demand for fine-tuning the distribution network
- VMI techniques
- Using sales and operations planning (SOP) for integrating marketing plans with the supply-chain management

Production Planning and Detailed Scheduling

Production planning and detailed scheduling assist in generating production plans and schedules that optimize the utilization of resources based on state-of-the-art methods like E. Goldratt's theory of constraints.

This component provides the facilities for the following tasks:

- Performing detailed material and capacity planning
- Performing forward and backward scheduling at multiple levels

- Synchronizing schedules and changes at multiple levels of BOM
- Performing a what-if analysis for different constraints
- Performing interactive scheduling and plan optimization

Supply-chain Cockpit

The supply-chain cockpit is similar in functionality to the management cockpit discussed in Chapter 20, "Valuing the Millennium Enterprise." It helps in managing the supply chain to provide a complete view of the entire length of the supply chain. The supply-chain cockpit is a graphical instrument panel for modeling, navigating, and controlling all nodes and links in the supply chain.

The supply-chain cockpit has facilities for the following tasks:

- Graphically representing the supply chain
- Zooming into segments of interest at any level of detail
- Monitoring material, capacity, and constraints in transportation and storage
- Maintaining performance matrices like delivery performance, throughput, costs, and so on
- Flagging predefined exception conditions by using event triggers and alarm conditions

SAP Business-to-Business (B2B) Procurement

The SAP business-to-business (B2B) procurement enables the procurement of non-production goods and services, including those for maintenance, repair, and operations (MRO). MRO is typically characterized as high-volume, low-value transactions for such items as office supplies, equipment parts and supplies, consumables, lubricating oils, and so on. It simplifies and manages the complete process by moving it to the desktop of the employees. It contributes towards enabling employee self-service, increasing accuracy, reducing transaction cycle times, and cutting costs while providing complete control and transparency to the purchasing department.

SAP B2B procurement caters to the following processes:

- The creation and maintenance of MRO requisitions
- The creation of purchase orders with or without catalogs
- The approval or rejection of the purchases
- The status and tracking of POs
- Desktop receiving
- Invoicing
- Performance reporting

Additionally, B2B leaves the purchasing department free to focus on the strategic sourcing and purchasing of direct material required for manufacturing and distribution requirements controlled by materials requirements planning (MRP) and advanced planning and scheduling (APS). SAP B2B can be integrated with SAP R/3 as well as work as a standalone while interfaced with non-SAP and legacy systems. SAP's B2B solution uses BAPIs (business application programming interfaces) to access and leverage the powerful business functionality and multilingual capability of the R/3 business backbone. SAP B2B is developed and deployed independently of the current release level of the core SAP R/3 system.

SAP Logistics Execution System (LES)

The SAP logistics execution system (LES) is a part of SAP's SCM initiative and covers the transportation and warehouse management requirements of a company. It can integrate flexibly with other functions like production, procurement, storage, distribution, transportation, sales, and service.

Transportation Management

Transportation management broadly covers the following functionality:

- **Scheduling**: this helps in rapidly preparing highly accurate schedules and route plans that enable optimal, reliable, and economical service to customers. It treats transportation as an integral part of your supply chain and therefore enables a company to optimize all transportation plans and routes. It provides facilities for planning shipments manually or automatically based on predefined rules.

- **Processing**: this helps in various aspects of shipment processing such as checking trucks in and out, making appointments for loading/unloading, documentation (including foreign trade documentation), and communicating with the carrier companies. SAP also supports an interface with global positioning system (GPS)-based tracking systems that help in tracking your shipments precisely. For cross-border activities, this takes advantage of SAP's powerful features for supporting multilingual, multicurrency processes. SAP LES enables you to exchange data with customs authorities using the automated export system (AES).

- **Costing**: this helps in all aspects of freight cost management including the calculation of freight based on various parameters and the management of freight tariffs, surcharges, discounts, and other freight agreements. The calculation of freight costs is flexible in nature and can be based on weight, volume, distance, mode of transport, freight class, or even customer-specific agreements. Calculations can also be made using one dimension like weight or multiple dimensions simultaneously like distance and weight. It also enables automatic billing and efficient settlements of accounts with service agents.

- **Monitoring**: this provides a wide range of monitoring and reporting features on shipments, 3PL, costs, delivery times, and so on.

Warehouse Management

Warehouse management broadly covers the following functionality:

- **Decision support**: this provides facilities for an overview of the expected workload, capacities, staff assignments, and scheduling. It also enables ad hoc queries, drill-down reporting, and analysis facilities including the ABC analysis of warehouse movements.

- **Inbound processing**: this supports reliable, accurate, and efficient management of orders placed with suppliers. This includes the plan and schedules for pick-ups and the receipt of deliveries. It also provides an easy interface to the SAP Quality Management (QM) module.

- **Storage and facility management**: this provides facilities for modeling the warehouse spaces to optimize the usage of available space. It provides great flexibility and visibility in terms of being able to manage different categories of stocks, depending on requirements like batches, vendor consignment, or goods in a quality inspection. It provides facilities for organizing bins randomly or in order based on certain criteria like the best-before date, hazardous goods, or bulk storage.

- **Warehouse technology**: this provides facilities for mobile data capture as well as interfaces to other technical warehouse systems like an automatic storage and retrieval system (ASRS).

- **Outbound processing**: this provides support for outbound processes including the order selection (stock transfer or production orders), picking optimization, and shipping documentation like delivery notes or bills of lading. This is fully synchronized with the transport management system.

Customer Relationship Management (CRM)

ERPs implemented within organizations are akin to a meticulously planned, designed, and executed electrical wiring infrastructure that has been put in place without installing bulbs, tube lights, fans, audio systems, ovens, and other appliances that make the electricity useful. ERPs provide all the data and information resources that are needed to drive various activities of the organization, but often they do not possess the functionality to process and use this information resource optimally for the benefit of the organization. Customer relationship management (CRM) and the manufacturing execution system (MES) are prime examples of such lacunas.

The success of the e-businesses and e-SCMs would not be assured without incorporating elements from customer relationship management (CRM), which is a holistic approach to identifying, attracting, and retaining customers. CRM deals with creating a customer-centric enterprise. This involves two major aspects: customer-centricity and customer responsiveness.

All activities must eventually provide value to the customer and this will be reflected in his or her willingness to pay for the products and/or services. Because customers have numerous other choices, non-value-adding elements should be excised swiftly in Internet time. This entails focusing all strategies, plans, and actions on the customer, rather than the traditional focus on the products and/or services. It is a question of transitioning from *zero defects to zero defections*. Additionally, enterprises must ensure seamless and real-time integration between customer demand and back-end demand, fulfilling intra- or inter- enterprise supply-chain processes. SAP's mySAP.com business scenarios, discussed later in this chapter, address this issue for a number of specific business scenarios that are vital for the success of a company.

An effective CRM strategy aims at achieving the following:

- Continuously attracting new customers
- Gaining customer insight and managing intimacy
- Retaining profitable customers and phasing out non-profitable customers
- Establishing long-term relationships with current customers
- Enticing the customer to spend more and also increase profits further by cross-selling other products and up-selling higher-end products to the same customer

In an era where the advantages based on products and services are shortened to a click of a customer (see "The Customer-triggered Company"), the key to success is to forge long-term, profitable relationships with customers. CRM aims at identifying the customers that are more profitable to the company and optimizes relationships with those customers. Although this leads to increased services and incentives for customers that provide the greatest returns to the company, it might also result in reduced services or even strong disincentives for non-profitable customers. Such customer differentiation is not really new; only the pace of the Internet that hastens this process makes such differentiation more visible. Thus, the Internet glaringly bares the profound fact of *competition among customers*: even customers compete for bestowing their business. Customer retention is extremely important for companies because it is more efficient and effective to retain a current customer than gain a new one. Companies can generate additional revenue and profits without incurring the costs for acquiring new customers.

To strengthen customer relationships, companies draw on and integrate information from a wide range of resources to develop insights into customer wants, needs, and values. These sources might include direct contacts, customer information systems, sales reports, call center data, market surveys, focus groups, billing data, demographic studies, and so forth. This may also include prior records and an analysis of customer interactions with the company. The customer might interact with different units of the business through different channels, but the company must have a coordinated, consistent, and complete picture of the customer available throughout the enterprise. All these impart a greater degree of stability, continuity, and predictability to the customer base, which eases the planning and operations all along the supply chain.

Customer relationships are like assets, which need to be tended to guarantee an assured return. In light of this, SCM can be better understood to be concerned with having the right product in the right place, at the right price, at the right time, and in the right condition for *the right customer.*

Customer responsiveness is an outcome of sharing current, complete, and consistent information on interactions with individual customers. Furthermore, it implies instantaneous, transparent connectivity and visibility between customer-facing processes with the order-fulfilling processes. This visibility not only permits the salesman to give accurate available-to-promise (ATP) information to the customer, but also enables him to assess for himself the latest capable-to-promise (CTP) status for a particular order before making any commitments.

In turn, the various members of the supply chain also have better visibility and understanding of the customer requirements and commitments made to the customer; these ensure on-time-delivery (OTD). The tight integration with the fulfillment processes enables coordination, monitoring, and managing of goods across the ECE. It also provides instant notifications and alerts on exceptions and problems that may delay the OTD of the order. Further, this integration also helps in matching the growing trend of customers postponing the buying decision closer to the purchasing decision with the corresponding ability of the enterprise to postpone the point of product-differentiation as close as possible to the point of demand by the customer. The difference between these two decisions is that a buying decision is a decision to posses or procure something even if you do not have money; a purchasing decision means deciding to actually pay for it.

Every action of the customer needs to be met by a highly automated and tightly integrated response across the supply chain to fulfill the need. More succinctly, one can say that "sell one, make one" has become the manufacturing watchword and corresponds closely to the current marketing watchword of "the market of one."

For a successful CRM program that produces bottom-line financial results, the customer centricity needs to pervade the entire supply chain. A process view, as embodied in SAP, assists in achieving this by seamlessly integrating the customer-facing processes with upstream supply-chain processes (see mySAP.com Marketplace later). As emphasized throughout this book, the process view cuts across the impeding organization boundaries to focus on business results for the satisfaction of the end-customer, who is the real owner of all business processes. The SAP Customer Relationship Management (CRM) initiative helps customer align their products and services with customer's preferences. This is constituted of the following:

- SAP Marketing: this provides functionality and tools for planning, executing, evaluating, and integrating marketing programs.

- SAP Sales: this simplifies and automates sales tasks, allowing the sales force to focus on the customer relationships and increased customer satisfaction. This includes a solution for mobile sales.

- SAP Service: this helps in increasing the efficiency and effectiveness of customer service to transform it into a competitive advantage. This caters to functionality like call-center-based support centers, parts and service delivery, and field service. Out of the 16-module CRM suite planned by SAP, the various SAP CRM applications that would be introduced initially are

  - Internet sales

  - Internet service

  - Field sales

  - Field service

  - Service interaction center

Additional CRM applications that will become available include telesales, telemarketing, marketing analysis, product and brand management, and Internet marketing.

Enterprise Application Integration (EAI)

Enterprise Application Integration (EAI) is the process of tying together multiple applications to support the flow of information across business units and their information systems. B2B integration is essential when creating communities of partners that collaborate in a variety of areas ranging from planning to distribution to customer service. It is necessary to leverage relationships with partners to reduce time-to-market, improve quality, reduce inventories, increase responsiveness, and also to expand in global markets. For a company, the key to creating value in an Internet-based economy is to integrate across the confines of an enterprise to the back-end finances, logistics, and even office applications of its value-chain partner suppliers and customers; a single business transaction might span multiple applications. This leverages and multiplies the ROI on investments made in such systems.

However, this entails integrating seamlessly with an unlimited number of heterogeneous and autonomous systems, databases, and protocols. This is also required when enterprises implement ERP in phases whereby the problem of integrating with remaining non-ERP systems becomes unavoidable. Middleware that has traditionally been associated with interfacing solutions has recently evolved into environments called enterprise application integration (EAI) that target integration with enterprise applications systems as their main focus. Using standards such as XML and Java, the new middleware bridges intra- and inter-enterprise applications spawned by the Web and e-commerce.

The interfacing approach of point-to-point interfaces between two applications would be prohibitively expensive for EAIs that might involve tens and hundreds of such interfaces. EAIs adopt the alternate approach of instituting an information broker whereby all systems communicate with the information broker by uploading data into the same while simultaneously translating it into a single format and protocols native to this central broker. Because information is routed through the information broker, rather than going directly among different systems, this simplifies the problem considerably and it becomes easy to connect disparate systems via their respective adapters that use the singular format and protocols of this central broker. Any future systems have only to devise one "adapter" to integrate with the central broker to start communicating transparently with all other systems. The exchange of data between the various systems provided by EAI is governed by the rules of the business process, which are defined by the user. The message broker routes the messages according to these rules. The data in the messages is translated en route into whatever format is required by the concerned application.

EAI with SAP is a significant effort for any company fueled by the increasing market-driven trend towards e-business and customer-facing applications. This is caused by the fact that it would be uneconomical for a company to Web-enable all of its business-critical applications including SAP, its legacy systems, and other specialized applications. However, it may also become imperative for a company to be able to access such business-critical systems on the Internet through Web user interfaces (WUIs) like browsers that are scalable, easy to access, easy to distribute, and also easy to use with minimal training. In such cases, EAI becomes essential to leverage fully on such proven corporate assets.

B2B integration is an enabler of highly coordinated business communities collaborating together with the speed and agility of a single, well-run organization. The customer-triggered company that is discussed at the end of this chapter is a competitive imperative today. Only EAI can enable such customer-triggered, real-time interactions among multiple companies that coordinate their actions to fulfill the customer's needs successfully. SAP works closely with its partners who have leading-edge EAI capabilities, technologies, and products. Appendix C gives a list of third-party solutions promoted by SAP.

Web User Interfaces (WUI)

In the course of his or her daily routine, a user might have to access the Internet, intranet, or several incompatible operational, business, and decision-support applications. Users might find themselves overwhelmed with information and technology options that may have to be exercised to move across these various resources. Users might dissipate enormous amounts of time and effort in switching between applications and entering passwords and other identification information every time. Enterprise information portals (EIPs) solve these problems by devising a single gateway to all such resources. Users have the convenience of a single sign-on accessible from anywhere using only a single password.

EIPs, or what I would term as WUIs, solve the problem of information logistics caused by the use of diverse applications. This enables users to focus more on the content, context, and relevance of corporate information, rather than on the complexities of accessing from diverse, autonomous, and often proprietary sources, which leads to better decisions. Inevitably, these later factors restrict the access of valuable information and hence deprive a majority of personnel from playing a more effective role in the organization. WUIs enable all users to subscribe, create, design, value-add, publish, collaborate, reuse, and share information using tools and formats with which they are more familiar and comfortable.

WUIs have the following efficiency and productivity-multiplying features:

- Interactive and secure access from anywhere

- Explicit and implicit subscribe and publishing facilities that enable users to schedule receipts when sending just-in-time (JIT) information from or to identified resources

- A single point of interactive access via a Web browser to both internal and external industry-specific and company-specific applications, content, and services

- A wide variety of information formats, including relational database tables, multidimensional databases, and decision-processing objects like queries, reports, word-processing documents, spreadsheets, images, video, audio, HTML and XML pages, e-mail messages, and so forth

- Personalized, easy, uniform, role-specific, company-specific, industry-specific user interfaces (with options for multiple roles)

SAP's mySAP.com Internet Environment

SAP's mySAP.com is a real-time collaborative, business solution environment that includes Internet-enabled applications like Web-enabled core components of SAP R/3, the personalized Workplace as an enterprise portal, the Marketplace as a global e-business hub, new enterprise and collaborative e-business scenarios, and services like application hosting. mySAP.com enables companies to move from integration to the next level of collaboration. In fact, the mySAP.com environment has been branded to invoke the following: "my" signifying the individualized, personalized and customized element, "SAP" signifying the backbone of robust SAP application solutions, and, ".com" indicating the Web-enablement of this empowering environment. mySAP.com offers companies seamless end-to-end integration of SAP and non-SAP solutions, originating at the point of customer contact and extending throughout business operations to provide a total e-business environment. mySAP.com comprises four key elements:

- The mySAP.com Marketplace, an open electronic business-to-business hub that enables inter-company relationships for buying, selling, and communicating

- The mySAP.com Workplace, an enterprise information portal that provides users with a personalized, browser-based work environment that offers everything they need on a routine basis

- mySAP.com business scenarios that enable collaborative, role-based, business-to-business, and business-to-consumer solutions through SAP and third-party software applications

- mySAP.com application-hosting services that provide a quick, cost-effective mechanism to adopt the full range of mySAP.com solutions

Figure 21.3 shows a schematic of the mySAP.com environment. I discuss each element in the following sections.

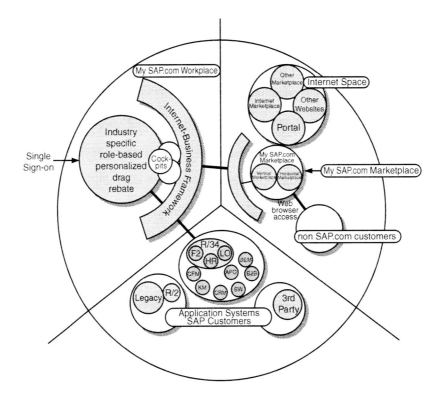

FIGURE 21.3

SAP's mySAP.com Internet Environment.

In the future, mySAP.com will incorporate products like SAP R/3, SAP's industry solutions, and new dimension products in the form of components. Thus, all SAP products will be available as independent products as well as components of mySAP.com. The advantage of the latter will be the all-in-one pricing. This pricing will be based on

- **Identifiable users**, who pay by subscription/ name, which will continue to be based on the number of users but will differ depending on the nature and extent of usage. The different categories of users are Manager, Professional, and Employee.
- **Software engines** that pay by records.
- **External sources** that pay by transaction.

mySAP.com Marketplace

The mySAP.com Marketplace is constituted of two aspects. First, it is the infrastructure that supports the collaborative mySAP.com business scenarios that enable different buyers and sellers to come together to exchange goods, services, and information as single-step transactions. Second, it is also the name of the Web portal hosted by SAP at www.mySAP.com providing industry-wide content, community, collaboration, and commerce.

This houses many industry-specific as well as cross-industry "communities of interest." The cross-industry areas of interest include basic business services like travel reservations, package shipping, document exchanges, business directories, online bidding, spot-market buying, RFP or RFQ matching, and general content (news, company profiles, annual reports, and stock quotes), as well as specialized services like SCM. There are two basic variations of online bidding: auctions and exchanges. In an auction, one seller gets bids from multiple agencies or individuals and controls the action; the later typically entails movement of prices in one direction. Exchanges, on the other hand, are operated and controlled by neutral parties who frame the rules for the buyers and sellers to meet and negotiate a deal.

The mySAP.com Marketplace features online catalogs and real-time auctions that enable companies to obtain real-time quotes based upon supply and demand, leveraging the opportunities of the Internet for one-step business. Formerly disparate business processes are synchronized across enterprises in the context of a single transaction. This leads to tremendous advantages in automatic aggregations, reconciliations, transparencies, real-time updates, accurate records, reduced costs of transactions, and so forth. The mySAP.com Marketplace provides the complete infrastructure, security architecture, e-commerce, and order fulfillment-enabling applications, services, and interoperabilities to conduct such one-step business transactions.

mySAP.com Workplace

The mySAP.com Workplace is a WUI that provides any user with a single, integrated, Web-based, role-based access point for software and information to improve personal productivity through the power of *personalized collaboration*. This is a personalized WUI that can be found on the desktops of individual members of a company and that provides a gateway to all business solutions, services, and information resources that are accessed frequently for daily operations. Users can access intranet self-service applications, extranets, and front office, back-office, and legacy applications all through a Web browser. They can also customize and configure the mySAP.com Workplace to suit their individual work styles and requirements. Furthermore, although the Web itself is stateless by nature, mySAP.com Workplace keeps track of the usage state of an application, permitting users to pick up applications exactly where they left off at any time.

An integrated user workplace is critical in collaborative business environments. The mySAP.com Workplace provides integration between Web-based resources and business applications. To cater to such requirements, mySAP.com Workplace provides drag-and-drop support across business applications and Web sites. For instance, a buyer using mySAP.com Workplace can drag and drop a rush purchase order onto an icon belonging to an overnight package delivery carrier in the same screen window. This simple action triggers mySAP.com Workplace to automatically access the carrier's Web site to obtain full details of the specific overdue shipment and display it immediately for reference on the screen.

The mySAP.com Workplace also provides a personalized portal for the mySAP.com Marketplace hub on the Internet at www.mySAP.com, providing content, community, collaboration, and commerce. It also provides integration with other ERP solutions and non-ERP information resources, including financial market data, news tickers, and industry-specific content. The Web-based collaboration enabled by mySAP.com Workplace is supported by the SAP Internet business framework, which provides a Web-based, flexible, and open infrastructure for all mySAP.com solutions through XML-based Web messaging through the SAP Business Connector and WebFlow. The SAP Business Connector maps and converts between SAP document formats and XML-based business documents; the latter are exchanged over the Internet.

mySAP.com Business Scenarios

The mySAP.com business scenarios are Internet-based, one-step business solutions that enable business collaborations by integrating process functionality, industry-specific knowledge, and necessary services essential for users to succeed in their business responsibilities. Business scenarios create significant values for companies by helping them implement new business processes quickly, increase operational efficiency and productivity, reduce costs and lead times, enhance decision support, and hence customer service.

The mySAP.com business scenarios provide companies with comprehensive, flexible, industry-specific collaborative solutions for areas such as e-commerce, CRM, SCM, and business intelligence (BI).

MySAP.com business scenarios that are available at present include

- Collaborative planning
- Collaborative forecasting
- Web-based selling and catalog hosting

- Web-based order fulfillment
- Web-based customer service
- Web-based billing presentation and payment
- Web-based buying and procurement

Role-based scenarios help a company in utilizing SAP applications as well as other data resources suitable for its personnel to perform specific individual roles within the corresponding business processes of the company.

mySAP.com Application-Hosting Services

The basic idea behind the Application Service Provider (ASP) computing model is that a provider hosts and manages applications that users can access over networks like the Internet. This is the final step towards software manifesting as a service. The market is evolving towards a state where companies will pay for the software as services on a usage basis, as they do traditionally with utility services like electricity and gas. This market was pioneered in 1998 by startups such as Breakaway Solutions, Corio, and so on. The ASP model typically involves lease-to-own options on software. It entails renting access, at a low rate, to the functionality of ERPs and other applications like CRM, SCM, and so on over the Internet.

In contrast, traditional outsourcing requires up-front purchase of software licenses and often charges large fees for contracted services. But, recently, many ASPs are also experimenting with other pricing models that involve charges for initial customization, migration, and integration plus a flat monthly fee depending on the use of functionality and services, or even a percentage of the customer's revenue. The ASP services could range from infrastructure, co-location, co-hosting, and dedicated hosting right through to even hosted businesses such as hosted buying services or even hosted customer management services.

Application Service Providers (ASP) present a real opportunity to replace the in-house IT department. Smaller companies also need the full functionality of high-end applications such as ERP, SCM, or CRM that they cannot afford. ASPs meet the needs of SMEs and the dot-com companies that cannot afford the substantial up-front investments in establishing the infrastructure, knowledgeable and experienced staff, on-going administration and monitoring services, better back-up and recovery methods, and so forth.

The top reasons that are cited by companies for renting applications are guaranteed performance levels, high availability, responsive service, and support. The cost of ownership of hosted applications can be 25% cheaper than managing the applications internally. Other criteria for companies to contract ASPs are lower up-front costs, faster implementations, higher redundancy, larger scalability of hardware and bandwidth, automatic upgrades, quicker distribution and deployment, and data storage, back-up, and recovery capabilities.

The mySAP.com application-hosting services enable customers to evaluate, implement, and operate mySAP.com solutions online. This enables companies to perform detailed evaluations prototypes, and company-specific solutions via the Internet prior to deciding on purchasing or actually purchasing the SAP product. Customers also have the facility to implement and continue using SAP functionality via the Web browser.

Outsourcing application services has many advantages, such as

- Enabling a company to concentrate on enhancing the competitiveness of its core functions
- Enabling a company to outsource the enhancing competitiveness of its non-core but still-critical functions like implementing ERP systems
- Reengineering critical but non-core functions and processes quickly
- Comprehensive industry-specific and company-specific evaluations
- Rapid prototyping of company-specific implementations
- Lower up-front investments in hardware and software, technical manpower resources, and training
- Reduced risks of initial erroneous decisions in pricing, reliability, scalability, bandwidth, and security
- Flexibility of options like hosting, co-hosting, and co-location
- Time-to-implement at a lower cost
- Time-to-go live at a lower cost
- Time-to-benefit at a lower cost
- Time-to-full ownership at a lower cost
- Time-to-deploy at other sites at a lower cost
- Higher service-level guarantees
- Better customer service
- Reduced administration, management, maintenance, and support costs

SAP, along with its application service provider (ASP) partners, provides the following services covering the entire customer solution cycle:

- **Internet-based demonstration and evaluation**: SAP reselling partners demonstrate and assist companies to evaluate SAP and industry-specific solutions on SAP-hosted systems. Even company-specific implementation prototypes are feasible on SAP-hosted systems.
- **Implementation**: SAP implementation partners configure, customize, test, and implement hosted systems.

- **Operations**: SAP ASP partners manage the operation, ongoing maintenance, and upgrades of the ASP-hosted system.

The Customer-triggered Company

The Internet has engendered a dramatic shift in the business environment from a production-centric model to a customer-centric one. It has led to a tidal wave that has swept the market beyond the model of a customer-driven company to the more recently witnessed phenomenon of what I term as the customer-triggered company. The outstanding potential for the survival and success of customer-triggered companies is amply demonstrated by the dizzying market caps enjoyed by the dot-com companies on our stock exchanges. In its wake, the Internet has created hundreds of millionaires overnight and, although technically temporal, those are real numbers. There is nothing virtual about those dollar signs.

Currently, more than computers and computing, it is the customer that is all pervasive. The pervasive customer wants the following:

- Personalized attention
- To buy in smaller quantities
- Customized products
- To postpone the buying decision closer to the purchasing decision
- To enjoy the buying experience at any convenient time or place with any convenient mode of payment
- Easy access to the status of the order
- Instant gratification
- Increased excellent service and support at a lower cost

In the Internet-based economy, success hinges on establishing a "pull." In this century, instead of the four P's of marketing (product, price, place, and promotion), the four C's (content, cost, convenience, and communications) would reign, all centered on the individual customers, rather than the products earlier. Figure 21.4 shows the old and the new marketing mix. The content includes the information on the products and services as well as the direct context of the presentation.

Never before has it been so easy for a customer to find a desired product or service along with contextual data necessary to make an informed purchase decision. Companies need to truly focus on sensing, feeling, thinking, relating, and acting to each individual customer. This is the best example of a "high-tech and high-touch" organization. Customers are no more than a click away from a world of comparative information about products, prices, and alternatives that are resulting in heightened competition among the suppliers. Companies need to respond rapidly and profitably to this generation of net-savvy and opportunistic customers who are perpetually on the verge of switching or clicking to alternate suppliers. The power of the customer will continue to grow to unprecedented levels with the ever-increasing ability to shop and buy anything from any one at any price at any time anywhere.

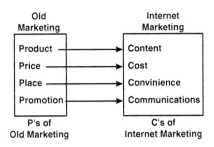

FIGURE 21.4

Internet marketing mix.

Unlike the make-to-stock strategy that has dominated since the '80s, the millennium enterprises must adopt the strategy of make-to-order, or even beyond to a "sense and respond" to the customized requirements of individual customers. In fact, the JIT philosophy for increasing the efficiencies and effective responsiveness of the supply chains would have to surpass itself to become synchronized with the actual event of an order being placed by the customer, which will truly become the universal point of purchase (POP). It is in this sense that the market is moving rapidly towards the event-driven enterprise where all actions are actually triggered by the click of the customer on the personalized WUIs of enterprises, such as the mySAP.com Workplace.

All actions of procurement, production, dispatch, and collection will result from the subsequent cascade of events triggered within the enterprise and the extended enterprise (see "Supply Chain Synchronization" earlier). The lines among the ERP, SCM, and front-office systems, such as CRM systems, are blurring. This will lead organizations to shed the monolithic, vertically integrated infrastructures of the past and embrace loosely coupled, independent, and Internet-agile organizations that engage collectively to address a momentary customer transaction.

The Internet and the Millennium Enterprises

Now that you've reached the end of the book, I would like to speculate on why the Internet is begetting the revolutionary changes that we are witnessing today. What gives it the power to drive the massive changes that have been witnessed in the last five years, while similar changes in the past have taken ages to sweep across the globe?

I believe the fundamental reason is that a *medium* is always more powerful than a *message*. It might be that, at certain stages in history, messages (and their messengers) have had a determining effect on the course of history, but these passages have been few and far between. The impact of the medium has always been more powerful and long lasting than *any* message. Throughout history, the powerful have always recognized this truth and have concentrated on controlling a medium as the most powerful facet of governance, rather than becoming martyrs as revolutionaries with a new message to tell to the world. The print medium has outlasted all ideological and technological revolutions seen in past centuries since the dawn of civilization. In one form or another, this has been a known fact in all fields of human endeavor, but Marshall McLuhan brought this out much more forcefully for the electronic media in the middle of the last century.

Computers were always positioned as *messages* of the new era, but it is clear that right from the beginning the Internet was a medium. Considering that the Internet is not governed or dictated by any specific authority and is one of the most democratic of institutions, one can be absolutely sure that the Internet is destined to herald the next major cultural revolution in human history.

Additionally, underlying all human endeavors lies the quest for immortality, the desire to transcend space and time forever. It might seem that this is only the concern of spiritualists and philosophers or mathematicians, relativists, and other scientists. On the other hand, it might also appear that all commercial endeavors are driven by the pursuit of money, but that could be wrong. At the base of all commercial transactions lies the fundamental concerns for transcending space and time.

All major technological advances, be they discoveries or inventions, that had lasting impact on the future course of human development had to do with one of the following:

- Sliding space and/or time in a direction that satisfied the basic urge to transcend space and time in practical terms and in a direction that was convenient.

- Altering space and/or time, that is, expanding or contracting space and/or time, to satisfy the basic urge to transcend space and time again in practical terms and in a direction that was convenient. Although such effects are not unknown in physical sciences, here I am referring effects that are psychological and experiential in nature.

Figure 21.5 shows a snapshot of the technological advancements witnessed in the last century interpreted in this new light. In the figure, the legend used is as follows:

- Sliding Space:

  +ve = Bringing Near

  -ve = Taking afar

- Sliding Time:

  _+ve = Bringing Near

  -ve = Taking afar

- Altering Space:

  +ve = Compressing Space

  -ve = Expanding Space

- Altering Time:

  +ve = Compressing Time

  -ve = Expanding Time

For instance, telephones permit you to converse with a person as if he were close (Sliding Space +ve and Altering Space +ve) and without waiting for a time in the future when you can meet him in person (Sliding Time +ve). It is a simple grid, but it enables us to understand in a powerful way the essential unity behind the technological advances in the last couple of centuries. It also gives rationale for the difference in the degree of impact that these technological inventions have had on human life and thought.

It is evident that its power on the consumer's mind comes from its unprecedented facility to slide and alter both space and time to a degree that is unlikely to be surpassed for quite some time in the future, and is matched only by that of printed paper.

Technological Advances in the Last Century

Description	Space				Time			
	Sliding		Altering		Sliding		Altering	
	+ve	-ve	+ve	-ve	+ve	-ve	+ve	-ve
Paper	X	X	X	X	X	X	X	X
Vehicles		X						X
Telephones	X		X		X			
Voice Mail	X	X	X		X	X		X
Photographs	X	X	X			X		
Transmitted Pictures	X	X	X	X	X	X	X	
Motion Pictures		X	X		X	X		
Audio/Video CDs	X	X	X		X			X
Audio/Video CD Players	X	X		X		X		X
Deepfreezers						X		
Microwaves					X		X	
Credit Card Payments	X	X			X			
Telephone Charge Cards	X				X			
Computers			X	X	X		X	X
Networks	X	X		X	X			X
Internet	X	X	X	X	X	X	X	X

FIGURE 21.5

Technological advances in the last century.

On the technological front, all these factors also translate into the reasons why Extended Markup Language (XML) is likely to be the most revolutionary papyrus in human history. The power of papyrus or printed paper has been mind-boggling; it has reigned supreme in its impact for so many centuries, but the impact of XML will be a million times more powerful. It will be more revolutionary than papyrus because it combines within itself the power of the printed document as well as the interactivity and experience of a screen.

XML has generally received attention for its potential as a universal standard for client-side document presentation and management systems. However, XML's greatest promise to revolutionize distributed applications does not lie in its being a portable and a universal standard for a data-interchange format (which in itself is great), and its potential to become a universal native *data storage format*. Data, in the context of XML, always means not only digits, but also generalized data in the sense of audio, video, graphics, and data as well. Furthermore, XML by its nature supports both data and metadata (information about data) in a flexible and hierarchical structure. Object databases might be a better fit for XML data, rather than the traditional Relational Database Management Systems (RDBMS), because they provide a scheme for storing information about data analogous to the way that XML tags give meaning to the data on the XML pages. XML's unlimited and user-defined tags fit much better into an object database than the set-oriented row-and-table metaphor of a relational system. Thus, one can envisage the World Wide Web Consortium's (W3C's) DOM (Distributed Object Models) models migrating seamlessly into any of the three distributed-object models: CORBA (Common Object Request Broker Architecture) from OMG (Object Management Group), DCOM (Distributed Component Object Model) from Microsoft, and EJB (Enterprise JavaBeans (EJB) from Sun Microsystems).

What about the future of SAP R/3? Populated CASE or repository-based applications like SAP would be collapsed into a single-layered XML database management system (XDBMS) package, which will be Internet-enabled by default, instead of existing in the three-layered architecture of

- A SAPGUI layer
- An application layer
- A database layer

Finally, it may sound clichéd, but with the advent of the Internet, e-commerce, and e-business systems, we seem to have traveled "forward into the past." Increasingly, e-businesses conducted in real-time and functioning on auction-based, dynamic pricing systems with facilities for aggregation and one-step business are reminiscent of the barter system of the ancient times. The only difference is that this time it is also between enterprises.

Appendixes

PART

VII

IN THIS PART

Selecting SAP Implementation Partners

APPENDIX

A

Selecting the right kind of implementation partner is very critical. For the successful implementation of SAP, it is crucial for a company to define the objectives and the role of the SAP consulting firm. The prime objectives for the firm should be

- To help and guide the SAP implementation
- To train the core implementation team of the company
- To transfer knowledge of the SAP product and functionality to the members on the implementation team

This ensures that the company can continue the momentum of the SAP implementation into its subsequent phases even after the exit of the consultants.

SAP implementation partners should be selected on the basis of

- A SAP implementation projects portfolio
- SAP consultants and their experience
- Industry-specific expertise
- Project-consulting experience
- An implementation methodology
- The location of additional office sites

It should be noted that, unlike the case of the projects in the past that were predominantly for Fortune 500 companies, the projects for millennium enterprises (with revenues ranging from $50 million to $1 billion) will require smaller teams with multi-skilled consultants. Millennium enterprises will not require or be able to afford individual consultants for every functional area.

SAP Consulting Partners in the U.S.

IN THIS APPENDIX

National Logo Partners

- Andersen Consulting
- Cap Gemini America
- CSC Consulting America (CSC)
- Deloitte & Touche (D&T)
- Dynamic Data Solutions
- Electronic Data Systems Corporation (EDS)
- Ernst & Young (E&Y)
- Hewlett-Packard Company (HP)
- IBM Corporation (IBM)
- Intelligroup, Inc.
- KPMG Peat Marwick
- Modis Solutions
- Origin Technology in Business
- PriceWaterhouseCoopers
- Resource Support Associate, Inc.
- Siemens Nixdorf Info Systems, Inc.

Implementation Partners

- Abacus Software
- ACSYS IT
- AG Consulting (Division of ADP)
- Akili Systems Group
- Application Partners, LLC
- Applied Integration Services
- Argus Integrated Solutions, Inc.
- Arthur Andersen, LLP
- Atlantic Duncans International
- Atlas Software
- Braun Technology Group
- BrightStar Information Technology Group

- Bristlecone, Inc.
- Bureau Van Dijk Computer Services, Inc.
- CAI/Advanced Solutions
- Cap Gemini America, Inc.
- CaRD America, Inc.
- CDG & Associates, Inc.
- Ciscorp
- Clarkson Potomac Group, Inc.
- Client Server Solutions, Inc.
- Complete Business Solutions, Inc.
- Computer Task Group, Inc.
- Conley, Canitano Association, Inc.
- Cybertech International Co.
- d.d.synergy USA
- DA Consulting Group
- Debis Information Services
- Delphi Consultants, Inc.
- Delta Consulting, Inc.
- Deno Morris, Inc.
- Dynamic Resources, Inc.
- EA Consulting
- Eisner Consulting
- EMAX Solution Partners, Inc.
- Executive Consultants
- Gamma Computer, Inc.
- Global Core Strategies
- Grant Thornton, LLP
- Grom Associates Data Processing Cons.
- Hewlett-Packard Company
- Holland Software Solutions LLC
- Honeywell, Inc.
- HPC Heck & Partner Consulting

- HR Link Group, Inc.
- IBM Corporation
- IDS Sheer, Inc.
- IMG America, Inc.
- IMI Systems
- Integration Associates
- Integration Software Consultants
- Intelligroup, Inc.
- International Management Group, Inc.
- IT Services, Inc.
- Kelly-Levey & Associates
- Knightsbridge Solutions, Inc.
- Kurt Salmon Associates, Inc.
- Litton PRC
- Logical Choice of Technologies, Inc.
- Magnus Management Consultants USA, Inc.
- Mahindra Consulting
- Management & Application Support
- Management Resources of Virginia, Inc.
- Meatra America, Inc.
- Metamor Enterprise Solutions
- Miracle Software Systems, Inc.
- Modis Solutions, Inc.
- Multivision International, Inc.
- Murray & West
- Nanobyte Software, Inc.
- Nexus Technology, Inc.
- OAO Technology Solutions, Inc.
- Optimum Consulting America, Inc.
- Osprey Systems, Inc.
- Pegasus System+B25s, Inc.
- Phaedra Software Solutions

- Plaut Consulting, Inc.
- POWERhaus Consulting, LLC
- Preimer HR Solutions, Inc.
- Prescient Consulting, LLC
- Prism Consulting Group, LLC
- Prism Consulting Services
- Radiant Systems, Inc.
- RCG International, Inc.
- realTECH, Inc.
- Realtime Consulting, Inc.
- Reed Business Systems Consulting
- Resource Support Associates
- RPM Associates
- RWD Technologies, Inc.
- Schmidt Vogel & Partner America, Inc.
- Science Application International Corporation (SAIC)
- Seal Consulting, Inc.
- Seltmann, Cobb & Bryant, Inc.
- Seimens Nixdorf Info Systems, Inc.
- SLI Consulting, Inc.
- Soft Guide International, Inc.
- Solbourne Solutions Consulting, Inc.
- Spearhead Systems Consultants (U.S.) Ltd.
- SPO America, Inc.
- Syskoplan Consulting Group, Inc.
- Technology Solutions Corporation
- The Amber Group, Inc.
- The Hunter Group, Inc.
- The INC Group, Inc.
- The Owens Group, Inc.
- Transaction Information Systems
- Triple-I

- TSI International Software
- VGS, Inc.
- Walldorf Technology Group
- Whittman-Hart, LP

Hardware Partners

- Amdhal Corporation
- Compaq Computer Corporation
- Data General Corporation
- Dell Computer Corporation
- EMC Corporation
- Hewlett Packard Corporation
- Hitachi Data Systems Corporation
- IBM Corporation
- NCR World Headquarters
- Sun Microsystems, Inc.
- Unisys Corporation

Technology Partners

- Informix Software, Inc.
- Intel Corporation
- Microsoft Corporation
- Oracle Corporation

SAP Third-Party Solutions

Company	Category	Product
Abaco		
ABC Technologies	Activity-based costing system	Oros 99Core, EasyABC Plus
Acsis, Inc.		
AppNet		
arcplan, Inc.	Data warehousing/ business intelligence (BI)	inSight, dynaSight
Ardent Software, Inc.	Data warehousing/BI	DataStage
Aspect Development, Inc.	Supply-chain management solutions	Aspect CSM, eSource, B2B eXpress Catalog
Authoria (Foundation Technologies)		
BMC Software	Enterprise management	PATROL, INCONTROL, RESOLVE, MAXM
BrightStar Information Technology, Inc.		
Brio Technology/ SQRIBE Technologies		
Business Object America		Business Objects
CIM Vision Systems		
Cognos Corporation	BI	
CommercePath		
Computer Associates Intl.	Enterprise management	Unicenter TNG
Compuware Corp.	Automated testing	QACenter, EcoSystems
Condor Technology Solutions		
Conley-Canitano	Accelerated industry solutions	Apparel and Footware Solutions (AFS)
CrossWorlds	Enterprise application integration	Customer interaction Software, Inc.
Dazel Corporation		
Documentum Inc.	Enterprise information portals	Documentum 4i
eOnline, Inc.		
Epic Data		
ESRI	GIS, vehicle-routing system	GIS, ArcLogistics Route

Company	Category	Product
ETI (Evolutionary Technologies)	Enterprise applications integration	ETI.EXTRACT
Extricity Software	Enterprise application integration	B2B integration
FileNet Corporation	Workflow/document management	
Gamma Computer	Web enablement for SAP	Robusta, Data Shuttle
Glyphica		
Gensys Telecom Laboratories, Inc.	Computer telephone integration	GENSYS CTI
Grainger Internet Commerce	E-commerce solutions	
HAHT Software, Inc.	E-commerce solutions	
HostLogic, Inc.	Applications hosting	
ICM America LLC		
i-Cube		
IDS Sheer, Inc.	BPR toolset	ARIES toolset
IMG Americas, Inc.		
IMPRESS SOFTWARE, Inc.	ITS-based solutions for the Internet	IMPRESS/OIS App. Server for SAP
INC Group, Inc.	Enterprise application integration	RealLink
Informatica Corp.	Enterprise application integration	PowerCenter
Information Builders, Inc.		
Innovision		
Insite Objects, Inc.	SAP documentation, change management, and training	DOCSITE, INSITE, EYESITE
Intactix International		
IntelliCorp, Inc.	Blueprint/Implementing cycle management	LiveCompass, LiveModel
	Enterprise application integration	LiveInterface, LiveTransfer
	Customer relationship management	Intellicorp CRM
Intermec Technologies		
Interpath		
INTERSHOP Communications, Inc.		
IT Services-Compuware		

continues

Company	Category	Product
iXOS Software, Inc.	Imaging and archiving solutions	iXOS-ARCHIVE
JetForm Corp.	Workflow software	
Litton PRC, Inc.	Testing solutions	Stress test analyzer
Luminate Software Corp.		
Macro 4, Inc.		
Manhattan Associates	Supply-chain execution App.	PkMS'99
MarketFirst Software		
MarketMAX, Inc.	Merchandise planning system	TMS/Enterprise
McHugh Software International	Logistics applications	DMplus, TRACS
MDSI	Workforce management system	Advantex enterprise gateway
MERANT	Data access in SAP	DataDirect for R/3
Mercury Interactive Corp.	Testing solutions	WinRunner QuickTest for R/3
Micrografx Inc.	Enterprise graphics solutions	iGrafx
Miracle Software Systems, Inc.	EDI system	EDI with RAPtor
Mobius Management Systems	Internet-based document viewing and customer care	DocumentDirect for the Internet, RemitDirect, Electronic Document Warehouse
Neoforma.com		
New Era of Networks Inc.		
Oberon Software Inc.	Enterprise application integration	
Open Text Corporation		
Optio Software	Output management solutions	Optio e.Com Series
OSI Software Inc.		
Pandesic Company	E-commerce solutions	
Partech, Inc.		
Peak technologies		
Plaut Consulting	Applications hosting	
Powersim Corporation	Business planning and simulations	Strategic enterprise management
Qwest Cyber.Solutions		
Rapidigm, Inc.		
RCM Technologies	Performance management	SAP performance management

Company	Category	Product
Recognition Systems Inc.	Customer relationship management	Protagona/SAP
Red Hat, Inc.	Linux	
Seqencia Corporation		
ServicePower		
Shipco Logistics, Inc.	RF Data Collection, Inc.	LogLink/RF for SAP R/3
Smallworld Systems	GIS Solutions	Smallworld GIS
SPS Commerce	EDI	
Sterling Commerce	E-commerce	
Sterling Software	EDI	
StreamServe	Output processing, formatting, and distribution	StreamServe
Symbol Technologies, Inc.	Barcoding	
Synsort, Inc.	Enterprise backup/restore	Backup Express
Syskoplan GmbH	Infrastructure management solutions	Integrated IT Mgmt., Call Center for R/3, SLAM, NOAH
Systems America	Enterprise app. integration	InterfaceONE
TAXWARE International ReMIT	Tax management apps.	SALES/USE Tax System,
Teklogix		
Telxon Corporation		
TIBCO Software Inc.	Enterprise app. integration	TIB/ActiveEnterprise
Time Link Corporation		
TimeVision		
Tivoli Systems, Inc.	Enterprise management systems	Tivoli
TOPCALL Corporation		
TopTier Software		
TSI International	Electronic data interchange (EDI), enterprise integration	
Vastera Inc.	Export/import trade application	EMS Global Passport
Vality Technology, LTD.	Data reengineering, BI	Integrity data reengineering
VeriSign Systems, Inc.		
Veritas Software		
Vertex Inc.		

continues

Company	Category	Product
Visual Edge Software		
VIT	Supply-chain performance	SeeChain
webMethods, Inc.	E-commerce solutions	
ZMAX/Eclipse Information Systems		

INDEX

A